The

EVERYTHING® Easy Crosswords Book

Dear Reader:

When I tell people I make crosswords, I often hear the same complaints: "Why are they so hard?" "Why are they so obscure?" "Why don't they seem to like people from my generation (I've heard this from both kids and oldsters)?" Or simply put, "Why is there so much crud in the puzzle?"

I made this book because I have a particular vision of how to combine "easy" and "fun" in the arena of crosswords that I feel will appeal to all ages, without too much repetition of words. Let me share some of my thoughts with you. Have you ever seen, for instance, a crossword with no proper nouns, multiword entries, acronyms/abbreviations, foreign words, crosswordese, or hard words? Well, that's the first three chapters. Want to decide for yourself if you want to know which clues have multiword or hyphenated answers? Those are Chapters 7–9. Hey, this could catch on!

Let me know what you think at my Web site: *www.themecrossword.com.*

Puzzlingly yours,

Douglas Fink

The EVERYTHING® Series

Editorial

Publishing Director	Gary M. Krebs
Managing Editor	Kate McBride
Copy Chief	Laura MacLaughlin
Acquisitions Editor	Bethany Brown
Production Editor	Jamie Wielgus

Production

Production Director	Susan Beale
Production Manager	Michelle Roy Kelly
Series Designers	Daria Perreault Colleen Cunningham
Cover Design	Paul Beatrice Frank Rivera
Layout and Graphics	Colleen Cunningham Rachael Eiben Michelle Roy Kelly John Paulhus Daria Perreault Erin Ring
Series Cover Artist	Barry Littmann
Puzzle Designer	Douglas R. Fink

THE EVERYTHING® EASY CROSSWORDS BOOK

Challenging fun for beginners!

Douglas R. Fink

Adams Media
Avon, Massachusetts

This book is dedicated to my wife, Susan, and daughter, Hannah, who had to put up with me shutting myself in the office while writing this book.

An Everything® Series Book.

Published by Adams Media, a division of F+W Media, Inc.
57 Littlefield Street, Avon, MA 02322 U.S.A.
www.adamsmedia.com

ISBN 10: 1-59337-045-8
ISBN 13: 978-1-59337-045-9

Printed in the United States of America.

20 19 18 17 16 15 14 13

Library of Congress Cataloging-in-Publication Data
Fink, Douglas.
The everything easy crosswords book / Douglas Fink.
p. cm.
An everything series book
ISBN 1-59337-045-8
1. Crossword puzzles. I. Title. II. Series: Everything series.
GV1507.C7F54 2004
796.732—dc22
2003027441

Contents

Acknowledgments / vi

Introduction / vii

Chapter 1 • **Over-Easy** / 1

Chapter 2 • **Easy as Pie** / 21

Chapter 3 • **Easy Going** / 41

Chapter 4 • **Easy as One-Two-Three** / 61

Chapter 5 • **Easy Street** / 81

Chapter 6 • **Easy Does It** / 101

Chapter 7 • **Take It Easy** / 121

Chapter 8 • **Easy Come, Easy Go** / 141

Chapter 9 • **Easier Said Than Done** / 159

Chapter 10 • **Common Denominators** / 197

Chapter 11 • **They All Scream Themes** / 215

Chapter 12 • **Clueless Crosswords** / 233

Chapter 13 • **Theme Party** / 241

Chapter 14 • **Just Being Silly** / 277

Appendix A • **Glossary** / 295

Appendix B • **Puzzle Answers** / 297

Acknowledgments

I would like to acknowledge the following for their help:

My family, for putting up with this crazy side passion of mine which makes me prone to obscure puns.

Various members of the crossword community (including Sandy Fein, Will Shortz, Cox & Rathvon, Nancy Schuster, Ray Hamel, and Arnold Reich), for their input and confidence (or in some cases for saying, "You said you'd do WHAT in a time span of just WHAT?"), and continued desire to proliferate this form of edutainment upon an unsuspecting population.

The staff of Penny Press, Inc., for my humble introduction to puzzle publishing.

The staff of Adams Media for their assistance, especially Bethany Brown, for trusting in a former newsletter/magazine editor who had never before published a book.

The freelance proofreading assistance of Valerie Shea, especially in the area of creative alteration. Also, to Kate Burgo for her added assistance.

The purchaser of this book, for making the publishing of the next book more probable.

Introduction

▶ CROSSWORD PUZZLES HAVE EXISTED for less than a century, but they have grown in popularity to become the world's leading printed puzzle type. They may fill your commute to work, make lunch a little more fun, or make that plane flight or DMV line seem not so long. In the year of the crossword's ninetieth anniversary, *The Everything® Easy Crosswords Book* gives you more than 200 puzzles, specifically created to avoid the crosswordese that has made so many crosswords unpleasant to the newcomer. Crossword puzzles are supposed to be fun. They should not be full of obscure rivers, uncommon animals, weather vane directions, or foreign words that are easy to build puzzles with but rarely used in everyday speech. So if knowing an ERNE from a TERN, a UTE from an OTO, or the AARE and AAR from the ISAR, ISER, ISERE, and YSER is something you'd rather avoid, you've come to the right place.

Furthermore, *The Everything® Easy Crosswords Book* will try to avoid variant spellings, prefixes and suffixes sitting by themselves (like OLA and ESE and STER and ADE), multiword partial phrases (like ONEI and TOA and INLA), plurals of names and abbreviations (like AVAS and EVAS and RONS), spelled-out letters (like CEE and ELL and ESS), weather vane abbreviations (like ENE and ESE), and of course, crosswordese (those words that you never see in everyday English, like SNEE, NENE, ATEN, ANOA, ANI, and ONER; these tend to be three- or four-letter words using one-point Scrabble letters, often starting with vowels).

There are seven general rules to American crosswords:

1. No unchecked squares (every white square is used in both an across and a down entry)
2. Mirror-symmetry (if you cut a puzzle in half and rotate it around its middle, the black and white squares match)
3. Interconnectedness (the black squares don't cut the diagram into multiple sections)
4. Two-letter entries are taboo.
5. Using of the same word or multiple forms of the same word in a grid is taboo.
6. Bigotry and suggestiveness in the entries and clues are frowned upon.
7. Newspapers standardize on specific grid sizes; keep this in mind when constructing for specific newspapers.

So, find a comfy seat, get yourself a nice sharp pencil (erasers or pens optional), relax, and dig into these puzzles.

The beginner puzzles have no proper nouns or hyphenated/multiword phrases (Chapters 1–3). The easy puzzles include proper nouns (Chapters 4–6). The medium puzzles also include hyphenated and multiword entries, but you can find out which ones they are by looking at the bottom of the page for help (Chapters 7–9). Themed puzzles have themes throughout their long entries, while theme crosswords have a common theme for all the entries throughout the puzzle. If you see a person's name without a blank, that means you've been provided with the last name, not the first name (so "Singer John" is ELTON, not DENVER).

Okay, off you go! You're on your own now. 

Chapter 1

Over-Easy

Where the deer and the antelope play

ACROSS

1. Where the deer and the antelope play
6. Bit part
11. Spoken
12. Drive like a maniac
13. Light-colored
14. Playful aquatic mammals
15. Start of a blossom
16. Tale
18. Even-Steven result
19. Not doing much at all
21. Relaxing place
22. Gel
23. Prom goer
24. Lids
26. Active one
28. Gotcha
32. Canine
35. Bikini top
36. Had on
37. Wise bird
38. Break with a beau
40. They might be classified
41. Brings together
43. Cavities
45. Adorn
46. Silly
47. Trick preventer
48. Dove's domiciles

DOWN

1. Bunny
2. Imply
3. Pasta piece
4. Pistol
5. Ripple
6. Siesta
7. Museum piece
8. Track events
9. Altogether ooky
10. Start, as in a disease
12. Klinger's rank
17. *
20. Completion
25. Give seeds a chance
27. Thing
29. Aussie bears
30. Passionate
31. Assents
32. Be unsure of
33. One who pays property tax
34. Move effortlessly
39. Slender
42. Four o'clock drink
44. Washington's bill

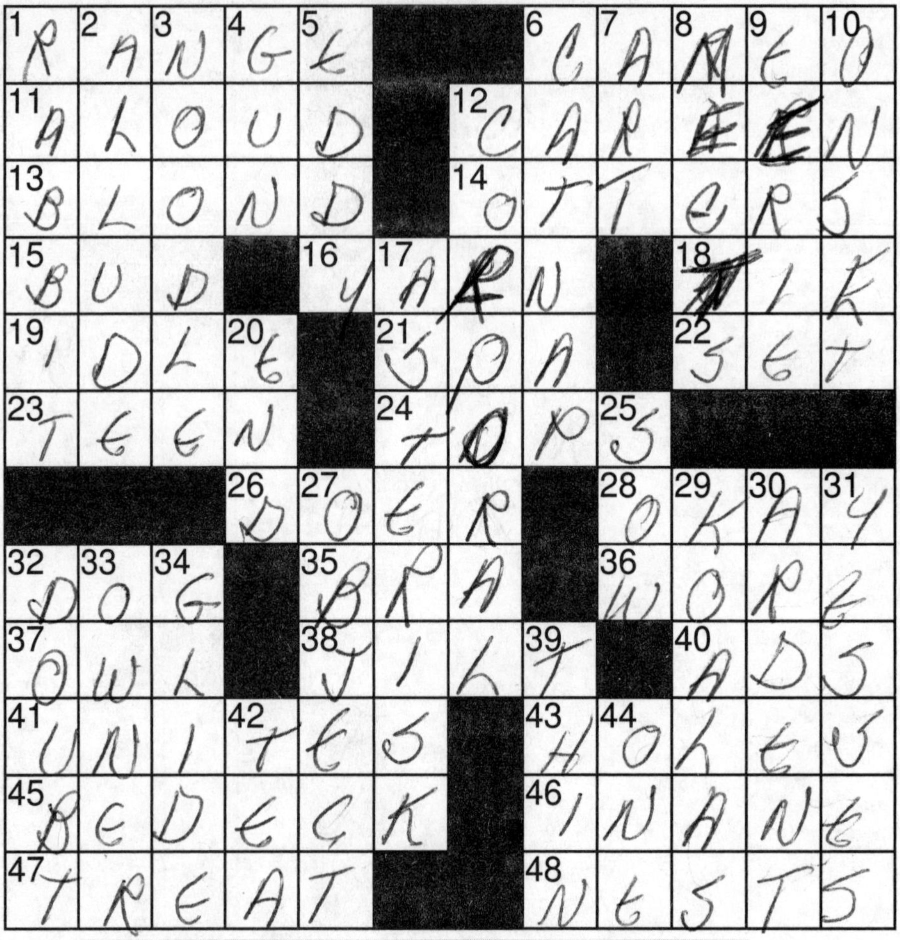

❖ **Solution on page 298**

We've been over these before

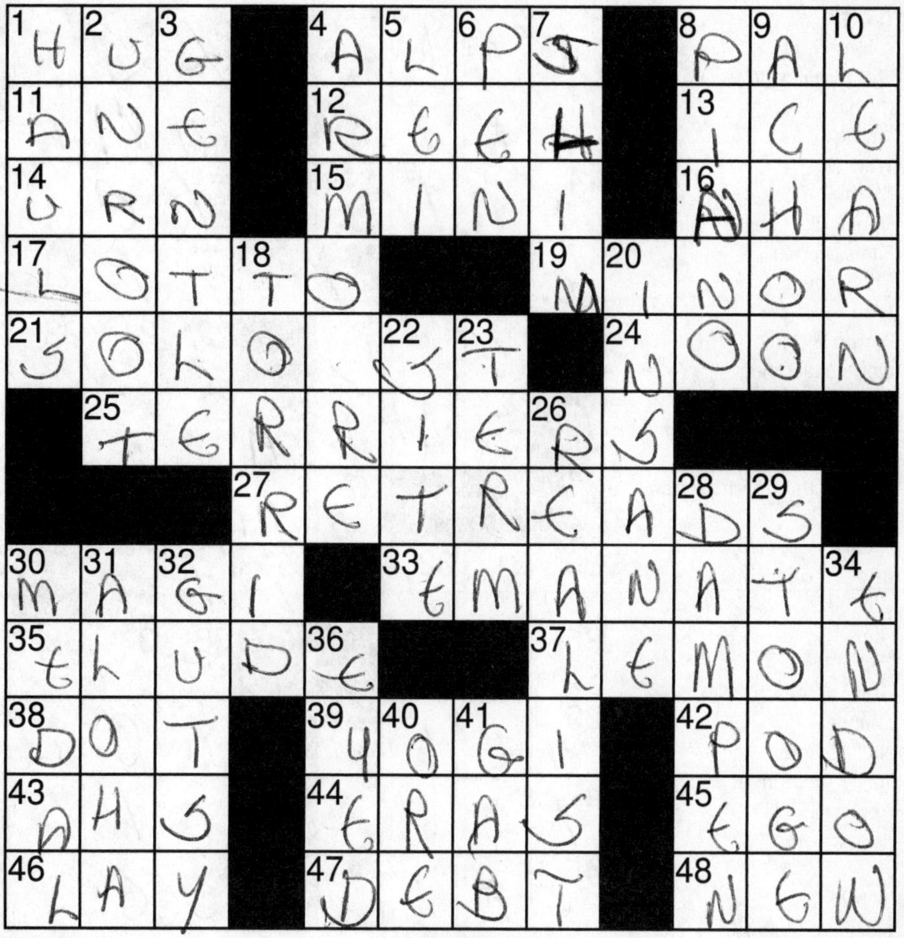

ACROSS

1. Embrace
4. Swiss mountain range
8. Buddy
11. Monkey's uncle?
12. Film holder
13. Diamonds, in gangster slang
14. Voluminous vase
15. Brief skirt, briefly
16. Eureka!
17. Gambling game
19. Youngster
21. One playing alone
24. When both hands meet during the day
25. Small dogs
27. We've been over these before
30. Wise men
33. Come forth
35. Evade
37. Tart fruit
38. Speck
39. Hindu mystic
42. Pea's home
43. Cries of content
44. Historical periods
45. Freud's focus
46. __ down the law
47. It's what you owe
48. Freshly minted

DOWN

1. Lugs around
2. Remove forcibly
3. Not too hard
4. Clothing cache
5. Hawaiian necklace
6. Ink-filled writer
7. Slender
8. It has 88 keys
9. Response to pollen, perhaps
10. Acquire knowledge
18. Steamy
20. Out of one's mind
22. Location
23. Semester
26. Pragmatic person
28. Make moist
29. Fall guy
30. General's badge
31. Hawaiian hello
32. Daring
34. Provide with funds
36. Noticed
40. Mined, but unrefined material
41. Chat

★ **Solution on page 298**

From D.C. to California

ACROSS

1. A long time
4. From California to D.C.
8. Cushion
11. We be
12. Wildcat
13. "A long time ___ "
14. Dance like Gregory Hines
15. Pants presser
16. Cherry center
17. With morals
19. Barroom drink
20. Oboe attachment
21. Called on the phone
24. Clothes for cool weather
27. Type of liqueur
30. Remove the unartistic part
33. Apiece
35. Family
36. In need of a drink
39. Combine
40. Ninny
41. Tree juice
42. Golf ball perch
43. Lounge
44. Night before
45. To ___ is human
46. Applications
47. Administered

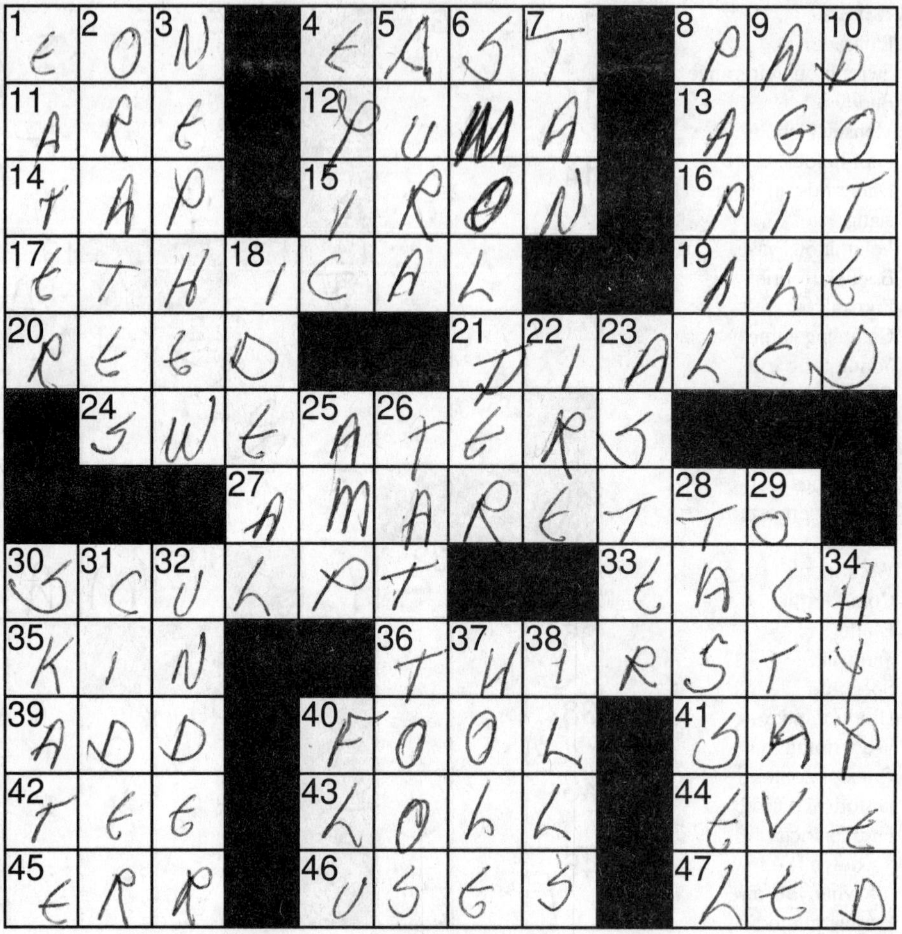

DOWN

1. Restaurant patron
2. Talks to be heard
3. Sibling's lad
4. Expensive movie
5. Subtle quality
6. Slow burn
7. Result of sun worship?
8. Like some religious decrees
9. Able to move about easily
10. Loved to excess
18. Perfect
22. Anger
23. Fall flower
25. Concert need
26. Body art
28. Graduate's frill
29. C to C
30. Fleming's footwear
31. Apple drink
32. Beneath
34. Oversold
37. Opening
38. The bad stuff
40. It'll make you sick

★ **Solution on page 298**

Lack of difficulty

ACROSS

1. Producer in a coop
4. Diamond bag
8. Scrooge's comment
11. Hatchet
12. Performs in a play
13. Ram's mate
14. Compete
15. Hone
16. Looker's leg
17. Not quite ancient
18. Old stringed instrument
19. Important period
20. Prison place
22. Tidy up
24. Large body of water
25. Put gas in a car
26. Part of a house
28. Lessen
31. Heist
34. In a little bit
36. Be indebted to
37. Surf and ___
40. Plaything
41. Bullfight "bravo!"
42. Disparaging word
43. Had a bite
44. Part of MPG
45. Lack of difficulty
46. Safety at the circus
47. Pig's place
48. Fruit grower
49. Uh-huh

DOWN

1. Mayhem
2. Napoleon and others
3. Sewing spike
4. Cry and cry
5. Painful
6. Breastbone
7. High regard
8. Have kids, biblically
9. Cognizant
10. Macho one
21. Animal fat
23. Copies
25. In fashion
27. Start
29. The study of plants
30. Baby's shoe
31. Basketball
32. He barely gives a hoot
33. Suspicious
35. Russian refusals
38. Decoy
39. Without cost

★ **Solution on page 298**

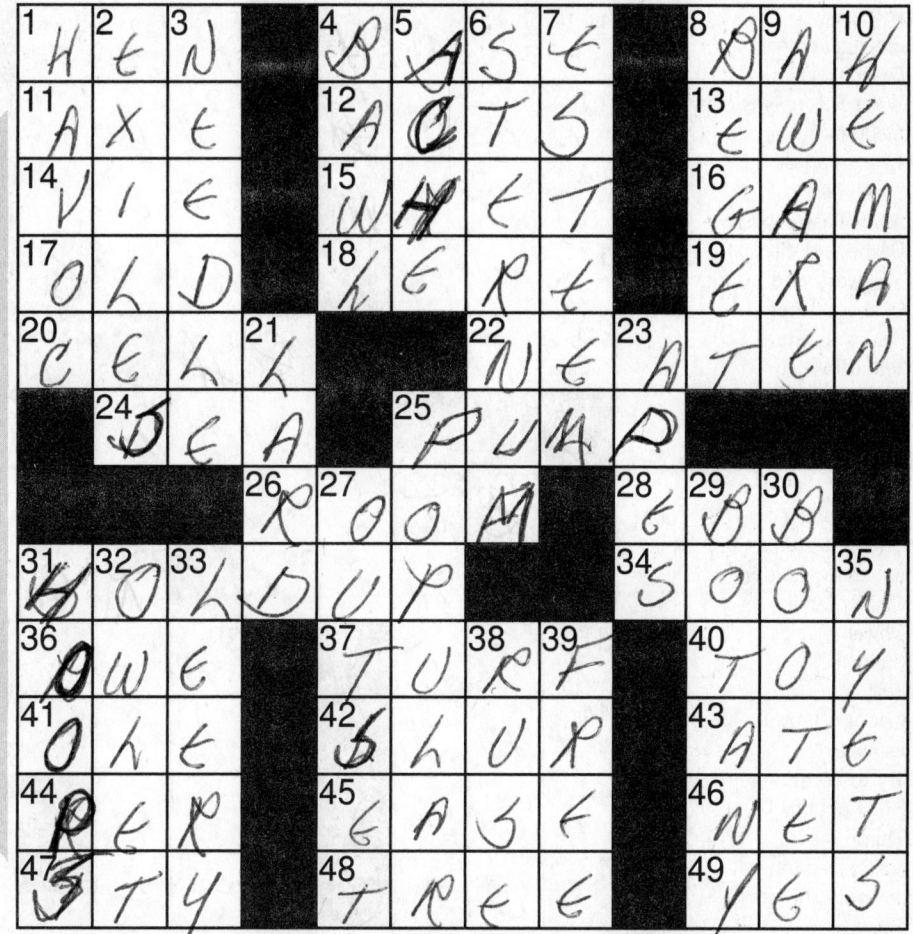

World that can be whirled

ACROSS

1. Elephant color
5. Baseballer's need
8. What 5 Across is often made from
11. Tibetan priest
12. Yuck!
13. Animal assemblage
14. Dashboard display
16. ___ work and no play . . .
17. Coal container
18. Realty measure
19. Tell a fib
20. A bit, to a dollar
22. Like an untended garden
24. Offshore
26. Motorist's need
27. "That's show ___!"
29. Doorbell sound
31. Ice cream holders
33. Courtly family
37. Dowel
38. Chums
40. Belly
41. Cry of discovery
42. Estrange
44. Try to court
45. 2,000 pounds
46. Thing
47. Neither's partner
48. Spy with the eyes
49. Minus

DOWN

1. World that can be whirled
2. Spokes of a wheel, perhaps
3. In the midst of
4. Sweet potato
5. Deli worker
6. Antiquer's aid
7. Tossed
8. Showy flower
9. One side in a game of eight ball
10. Like Swiss cheese
15. Consumes
21. Fog
23. Like quiche
25. Flight provider
27. Weepy cry
28. Like a game under a dome
30. Sniffer
31. What Jack broke when he fell down
32. Petty quarrels
34. Playing marble
35. Minstrel's instruments
36. Flower parts
39. Skin soother
43. Nothing

★**Solution on page 298**

Words of praise

ACROSS

1. Pickle holder
4. Tater
8. Little bit
11. Purpose
12. Dunce cap shape
13. Overwhelm
14. "Let 'er ___!"
15. They make a circle
16. Place to get a drink
17. Words of praise
18. Quantum ___
19. Sphere
20. Prepared
22. Not a soul
24. Like a fox
25. "I'm ___ you!"
26. Feel green?
28. Central control
31. Golfer's sidekick
34. Talent
36. Trouble for Shakespeare
37. Pappy's spouse
39. Green veggie
40. Disencumber
41. This spot
42. ___ port in a storm
43. Plead
44. Secretly follow
45. Vote in favor of
46. Take to court
47. ASAP
48. Request

DOWN

1. One of twelve people, often
2. Comments to the audience
3. Rub out a ratification
4. Like a reptile
5. Tiny opening
6. Eerie
7. Tyrant
8. Forbidden
9. Prize
10. Horse race
21. Given a new color
23. Tremendous benefit
25. Have too much of a good thing
27. Starry times
29. Green tropical fruit
30. Parts of an act
31. Dr. Atkins wants them limited
32. Farewell, mon ami
33. Elude
34. Prepared to propose
35. Boat that goes both ways
38. Diva's number

★**Solution on page 298**

Infatuated

ACROSS

1. Fodder for a dirty magazine
5. You might have it sunny-side up
8. Taste, as in wine
11. Neighborhood
12. Pigeon's purr
13. One-spot
14. Camera picture
16. "___ the season . . ."
17. Owns
18. Married
19. Shade
20. Off-key
22. What a beatnik beats
23. Infatuated
25. Where the grapes grow
28. Lots of land
31. Entrance halls
33. Spoken
34. Card game, or what you say when it ends
35. Space
36. Go bad
37. Banister
39. Little piggy
40. Common survey question
41. Forearm bone
42. ___ *Now for Something Completely Different*
43. Angry
44. Where to lay an egg

DOWN

1. Turkish title
2. Decorative
3. Explanation
4. Snippet of sleep
5. Management level
6. Less than better
7. Achieved
8. Silky fabric
9. Cake cover
10. Green sauce
15. Hindu mystics
19. Now
21. Kind of orange
22. Farther than
24. Classy
26. Entertain lavishly
27. Saps
28. Main artery
29. Sing
30. Like most movies
32. Sidewalk sound
34. Go ___ for
37. Overactive actor
38. Stocking slit

★ **Solution on page 298**

Dagnabbit!

ACROSS

1. Leather piercer
4. Jabber
7. Gush
11. By way of
12. Cooking liquid
13. Part of a foot
14. Trespass
16. Where to get a BLT PDQ
17. Pain
18. Have a bite
20. Made a lap
21. Require
22. Bombing run
24. Concealed
27. On tape
29. 100 centimes
30. Dagnabbit!
34. Choose
35. What this and that make
37. ___ and legend
38. In the vicinity
40. Galleries
42. Info
43. Cleopatra's snake
44. "___ in a million years!"
45. Hodgepodge in a pot
46. Bashful
47. Nonalcoholic

DOWN

1. Birdlike
2. Flinch
3. Wood spinner
4. "___ Are There"
5. Assistant
6. Glad
7. Depressed
8. Abracadabra
9. Custard-filled pastry
10. Ivory-colored
15. Lessen
19. Ripped
23. Puzzling question
25. Properties without buildings
26. Anxieties
27. Say again
28. It's left in a will
29. Spots for frogs
31. Circular
32. Knight's outfit
33. Irritable
36. Dogsled command
39. Like sushi
41. Secret agent

★**Solution on page 298**

Apprehend

ACROSS

1. Places to hit the hay?
6. Challenged
11. Radiant
12. Not bugged
13. Playwright's product
14. Tiny tabby
15. Nonetheless
16. British bumbler
18. Mugger repellent
20. Tales
25. Ground, as one's teeth
28. Appearance
29. It's often said with a raised hand
30. Soft
32. Follows
34. They're on a janitor's ring
35. Expert pilots
37. Number in a pair
40. Catered event
44. Use 4-letter words
46. Almost
47. Like a haunted house
48. Manuscripts
49. Bird buildings

DOWN

1. Lord's companion
2. Shrek, for one
3. Brit's apartment buddy
4. Male cat
5. Fabric sample
6. Worshiped one
7. Appear onstage
8. Often-traveled path
9. Before, once
10. Reading room
12. Go down the slope
17. Cry
19. Like a fireplace
21. Someone you can count on
22. Nature's alarm clocks
23. At this time
24. Wild blue yonder
25. Sticky bit
26. Apprehend
27. Water barrier
31. Minimize
33. Leaves port
36. Shed tears
38. "___ for me!"
39. Mined-over matters
40. Picnic pest
41. Admission charge
42. One way to send a picture
43. Handicraft
45. Petite

★ **Solution on page 298**

Suspicion

ACROSS

1. Military branch
5. Evian, for one
8. Low on funds
12. Boyfriend
13. Pot top
14. Earring's locale
15. Indoor light source
16. Freud's find
17. "Once ___ a time . . ."
18. Go by, like time
20. Done in the dishwasher
22. Suspicion
24. Pulverize in the food processor
27. Put in through the keyboard
31. Raw material
32. Words to live by
34. Sailor's assent
35. Appeals to
37. Continue a subscription
39. Have reference
41. Picture taker
44. Kisses loudly
48. Roast roaster
49. Annoy
51. Lion's facial encircler
52. Medicine tablet
53. Strong cleaner
54. Fairly matched
55. Crosscurrent
56. Use a needle
57. Bawdy

DOWN

1. Competent
2. Actual
3. *Y Tu* ___ *Tambien*
4. Starbucks connoisseur
5. Glossy
6. Arnold of *Green Acres*, for one
7. "I'd like to thank my ___ fans"
8. Dive
9. "My mistake"
10. Woodwind instrument
11. Shred
19. Sports shoe
21. Meantime
23. Minimal
24. Luau chow
25. Coffee container
26. Gun, like an engine
28. Jogged
29. Tear maker
30. Beads on the blades
33. More than sidetracks
36. Not covert
38. Tooth covering
40. Out of kilter
41. Try to adapt
42. Fanatical
43. Come together
45. Lair for a bear
46. Was privy to
47. Transmit
50. Bread sounding like a sense of humor

★ **Solution on page 299**

More than just a job

ACROSS

1. Vulgar
7. Make a sheepish comment?
12. Kind of lizard
13. Cause to do under duress
14. Unlikely to stand up
15. Source
16. On edge
17. Male child
18. Like 3 or 7
19. Fiddle with
22. Sauce seasoning
26. Recent
27. Put up in poker
31. Good's opposite
32. Hot or iced beverage
33. Wet weather
34. Office notice
35. "To ___ is human . . ."
36. Espied
37. More than just a job
40. Tap lightly
43. It'll come and go
44. "___ ho!"
49. Nuclear
51. Head cushion
52. Dairy snack
53. Caught con
54. Digging tool
55. Tries for a ringer or a leaner

DOWN

1. Prepare flour
2. Leer at
3. Destroy
4. Water walls
5. Map within a map
6. 24 hours
7. Carried
8. Living necklace
9. Therefore
10. Base's counterpart
11. Cultivate
13. Pots and pans
17. Showed scorn
20. Relate with each other
21. Uncommon
22. Skirt edge
23. Night's start
24. Edge of a golf hole
25. Group that functions as one
28. Type of 47 Down
29. Part of a suit
30. Finale
38. Burning
39. Animal with a horn
40. Gives money to
41. Upon
42. Frat party attire
45. Shade trees
46. "___ poor Yorick . . ."
47. Congressional noun
48. Barnyard birthers
50. Pigs like to wallow in it
51. Poe's pendulum place

★ **Solution on page 299**

Search for gold

ACROSS

1. Study at the last minute
5. Implore
9. Strawberry seed
12. Ace in the ___
13. Easter animal?
14. Mesozoic, e.g.
15. Foal food
16. Listen up!
17. Comes before la
18. Search for gold
20. Sole
21. Highly trafficked place
23. Sermon spots
27. Peruse again
31. Bosc and Anjou
32. Pageant topper
33. Closer to pushing the envelope
35. Holy
36. Shrimp dish
38. Zits
41. Disobeyed
46. Cow's comment
47. Ticklish color
48. Trendy tea drink
49. Explorer's need
50. " . . . but just this ___"
51. Word on a towel
52. Cry at a bullfight
53. High school attendee
54. Desires

DOWN

1. Use a knife in the kitchen
2. Noise from the crowd
3. Low female voice
4. Predicament
5. Theater workers
6. Do a double take
7. Hose holder
8. Large deer
9. Coin for Carlos
10. It might rust
11. Imported ___ ale
19. Astronomer's unit
20. Songlike
22. Not wholesale
23. King Kong, for one
24. Was CEO for
25. Chasing game
26. End one's slumber
28. Carol Burnett's thing to tug
29. "We ___ the World"
30. Mom's mate
34. Canyon
35. "Wiser words were never ___"
37. No-no for words
38. Armory stash
39. Santa's "Sorry!"
40. Not yup
42. Twinging
43. "My Country 'Tis of ___"
44. Get via hard work
45. Badmouth
47. Cauldron

★ Solution on page 299

Shine

ACROSS

1. Thay it like tho
5. Femme fatale
9. Scott Joplin piece
12. "___ us a child is born"
13. Sunburn soother
14. Follower and preceder to "in"
15. Storage spot in the backyard
16. Forgetful actor's request
17. Personal write-up
18. Paving substance
19. Flower part
20. Ram's remark
21. Draw out
23. Succeed in Lent
25. Artifact
26. Neutral hue
27. Scout group
28. Homer's harrumph
29. The gift of ___
32. Tribal unit
34. Cat-o'-nine-___
36. Move nonchalantly
39. ___ waste
40. Dutch ___ disease
41. Like an approach to a loop-the-loop
43. Flower appreciator
44. A long time ___
45. Conceal
46. Record a TV show
47. Gym surface
48. Radiate
49. Computer person
50. Understand
51. Stage scenery
52. Garden spots

DOWN

1. Shine
2. Breathed in
3. Like an operating room
4. Seed holder
5. Personal servant
6. Landed
7. Ruler
8. Apple tool
9. Jewish scholar
10. Pseudonym
11. Rub it in
19. Film, for short
22. Piece of cake
24. Common sweetener
26. A really long time
28. When the sun's out
30. Military pilot's post
31. Censored
33. Hair on your lids
34. Source of domestic water?
35. "Yeah, right!" reactions
36. Where things are sewn together
37. Tiny pond plants
38. Killed in the Bible
39. Borscht necessity
42. Revise a manuscript
46. Where to rub-a-dub

★ **Solution on page 299**

Flashy

ACROSS

1. Measure of gold purity
6. Intentions
11. Spring flowers
13. Baseball group
14. Silver confetti
15. Flashy
16. Rim
17. Give a lecture
19. Metal man
21. Openhanded blow
25. Prickly desert items
28. Gotcha!
30. Wood chopper
31. Relative of 28 Across
32. Honkers
34. Sickly
35. Stick
36. Assembly is required for this
37. Everglades bird
39. Putin's veto
41. By law
43. Strange
45. Smallest particle
49. Hope to achieve
52. Fleet
54. College employee
55. Petty officers
56. Polka dots
57. Media people

DOWN

1. Go fly a ___
2. Like the Kalahari
3. Boxing place
4. Make yourself heard
5. Player's peg
6. Sassy
7. Bowling alleys
8. Turkish title
9. Cashew, for example
10. Observe
12. Neatnik's least favorite companion
13. Hate hate hate
18. Chicken choice
20. Swine's sound
22. Lion's home
23. Car bar
24. Animal fur
25. ___ on the cob
26. Greeting to Sinbad
27. Cryptographer's case
29. Like people who say 26 Down, often
33. More smarmy
38. Compelling charm
40. Chubby Checker's dance
42. Aussie aloha
44. Time periods
46. Domesticated
47. Arty tributes
48. ___ best friend
49. Tummy muscles
50. Have dinner
51. Champion
53. Sales ___

★ **Solution on page 299**

Blossom

ACROSS

1. Ignited
7. Pressed suit
12. Blossom
13. Act like a coward
14. Shopper's bonus
15. Beaten in a fight
16. One who is in the red
17. Thief
19. No longer chic
21. Canyon's effect
25. Cries of recognition
28. Join in matrimony
29. Pancake topper
30. Black or Red
31. Mature one
33. Ginger ___
34. Steep in cost
36. Doves do it
37. Prohibition
38. Band member's highlight
39. Cat calls?
41. Chem lab container
43. Get an acceptable grade in
47. Casual shoe
50. Wintry hanger
52. Beat at the buffet
53. By a ___ margin
54. Dog show category
55. Says "hi" to

DOWN

1. Bushy do
2. Took a plane
3. Brain part
4. Hugo or Tony
5. Bumped into
6. Built a building
7. Threesome
8. Lime ___
9. Printer's need
10. Improve with ___
11. Was in charge
13. Oaf
18. Breaks down
20. Be off with you!
22. Grouch
23. ___ hoop
24. Unseal
25. Poisonous snakes
26. Hoagie
27. Wind gatherer
29. Stash
32. *Through the ___ Glass*
35. Sleepy one's request
39. Purchasing place
40. Steeple
42. Take control
44. Land measurement
45. Place to stick mail
46. Does embroidery
47. Tennis ploy
48. ___ *Miss Brooks*
49. Did lunch
51. Coupe or sedan

★ **Solution on page 299**

Right now!

ACROSS

1. "___ and good morrow!"
5. Use a swizzle stick
9. Halloween shout
12. Opera song
13. Senator's assistant
14. "Shut yer ___"
15. Teller's stack
16. Medicine dispensers
18. Diner goer
20. In addition
21. Totals numbers
23. Fuzzy fruit that's green inside
27. Solar power source
30. Enmity
31. Four-door car
32. Nook and ___
34. One with a wee one
35. Irritate
36. Large
37. *Much ___ About Nothing*
38. Russian ruler, once
39. Yuletide purchase
40. Root for poi
42. Attain
47. Elevated region
51. A psychic might read it
52. Conquer a test
53. Flaky rock
54. Right now!
55. "Quiet on the ___!"
56. One who looks down their nose
57. Helps off the highway

DOWN

1. Not merely dislike
2. Region
3. Dryer collection
4. At ___ (relax)
5. Feeling blue
6. Soapbox speech
7. Worshiped ones
8. Company spokespeople
9. See ya
10. Boating tool
11. HQ
17. Fireplace tool
19. Like some dark days
22. No longer wet
24. What a light bulb signifies
25. Magician's stick
26. Fascinated by
27. Amscray!
28. Footed vases
29. Partner to gramps
31. More wise
33. Toward Santa, most of the year
34. Key lime ___
36. Rodeo critter
39. Part of a wedding gown
41. ___ for the poor
43. Right on a map
44. Highway goer
45. Stick in one's ___
46. Haberdashery wares
47. Possesses
48. Drink coolers
49. Understand
50. Dainty dollop

★ **Solution on page 299**

Honor

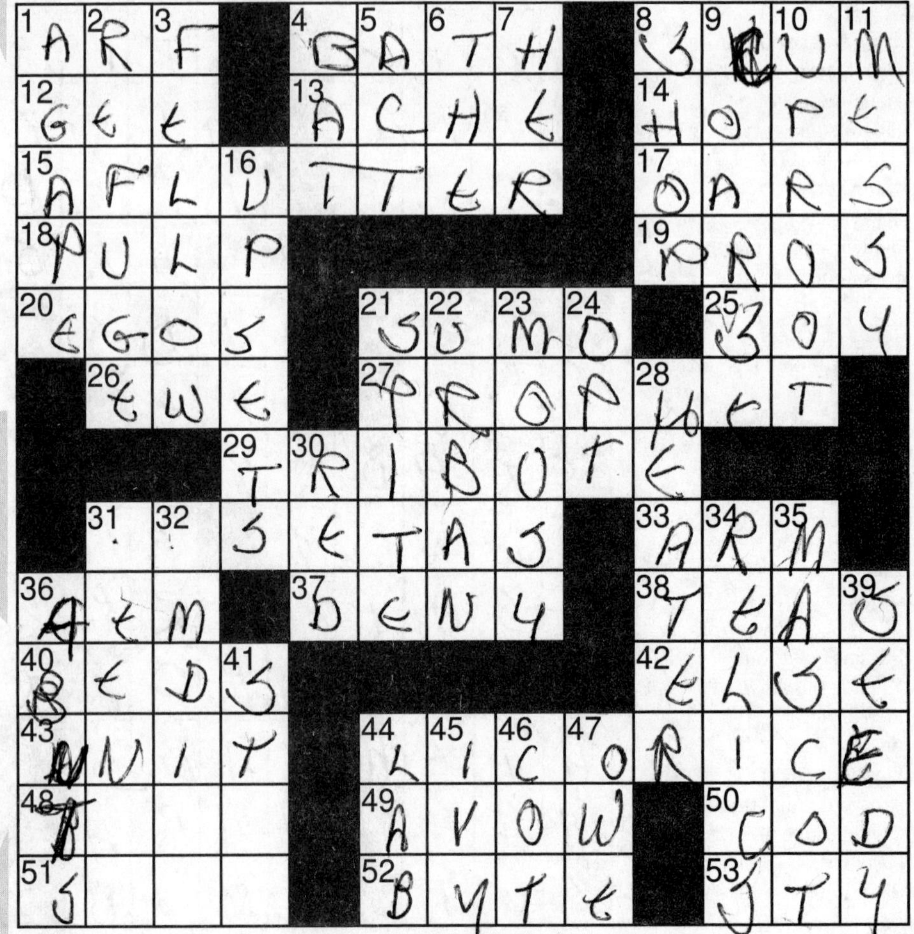

ACROSS

1. Spot's statement
4. Tub event
8. Cleanser target
12. ___ whiz
13. Hurt
14. *Ryan's ___*
15. "My heart's all ___"
17. Rower's needs
18. Unstrained OJ has it
19. ___ and cons
20. Snobs have inflated ones
21. Type of wrestling
25. ___ sauce
26. Woolly mama
27. Biblical seer
29. Honor
31. Coins in Mexico
33. Provide with guns
36. Semiprecious stone
37. Say "no" to
38. Darjeeling and pekoe
40. Story sites for kiddies
42. What ___ is new?
43. Troop group
44. Black or red candy
48. Currency used by much of NATO
49. Assert
50. Cape ___
51. Word that precedes and follows "by"
52. Computer unit
53. Pig's digs

DOWN

1. Hanging open
2. Sanctuary
3. Chap
4. Cricket need
5. Make-believe
6. *Beauty and ___ Beast*
7. That girl
8. Patronize a store
9. Raspy
10. Snag a weed
11. Like Oscar Madison
16. Victories over a champion
21. Malice
22. In the city
23. Quite reserved
24. Select
28. Winter need
30. Roulette color
31. Food allergen
32. Dynasty
34. Historical pieces
35. Team's symbolic pride
36. Attaches
39. Like the wrong side of town
41. Word in an octagon
44. Bunsen burner's place
45. Old college growth
46. Temporary bed
47. Take out a mortgage

★Solution on page 299

Wily

ACROSS

1. Share gossip
5. Cry before using the iron
9. Rear of a ship
12. Lasso material
13. Controversial wedding vow word
14. Attempt
15. Poker cheat's sleeve stash
16. Arrived like the sun
17. Felt-___ pen
18. Identical
19. Class cost
20. Pedestal
21. It might be on a pedestal
23. Loud vehicles, often
25. Tokyo tender
26. Nada
28. Like cinders
29. Bits of news
31. Shed like a bird
34. It might be between your teeth
35. Taste a drink
38. Tropical fruit
40. Spitfire
42. From the top
43. Tourist's destination
45. High mountains
46. Person of habit?
47. Not false
48. Bird calls
49. *My ___ Sal*
50. Ties the knot
51. Leg covering
52. Wily
53. Bauxite and others
54. Place next to the decimal point

DOWN

1. Saucy
2. Find
3. Yeti, perhaps
4. Under siege
5. Throw in the towel
6. Slender woodwind
7. Bowling button
8. Watch
9. Stick onto an e-mail
10. Like some kittens
11. Uses a keyboard
20. Public transport
22. Togetherness
24. Like a sore throat
27. Part of a journey
30. *The ___ of King George*
31. How-to book
32. For all to see
33. Statute
35. Scene for a barroom brawl
36. Intrude
37. Vigilante groups in Westerns
38. Painful desires
39. NPR or NBC
41. Mexican chip
44. With nary a stitch
47. Tango requirement

★ **Solution on page 299**

Chapter 2

Easy as Pie

Getting closer

ACROSS

1. Talk all at once
5. Rolling stone's lack
9. Shape of a St. Louis landmark
13. Toss in a chip
14. See 56 Across
15. Nasty
16. Matinee megastar
17. Eden attire
18. My word!
19. Knock over
21. Getting closer
23. Princess peeve
24. Cue to a hubby
25. Prizes
28. Put in the oven
30. ___ *the Dog*
31. Before I'm ready
33. ___ and flow
36. Soapmaker's substance
37. Fit for a king
38. Needed back at the library
39. Offered, as a farewell
40. You might mix granola into it
43. One that's mighty pretty
46. Baseball's path
47. Accounting books
50. Takes another base
53. Like some tests
54. Scuttlebutt
56. See 14 Across
57. Use a towel on
58. Statement of what you owe
59. Singe
60. Sees as profit
61. Kid's throwing game
62. Water wavelet

DOWN

1. Horse's pace
2. Cancel
3. Gridlock
4. "Mother's Little ___"
5. Double agent
6. The loneliest number
7. Kind of party
8. Comfy seating
9. Path
10. Firm
11. Trolley sound
12. ___ your bets
20. "When I was a ___"
22. Black
25. The hole thing
26. Method
27. Acorn, for one
28. Car cover
29. Someone you can rely on
32. ___ of reason
33. Taught
34. Pricker
35. Wager
37. Hourly worker's concern
39. Reveille items
41. Kind of bran
42. Lube job necessity
43. Uncovered, as a cover
44. Like places Scooby Doo goes to
45. Conform
48. Meat lovers' messy grub
49. Use a scissors on
50. Auction end cry
51. Put ammo in
52. Agile
55. It might put you in bed

★ **Solution on page 300**

So be it!

ACROSS

1. Knight's weapon
5. Male tykes
9. ___ the hogs
13. Press a suit
14. Cooperate in a crime
15. Busy place
16. Tuna treat
17. Engine's happy sound
18. So be it!
19. Emcee's speech
21. Net draggers
23. ___ the joint (spied on)
24. Vision
25. Throw in
27. Conceit
28. Unit of homework?
31. Like Felix Unger
34. Nobleman
36. Sport where horses aren't in water
37. Part of the eye
38. Run away
39. Took out a loan
40. American amigo
41. Ball
42. Column's counterpart
44. Dame
46. Yellow fruit
50. Come together
53. Unmanned plane
54. What a temptress does
55. Work hard
57. *Mission: Impossible* symbol
58. Gets your goat
59. Theorem word
60. Not new
61. Hey, you!
62. Mar a car
63. ___ *Make a Deal*

DOWN

1. Copycat
2. Field for fighting
3. Young horses
4. Beseeches
5. Racing unit
6. Neighbors
7. Rump
8. One not in the lead
9. Commandment word
10. Counterpart to 46 Across
11. Completed
12. Writing utensils
20. Peculiar
22. Owl's question?
26. Took out of the freezer
28. Take a trailer
29. José's hurray
30. Show you agree
31. ___ it in the bud
32. Distinctive period
33. Not do well
35. Kind of tuna
36. Strong
41. Galena, for one
43. Experienced
44. Hallowed
45. Condescend
47. Mickey ___
48. When it started
49. Requirements
50. Select coupons
51. Mine and yours
52. Big boats
56. Parking ___

★ **Solution on page 300**

Hey!

ACROSS

1. Bloc's agreement
5. At a distance
9. Social slight
13. Shampoo additive
14. Uh-uh
15. Manuel's money
16. Eat in splendor
17. Dancer's duds
18. Lopped off
19. Tracing aid
21. Guard
23. Hey!
24. The Boston ___ Party
25. Common breakfast ingredient
28. Weak, like an excuse
30. Work for the copy center
35. Container in a coven
37. With the fat removed
38. Aggravate
39. "Scarborough Fair" herb
42. Like a rejected draftee
44. Babe's cart
45. Gender
46. Unpleased response
48. Keep a ___ on it!
50. However
54. Surgical sewing
58. Passageway
59. Leave out
61. Go elsewhere
62. On an ___ keel
63. Bargain event
64. Ballerina's move
65. Flat-topped hill
66. Stepped on
67. Kennel cry

DOWN

1. Paw parts
2. Came to earth
3. Megaphone shape
4. Itsy-bitsy
5. Not hawklike
6. Ump's cry
7. Befitting
8. Recycling aim
9. Bridge bit
10. Queue call
11. Netizen
12. ___ of work
20. Arctic weather
22. Muff preceder
24. Choir member
25. Shade of brown
26. Profit
27. Big gap
29. Special effect
31. *A Nightmare on ___ Street*
32. Like two ___ in a pod
33. Like steak tartare
34. Jet black
36. Luau loop
40. Paid respect to
41. Give off
43. Harbor craft
47. Easy Halloween costume
49. Unlike an Amazon
50. Those folks
51. Got
52. Corrida cries
53. Elbow-wrist connector
54. Missile site
55. Part in a play
56. Up to no good
57. Ooze
60. Damage

★ **Solution on page 300**

Gain knowledge

ACROSS

1. Don't match
6. Pricy
10. Just hang out
13. Hard to believe
14. Marathon
15. Chop
16. Ferris Bueller specialty
17. Gumbo need
18. Place with a pool
19. Landlord's customer
21. Copy fixer
23. Sailor
24. Tannery tools
25. Willing
28. Ailing
30. Green hue
34. Function
35. October gem
36. Relinquished
37. Gain knowledge
39. Corner chess piece
41. Straggler's verb
42. When bears beat bulls
43. Lifter's locale
44. Depend
45. Credo
47. *All About* ___
49. Plot
52. Snuggle
56. I see what you're up to
57. Picture
60. More slippery
61. Spanish nobleman
62. Lymph ___
63. Kind of eclipse
64. Primate
65. Got bigger
66. Leaks out slowly

DOWN

1. Informal talk
2. Come in less than first
3. Similar
4. Help to relax
5. Laughing one
6. ___ football
7. Acorn's aspiration
8. Boring device
9. Wrestling hold
10. Expansive
11. Convention-like event
12. Park or neutral
20. Vacation
22. Vacation spot
24. Metal mixture
25. Swallow
26. On the briny
27. Not nice
29. "Medium" at the movies
31. Keep it in neutral
32. Osso buco need
33. With jitters
35. Like some traffic
38. Sushi need
40. Sign of bad things to come
44. Bring to safety
46. Furnishing style
48. Hat hangings
49. Sweet beverage
50. Judo move
51. Sharpen
53. Fork prong
54. Vault
55. Makes mistakes
58. Honorary writing
59. ___ and improved

★ **Solution on page 300**

I would, would I?

ACROSS

1. Road ___
4. Mire
7. De-energizes
11. In the past
12. Haunted house sounds
14. Look at in a funny way
15. "Ode on a Grecian ___"
16. Dreadful
17. Virginia dance
18. Cautious
20. Starry
22. Ransomed one
26. In need of a massage
29. Objective
30. In the know
35. Buddy
36. Use needles
38. Gave a chill to
39. Spun yarn
40. Like an omelet
41. Little holdup
42. Card suit
44. Trim a tree
45. Not there
46. Not a pretty sight
49. For a time
53. Just sat
57. Crazy bird
58. Helpers
62. Like some rinks
63. Roger Rabbit, for one
64. "I would, would I?" look
65. This gal
66. Does a hit man's job
67. Each
68. ___ person (one who's not himself)

DOWN

1. Move something heavy
2. Fairy tale baddie
3. No longer 45 Across
4. Archer's need
5. Klutz
6. Creature that doesn't sound old
7. Ilk
8. Distiller's need
9. Comment to the court
10. Vend
12. Sandwich spread
13. Ore's waste
19. Wined and dined, for instance
21. Body of water
23. For Pete's ___!
24. Sensation
25. *The Three ___*
26. Biblical book
27. Fellow
28. Wahine wiggle
31. Used a certain well
32. A problem for Noriega
33. Not the front
34. Embroidery place
37. Key problem
43. Slippery fish
47. Votes for
48. Jeopardy
49. Choral singer
50. Fido's remark
51. Horseshoe's place
52. Cozy places to stay
54. Sylvester's weakness
55. Reverb response
56. ___ in the wool
59. Mischievous one
60. Playing cube
61. Make a typo

★ **Solution on page 300**

Legitimate

ACROSS

1. One place to sleep
5. Refreshing calls
8. Stooge
11. Ambience
12. Religious painting
14. Tennis shot
15. Feed into a fax
16. White collar folk
17. Annoyance
18. In this manner
20. Extra in a Western
22. Fraternal member
24. Title title for Poitier
25. Commercial spots
28. Mood
30. Freud's prop
34. Egg on
36. Boeing concern
38. Gives rise to
40. Lingerie item
41. Note taker
42. Truckstop truck
44. It means trouble, my friends
45. Teacher temp
47. Medico
48. Unproven
52. Picked up on
57. Pitching ___
58. Sued one's claim
60. Legitimate
61. Wall hanging
62. Big books
63. Workshop holder
64. Affirmative
65. Minuscule
66. Tarzan's pals

DOWN

1. Endure
2. You hit me!
3. German lady
4. Sits in the sun
5. First ___
6. Clothing seams
7. Messy places
8. Boater's tarp
9. *God's Little* ___
10. Look
12. Missile ammo
13. Buffoonery
19. Allow
21. Takes a pratfall
23. Benders in the legs
25. "Rock of ___"
26. "___ Rock the Boat"
27. Guru
29. Needed an eraser
31. Festive event
32. Amino ___
33. Hock shop item
35. Thick
37. Gradual absorption
39. Candy substance
43. Put a cold pack on
46. Underneath
48. Not home
49. Folk history
50. Scads
51. Tenth of a buck
53. Star that goes boom
54. Bounce stones off the water
55. Let up on
56. Salon supplies
59. Spelling event

★ **Solution on page 300**

Balderdash

ACROSS

1. Raised animals
5. Stable food
8. Gloom
13. Sales pitch
14. Bit a burrito
15. American bird
16. Bookie's concern
17. Decay
18. Opted for
19. Seven days
20. Pedro's pal
22. Gardening supply
23. Bad biters
25. Sandwich bread
27. Mason ___
29. Edition
32. '60s hairstyle
36. Get up
38. ___ takers?
39. Victory
40. Vintner's specialty
41. Hill dweller
42. That bunch
43. It's a long story
44. Hollow rock
46. Bo Derek's number
47. "In ___ beginning . . . "
49. Get the sowed stuff
51. It might say "Welcome"
54. Casa cover
57. Trudge
60. Certain somethings
62. Exchange vows
63. Go into the shallow end
64. Half of a heightening set
65. Annoying one
66. Grocery list entry
67. Balderdash
68. Good name for a lawyer
69. Army meal

DOWN

1. What the wind does
2. Amusement park attraction
3. Lovable
4. Spots for students
5. Irritate
6. Particle
7. Himalayan Sasquatch
8. 34 Down
9. College cheer
10. Divas have them
11. To boot
12. Hollow shoot
21. Dull color
24. Kind of chart
26. Per
27. The first summer blockbuster
28. Solo at La Scala
30. Rational
31. Biblical preposition
33. Treadle
34. 8 Down, essentially
35. Available for business
37. Senate position
41. Elderly
42. Casual shirt
45. Deepen, as a channel
48. Rapid
50. Drowning
51. "Monster ___"
52. Mercury or Saturn
53. Tony Orlando and Dawn, for one
55. Holds the deed on
56. Suitor
58. English 101 readings
59. Precious ones
61. Porter or stout

★**Solution on page 300**

Grand tale

ACROSS

1. Volcano output
5. Goblet feature
9. Entrance to 27 Down
13. Good times
14. Sushi fish
15. Cozy place
16. Ousted
18. Mercenary's need
19. ". . . happily ___ after"
20. Talk back
21. Pond scum
24. Gee whiz!
27. Place for a nature walk
28. Escaped info
29. Break
32. Make it read better
33. Trifling
34. ___ *American Cousin*
35. Believe it or ___!
36. Hindu honorifics
37. Marmaduke's treat
38. Bring to court
39. Grand tale
40. Timeworn
41. Freshwater fish
42. Edens
43. Not a big talker
46. Congratulate
48. Bad smell
49. Drink with tequila
54. Kid
55. Carve
56. Admit frankly
57. Something to swear
58. Empty ___
59. Kind

DOWN

1. Called the shots
2. *You ___ There*
3. Cauldron
4. Fiery remnant
5. Where to find 4 Down
6. Fix a piano
7. Peppy
8. Infuriated
9. Brief light
10. Priest of the East
11. Goals
12. Those in the know
17. Not fictitious
21. Love
22. Churchgoers
23. Vamoose
25. Mare's meal
26. It's the limit
27. Brief home
28. Make rules
29. It lays an egg
30. Female family members
31. What is sought
33. Nickname for Dad
36. "___, though I walk . . ."
37. Vehicle in *Speed*
40. Common first (or second) word
41. Train bunk
42. "There ___ to be a law"
43. Austin Powers's aura
44. Thought
45. Practically all
47. Pendulum paths
49. Chess pieces
50. *Brother ___*
51. Wall creeper
52. Summit
53. Wow

★**Solution on page 300**

Overwhelmed

1	2	3	4	■	5	6	7	8	■	9	10	11	12
13				■	14				■	15			
16				■	17				■	18			
19				■	20			■	21				
■	■	■	22	23		■	24	25			■	■	■
26	27	28			■	29					30	31	32
33			■	34	35				■	■	36		
37			■	■	38				39	■	40		
41			42	43				■	44	45			
■	■	■	46				■	47			■	■	■
48	49	50			■	51	52		■	53	54	55	56
57				■	58				■	59			
60				■	61				■	62			
63				■	64				■	65			

ACROSS

1. Use the phone
5. Airport queue
9. Talking-doll word
13. Clarinet's cousin
14. Kind of tradition
15. Italian desserts
16. Too bad!
17. Extremely
18. Earth inheritor
19. Camera part
20. Corrode
21. Party givers
22. Eternity
24. Night times
26. Carved gem
29. Cel blocker
33. Have a tab
34. Ship areas
36. Regret
37. Corral
38. Ask on one's knees
40. Monty Python opener
41. Teacher
44. Inner torment
46. Grocery need
47. Needle part
48. Birth day event
51. Operate
53. Stereo pieces
57. Alimony collectors
58. Take care of
59. Saw or bit
60. Happiness
61. ___ *the Woods*
62. Otherwise
63. Put in the mail
64. Fret
65. More than want

DOWN

1. Fossil fuel
2. Qualified
3. Temporary gift
4. Renter
5. Women's group?
6. ___ 51
7. Moe, on *The Simpsons*
8. Crafty
9. Brunch drink
10. Super serves
11. Encounter
12. Requests
21. Shorten
23. Lookie!
25. Passport stamp
26. Deal
27. Overwhelmed
28. Windows pull-down
29. Portion
30. Math class
31. Pitcher's goals
32. Remainder
35. Elects
39. Groundhog ___
42. Shut
43. Broadcast
45. Make shipshape
47. Wealthy alums do it
48. Stamina, in *Variety*
49. Wheel shaft
50. "How long has it ___?"
52. Feed the kitty
54. Gopher kin
55. Sit for a portrait
56. Downhill racer
58. "Whether ___ nobler to . . ."

★ **Solution on page 300**

With sprinkles

ACROSS

1. Between
5. "___ and Circumstance"
9. Hair holders
13. Took a trolley
14. To no ___
16. Suit
17. Golf club
18. With sprinkles
19. Baby bag item
20. Ethnic eatery
21. ___ or nothing
22. Bad to the core
24. Cobbler's tool
26. Dominant
28. Got it?
29. Take on workers
32. Like a parabola
34. Gotcha in the galley
35. Layer with a hole
37. Story starter
41. Ingenue
43. Trendy salad green
46. Via, on a sign
47. Fireman's supplies
49. One off their rocker
50. Errand person
53. Brings to a close
55. It has a honker
58. Sported
59. *The ___ Couple*
60. Endowers, often
62. State veep
64. Exercises outside
68. Raced
69. Use a razor
71. Word processor key
72. Blacken
73. Aerial
74. Wild guess
75. Healthy
76. More than you can imagine
77. Xmas expectation

DOWN

1. Very dry
2. Request for seconds
3. *American ___*
4. Prerecovery stage
5. ___ with fear
6. Racetrack shape
7. Cliff Claven, for one
8. Diaper fastener
9. Eyed ingredient?
10. Uses the egress
11. Home on the range
12. Acted-out event
15. Song segment
23. ___ day at a time
25. Ram cushion
27. They might be designated
29. *___ of Eden*
30. Ancient tale
31. Fig-figured fruit
33. Preceder and follower for "eat"
36. Questionnaire option
38. They're sisters
39. Piece for a P.I.
40. Chows down
42. Bad toupee
44. Gets better
45. Like a resale item
48. Italian spice
51. Have a deed for
52. Palm off
54. Tweak
55. ___-22
56. Oahu welcome
57. In the boonies
61. "A ___ formality"
63. A bun in the ___
65. Latch ___
66. Reception to a roo
67. Sheds tears
70. Gilligan's home

★ **Solution on page 301**

I like that!

ACROSS

1. Thrift ___
5. A needle pulling thread
8. Flame watcher
12. Kind of duck
13. Tot's bedtime
15. Portuguese purchaser
16. Spring flower
17. Cheer up
18. Let go of
19. Went another way
21. Arm joints
23. I like that!
24. Lamb's lament
25. It's fate
28. Represent
32. Obligations
33. Golly!
34. Cattle call
35. Skilled
36. Croc doc
37. Desolate
39. May honoree
40. Feel bad
41. *A ___ of Their Own*
42. Soul
45. Bicycle built for two
46. Fella
47. "You're the ___"
48. Disco effect
51. Garden herb
56. Like a tug-of-war rope
57. Agenda
59. Rash treatment
60. Goad
61. Supported
62. Prep soil for planting
63. Worker's manager
64. Crib or cot
65. Procedure part

DOWN

1. Went downhill
2. Tortoise competitor
3. Drop out
4. Cancun cash
5. Choose
6. Steer clear of
7. Moistened
8. Road divider
9. Not theirs
10. Hot to ___
11. Brewer's need
13. Things in a row
14. Plebe
20. Like impossible goals
22. Cleaning item
25. Congrats
26. They're on the agenda
27. Sample soda
28. *Desk* ___
29. Something you project
30. Public assembly
31. Oxen harness
32. "There Is Nothin' Like a ___"
33. Stylist's stuff
36. Go head-to-head
37. Touch or hear
38. Bit
40. A way in
41. Ran out
43. Acts like Shatner
44. Capture
45. ___ one's own horn
47. Swap
48. Hurt, as in a toe
49. Tropical tuber
50. Carpets
52. Welcome items
53. Dismounted
54. ___-playing game
55. Schnauzer's SOS
58. Women's ___

★ **Solution on page 301**

Go up and down

ACROSS

1. World-weary
6. Barbecue needs
10. Shaker filler
14. Grammarian's concern
15. Milky gem
16. Gullet
17. Highway sign
18. Can in a machine
19. Pol's office worker
20. ___ on the back
21. Complainer's sound
23. Spirits
25. Peter or Ivan
26. Put back to normal
27. You of old
30. Magnate
34. It's between here and there
36. Really steam
37. ___ a plea
40. "___ be back!"
41. It ruins the ending
44. Color
45. Tissue layer
46. ___ of conduct
47. Everyday riser
49. Met set
52. Mental faculties
53. Following
57. Unabridged dictionary, for one
59. Crepe kin
61. Go up and down
62. ___ sum
65. Parent's sister
66. Symbol
68. Having a lot to lose
70. Stadium level
71. Greek garb
72. They get you in deeper
73. It has a ripple effect
74. Where to plant
75. Way to a man's heart

DOWN

1. Use a trampoline
2. Fishing, perhaps
3. Pub missile
4. It might be over easy
5. Judges
6. Sinner's unit
7. Story's second word
8. Good and ugly alternative
9. Throw down
10. Frighten
11. Operatic solos
12. Dispense soup
13. Canary comment
22. Granola grain
24. Unpleasant
25. Nudge alternative
27. Do a pratfall
28. College residence
29. Just
31. "Hear ye" guy
32. It might be crude
33. Juan's "Whee!"
35. Companion
37. Indian tea
38. Boot out of office
39. Casa critters
42. Mom's mate
43. Tribute
48. Baa ma
50. Like many drunk singers
51. Tofu bean
53. Lessen
54. Brake ___
55. Like a pitchfork
56. Item in a crossword grid
58. Simoleons
60. Annoying spots
61. One like a lama
62. "___ Santa . . . "
63. Ain't right
64. Lookout spot
67. Pigeon patter
69. Ghost's "Gotcha!"

★**Solution on page 301**

Hurrah

ACROSS

1. Rhyming food for Paco
5. Stage strutter
8. Tend crops
12. Neutral color
13. More recent
15. You might fly into one
16. Doctor's deed
17. Ticked off
18. Bourbon Street veggie
19. Key master
21. Fled
22. MTV viewer
23. Postal-creed word
24. Vote for
26. Yule drink
29. Wacky
32. Stoles
33. More out of line
36. Table part
38. "___ of Good Feelings"
39. "In tonight's ___ . . . "
41. Hurrah
42. Mole
43. It goes on a screen
44. Hair treatment
45. Road haulers
47. Converted
50. Common wedding spot
53. Zilch
54. Porno
57. I've found you out!
58. Did hard work
62. Tuneful cadence
63. Vertigo spot
65. Doctor's miracle
66. Whiteheads
67. Kind of campaign
68. Make money
69. ___ shift
70. Bawl
71. Do a maid's job

DOWN

1. Acid ___
2. Needing a massage
3. Farmer's produce
4. Excursions
5. "Eating ___ curds and whey . . . "
6. Like an attentive one
7. Heavy ___
8. Capri attraction
9. Do fall work
10. Bad boss
11. End one's dependence
13. Dangerous liquid
14. Went back
20. Lad
25. Inedible apple part
26. Common Market money
27. Process cheese
28. Diagram on this page
30. Pilot
31. Desire
32. Given food
34. Take advantage of
35. A way out
37. Where dumbbells are
39. Satanic
40. Duel items
44. Kept order
46. Concern
48. The return key
49. It's all about you
51. Buttinsky's sounds
52. Cowboy contest
54. Refinery refuse
55. Rats
56. It's near the radius
59. Maui meal
60. Has an accident
61. Bruise a cruiser
64. Chatter

★ Solution on page 301

Gets all gussied up

ACROSS

1. Tex-Mex sauce
6. Slight lead
10. Doe beau
14. Turn over
15. Lunch time
16. Visit
17. Plateaus
18. Big brass
19. ___ beer
20. You there!
21. Poetic eye
22. Prop gun supply
24. Diamond unit
26. Left on a piano
27. Lug
29. Copy
33. Bedspreads
34. Eliminate
35. Fish 'n' chips fish, sometimes
36. Young'un's nickname
37. Piehole
38. Home preceder
40. Resentment
41. Stone worth stealing
42. Gets all gussied up
43. Boring
46. Unpleasant
47. Needed back at Blockbuster
48. Attempted
49. Gives entrance to
52. Unlikely beauty queen
53. Get a ___!
57. Salermo sayonara
58. Spit out
60. Bell
61. Damage
62. Good name for a nobleman
63. Signed a contract
64. Fraternal members
65. Alters a shirt
66. Makes a home

DOWN

1. ___ pump
2. Primatologist's subjects
3. Without
4. Kidnapped
5. They might be personal
6. Capture
7. Think not
8. Clump
9. Made possible
10. Write badly
11. Foghorn Leghorn, for one
12. One way to run
13. Apprehends
21. Slag secreters
23. Cut
25. Sax type
27. Hobbit's home
28. Handed over
29. Get a run in
30. More chilly
31. Like some humor
32. Puts in
33. SNL segment
34. Collide
37. Proposer's hoped-for answer
38. Leaf holder
39. Newsprint screamer
41. Was on *The Price Is Right*
42. Prudish one
44. Toughies for ESL students
45. Please leave!
46. Standouts to Yankees
48. Caring word, when doubled
49. Yearn
50. ___ *M for Murder*
51. Con artist's target
54. Gets one's dander up
55. Yard components
56. Means justifier?
59. ___ one's respects
60. One of seven

★ **Solution on page 301**

I hated this movie

ACROSS

1. Football maneuver
5. Roman ruin feature
9. Handle with ___
13. Sitting on
14. Ricochet
16. At an end
17. Have a go at again
18. African charger
19. One-time dance craze
20. Lode load
22. "All ___ are off"
24. Bankroll
25. Jab
27. Skirmish
29. Game participant
31. Artist's attire
33. Groove
34. More than partially
36. Weld
40. Clergy's closer
42. Noble steed
44. Urgent
45. Scout's badge
47. *Strangers on a ___*
49. Blemish
50. Crunchy
52. Local, to a tourist
54. Oompah dances
57. Knob
58. Bitter brew
59. Innocent or guilty
62. "I hated this movie," e.g.
63. Donate
65. Ooze
67. Hiatuses
71. Level
72. ___ tots
73. Subject for a class
74. Swamp grass
75. Monastery member
76. Nervous

DOWN

1. Golf goal
2. Scarfed down
3. Grass square
4. Like an X-File
5. Land parcel
6. "Go team!"
7. Tot spot
8. Whet
9. Gear component
10. Declares openly
11. Majestic
12. Wear away
15. Slogan
21. The Great Barrier ___
23. Thus and ___
25. Feather
26. Western
28. Halt, but leave marks
29. Brit's baby buggy
30. Daiquiri liquor
31. Show bad table manners
32. Talking bird
35. Oodles
37. Skittish
38. Really want
39. Agreeing word, when doubled
41. Small cut
43. Inexpensive metal
46. Capture
48. Doting babysitter
51. Small key
53. Lollipop licker
54. It might vibrate
55. Oil producer
56. Flood foiler
60. Pupil's poser
61. Model T, e.g.
62. Benefit
64. This ___ up
66. A ___ of thieves
68. What happened next?
69. Babe, for one
70. Home to a 69 Down

★ **Solution on page 301**

Fuss and bother

1	2	3	4	5	■	6	7	8	9	■	10	11	12	13
14					■	15				■	16			
17					■	18				■	19			
20			■	21	22			■	23	24				
■	■	■	25				■	26			■	■	■	■
■	27	28					■	29			30	31	32	■
33						■	34			■	35			36
37					■	38			■	39				
40				■	41			■	42					
■	43			44			■	45						■
■	■	■	■	46			■	47				■	■	■
48	49	50	51			■	52				■	53	54	55
56				■	57	58			■	59	60			
61				■	62				■	63				
64				■	65				■	66				

ACROSS

1. Despise
6. Xmas tale starter
10. Netizen's room
14. Sledding site
15. "Ticket to ___"
16. Company picture
17. Injures
18. Not an easy thing to split
19. Help, like a henchman
20. Money for miso
21. Another meaning for 20 Across
23. Pay no attention to
25. Go for a dash?
26. ___ day now . . .
27. Picture dots
29. Occur
33. Dog
34. Bump
35. Put down
37. Stop at sea
38. "As I ___ saying . . . "
39. Half of a sawbuck
40. You might pitch one
41. Not many
42. Like a sheep
43. Lust
45. Rough
46. Swimming segment
47. Circus performances
48. Tokyo theater
52. Cut hair
53. Industry
56. The Gay '90s and others
57. Old harp
59. Domicile
61. "What's your sign?", e.g.
62. Golf gadgets
63. Workshop items
64. Increases, like a bill
65. Tibetan beasts
66. Wading bird

DOWN

1. Pale
2. Sad color?
3. It's meant to be blown
4. Pick
5. One who lives there
6. Land parcels
7. Accompanying
8. Fuss and bother
9. Work class
10. Part of an Auel title
11. Tramp
12. Time or stress
13. Kind of bag
22. Ceramic piece
24. Cheat
25. Is
26. Cries of surprise
27. Like some driveways
28. Simply ridiculous
30. Grippy puller
31. Roof rims
32. Sibling's daughter
33. It may need belling
34. Not the J in TMJ, but a good guess
36. Arid
38. Show remorse
39. Rupert's roomie
41. "___, thy name is woman"
42. Things to look at
44. Kind
45. Hold lovingly
48. Seaweed
49. Melody
50. "I'm with the ___"
51. Capitalizes on
52. *Star* ___
53. Rude dude
54. Not busy
55. Gusto
58. Senate vote
60. Swamp

★ **Solution on page 301**

Eccentric

ACROSS

1. Chunk
5. Astonishes
9. Marshmallow holder
14. Rain cats and dogs
15. Answering machine sound
16. :
17. Linc had one
18. Shout
19. Common salutation
20. They go up or down
22. Netizen's nook
24. Its teeth can cut
25. Religious leader
27. It waits for no man
29. Attendant
32. Approached
36. Activist
37. Eccentric
39. Yokel
40. Lodging house
41. Four after do
42. Ploy for Serena
43. Waistband
45. Show you may have seen before
47. Polite bloke
48. Fold
50. Window dressing
52. Multipurpose
54. Astute
55. Sippy
58. Prissy
60. Lives
64. Take by force
66. Lunch or brunch
68. Part of a 66 Across
69. Ward off
70. Party pooper
71. ___ of Man
72. Persevere
73. Ran a tab
74. Two-by-four

DOWN

1. Resorts
2. Upper level
3. Atmosphere
4. Part of a stove
5. Hopelessly bad
6. Itsy bitsy
7. Shocking fish
8. Banana ___
9. Conspirator's plan
10. ___ the line
11. Misfortunes
12. Fizzy drink
13. Believe
21. Uncut
23. Teensy
26. Popped up
28. Lend an ___
29. Sub spotter
30. Keyed up
31. They might be ajar
33. Measuring stick
34. "___ and Ivory"
35. Cause for Chapter 11
36. Platter
38. Strum
44. "If I ___ a Hammer"
45. Raise
46. Razzed
47. Origin
49. Easily bent
51. Just hired
53. Low dance
55. Road side
56. Chatroom being
57. It's just a stage
59. Siamese saying
61. Missing
62. Corker
63. Raced
65. Prepare to drag
67. "People ___ Strange"

★ **Solution on page 301**

We are family

ACROSS

1. Stockpile
6. Sing like Ella
10. Clean
14. Mistake
15. That hurt!
16. Fair
17. Put up with
18. Pretentious
19. Bard's lament
20. They come before dos
21. ___ of the court
23. Tranquil
25. Cook slowly
27. Craft
29. ___ test
31. *Arsenic and ___ Lace*
32. Baden-Baden, e.g.
35. Wanted
38. Bistro
39. Don't have one, man
40. Kind of closet
41. School dance
42. Don't waste
44. Break the ___
45. Jacob had one
47. Held responsible
48. Church seat
49. Grounds keeper?
50. Responds to the moon
51. Hinder
53. Croquet site
57. Cloisters
61. Nerd
63. Douglas ___
64. Get better
65. Melt
67. Ingenuous
69. Perot features
70. Tardy
71. Nasty ones
72. Inspiration
73. Black-___ Susan
74. Red veggies

DOWN

1. Puts on a burner
2. Go around
3. Greet the day
4. Curtain fixture
5. Made a picture
6. Flew high
7. ___ and whey
8. What Daryl Hannah and Ethan Hawke do
9. A good person to know
10. It's starting to ___ thin
11. Crossbar
12. Reach across
13. They might get a run
22. Fervent
24. Golden aged
26. Stadium activity
28. *General Hospital*, e.g.
30. 100 years
32. Lowlife
33. Stance
34. Lost in wonder
35. Pace
36. Chinese staple
37. From scratch
38. Bilk
41. "You're getting warmer," e.g.
43. Part of this book's title
46. Struggle
47. Expressed, as a farewell
50. Made coffee
52. Striped stone
54. Blazing
55. Rosie's bit
56. Woman's wear
57. Excuse me!
58. Better half
59. Prohibits
60. Or ___!
62. Door part
66. Mare munchie
68. Ripen

★ **Solution on page 301**

Chapter 3

Easy Going

Intrude

ACROSS

1. Firmly embedded
6. Those who excel
10. Head-over-heels
14. Showy flower
16. All-night party
17. Pomposity
18. Conjures up
19. Snowballed
20. Flower bed
21. British yea
22. Intrude
24. Record holder
26. Biblical book
29. Viper
30. Heroic tale
33. Veggie holder
35. Recital star
37. Server
38. Kind of scientist
41. Familiarize
42. Solutions
43. Mare or ewe
44. Clumsy crafts
45. Long in the tooth
47. Made smooth
49. Deli bread
50. It hangs out
51. Romanov royal
52. Tell
54. Checked over
55. Response to a cat, perhaps
59. Wear away
61. ER concern
63. Flub
64. *L.A.* ___
67. Final
68. Living-room piece
71. Sweater material
74. Chip in
75. Rope arrangement
76. Not impartial
77. Sign spotter
78. Alluring
79. Court cries

DOWN

1. Concept
2. Kind of bean
3. Pump or mule
4. Antlered one
5. Formal dining need
6. Sock pattern
7. Roller coaster compartment
8. 12/24 or 12/31
9. Puts in stitches
10. Hung open
11. Felt poorly
12. Orchard
13. Daisylike bloom
15. Nile nippers
23. Engrossed
25. Luck, in a song
26. Pest
27. Caught a king
28. Nimble
30. "Nothing personal"
31. Analogous
32. "Anything ___"
34. Sahara spring
35. Zoom skyward
36. Hackneyed
38. Craze
39. Fix a law
40. Crib cry
42. Skewered steak
43. Additional
46. Big bash
48. Out of the ordinary
50. ___ *Here to Eternity*
51. It might be shed
53. Pact
55. Rand-McNally book
56. Construction machine
57. Waste maker
58. *The ___ Limits*
60. Humdrum
62. Shows curiosity
64. Misplace
65. Kind of code
66. Bankrolls
69. Hole in ___
70. Sly one
72. Playful bite
73. Guy's date

★ **Solution on page 302**

Phooey!

ACROSS

1. Ship's pole
5. Balm target
9. *The 39* ___
14. Skunk's weapon
15. Tinge
16. Lawful
17. ___ of the valley
18. "Nevermore" quother
19. "The ___ has landed"
20. Links item
21. Orthodontist's concern
22. Spoke like a snake
23. Total
24. Outspoken
25. Funny fellow
26. Growl
28. Stifled
34. Guitar ridge
36. "Nice fireworks!"
37. Bossa ___
38. Popular, in *Variety*
41. "Holy moley"
43. Cat habitat
44. Shining
45. Scale member
46. Wedding cake layers
47. Slanderous statement
48. Admirer
49. Phooey!
51. Baby plants
54. Shoots from the green
57. Break a fast
58. A black cat, perhaps
60. Part of TGIF
62. Practically
66. *And Then There Were* ___
67. Kid's toy
68. Controls
69. Plank
71. No ___ Traffic
72. Sample
73. Detroit products
74. Improve a garden
75. Eating utensil
76. Nana
77. Chances

DOWN

1. Removes one's coat
2. French farewells
3. Serious
4. Stab
5. Box in a hold
6. Sanctuaries
7. Expert
8. Coop
9. Santa's ride
10. What a 5 Down in Boston Harbor might hold
11. Cooks fold them in
12. ___ by comparison
13. Toboggan
15. Tic-tac-toe goal
21. Take on debt
22. Shakespearean verb
25. Stiff
27. Have the means for
29. Castle circle
30. Join up
31. Gigi or Lili
32. Fairy tale's second-to-last word
33. *Happy* ___
35. Rent payer
38. Kind of drum
39. Eye amorously
40. Chimney channel
42. Instrument for Chuck Barris
43. Harmonize
48. Decree
50. Flips
52. Taper off
53. "Moonlight ___"
55. Gave a tenth
56. Put in a shed
59. Unlikely think-tank member
61. Taters
62. They might be liberal
63. Bound
64. Sushi side dish
65. ___ the matter at hand
69. Carousel rider at the airport
70. ___ *Town*
71. Snake eyes

★ **Solution on page 302**

Hot spot

ACROSS

1. Thing on a menu
5. Like Kojak
9. Golf or hockey
14. Created
15. " . . . and all is well" person
16. Antique store find
17. Touched down
18. Blood line
19. Get used to
20. What have you ___ there?
21. Mule pule
22. Uses mouthwash
24. Saw to it
26. Montego ___
27. Famous
29. Kid
30. Fossil fuel
33. Talk
36. Appointed
38. "___ Meets West"
39. Recovered from cryogenics
41. Neck part
42. Shiny rock
43. Mortgagee's concern
44. Whirlpool
46. Tend to
48. Not now, but I ___ to
49. Synthetic fiber
51. Takes five
52. Bowling pin count
53. Nanny's newbie
54. Thin crest
56. Teary-eyed
57. Lord's lessee
61. Less slow
65. Rotate
66. Forbid
67. Soprano's hits
68. Expect
70. Wander
71. Trace
72. Not the M in ATM, but a good guess
73. Hot spot
74. Lawn tool
75. Social equal
76. Join

DOWN

1. Politician's concern
2. Claw
3. Removes a colon?
4. Came upon
5. Enlarge
6. Buoyant
7. Permitted
8. Go slowly
9. Egyptian charm
10. Rotund
11. Not injected
12. Ready to eat
13. Young'uns
15. ^
21. "If it ain't ___ . . . "
23. Went along
25. Underwhelmed
28. "I'm a Yankee Doodle ___"
29. Agent, briefly
30. Trot and gallop
31. Fancy tie
32. Tinseltown types
33. ___ one's stuff
34. Just something you're going through
35. Had a bite
37. Local veep
38. Show starters
40. Ridicule
45. Pop
47. Church item
50. More chilly
53. Kind of roll
55. Isis or Osiris
56. Mobile Western prop
58. On top of
59. Belly dancer's feature
60. Tendency
61. Dislike intensely
62. Waterless
63. Rat out to the cops
64. Knievel prop
65. Reasonable
69. ___ is me!
70. Song start, when tripled

★**Solution on page 302**

It's mindless

ACROSS

1. Ice ___
5. They come out of a joke writer's mouth
9. Holiday precursors
13. Advance
14. Wage ___
16. A secretary might take one
17. It locks an ox
18. Naughty netizen
19. Elite alternative
20. They charge
22. Hatchet, or that there lumberjack
24. Harry Potter's specialty
26. Sufferer's question
28. Valentine's Day gift
29. Hyped a film
30. Like custard
32. Joins forces
34. Outdoor living room
36. Commie
39. One not kept in stitches
40. Betwixt
41. Test run
42. Soft stone
43. Scratchy voice
45. It's mindless
47. Clever
48. Stops marching
49. Tzatziki base
50. Shops
51. The ___ of society
52. Desert request
55. Stick in the water
58. V flyers
59. Moral compass
61. No-no olio
63. Titles for knights
64. Homes
66. Surgical reminder
70. Annoying one
71. Scrub
72. Buyer in Britain
73. Takes to court
74. Bad mark
75. Manually skilled

DOWN

1. Shoo-___ pie
2. Where Brits go
3. Charter hider
4. Full of vim and vigor
5. Close in on
6. Archer's object
7. Grate together
8. Play place
9. Use
10. Widow covers
11. Host
12. Flies through the air
14. It's a long story
15. Diamond expert
21. Takes cover
23. Part of QED
24. Not automatic
25. With rapt attention
27. Mountain man?
29. Litter's littles
31. Happy-go-lucky
33. Wander
34. ___ due
35. DJ gear
36. Hodgepodge shows
37. Exit
38. Morons
41. Gotten off the point
44. Too
46. It might have clowns
48. Pitch
50. Hooligans
52. Faint traces
53. Bye-bye, Gigi
54. Short on words
56. Bikini, for one
57. Commuter's news source
58. Wow, in the '50s
60. Dispirit
62. Oscar word
65. Go for an apple
67. White ball
68. Sandy's statement
69. . . . and all that ___

★**Solution on page 302**

What a relief!

ACROSS

1. Tunnel end signal
6. Helmsman's hello
10. ___ *Hour*
14. Glistening
16. Like a bum leg
17. Office shape
18. Cold and damp
19. Disbeliever's cry, when doubled
20. Happy cloud number
21. Too long to wait
22. Bridge partner?
24. Moose kin
25. Bugs Bunny's addressee
26. What a relief!
27. ___ and flows
30. Rhinestone
32. Black hole's beginning
33. Snoop
36. Open
38. Football or fishing term
40. Trembled
43. Put on a scale
45. Cowardly critter in Oz
46. Alter a window
47. Get on your knees
48. Frolics
49. Waif or sea creature
51. Like totally cold
53. Comb user
54. Carmine and rose
56. Distressed one?
59. Like morning grass
60. They might get struck
61. Bottom line
63. Not at hand
66. Safecracker's soup
68. Asphalt
69. Pesky
70. South Seas staple
71. Update
74. Forest member
75. Run ___
76. Pizza pieces
77. Scorch
78. Mother Hubbard's lack
79. Nourishes

DOWN

1. Put on, as skates
2. Homes with domes
3. Quick look
4. Clothing line
5. Fisherman's hat
6. Let
7. Stones in the air
8. Buffet item
9. Yup
10. Areas
11. Like a sinner
12. Soldier stat
13. Bullfight bravos
15. Legendary
23. Fame
26. Dirty Harry addressee
28. Tub cleaner
29. Support for a bust
31. Said like Poe
32. One going downhill
33. Like some milk
34. Alka-Seltzer sound
35. Cravings
37. Skin-diving sites
39. Dirt clumps
40. Cinema souvenir
41. Take on
42. On a sole occasion
44. Motorless transport
47. *The Man Who ___ Too Much*
48. Crater edges
50. Dander
52. Kin to crocs
55. Powerhouse
57. Lure
58. Rented out
59. Laundry machine
60. Feed the fire
62. Ponytail
63. Tiny tunnelers
64. Tiger's cry
65. With the buoys and gulls
67. Depleat
70. Bar brokerage
72. Magical being
73. Do battle

★ **Solution on page 302**

Help out

ACROSS

1. Ballet skirt
5. Narrative
10. Piercing tools
14. Fiery gemstone
15. Reception
16. Stealer's stash
17. Person, place, or thing
18. It isn't easy
19. Was shotgun
20. Necessitated
22. Dodge verbally
23. Move like a crab
25. *Roger Rabbit* henchman
26. Chew out
29. Ran the show
31. Like an unlikely coincidence
32. Uproar
36. They may be consenting
38. Curve
39. Plus
40. Wee bit
41. Even
43. Barely furnished
46. Sports gear
49. Green fruits
50. Moved like a mamba
52. Exploded
53. Visit a pit stop
56. ___ pole
58. *Home* ___
59. At fault
64. Bit of cottage cheese
65. Help out
68. One way to travel
69. Outskirts
70. Creeps
71. Stuff
72. Like a ___ in headlights
73. Oversells
74. Not his

DOWN

1. Muscle ___
2. "When You Wish ___ a Star"
3. Stretched out
4. Fibula's counterpart
5. Studied
6. Fill with bullet holes
7. Slag source
8. Sailing spot
9. Lamprey
10. Enough ___!
11. Forest
12. Fraternal order spot
13. Detroit need
15. Firm
21. Getaway spot
22. Boot part
24. Put the media with the troops
25. Puts the metal to the metal?
26. 4-door car
27. Petroleum product, with 28 Down
28. See 27 Down
30. Is able to
31. Has a wrap
33. Injures
34. Beginning
35. Lyric verses
37. One way to get home
38. Assail
42. Peeve
44. Like a tomato
45. Melody
47. One way to be torn
48. Place for a pad
51. Tame
52. Stiff drinks
53. Went like the wind
54. Stay away from
55. Smith's need
57. Elephant's standouts
60. Bend
61. In one's birthday suit
62. Tall tale teller
63. Trees of shade
65. Fireplace debris
66. Place for a kite
67. Have an evening meal

★ **Solution on page 302**

It may be golden

ACROSS

1. Like storm clouds
5. Burn balm
9. Where knights battle
14. Jazz instrument
15. Leverage
16. Audible
17. Toilet paper holder
18. Smug
19. Tux store customer, often
20. Use a stool
21. Make a vroom
22. Do a garden chore
23. Something to stroke
24. Abrade
26. Spoken
28. Unrehearsed exercise
31. Hummus, e.g.
33. Payable
34. ___ peeve
36. Flowers for Nero Wolfe
39. It may be golden
41. Bread staple
43. Conceal
45. Tilt
46. Undesirable
47. Slingshot missile
48. Fall movie, often
50. ___ *Done Him Wrong*
52. Mother Teresa, e.g.
53. Valued
55. Firstborn
57. Uncooked
60. Nimble
62. Sonnet's kin
63. Surprise title to a 20-something
64. Deface
65. Move while waiting
69. Small child
71. Hang in a hammock
72. Verify
73. Proofreaders catch them
74. It's been ___!
75. Father
76. Covers with a blanket
77. Sleep spots
78. Loose ___

DOWN

1. Freckles
2. Get next to
3. Ill one's gear
4. Fish that's big enough
5. Endorse
6. Enticed
7. Antipasto ingredients
8. Slippery tree
9. Fast cat
10. Dearie
11. Go into
12. Attack
13. Cape Cod treat
16. Keep safe
22. Crowd cheers
25. Knot maker
27. Decree
28. Revered one
29. Stubborn ones
30. Use a bike
32. It often rhymes
35. Hair snare
37. Proceed monotonously
38. Head cavity
40. Not competent
42. Forest hopper
44. Folded
46. Liquor shop supply
47. Bear's advice
49. Students clap them together
51. Woman in a will
54. Wreck
56. Oust
57. Hard books to carry
58. Embellish
59. Printer's proof
61. Stared
66. Related
67. Wag
68. Binocular users
70. Wham!
71. Beaker room

★ **Solution on page 302**

This instant!

ACROSS

1. Destroy
6. Hubbub
9. What stars have
13. Precipice
14. It's out of control
16. The yoke's on them
17. A tale told by an ___ . . .
18. Pizzazz
19. Shred
20. Poker place
21. Atremble, perhaps
23. Secure
25. Whipped-up dessert
27. Impressive acts
30. Amulet
32. Space streaker
35. Sideline Snidely
36. Scrapbook filler
39. Spouse
40. Trick
41. Gullible rustic
42. Vampire's fear
43. Elect
44. Cocoon creator
46. This instant!
47. Slimy something
49. Spring up?
50. Strokes
51. Love song
53. Dodge
55. It pours slowly
56. When to say grace
59. Mix
61. Drink order word
62. Kid's card game
65. Religious scholar
68. Grans
70. Ghost writer?
72. Impresses
73. Hagrid, for one
74. School report
75. Track event
76. Repair hair
77. Sign spotters

DOWN

1. Paper ___
2. Have at again
3. Reduce a sentence?
4. "Long" follower
5. Sky streaker
6. Bosun's howdys
7. Water blocker
8. Beg your pardon!
9. Prepare
10. You might have one to grind
11. Shakespearean troupe members
12. Terminus
14. Machinery bits
15. Elevator passages
22. Squat
24. Charge
25. Like 11 Down
26. Buffet types
28. Lit
29. Put into a position
30. Square dancers
31. School class
33. Undo a riddle
34. Repair shop assignments
35. Hoppers
37. Punctured
38. Passed through final inspection
45. Circus site
46. Fight
48. Continue
49. Type of hole
52. Screwy place
54. Kills a bill
57. Insipid
58. Where to bring worms
60. Surprise attack
62. Sage
63. Slightly cracked
64. You might catch them at the beach
65. Orange spud
66. Have chits out
67. Gosh!
69. Not yea
71. Purpose

★**Solution on page 302**

Skedaddle!

ACROSS

1. Profit from
5. Skedaddle!
9. Ball goers
13. Rod in a hot rod
14. Cool dessert
16. Unbleached color
17. Work soil
18. Deal maker
19. I'm talking to ya!
20. Obscure
22. Becomes less wide
24. Messy place
25. Bud
26. Mixing place
27. Issue
29. Male kin
33. Take an oath
37. Foil
39. Key hider?
40. Self-sacrificer
42. Round beads
43. Protein for vegans
44. Storybook being
45. When all ___ fails . . .
47. Tightened text
49. As well
50. *X-File* extras
52. Tetris players, probably
53. Provoked
55. Knitted
57. Stay put
58. Live and breathe
59. Plie path
62. Arty buildings
66. Happy
68. Junk hauler
69. It often gets flushed
71. Script part
72. Foot holder
73. Request for more
74. Length x width
75. Watch over
76. Televisions
77. Evaluate

DOWN

1. Hotel-door posting
2. Be
3. Pewter or brass
4. Pommel
5. Request
6. Captain Hook's fear
7. Workout spot
8. ___ *Wolf*
9. Lack
10. Say again
11. Make a pot
12. Accumulations
14. Git!
15. Venture across
21. ___ board
23. Spellbound
28. The ones over there
29. Catch a con
30. Express strong feelings
31. Sliver snack
32. Macho men
33. Killed, like Goliath
34. Cart
35. Trial go-with
36. Had a little lamb
38. Small songbirds
41. Classify
43. "My Country ___ of Thee"
46. You might flip yours
48. Sand mounds
50. Like fine wine
51. Deck needs
54. Sworn
56. Put on paper
59. In flames
60. Crypt cryptics
61. Sod spoiler
62. Hey, buddy!
63. It might need a rub
64. Hooligan
65. Potential heirs
66. Dab
67. Strip
70. Titanic problem

★ **Solution on page 302**

Life story

ACROSS

1. Aesop's tale
6. Hearty meal
10. Meat loaf serving
14. Like a firefly
15. Hi-fi piece
17. Mexican munchie
18. Light pancake
19. Illness
20. Has title to
21. British ritual
22. Resume item
24. Quarry items
26. Religious faction
28. Put off
30. ___ sale
31. Reduce
33. Priest
37. Stale
38. Feathered friend
39. Eye, poetically
41. Disorder
44. Like a diva
45. Life story
46. Precious one
47. Chico's chum
49. Part of a trip
50. Shrill bark
51. Male singer
53. One way to run
57. Deposit
58. Taverns
59. Goat's goodbye
60. Pigeonhole an actor
63. Side of the head
66. Give a reason to edit
67. Pizza need
69. Auction cry
71. Like a dazed look
74. Diagonal mark
76. Train segment
77. Upper room
78. Concert souvenir
81. Ease up
83. Zoning unit
84. Slims down
85. Ousts a king
86. "The Lady or the Tiger" choice
87. Dessert in Wonderland
88. Removes a layer

DOWN

1. *The ___ of Life*
2. Concurs
3. Whiten
4. Prune
5. Flock members
6. Corn holder
7. One who does windows
8. Paleontologist's concern
9. United
10. Larry or Moe
11. Croquet site
12. Facial distorter
13. Superior
15. Funny look
16. Rockefeller and others
23. Well, yes and no
25. Not on time
27. Trampled
29. Edit code
32. Not up to par
34. Type of shield
35. Dignified
36. Toweled off
40. Cranberry source
41. Fine looker
42. Depleted
43. Divine food
44. Type of evergreen
46. Rip-off
48. Like some rocks in the water
51. Stories
52. Hide from other spies
54. Assists an assassin
55. Moll's feature
56. Openings
61. Torment
62. Samples products
63. Russian royals
64. Pinpoint
65. With glee
68. Vigilant
70. Attire
71. Happy
72. Like Lucy, to Desi
73. Height increaser
75. Stage stealers
79. Cereal grain
80. You might get a treatment there
82. Grump's harrumph

★ **Solution on page 303**

There oughta be one

ACROSS

1. Tree or human part
5. Where to see a ham
9. 2-door car
14. Stench
15. Mystiques
16. Storage bin
17. Belatedly hocked
18. Approaches
19. Kind of bar
20. Least difficult
22. It blows
24. Pub pint
25. There oughta be one
26. Slowly escape
27. Unclad
29. Pig out
32. One with lots of interest
34. Lost traction
35. Baker's sense of humor?
36. Needing a loan
37. Append
38. Convenience
40. They don't take stock
43. Garden pest
45. One way to learn
47. Oriental combat
49. Curvy
51. Scanned
52. Fella
53. It might be mulled
55. Forest forager
57. Up to the task
58. Pass
60. Middling?
62. Southern side
63. Sot
66. Misjudge
67. Parking place
68. Say it ___ so
69. Baby gear
73. Swear
76. Less bright
78. Display
79. They don't hold water
80. Pressing needs
81. Greater area phone book, e.g.
82. Metal fastener
83. Column near the decimal
84. Naval vehicles

DOWN

1. Folk history
2. Inspiration
3. Swabs
4. One way to have fish
5. Tandem song
6. Time period
7. Jumbo
8. Problem
9. Hard to get
10. Control location
11. Comprehension
12. Kitchen gadget
13. Misstepped
15. Reply
16. Stolen
21. Drum holder
23. Goad
26. Seafood treat
27. Microwave
28. Regions
29. Further from birth
30. Screened stuff
31. Those in favor
33. Weeps
34. Musical tool
36. Urge
39. Chinese sauce
41. Latin dance
42. Teeny
44. Gold coin
45. Shooter's call
46. Not up to much
48. Number for the road
50. Tiny bites
54. Wiggly ones
56. Does doughs
57. Takes in
58. Arousing
59. Group of pups
61. Hear a suit
62. It may be half full or half empty
64. 4-F
65. Gaze
68. Start of a birth announcement
69. Eye part
70. *O Brother, Where Art ___?*
71. Aboveground burial spot
72. Farm females
74. When to turn on lights
75. Do embroidery
77. Put on

★ **Solution on page 303**

Local star

ACROSS

1. Walking stick
5. Vipers
9. Greetings
12. Not normal
15. Pay attention to
16. Kind of meet
17. Metal container
18. It might be pitched
19. NIMBY locale
21. Sloppy copy
23. It comes before the com
24. Listened to
25. It might cause a delay
26. Local star
27. Divisive word
28. Sagas
31. Intend
33. Carved
37. Bugle tune
39. Mandolin-shaped fruit
41. Bagel topper
42. Tot spot
43. Fine meal
46. Meter or liter
48. Flightless bird
49. At all
50. Compensates for
53. Oil effect
54. Dessert vehicle
55. Paranoid one's fear
56. Like this entry
58. Press profits
59. High or low card
60. Teen dance
61. One of no concern
63. Like DNA
65. Injures
68. Jungle tree hanger
70. Part of a series
72. Have something
74. Friar
76. Where the pedal is put
77. Unlikely attire for the ASPCA
78. Let go
81. Namelessness
83. Amazement
84. Sever
85. Celeb, perhaps
86. Till fill
87. Tent stake
88. High school course
89. It talks back
90. Nudnik

DOWN

1. Dorm dwellers
2. Flowering
3. Curl up
4. It tends to get lashed
5. Pale
6. Mom's cool request
7. Echo
8. Hustled
9. Centers
10. Decreased?
11. Pesky one
12. Late-nighter
13. A deer, a female deer
14. Woofer
20. Complains
22. Unwise one
29. Cat of many colors
30. Produces
32. In pieces
34. Bunch
35. Put an edge on
36. Theater sign
38. Operatives
40. Over
43. Summary
44. Gets around
45. Certain someone
47. Ruthless ruler
48. Destiny
51. Ruckus
52. Points of interest
57. Attractive
60. Troop group
62. Moniker
63. It picks up on things
64. Bureau
66. Make oil or sugar
67. Browns in butter
69. Tree dweller
71. Food from heaven
73. Rendezvous
75. Maintained
76. Impair
78. Knock
79. She-sheep
80. Stool stick
82. Janitor's tool

★ **Solution on page 303**

Value

ACROSS

1. Foreboding
6. Sow's sweetie
10. Value
15. Gamut
16. Make happen
17. Hula hello
18. Broad expanse
19. Mini map
20. Couch potato
21. Soup veggie
22. Caboodle companion
24. Deck of fate?
26. Response to a mouse
27. Logician's word
29. Hooray for our side
31. Ring holders
33. Coastal
35. Inventor's inventory
38. Like some seats
40. Speaketh
42. *ER* crew or prop
44. Job hunter's pursuit
45. Trunk tire
46. Best bud
47. Bomb that bombs
48. Aries symbol
49. Edits out
52. Country estate
54. Golfer's hazard
56. Understudy's hope
57. Goer
59. Reading room
61. Word for a herd
64. Highway hauler
65. Drink slowly
66. Stumbling block
68. Unlikely acrobat
71. Reason for a bigger house
74. Just out
76. Ill will
77. Where to catch some zeds?
79. Leg up
81. Consumed
83. A 59 Across may have readers for this
84. Stripes
85. Totally wiped
86. Knight's need
87. Threat ender
88. Lab work

DOWN

1. Hang loosely
2. They're in a rush
3. More than aggravate
4. Ring count, for a tree
5. Typist's spot
6. Prevent
7. Fling a king
8. Out of port
9. Tired tires?
10. Actress's other job
11. Past one's prime
12. Aunt Eller or Auntie Em
13. Quaker's pronoun
14. Hear ye
16. Fortress
23. Camera part
25. Black Beauty's bit
28. Dinghy duo
30. What you get from your parents
32. Go berserk
34. Kit
35. They have something to sell
36. Prop for a princess
37. Fastener
39. Bond holder
41. Seamy locale?
42. Ship of the desert
43. Why you didn't do it
46. Escape capsule
50. Butter holders
51. Full of anxiety
52. Likely to change
53. Consecrates
54. Typical number of piggies
55. Wine cellar supply
58. Pull one over on
60. Audio accessory
62. Marries
63. Child provider
67. Restroom label
68. Makes a hit
69. Finished gliding
70. Confront
72. Mattress part
73. Longer than you want to wait
75. Left on the map
78. Everyday article
80. I told ya so!
82. Old Samsonite ad actor

★ **Solution on page 303**

Slivered side

ACROSS

1. Animals
6. Suggestion
9. Puts in the form of a question
13. Be compulsive
15. Church law
17. Slivered side
18. Detest
19. Quitter's cry
20. Cocoon dweller
21. Made a hole
22. It's poured hot
24. Greedy one
25. Routine routine
26. Spy's skill
29. Edits a screenplay
32. Balls
34. Fabric shop purchase
36. Most ornery
38. Kind of mark
42. Nursery item
43. Drink purchases
45. Bond, i.e.
46. Pay to play
47. Gold standard
48. Skedaddle
49. It's often needed before a long drive
50. Wayward one
52. Star quality
54. Like some marriages
56. Brings forth
58. Weeps
59. Place to grab a bite
60. Hidden cave
63. They spray
67. Fireplace item
68. Boxer's umpire
71. Miniature
72. Minting plate
73. Hole makers
75. Send away
77. Compete
80. Make a big stink
81. Ventured
82. Praised
83. Current event?
84. Got together
85. Nuisances

DOWN

1. Closes shop
2. ___ *a Boy*
3. Accepted practice
4. Tennis barrier
5. Shade of gray
6. Summer skin hue
7. Part of a foot
8. Mallet game
9. African menace
10. Soup sound
11. On the blink
12. Hunts flies
14. Pioneer
15. Mean mutt
16. Canceled out
23. Triumphant cries
27. Like an open mouth
28. Boulevard
30. Badmouth
31. Strong lifter
33. Fibers
34. Times itself
35. Nana's daughter
36. One down under
37. BBQ enthusiast
39. A place to get away to
40. Sport events
41. Da opposite
42. Stats
44. Quest of a 36 Down
47. Baby bouncer
48. Tease
50. Tizzy
51. Paid no attention to
52. Least large
53. Specialists
55. Likely
57. Citrus fruit
60. Night driver's problem
61. Maneuvered a boat
62. Acted like a 48 Down
64. Polishes
65. Metal fastener
66. Grower's supply
69. Blue book event
70. Frankenstein fear
71. Tied the knot
74. Plane's place
76. Court call
78. Best
79. Lament

★**Solution on page 303**

Up for discussion

ACROSS

1. Benefit
6. Telegram terminator
10. Bricklayer
15. Outdoor outing
17. Cone seepings
18. Overhead
19. Relaxing chair
20. White shirt wearer
21. Less polite
22. Flamenco shout
23. Kingdom
25. Lose a lap
26. Catch a few winks
27. Stepping styles
28. Zounds, à la Homer
30. Commencements
32. Arouse
36. Secondhand
39. Invigorate
41. First coat, often
44. Attire
46. Star's coming-out
47. ___ *Gang*
48. Up for discussion
52. Beer barrel
53. Lug
55. Cuts by Keats
56. Turf tools
58. Repay
61. Joint, when out of joint
63. Authorized
64. Brings upon oneself
67. Stein
69. Stopover
71. At least two eras
73. Rapscallion
77. Primitive fellows
79. Clown missile
80. Polite
81. Somersault
82. Aplenty
85. Make amends
86. Dropped
87. Got a goal
88. Less outdated
89. Like 79 Across
90. Telethon giveaways

DOWN

1. Kitchen garb
2. Cello's cousins
3. Allow
4. Tough stain
5. Bear false witness
6. Had a snoozer
7. Goes down the runway
8. Pilot's period
9. Waited nervously
10. Western hero, often
11. Border on
12. Pop
13. Kiln
14. Unlikely Don Juan
16. Animal
24. Baseball strike
27. Envy
29. The O in BYOB
31. Slot machine feature
33. We are family
34. Summon up
35. I refuse!
37. "Good gravy!"
38. Camel food
39. Recede
40. Bugs or badgers
41. Husks
42. Bucolic
43. Peeved
45. Hoarse talk
49. Tyke
50. Decision decider
51. Statute
54. Jazzman's job
57. African antelope
59. Candy combo
60. Winter woe
62. Go up
65. School assignment
66. Quite a party
68. Blunder
69. Obscures
70. Suggest
72. Has to have
73. Use an MRI
74. Use in a reference
75. Promise
76. Explosive item
78. Defense motion
83. Sham
84. Brit's bathroom

★ **Solution on page 303**

Once more

ACROSS

1. Kind of history
5. Tanner's ware
9. Animal trainer's supply
14. Shout on the links
15. Once more
17. Songbird
18. Fiction alternative
19. Regal one
20. Leaning
21. Rubbed out
23. Styx classic
25. Benevolent ones
26. Alert color
27. Hightailed it
29. Show one's anger
31. Suave
34. July 4th cry
35. It might be hailed
38. Go with the flow
39. Pea or lentil
41. Give up
43. Knowledge
45. Dropped in status
46. Pickle
47. Projectors project it
49. Storage containers
50. Crafty one?
53. Firer
54. Hill hurrier
55. Holler
56. Sib's gal
58. Wagon ride material
59. Indigestion
61. Halloween decoration
64. Somewhat off
66. Commotion
67. Dear
69. Nearly all
73. King's title
74. Toe, at the pool
76. Supply a lung
78. Half-widths
81. Office worker
82. "He ___ me"
83. Hits with phaser fire
84. Enemies
85. Like a resume
86. Put in the mail
87. They may be loose

DOWN

1. Home seller's hope
2. Acted like a lion
3. Video ___
4. Response to "Shall we?"
5. Babushka
6. It might be inflated
7. Large dog
8. Farming need
9. Lots of laughs
10. Give the once-over
11. October's stone
12. Medium, often
13. Adjusts
16. Approach
17. It's sprung around in spring
22. Create a canyon
24. Batman and Robin, i.e.
28. Meal ender
30. Not us
32. Unlikely hero
33. Object
35. Looker
36. Edit
37. Spots in the garden
40. Wine holder
41. Around
42. 42 Down, i.e.
44. Old horse
45. Declared untrue
46. Wingding
48. Bit of schmutz
51. Lengthy narrative
52. Accumulated
54. Public spat
57. Snob
60. Do a slalom
61. Informal attire
62. Automotive extra
63. Indispensable
65. Goes the wrong way
68. Hair collective
69. Fog
70. Without siblings
71. She of the sea
72. Subdued
75. Out of trouble
77. Took the helm
79. Kind of process
80. Roadside hotel

★ **Solution on page 303**

Push over

ACROSS

1. Biters
5. Feature of some coasters
9. Does well at retail
14. Topical treatment
15. Push over
17. Skirt fold
18. Arm bone
19. Get
20. Wow
21. Wayne's word
22. Lament loudly
23. Crowbar
25. Enthusiasm
26. One and one
27. Outtakes
29. Play place
31. Half of a sports pair
33. Strokes of genius
36. Porch swing
38. Stymies
40. Sire
42. Place to relax
44. Unpleasant weather
45. Shoot down
46. Complacent
47. Gringo's ole
48. Like a Pisan tower
51. Honda honker
52. Gulf
55. Attack
57. Strut
59. Stop going
60. Temp wheels
63. Scuba site
65. Oddball
66. Goal
68. Kin of pecs
71. Georgian fruit
73. Single sunbeam
74. Sticky stuff
75. Line dance
77. Spoken
79. Not so easy
80. Numbskull
81. Main dish
82. Choir voice
83. Profound quality
84. Singing standards
85. Eatery at sea

DOWN

1. Pleasure trip
2. Permits
3. Chinese dumpling
4. Mermaid habitat
5. Petitioned
6. Make a choice
7. Milky gems
8. Ballet bend
9. Small songbirds
10. Lawn tree
11. Go over a hurdle
12. Couch potato's specialty
13. Footfall
15. User's package
16. Bit of greenery?
22. Fish fleck
24. To ___ his own
28. Magician's word
30. Two-part
32. Easter edible
34. Quarries
35. Cook crabs
37. Growls
38. Smidgen
39. Pig pen
40. Small samples
41. Live
43. Closing
45. Fetch a felon
46. "Ain't ___ Sweet"
49. Pinocchio, for one
50. Mindreader
52. Travesty
53. Like a super super
54. Privateer's pro vote
56. Kind of club
58. Wingdings
61. Wine and dine
62. Piggish responses
64. Preference
65. Ghostly hue
67. Nitwits
68. ___-washed jeans
69. Foreshadow
70. Quick cut
72. Cause amnesia, perhaps
76. "Ain't We ___ Fun?"
78. Aha or oho
79. Radio man

★ **Solution on page 303**

Excellence

ACROSS

1. Yawns
6. Crete or Capri
10. Brainy
15. Fresh pie's lure
16. Spanish dessert
17. Intentional loser
18. Excellence
19. Video effect
20. One way to treat a problem
21. Jabbers
22. Part of a septet
23. Go together
25. Wimple wearer
26. Aspiration for 25 Across
28. It might be candied
29. Advance
30. Pantry items
32. White water
34. Entertainment center items
35. Herding dog
37. Acts like a 25 Across
38. Full of suds
40. It bites
43. Get in one's sights
44. Manipulate
45. Fellow
47. Alley call
50. 15 Across, basically
52. Overused
54. Tailor's concerns
56. Rank
58. Petty person
60. Cooking device
61. Mary's pet
62. Loll
64. Concert site
65. Gobbled
66. Mend a sock
67. Auction action
68. Inform
72. ___ of proof
74. Mitch Miller's instrument
76. Impish sort
77. Body parts
78. Othello, i.e.
79. Makes level
80. 74 Across set
81. Eternities
82. Musical marks

DOWN

1. Like some meat
2. Sector
3. A white meat
4. Diplomat
5. Temped with a baby
6. Uncertainty
7. Points of view
8. Stripling
9. Combatant
10. Resigned response
11. Feminist's complaint
12. Made up for
13. Summer fodder
14. Pattern
17. Dreadful
22. Storage building
24. Too soon
27. Parodies
29. Debt fret
30. Doctor's request
31. Game groups
33. It comes out of a pen
34. Curative spring
35. Legal load
36. Cracked
39. Smart response?
41. Spry
42. Teacher
46. Appetite
48. Iodine spreader
49. Toy soldier material
50. Cattle
51. Scottie and Airedale
52. Lean
53. Part of the family
55. Places to sit
57. Like most colleges
58. Grown up
59. Come forth
60. African primate
61. Baby production
63. Lawn being
66. Reader's retreats
69. Ava and Ari
70. Fluff
71. More, so they say
73. June honoree
75. Halloween heckle?
76. A pop

★ **Solution on page 303**

Chapter 4

Easy as One-Two-Three

Calm

1	2	3	4	5	■	■	6	7	8	9	10
11					12	■	13				
14						■	15				
16				■	17	18				■	■
■	■	■	19	20			■	21		22	23
24	25	26					27	■	28		
29			■	30				31			
32			33	■	34				■	■	■
■	■	35		36			■	37	38	39	40
41	42				■	43	44				
45					■	46					
47					■	■	48				

ACROSS

1. Minstrel's strings
6. Jazz variety
11. Spotted cat
13. One that's sent away
14. The magic word
15. Harass
16. Bridge position
17. Pond sucker
19. Balanced
21. House party seat
24. Foresees
28. Batman sound effect
29. Singer Charles
30. Merry-go-round
32. Was indebted to
34. Washer foam
35. Troublesome tykes
37. Rights group, for short
41. Calm
43. Forbidden things
45. Felt awful
46. Do reel work
47. Puts the metal to the metal
48. Pavarotti, for one

DOWN

1. Run like a rabbit
2. Home of the Bruins
3. Casual shirts
4. Cheered up
5. Call for help
6. Actress Neuwirth
7. Upper management
8. Chessmen who use diagonals
9. Rah for Raoul
10. ___ peeve
12. Put on the tube
18. Hands over authority to
20. Singer Damone
22. Villain
23. It's for boring people
24. Ace
25. Kind of bar
26. Stare at
27. Lawn piece
31. Fit for service
33. Like raisins
36. Does arithmetic
38. Nickel or dime
39. Plumb crazy
40. One on the Web
41. Dust maker
42. Bind
44. Suitable

★ **Solution on page 304**

What fun!

1	2	3	4	5	■	■	6	7	8	9	10
11					■	12					
13					■	14					
■	■	■	15		16		■	17			
18	19	20	■	21			22		■	■	■
23			■	24					25	26	27
28			29					■	30		
■	■	■	31					■	32		
33	34	35		■	36			37	■	■	■
38				39		■	40		41	42	43
44						■	45				
46					■	■	47				

ACROSS

1. Capital of Idaho
6. Gushes forth
11. Dental patch
12. Congrats in fencing
13. Dance deb
14. Minus, in appearance
15. Ruthless ruler
17. Pound or Frost
18. Prohibit
21. Way above average
23. BBQ item
24. Atom smashers
28. It tastes like almonds
30. Caustic cleaner
31. Autumn bloomer
32. Beads in the morning
33. Shock
36. Move slowly
38. High-kick dance
40. Utah senator
44. Playing pretend
45. Wipe out
46. Running hot and cold
47. Make a dance tape, perhaps

DOWN

1. Simple chest shield
2. Ten minus nine
3. ___ be seeing you!
4. Season
5. Unpleasant sights
6. Tofu source
7. Hand-held performer
8. It bounces back
9. What fun!
10. Faxed
12. More than warn
16. Conspiring with criminals
18. Bikini part
19. Destination
20. Hoop group, for short
22. Hot day
25. Dated
26. It might be seeded
27. Embroider
29. Inedible
33. Urban legend
34. Lunch for Lupe
35. " . . . a law ___ themselves"
37. Tortoise foe
39. ___ *Which Way But Loose*
41. Scottish beret
42. Forensic drama
43. Curse

★ **Solution on page 304**

Success

ACROSS

1. Expense
5. Fairy tale baddie
8. Vim and vigor
11. Tug-of-war need
12. ___ Baba
13. Durocher of baseball
14. Rephrase a phrase
15. Student supplies
17. Holiday helper
18. Success
19. Stopover
20. Drubbing
22. Quenches
23. Compassion
25. Like many car features
28. Peace
31. Lacked
33. On this spot
34. Assist
35. Spoil
36. Answer sheet smudge
38. Become exhausted
39. Exploit
40. This guy's
41. Remains holders
42. Make a new shade
43. It might be unsaturated
44. ___ Trueheart

DOWN

1. Words to live by
2. Gobs
3. Fancy
4. Vietnamese New Year
5. Where you are
6. Got down
7. Card game
8. Kilt crease
9. Creepy
10. Adds to a blog
16. Role on *A Different World*
18. With a smile
21. Expresses feelings
22. Worked on a horse
24. Most microscopic
26. Look up to
27. Gets the idea
28. In the lead
29. Compassion
30. In a snit
32. Garb
34. Met number
37. Over 13 acronym
38. Steve Martin song honoree

★ **Solution on page 304**

Stay in the game

ACROSS

1. October stone
5. The long ___ of the law
8. Stern
11. In need of liniment
12. Nexus
13. Cow call
14. Concise
15. Marina
17. Commence
19. Stay in the game
20. Prepare to race
21. Traces
25. Chucked copy
27. Like a postal extra
30. 26 miles, 385 yards
33. Was at the helm
35. What Dorian Gray's picture does
36. Military mistake
38. Kidney-shaped nuts
42. Big production
43. Had 38 Across
44. Mary's boss
45. Out on a dinghy
46. Damp
47. Janitor's stick
48. "This has been a ___"

DOWN

1. Academy Award
2. Directed liquid
3. Get there
4. "___ Misbehave"
5. Responses to a masseuse
6. "You'll ___ the day"
7. CEO's degree, often
8. Surrounded by
9. Specialty
10. Telethon gifts
16. They hurt
18. Hyped thing
22. Engrave
23. Farm building
24. They're locked up in cels
26. Pet line
28. Advance
29. Flies in the face of
30. Talkative bird
31. Type size
32. Undo
34. Old gold coin
37. Not on the rocks
39. Lawn tree
40. It might be pitched
41. Have an evening repast

★ **Solution on page 304**

Show of support

1	2	3	4	5	■	■	6	7	8	9	10
11					12	■	13				
14						■	15				
■	■	■	16			17			■	■	■
18	19	20					■	21	22	23	24
25			■	26			27	■	28		
29			■	30				■	31		
32			33	■	34			35			
■	■	■	36	37					■	■	■
38	39	40			■	41			42	43	44
45					■	46					
47					■	■	48				

ACROSS

1. Talking birds
6. Mob
11. Rang
13. More than unpopular
14. Bid at the bazaar
15. Puts in the pot
16. Even though
18. Covers
21. Bridge feat
25. Pirate approval
26. Vampire author
28. Diamonds, slangily
29. Got to know
30. Line from a tailor
31. Initial group for Gretzky
32. Verbal nudge
34. Made eyes at
36. Totally mad
38. State coffer helper
41. Tempest's place?
45. Bull session goals
46. Surround
47. Old kind of candy
48. Hurled

DOWN

1. Road sign acronym
2. Show of support
3. Slow steed
4. Pond cover
5. Bearish ones
6. Indian drink
7. Harangues
8. Heavy hitter of the '30s
9. A ___ bit
10. Crown giver's degree
12. Meets with an operative
17. Raise
18. Intro music
19. A sight for sore ___
20. Eeler's needs
22. Schmutz
23. Migraine, for one
24. Vulcan mind ___
27. Leading
33. Giant, but not like 8 Down
35. Oral B rival
37. Tending to snoop
38. Border
39. Work by Keats
40. Top ___ List
42. Bridge crosser
43. Intention
44. Sermon seat

★ **Solution on page 304**

It sets a trap

ACROSS

1. In the distance
4. Michael Jackson album
7. It sets a trap
11. It might be inspired
12. Vigoda of *Barney Miller*
13. Bone by the bicep
14. Wilde wile
16. Use 14 Across crudely
17. Actual
18. Cape ___
20. Amscray
21. Governing party
23. Hit by the Association
25. Thriller's quality
27. Tools
29. Garden implement
30. Glistens
34. Ralphie-boy's pal portrayer
35. Pacific ___
37. Pic piece
38. Sites for buildings
40. Bring back
42. Store sign
43. Staining substance
44. Nest egg recipient
45. Zone
46. Place for slop
47. Put in

DOWN

1. Food refrains
2. Conscious
3. Black-and-white show, today
4. Sound for Old MacDonald
5. Tooth woe
6. Mock up
7. Blossom beginning
8. Puts in a row
9. Like embedded journalists
10. Yummy
15. Came to a halt
19. Reside
22. Aerial, for one
24. Bug or butterfly
26. Palette blob
27. Ruckus
28. Rat
29. Tex-Mex topper
31. Oahu hola
32. Stuck in the mud
33. Exhaust
36. Pupil's place
39. Salty body
41. Heavens

★ **Solution on page 304**

Practice

ACROSS

1. Cookie Monster, for one
6. Different
11. They might be green or black
13. Move drunkenly
14. Katmandu resident
15. Plant, like a bug
16. Wet and cold
18. Goals on holes
19. Debut
22. Flatten
24. Grasshopper or key lime
25. Spot in the sea
27. 911 letters
30. Hot tub spot
31. You'd swear it
32. Comic Taylor
33. Was a snitch
35. Glue
37. Stolen spoils
39. A long way off
41. Pester
43. Military practices
47. Tip the ___
48. Go at
49. Archer and apple holder
50. Gas gauge reading

DOWN

1. Unpleasant wait
2. Bitter brew
3. Bit of advice
4. Do well in dodgeball
5. Family member
6. Part of IOU
7. Rate
8. Hot pepper
9. "Be it ___ so humble . . . "
10. Cincinnati team
12. Reason for a rosary
17. Tartan attire
19. Command center
20. Jot from a jigger
21. Like many dinner specials
23. Practice
26. Epic tale
28. Talk to all types
29. Do detective work
34. Coral island
36. Rainbow maker
37. Closing
38. ___ in a blue moon
40. Phen-fen foiling acronym
42. ___ or no
44. Drink like a cat
45. Glowing
46. Devious

★**Solution on page 304**

Cry at a clue

ACROSS

1. Opie portrayer
4. Taper's letters
7. Chin hair, perhaps
11. Good bouncer candidate
12. Cry at a clue
13. 1952 Olympics site
14. Imagine that!
15. Sticky stuff
16. G-note
17. They go with odds
19. Coalesce
21. Misbehave
22. Huckster
24. Seers may see them
26. Pragmatic ones
28. Not-so-sharp one
31. Understanding
34. Starts a set
36. Alert color
37. Saucer occupants
39. Sitcom about Tates and Campbells
40. Acknowledge
42. Ventilate
44. Animosity
45. 100%
46. Lovebird utterance
47. Racket
48. Regard
49. Explosive letters
50. Combo

DOWN

1. Shows animosity
2. It cuts a can
3. Shot provider
4. Coven cookware
5. Horror
6. Like a blue moon
7. Wee one
8. Seat specialist
9. It grows
10. Vacation venues
18. Meatloaf servings
20. Carver's tool
23. Run away together
25. IT types
27. Conference
29. Stays away from
30. Hon
31. Chart
32. Show by "The Capitol Steps"
33. Be fond of
35. All worn out
38. Verbal refinement
41. Put together
43. Ferment

★ **Solution on page 304**

Quite an accomplishment

ACROSS

1. Prereq, often
6. Go bad
11. Blade trimmer
12. Rival of Athens
13. "___ to Be an American"
14. Iconoclasm
15. Discriminating
17. Patriotic church watcher
20. Squishy
24. Feller's need
25. Try a lollipop
28. ___ West
29. "Car Talk" airer
30. Crocheter's need
31. Music store section
32. Oodles
34. Put the bubbly in bubbly
36. Baseballer Reese
39. *Gilligan's Island* locale
42. Spelunking sites
46. In the vicinity
47. Bon voyage
48. They're outstanding
49. Biblical passage

DOWN

1. Pesky tyke
2. Negative conjunction
3. Pair
4. Recycler's goal
5. Hospital worker
6. Blueprint
7. Doohickeys
8. It might be lode-bearing
9. "___ the economy, stupid"
10. Enron fouler
12. This boat
16. Carrie Fisher role
17. Word with "You" for Lurch
18. Place to see big veggies
19. Word of action
21. Stew or soup veggie
22. Quite an accomplishment
23. Hit the keys
26. Gullet
27. Lower joint protector
33. Teapot part
35. Traverses text
37. Expectant one's waits
38. Doomsday fear
39. Little Rascal, but not Darla
40. *Where the Wild Things* ___
41. Lump
43. Through
44. Sushi fish
45. Add together

★ **Solution on page 304**

Put in good humor

ACROSS

1. Arty amphibians
6. ___ for business
11. Touch the sky
13. Sean Connery has one
14. Pulled at
15. "She's Come ___"
16. Mystery
18. Represent
20. Fleet Street's demon barber
24. Be ill
25. Male heir
26. Diamond dalliance
28. Delayer
30. Boxing official
32. Clown name
33. One of several openers
35. "What, this old ___?"
37. 'Net
38. Where they cut the mustard
39. Dr. Moreau's property
41. Juice
43. Flowering shrub
47. Chewed the scenery
51. Hole maker
52. Cowboy game piece
53. Managers watch them
54. Available spread

DOWN

1. Veto vote
2. Actress Marie Saint
3. Get the gold
4. UFO miniseries
5. Shorthand specialists
6. Detailed
7. Cozy coop
8. Politician's pride
9. Devoted one
10. Poker verb
12. Word whittler
13. Like some raps
17. No-name
18. Ate in luxury
19. Put in good humor
21. *Sleeper* gratifier
22. ___ in paperwork
23. Caught some Z's
24. Nile nipper
27. Borrow without permission
29. "Me and My ___"
31. Missed a meal
34. Sheets and such
36. Fashion
40. Nose detection
42. Nibble
43. Jeanne d'___
44. Animal collection
45. They pay for shows
46. " ___ It Be"
48. Man material in Oz
49. Chang's twin
50. *Meet John* ___

★**Solution on page 305**

You can dig it

ACROSS

1. Be certain of
5. Discover a banana peel
9. Like the Beatles
12. Mystical quality
13. "Penny ___"
14. You can dig it
15. Goody-goody
16. Equal
17. Cheat at
18. ___ discretion
19. Ginger ___
20. First or third
21. Saw to
23. Skeet, for one
25. Put away
27. Kids make them from mud
28. Sang Noels
30. Bitty branch
32. They're on the go
35. Unsuccessful
37. Skill
39. Fill with rage
40. Fall from a front
42. Repeated *Star Wars* adjective
43. ___ *Yeller*
44. Soy-based soup
45. Talk show need
46. Scale member
47. Stove compartment
48. Banker's bundle
49. Endeavor
50. Spheres for soup
51. Garden plots

DOWN

1. On the fritz
2. Hospital workers
3. Align
4. Bon mot maker
5. Trim
6. Etna outflow
7. Blundering
8. Write
9. Seek
10. Happens
11. Father
19. It needs treatment
20. Kind of shower
22. Unlikely to attack
24. Tarzan, for one
26. Comedian Adams or Knotts
29. UV protectors
30. Clothing alterer
31. Like a savage
33. Give meaning to
34. Weaved
35. Winter dew
36. Pilot
38. Impossibility for the bald
41. In a calm, perhaps
44. Do maid's work
45. *Married to the* ___

★ **Solution on page 305**

Verbose

ACROSS

1. Shatter
6. Talmud teacher
11. Pupil hider
13. Echo
14. Summer treat
15. Joins a contest
16. Deem
18. Freddy's street
20. Ticket risker
24. It hooks in the back
25. Let out
27. Fancy holders
29. It comes and goes
30. Fine-tune
31. Noise number
33. It might be a kneeler
34. It's in the fine print
36. Darn
37. Antenna owner
39. Supernatural
43. Builds
47. Wakes up
48. Product documentation
49. Campfire glower
50. Verbose

DOWN

1. Panhandle
2. Ham on ___
3. Slender swimmer
4. It might be raised
5. It often has a tail
6. Convert
7. Pertinent
8. Bonnet buzzer
9. Slot symbol
10. "___ beginning to look a lot . . . "
12. Barkers
13. Go through again
17. Makes one's flesh creep
18. Did the wrong thing
19. Knight's weapon
21. Simpson's "my bad"
22. Marry in a hurry
23. ___ one's vows
24. Al Bundy's son
26. Morning moisture
28. Employ an ottoman
29. Fencing falsities
32. One who doesn't stay on
35. Look
36. Office pool member
38. Gut
39. Metal yielder
40. E-mail address suffix
41. Baby bear
42. Spend
44. Dastard
45. Lincoln's son
46. Underhanded

★ **Solution on page 305**

Curious

ACROSS

1. Well-worn path
4. Shout
7. Pass along
12. Back in time
13. It's flushed in a flat
14. Leak
15. " . . . and ___ hangs a tale"
17. Pioneer's transport
18. Flight-related
20. Come to
22. Like some laces
26. One who showed up
27. Curious
28. Time for a tan
29. At the center of
30. "A Boy Named ___"
31. My liege!
32. ___ guzzler
33. Bed on rollers
34. Tell off
35. Followed
37. Not for polite society
38. Turtle type
40. They go on
43. Opening
47. Chum in Chile
48. Warlocks, essentially
49. Arabian flyer?
50. Doctor's device
51. Nail
52. Frat party need

DOWN

1. Plea-bargainer, perhaps
2. Blech!
3. Nail holder
4. Smart
5. Locksley lad
6. Go to extremes
7. VCR button
8. Precise
9. Dunderhead
10. Bit of trouble
11. Kyoto cash
16. Did yard work
19. Art example
20. Lady
21. Not right
23. Nonliteral phrase
24. Before it's due
25. Colored anew
26. Actor in two Vegas films
27. Not anteing
30. Baking ___
31. Muffler
33. Bleeper
34. Believing, they say
36. Custom
37. Binge
39. Splendor
40. Flim-flam target
41. Physician flock, for short
42. Jazz booking
44. Get under one's skin
45. Actor assist
46. White ovoid, often

★**Solution on page 305**

Can I have one?

ACROSS

1. Wayne's word
4. Snow slider
8. Choose from a menu
11. Inventor Whitney
12. Rash
14. Catcall cry
15. Last will and ___
17. Common address
18. Eyes, to a poet
19. Church closers
21. Not a family car
24. Wand word
25. Infomercial verb
26. Piano pieces
29. Beaming
31. Can you ___ it?
32. Alter windows
35. Drew casually
38. Can I have one?
39. Displeased looks
41. Newman or Travis of song
43. Goes around
44. Sighed word
46. Coffee container
47. Puts into code
52. Come to an end
53. Tenacity
54. Pompom pronouncement
55. Land cover
56. Garden gremlin
57. Author Tan

1	2	3	■	4	5	6	7	■	■	8	9	10
11			■	12				13	■	14		
15			16						■	17		
■	■	■	18				■	19	20			
21	22	23			■	■	24					
25			■	26	27	28					■	■
29			30	■	31			■	32		33	34
■	■	35		36				37	■	38		
39	40					■	■	41	42			
43					■	44	45			■	■	■
46			■	47	48					49	50	51
52			■	53					■	54		
55			■	■	56				■	57		

DOWN

1. Goal garb
2. Fiesta cry
3. Third word of "America"
4. Broker's ware
5. It hangs from a tree
6. Times to see stars
7. Reading spot
8. Crosswords, to some
9. Indicate
10. Mannequin middle
13. ___ your engines!
16. Uppermost
20. Vegan's avoidance
21. Gear
22. Athena's pet
23. Bare
24. You're looking at one
27. Bookie's business
28. Zippo
30. Like this entry
33. Give assent
34. "___ kingdom come . . ."
36. *Daily Planet* employee
37. Hung
39. Wood in walls
40. Knickknack
42. ___ Wednesday
44. It's part of a plot
45. As it happens
48. Like a leaf to turn over
49. Period of note
50. Shove
51. Timid

★ **Solution on page 305**

What else?

ACROSS

1. Soap ingredient
4. Tater
8. Creep
12. Dinghy diary
13. She goes with gramps
14. Singular
15. The Dynamic ___
16. In need of an oasis
17. Crazy one
18. GPA determiners
20. Makes one's way
21. ___ *We Dance?*
23. X out, editorially
25. Abe's coin
26. Huff
27. "Takin' Care of Business" group, for short
30. Cal Ripken, for one
32. Community
34. TV filler, for short
35. Wrigglers
37. Golfer's goal
38. Let's go to the ___
39. Takes along
40. Tried to say hi
43. Rubbish
45. Is outstanding
46. Lex Luthor's assistant
47. Pound sound
50. Musical based on *La Bohème*
51. Celebration
52. Color
53. Strum in a stream
54. Release from bondage
55. What else?

DOWN

1. Lawyer's letters
2. The current solver, to me
3. It's I-dazzling
4. Fishing flop
5. Natural setting
6. Togetherness
7. Randolph, to Patty
8. Secluded spot
9. Common lunch time
10. Oaf
11. Hatchling hatchers
19. Species of sax
20. ___ respect to
21. Nae-sayer
22. Trumpeter Alpert
24. Close call
26. Sweat
27. Hubbub
28. Let in on
29. Tributes
31. Prime player
33. Cries of discovery
36. Alif or aleph
38. Hotheaded
39. Waste maker, they say
40. Eroded
41. Thoroughly impressed
42. Merchandise
44. Take a stand?
46. Switch setting
48. Scoot
49. Provided with pizza

★**Solution on page 305**

Impressive!

ACROSS

1. Scrooge statement
4. Facial sites
8. Hit 28 Across
12. Impressive!
13. Freelance
14. Drop from crying
15. Precious stone
16. Diva ditty
17. Ornate
18. Aroma
20. Party pooper
22. Pandora's box contents
24. Divided dogmatists
28. Store conglomerate
31. Where Jews are gentiles
33. Whopper
34. Tapers off
36. Olden
38. Newsman Koppel
39. Rider's cry
41. Antiquing liquid
42. Glamor
44. Poor box offering
46. Egyptian biters
48. Eye-related
52. Rocker Lou ___
55. "___ She Sweet?"
57. Detective Ventura
58. Raceway shape
59. Chair part
60. Actor Steiger
61. We are united
62. Tit for tat?
63. Just ___ of those things

DOWN

1. Cranberry places
2. Psst kin
3. Place to steal
4. Horse holder
5. One ___ customer
6. In the crowd
7. Fight before the fight
8. Put on
9. That ship
10. Trigger tidbit
11. Inquire
19. Merry melody
21. Like a campfire
23. Liquor lover
25. Dancing shoe
26. Fork finger
27. Clairvoyant
28. A good place for tumblers
29. Assist an assassin
30. Miss
32. Cain's bane
35. Fleecy femmes
37. "Oh my!" reaction
40. Without difficulty
43. Soup server
45. Watchword
47. Kind of tense
49. Root vegetable
50. Celeb
51. Surrender
52. Fit or snit
53. Actress Arden
54. It has a drum
56. Baby's break

★ **Solution on page 305**

Say it again

1	2	3	4	■	5	6	7	8	■	9	10	11
12				■	13				■	14		
15				■	16				■	17		
■	■	■	18	19			■	20	21			
22	23	24			■	25	26			■	■	■
27			■	28	29			■	30	31	32	33
34			35			■	36	37				
38				■	39	40			■	41		
■	■	■	42	43			■	44	45			
46	47	48			■	49	50			■	■	■
51			■	52	53			■	54	55	56	57
58			■	59				■	60			
61			■	62				■	63			

ACROSS

1. Counterfeit
5. Tuna sandwich
9. Almost empty
12. Excited
13. Calamine substitute
14. Boise's state, for short
15. Out-of-this-world drink?
16. Horse race start
17. Supporting
18. Discharge
20. Pipsqueak
22. Kid's alphabet book animal
25. Say it again
27. Ogle
28. It might be high or low
30. Angry speech
34. Bandies words
36. Like a contortionist
38. Not as much
39. Actress Carter
41. Actress Thompson
42. Downs a donut
44. On the wrong side of the tracks
46. Spin
49. "___ Miner's Daughter"
51. Chick magnet?
52. Like court statements
54. Picard crewmate
58. Ararat artifact
59. Crosby partner
60. By Jove!
61. Tinker
62. The ___ have it
63. Make asunder

DOWN

1. Dieter's concern
2. *Evening Shade* role
3. Family reunion crowd
4. Painting tool
5. Star worshipers?
6. Relieved
7. His wife was a pillar
8. Pearly whites
9. Mikey's cereal
10. Stink
11. *Star Trek* speed
19. Win at chess
21. Computer fouler
22. Fervor
23. Rochester's love
24. Implores
26. Terror unit
29. "___ It Romantic?"
31. Skilled
32. Not just crave
33. Cafeteria carrier
35. Hacker
37. Ingrid's role
40. Get away
43. Island 'allo
45. More senior
46. Huh?
47. Impressive person or sandwich
48. Black
50. Charo cheers
53. *Wings* role
55. The Golden ___
56. Unhealthy acquisition, to the ACS
57. Tally up

★**Solution on page 305**

Benevolent

1	2	3	4	■	5	6	7	8	■	9	10	11
12				■	13				■	14		
15				■	16				17			
18				■	19					■	■	■
■	■	■	20	21				■	22	23	24	25
26	27	28			■	29		30	■	31		
32					33	■	34		35			
36			■	37		38	■	39				
40			41	■	42		43			■	■	■
■	■	■	44	45				■	46	47	48	49
50	51	52						■	53			
54			■	55				■	56			
57			■	58				■	59			

ACROSS

1. Extreme slight
5. Plaything
9. Curious inquiry
12. Cellar dweller
13. Bring up, or what you might bring up
14. It's ground-breaking
15. Battery fluid
16. Stop sign shapes
18. Rats, to Willard
19. She knows best
20. Sprout
22. CPA skill
26. Baseball deal
29. Piglet, to Pooh
31. Ring around the collar
32. Girl clubs?
34. Slips
36. Be a doer
37. Ground for Gretzky
39. Von Bulow portrayer
40. *Empty* ___
42. Newsboy's cry
44. ___ Centauri
46. Mischievous children
50. *General* ___
53. It's put on 37 Across
54. Stand in ___ of
55. Put on eBay
56. A Great Lake
57. Nay rival
58. Carnivore's capture
59. Judge

DOWN

1. Same as 26 Across
2. Benevolent
3. Syllabus segment
4. Doctor's ___ manner
5. Scenes for teens
6. ___ a loss
7. Soft breakfast
8. Brit buggy
9. ___ asked you?
10. Sweetie
11. "___! We Have No Bananas"
17. Workout place
21. Big rig
23. And not only that . . .
24. One with angst?
25. Snake sound
26. Better late ___ never
27. Humans, for one
28. ___ and crafts
30. Dragon's ___
33. Power rod?
35. Gave a rave
38. *Waiting to* ___
41. Faucet
43. Final count
45. Tommy had one in *The Music Man*
47. Maned mom
48. Dance position
49. Emanate
50. ___ fever
51. Carry a tab
52. Red or Dead

★ **Solution on page 305**

Chapter 5

Easy Street

Pacify

ACROSS

1. Worry oneself
5. Undergarment
9. Walked
13. Kind of excuse
14. Pull-down, perhaps
15. Baseball's Berra
16. Mercenary's wares
17. Toward sunrise
18. Pacify
19. Police patrol
20. Red or black one
21. Hearts
22. Malfunction
24. Linc's locks
26. Open-mouth look
29. *Animal House* role
33. Like a ___ of bricks
34. Bells and whistles
36. Yes in the mess
37. Vexation
38. Bathtub cry
39. London terminal
40. Did editing
42. Merit badge duties
44. Over one's head
45. Prepared
46. Playground item
49. Home-helper's stat
51. Chocolate or potato item
55. *The ___ Ranger*
56. Accomplishes
57. ___ Krishna
58. Flat boats
59. Job had them
60. Shady shelterers
61. Least bad
62. Dubious
63. Catbird, for one

DOWN

1. Organism's overhang
2. Infrequent
3. Title role for Gwyneth
4. Perfume sample
5. Muckraker's job
6. Trim
7. Seated
8. Placed
9. Baron
10. Crowd sound
11. Give a sly eye
12. Lessens
21. More than a mission
23. Judge
25. ___ music
26. Fidget
27. Lacerated
28. From the start
29. Like asbestos
30. Throw for a loop
31. Gave an 11 Down
32. Beatty pic
35. Tactless
41. Least traditional
43. Makes an impression
45. Fraidy-cat
46. Scully's surface
47. Tales of long ago
48. Pen refills
50. "Where's the ___?"
52. Colonial patriot
53. Food fan Rombauer
54. Nuisance
56. MADD concern, for short

★ **Solution on page 306**

Get over here!

1	2	3	4	■	5	6	7	8	■	9	10	11	12
13				■	14				■	15			
16				■	17				■	18			
19				20	■	21			22	■	23		
■	■	■	■	24	25			■	26	27			
28	29	30	31			■	32	33			■	■	■
34				■	35	36					37	38	39
40				41					■	42			
■	■	■	43				■	44	45				
46	47	48			■	49	50			■	■	■	■
51			■	52	53			■	54	55	56	57	58
59			60	■	61			62	■	63			
64				■	65				■	66			
67				■	68				■	69			

ACROSS

1. Air
5. Makes a selection
9. Rubs out
13. Printer's concern
14. Prep a pear
15. Deplaned
16. Mimics
17. English
18. Monk's garb
19. Landlord income
21. Attends to business
23. Star dealer
24. Nasty to behold
26. Siberia senders?
28. Grand ___ Island
32. Vittles
34. *Stanley &* ___
35. Communications specialists
40. Booted from office
42. Protective barrier
43. ___ Grey
44. Like sandpaper
46. Paper deliverers, often
49. I had no ___!
51. British brew
52. ___ a nice day!
54. Farm fool
59. Cat comment
61. ___ to other matters
63. Top of a tale
64. Actress Adams or McClurg
65. Atop
66. Vehicular voicer
67. Watermelon missile
68. Get over here!
69. Macho man

DOWN

1. Tree topper
2. Media madness
3. ___ and shut case
4. Batman portrayer
5. HQ
6. Like the Popemobile
7. Tyke's toy
8. Put in the mail
9. Stick in the water
10. Most of them like the sun
11. Food for regular people
12. A.A. has 12
20. Added amount
22. Halt
25. Croc's kin
27. Hindu honcho
28. Bridge bet
29. You and me be
30. Strike
31. Ghostly
33. Clay for Mr. Scissorhands
36. Adds verve to
37. Tater ___
38. Cat prop for Seuss
39. Babe's abode
41. Sumac effect
45. Author Bradbury
46. Some court evidence
47. Steer clear of
48. Like some coincidences
50. You might hammer them out
53. Straddling
55. Sounds at stunts
56. Sailor's speed
57. Grayish yellow
58. ___ a hand
60. Traffic light color
62. Daughter of Hi and Lois

★ **Solution on page 306**

For beginners

ACROSS

1. Morse code morsel
5. Zsa Zsa's verb
9. Right this instant!
13. It comes back to you
14. Bobs
15. Roll on a runway
16. It might have a head on it
17. For beginners
18. Helmsley show
19. Graceful one
21. 18 Across, for one
23. Stream
25. Parch
26. Gosh, guv
27. He makes the call
28. Concealed
31. It might make you cross
32. Early event in *Romancing the Stone*
34. Made eyes at
37. ___ Age
38. Be all over
39. Tinman's request
40. Without risk
42. City floater
43. Author Anthony
44. Union action
47. Splints
48. Casino coin
49. Be contiguous
51. You might strike one
55. Beseech
56. Lady's man
57. Funny Arkin or Sandler
58. Tousle
59. More than hip
60. Succeeding

DOWN

1. Cotillion comer
2. The ___ of spades
3. Female
4. He might have a nag
5. Like Pete, perhaps
6. Bank offering
7. You might take them out
8. Enthusiastic
9. It comes in books
10. Docile
11. Cut a budget
12. Microscopic
20. Teensy
22. Clumsy ones
23. Class ___
24. Unshakeable
25. Muck
26. 2 bits, times 4
28. Job maker
29. Revered ones
30. Just say no
32. Become one
33. Time to do things
35. Eccentric
36. Totem pole's tale
40. Incomplete
41. Lend a hand
42. *Reality* ___
44. Relative of 25 Down
45. Sign preposition
46. Jury-___
47. Ladder louver
50. Place to hit the hay
52. A nice thing to say
53. Clinton's brass
54. Ambulance aide, for short

★ **Solution on page 306**

Start

1	2	3	4	■	5	6	7	8	■	9	10	11	12
13				■	14				■	15			
16				■	17				■	18			
19				20	■	21			22		■	■	■
■	■	■	23		24		■	25			26	27	■
28	29	30	■	31			32	■	33				34
35			■	36				37	■	38			
39			40	■	41				42	■	43		
44				45	■	46				■	47		
■	48				49	■	50			51	■	■	■
■	■	■	52			53		■	54		55	56	57
58	59	60		■	61			62	■	63			
64				■	65				■	66			
67				■	68				■	69			

ACROSS

1. Item at a bank auction
5. Put up
9. ___ of arms
13. Plow pullers
14. Declare true
15. Be in charge
16. Sticks in the ground
17. Where heroes are born
18. Title film role for Julia
19. You might turn its head
21. Apology bundle
23. Duck
25. Brought through the airport
28. They get crunched
31. They're often inflated
33. Tries to abut
35. Crackpot
36. Ones of no concern
38. Ransom spot
39. Soviet shah
41. Ditches class
43. Neither's mate
44. Apron part
46. Get the UPC
47. One might have a cover
48. T-bar user
50. Radio control
52. Harold's partner
54. Impudent
58. Johnson of *Laugh-In*
61. Trifle
63. Boarding preposition
64. Disaster
65. Sugar source
66. Football maneuver
67. Circus site
68. Throws in
69. Oktoberfest containers

DOWN

1. Decays
2. Golden parachuter, often
3. One in a similar position
4. Start
5. Seat softener
6. Scenic spots
7. Leia rescuer
8. Dance for Checker
9. Hit a max
10. ___ *Man in Havana*
11. Recent Olympic torch lighter
12. Bo's no.
20. Show grief
22. Many millennia
24. A long time
26. Gets from toil
27. Slouch
28. Them, in *Them!*
29. Breaks apart
30. ___ naked
32. Almost held back a laugh
34. Light on one's feet
37. Bridge section
40. Clothing item
42. Uppity one
45. Thick as ___ soup
49. Cuban dance
51. Like some tea or walks
53. Title
55. Diarist Frank
56. Doe's beau
57. Beermaker's need
58. But is it ___?
59. More than apologize
60. ___ Pan Alley
62. *Men in Black* concerns, for short

★ **Solution on page 306**

Passion

1	2	3	4	■	5	6	7	8	■	9	10	11	12
13				■	14				■	15			
16				■	17				■	18			
19				20		■	21		22		■	■	■
23					■	24				■	25	26	27
■	■	■	28		29		■	■	30	31			
32	33	34		■	35		36	37					
38				39					■	40			
41					■	■	42		43		■	■	■
44			■	45	46	47		■	48		49	50	51
■	■	■	52				■	53					
54	55	56		■	57		58		■	59			
60				■	61				■	62			
63				■	64				■	65			

ACROSS

1. Wine valley
5. Insufficiency
9. Yodel sites
13. Alimony recipients
14. Bestriding
15. Form of travel
16. Faint display
17. It might be dominant
18. Like a soufflé
19. Scores
21. Arp's art
23. Sweet sandwich
24. It doesn't ___ well
25. Kind of truck
28. Easy Halloween attire
30. Make amends
32. Hirschfeld hider
35. Ache aid
38. Mile measurers
40. Passion
41. Studied studiously
42. Scruff
44. Dutch ___ disease
45. Increases a phone bill
48. Pipes up in church
52. Concealer
53. Skimpy
54. Better half
57. Spielberg's first full film
59. Put in 60 Across
60. Hot spot
61. Proof word
62. Avoided the truth
63. Duma denial
64. Stash in a cache
65. Heels

DOWN

1. They have eyes for witches
2. Postulate
3. Basil sauce
4. Nutrasweet, today
5. Takes a trunk
6. Impersonate
7. Flat on the beach?
8. Massage
9. Kind of rug
10. Avoid the lead
11. One in a poke
12. Stone or Stallone
20. Grace's hubby
22. Please be a ___
24. Children's farm-animal film
25. Vegan staple
26. Singles
27. Got away from it all
29. Go on, now
31. No great shakes
32. Casual denial
33. You might bow to one
34. *Cheers* cry
36. Ash holders
37. Helpful ad, for short
39. It might be sharp
43. How the weasel goes
46. They're here to help
47. Say suddenly
49. Truth quantity
50. *You ___ for It*
51. "The ___ of the many . . . "
52. Blow off steam
53. At a mired pace
54. Got top prize
55. College creeper
56. Part of USF
58. It drives a mad scientist

★ **Solution on page 306**

Adore

ACROSS

1. Highway accesses
6. Put a question to
9. College employee
13. Glorify
14. Trouble
15. Fishing spot
16. Surface growth for 15 Across
17. Become less severe
18. Unfriendly one
19. Failures to accept
21. Proposal
23. Taking a break
24. Court gp., for short
25. Tiller's place
27. Snacked
29. Precarious
34. Lefty
37. Hot spot
38. Broadcast portion
39. Time at school
41. Groom
42. Give it a go
43. Long text, for short
44. It might be panned
46. Catcher
49. In front of
53. Adore
56. Doozy
57. Discoverer's call
59. Work by Shakespeare
60. Periods
61. ___ tent
62. Overact
63. I ___ do it!
64. "___ Loves You"
65. Speeds

DOWN

1. Perused
2. Shaft
3. Strength
4. Kilt pattern
5. Go for another plate
6. Makes dumbstruck
7. Blake Edwards film
8. Middle Eastern treat
9. Sit with a sound
10. Road ___
11. Pod veggie
12. Have a hunch
20. Go like Samuel Beckett
22. Old hat
24. Less 22 Down
25. Memo stat, for short
26. Pecks in a bushel
28. Epicure's concern
30. *The Eagle ___ Landed*
31. Otto, in a 1980 film role
32. Banjo's place
33. Scotland ___
35. It often has a pin or clip
36. Deep respect
40. It's been told before
45. Harvests
47. Allude
48. Something detectable
49. Went like the wind
50. New currency
51. Eggy treat
52. Overthrow
53. Vampire's garb
54. Spot
55. Attacks clods
58. Can you repeat that?

★ **Solution on page 306**

Happiness

1	2	3	■	4	5	6	7	■	8	9	10	11	12
13			■	14				■	15				
16			■	17				■	18				
■	■	19	20					■	21				
22	23					■	■	24			■	■	■
25					■	26	27			■	28	29	30
31					32				■	33			
34				■	35				36				
37			■	38				■	39				
■	■	■	40			■	■	41					
42	43	44			■	45	46					■	■
47					■	48				■	49	50	51
52					■	53				■	54		
55					■	56				■	57		

ACROSS

1. Pinup's kicker
4. Sicilian spouter
8. Passion
13. "Born in the ___"
14. Workers onboard
15. Onion's kin
16. "The Puzzler Presents" airer
17. Half of a Jim Carrey movie
18. Wears or spares
19. Happiness
21. Sitting like a lump
22. Slogs along
24. The Bronx has one
25. Fast ones
26. Depth of beauty?
28. Pendulum go-with
31. Moving about
33. Go in the snow
34. Husk
35. Not certain
37. Bambi's mother, for one
38. Recalled
39. One in charge
40. Sit like a lump
41. Create
42. More than mince
45. Way more than a mile
47. Take by force
48. Cupid
49. "___ Now or Never"
52. Pasta quills
53. Spots on the face
54. Reference word
55. Daisy kin
56. ___ light on
57. Strain, or cause of stress

DOWN

1. Pellet pusher
2. African attacker
3. Bread spread
4. Overshadow
5. Gives it a go
6. Spiffy
7. Out of order
8. Director's cry
9. Big beast, briefly
10. Grim
11. Game ___
12. Sit a spell
20. Change a charter
22. It's before home
23. Relation rate
24. Italian tube
26. Put in the bank
27. Be familiar with
28. Hyper
29. Beach locales
30. Calming words, when doubled
32. Hit the buzzer
33. Purple hue
36. All dolled up
38. Custodian
40. Sci-fi pioneer
41. Bee peon
42. Time of great change
43. Duct tape has many
44. Litter's littlest
45. Pod members
46. Chief
50. Sipped substance
51. Topic for Dr. Ruth

★ **Solution on page 306**

Festive

ACROSS

1. Festive
6. Rock that rolls
10. Authority
13. In on
14. Spin center
15. Reporter's question
16. Black
17. Hodgepodge
18. ___ see you later
19. Shirt colorers
20. They get in the way
22. Posed
24. Be a bit under
25. Impressed cries
28. Yen
31. Game with numbers
35. Mexican hats
38. Spotted
39. Lug
40. Bronx cheer
42. Praise
44. Necessary stuff
45. Stir
46. Untrue top
48. Baseball hat
50. Be bearish on
55. Becomes less strong
59. Lennon's mate
60. 60 minutes
61. Dancer/singer Abdul
62. Tundra critter
63. London art gallery
64. *Green* ___
65. *Catcher in the* ___
66. Winter white
67. Tears at

DOWN

1. Difficult
2. Not here
3. Make a sidewalk
4. Button action
5. Impulse
6. Souvlaki meat
7. They chop
8. It's quite a view
9. Attack
10. Groundhog of note
11. Character
12. Night birds
20. Pip or Pop
21. Seal
23. Tire filler
25. Tennis great
26. Fraud
27. XXX wares
29. Cliff projection
30. Fireman's need
32. Semester, perhaps
33. Actress Garr or Hatcher
34. Black stone
36. What a cover might be
37. *Star Trek* opener
41. It holds things up
43. Gaffer or best boy's concern
47. Lurch's usual response
49. We come in ___!
50. Mover and shaker
51. Today ___!
52. Roused
53. It's driven
54. Actress Barrymore
56. Stay on fire
57. Oozed
58. Fresh talk
61. On a ___ with

★ **Solution on page 306**

Have fun

ACROSS

1. Rapid
5. Buck
9. Sound devices
13. Yosemite Sam need
14. One you're aligned with
15. ___ canal
16. "Runaround Sue" singer
17. Stormy weather
18. Carbonated beverage
19. Moved slowly
21. Vegan's bane
23. Patronize Okemo
24. Mideast gulf
26. Indian, for one
28. ___ lizard
32. Salty salute
34. Or ___ what?
35. Fixed fee
37. Carp or shellfish
41. Antlered animal
42. Checklist member
43. Dalai ___
44. BSA oath word
46. Sasquatch
48. Cut a budget
51. It might be cracked
53. Cracked
54. Moderate
56. Kind of cash
61. Man Friday
63. ___ *High*
65. Certain something
66. Mull
67. VH1 show
68. Cut curls
69. Evil alter ego
70. Have fun
71. Military closer

DOWN

1. Film effect
2. In
3. Bos-Wash problem
4. I don't like your ___
5. Jam ingredient
6. Andes animal
7. Keep at arm's length
8. Perch talker
9. Blood takers, for short
10. Bullwinkle, for one
11. Oktoberfest dance
12. What red wine does
20. *American Idol* nickname
22. Also
25. BSA badge
27. Take a ten-speed
28. Helmed
29. Flamenco finish
30. Option
31. *Revenge of the* ___
33. Muscular fellow
36. Not the norm
38. Bump
39. Healers homogenized, briefly
40. Don't allow
45. Weird Al movie with Kramer as a janitor
47. Kind of rally
48. SRO event
49. Flock members
50. Thrown in
52. Area of focus
55. The COLA-concerned
57. ___ India Company
58. Ahi, for one
59. Chevy Chase action
60. Chatters away
62. Flock female
64. Kite site

★ **Solution on page 306**

Blown away

ACROSS

1. Party
5. Onrush
10. It's usually accepted
14. "Chantilly ___"
15. Door evener
16. She's deep
17. It needs to be kneaded
18. Cancel out
19. Edict
20. Common article
21. Show bravado
22. Honkers
23. Earth inheritors
25. Wavering water
28. Org. for Orr, for short
29. *Evening* ___
31. Klutzy call
33. Jaunt
35. Cooker
36. Converse casually
40. Move like Tinkerbell
41. Dodge
43. Jumbo
44. Shell food?
45. *A ___ Good Men*
46. Aides asea
48. Breach
50. Nullifies
51. Dejected
54. Cat call
56. *Lost in Space* role
57. What hot dogs do on the grill
59. All ___ Caesar!
61. Like some roads
64. Don't win or draw
65. Leguizamo film
67. Ball
68. Pot stuffer
69. Had a bug
70. Director Egoyan
71. Pop quiz
72. Like untended gardens
73. "Shall we?" response

DOWN

1. Not sharp
2. A pop
3. Blueprint
4. Green wood
5. Little light
6. Humerus neighbor
7. Spectrum
8. Serengeti beast
9. Water weaver
10. *Bagdad* ___
11. Sci-fi shocker
12. Secret supply
13. ___ *California*
21. It's ___ a pleasure
22. Con
24. Sentence reducer
26. It hinges on something
27. A bit eccentric
29. Tender
30. Luau dance
32. Academy
34. Flub
35. Long bench
37. Embarrass
38. Like some cheese
39. Sawbucks
42. Bush block
47. Vader's way
49. Little terror
51. Messy landing sound
52. Without anyone else
53. Cleans the house
55. Moby Dick, for one
56. Like Chicago
58. . . . and never the twain shall ___
60. Blown away
62. Cake
63. Southern spuds
65. Noticed
66. ___ à la mode
67. ___ Friday

★ **Solution on page 307**

Fitting

ACROSS

1. Dash
5. Joke
8. Cobras' kin
12. The sun, to newsprint
13. Puts out in the sun
15. Circuit
16. Skirt type
17. Mountain call
18. Steal
19. Parts of a whole
21. Hitched on the run
23. Ply a needle
24. Stew site
25. "Those Were the ___"
26. Fix in one's mind
28. Insert ___ A in slot B
31. ___ *Royale*
34. Card at a 31 Across
35. Apple slag
36. Put up
37. Try to win
38. Comely one
39. Queue or cue
40. Pigeonhole
41. Tatters
42. Jot
43. Like soda cans, often
45. Hollyhock holder
46. Fabricate
47. Fox show on CBS
50. Mark of rank
53. Grumble
55. Tight
56. Flirt
58. Golf swings
59. Napoleon's destination
60. With weapons
61. Plow pairer
62. Unwrap
63. Fitting
64. Vegas device

DOWN

1. They might be grand
2. Like an acrobat
3. Continue
4. Clip
5. Small cave
6. Lends a hand
7. My word!
8. Ladies of depth
9. Bathroom bar
10. Nudge
11. Hightailed it
13. Hard worker
14. Low-life
20. Occurrence
22. Drain drainer
25. Game need
26. Blind ones in rhyme
27. Like April days, often
28. Schlep
29. Dry
30. Comb users
31. Highland Scot
32. *Salome* solo
33. "___ in the Clowns"
35. Muffet bit
37. *Miami* ___
38. Bird word
40. Pamplona penny
41. Gotten in *Ghostbusters*
43. Beat the ___
44. Stashing site
45. Very important
47. Yuletide song
48. Perv
49. Embedded item
50. Routine part
51. Impressive story
52. Cartoonist Goldberg
53. Like *Hairspray*
54. ___ an egg
57. NOW concern, for short

★**Solution on page 307**

Enthused

ACROSS

1. Desert navigator
6. Small note
10. Enthused
14. Humble home
15. Sign of a future event
16. Grammie
17. Super-moist fruit
18. Big nibble
19. Present
20. Facial orb
21. Artisan
23. Kind of salami
24. Enthusiasm
25. Flattened circle
27. Tied bundle
30. One to be followed
32. Acronym sandwich
35. Come out
37. Outfield item
38. Ole in Ohio
39. Difficulty
40. As easy as ___
41. Wipe from memory
43. It's kept in a nest
44. Surveyor's unit
46. Does lab work
47. Kite or kazoo
48. Penetrate
50. Piqued
51. Crumbly cheese
52. Molten
54. Waiter handouts
57. "Are we there yet?", for one
59. Do yard work
62. Neck and neck
63. Get less than a D-
64. Title role for Snipes
66. Knit
67. Old strings
68. Artificial fabric
69. Grandiose
70. From a resale store
71. Oscar or Tony

DOWN

1. Oscar or Tony
2. Controversial vow word
3. Tunnel user
4. Hoopla
5. Tightly packed
6. On the road
7. Give off
8. Step-by-step
9. Person
10. Gate passer
11. Carly Simon adjective
12. Bits at a briefing
13. 12 Down, essentially
22. XY being
23. Wedding ring?
24. Goose egg
26. Flock doc
27. Henri's hat
28. Felipe's friend
29. With good gams
31. *Jurassic Park* rock
32. Opera encore
33. Focused beam
34. The group by me
36. Wrathful fruit?
40. Lowly positions?
42. Cheerful
45. Camp aide, for short
46. Someone of no importance
49. Wound
51. Uproarious
53. Striped horse
54. Neighbor of Phoenix
55. Happily ___ after
56. *Aliens* role
58. Take on
59. Author Angelou
60. It's nasty on the nose
61. Weave
63. Vaccine target
65. Attorney's forte

★ **Solution on page 307**

Oh my!

ACROSS

1. Gives a title to
6. Slant
10. Cinema souvenir
14. It's to be remembered
15. Tailor's unit
16. Charlie Brown frustrator
17. Snooped
18. Potter's supply
19. Grub
20. Future observer
21. Pay attention to
22. Mature sapling
23. Taken in
26. It goes with a horse
27. Escapades
30. Crush
32. Tolerated
33. Entrenched
34. Be immoral
37. Perch
38. Lots of salt water
39. Way more than average
41. Guys
42. Oh my!
44. Sage
45. Play item
46. Tipped off
47. Federal veep
50. Stifle
52. ___ *Alone*
53. Towel word
54. Hoodlum
58. Is in hock
59. Pleasant
60. Envelop
61. Candy flavor
62. They might hold you up
63. Heart line
64. Baja buck
65. Bit of change
66. Mixed metal

DOWN

1. Little snoozes
2. Healing rub
3. Compose
4. Green gems
5. Lawn lump
6. Athlete's pride
7. Fishing locale
8. Professor's forte
9. Skittish
10. SNL bit
11. Sparkly headpiece
12. Speak
13. Surrounded
21. Worked on weeds
24. One who wants to lose
25. Acronym for a patriotic org.
27. McDonald's place
28. English horn kin
29. Leo, for one
31. Fireside treats
33. Provided for
34. Religious subset
35. Bit of land
36. Necessity
38. Blue gem
40. Drinker's perch
43. Yucky stuff
44. Pamplona cries
45. Voilà
46. Take into custody
47. ___ at the bit
48. Gadzooks!
49. Final words
51. Pie nut
55. Wayne's word
56. Do ___ others . . .
57. Outback 'allo
59. *Today* place
60. Sheepish remark

★ **Solution on page 307**

Prized

ACROSS

1. Amount of evidence
6. Breakfast order
10. Flower part
14. Forgo
15. Complain
16. Biblical pronoun
17. Santa's helpers
18. White stone
19. Take out a video
20. Actress Gardner
21. Relations
23. Most small
25. Tattle
27. Prized
29. Oven mmm's
31. Verb form
35. Just friends
38. Have obligations
39. Put out on the media
40. Pantry unit
42. *The ___ Suspects*
44. Acquire
45. Wet weather
47. It ends with a conclusion
50. Eye part
51. Did NSA work
53. Mesmerized
57. Finger-pointing
60. Writer
62. Besmirch
63. Veg
64. Court claim
66. ___ *the Other Reindeer*
68. Blinds part
69. *The Donna ___ Show*
70. Ballot box entries
71. Choice before showing fingers
72. Puts a bee in one's bonnet
73. A big yawn?

DOWN

1. Show of effort
2. Cut in two
3. Foe
4. Genesis gal
5. Work place
6. Fiscal
7. It might be between teeth
8. Preps cheese
9. Like some ends
10. Long step
11. It goes with 16 Across
12. Long waits on hold
13. Jeff's pal
22. Graphic
24. Take down, fiscally
26. Past due
28. Formerly occupied
30. Director Serling
32. It might be proper
33. Sultan of ___
34. They're shocking
35. Buzz by phone
36. Golf landings
37. Part of B.A.
41. Memo sites
42. Brew house?
43. Brand
46. Rollercoaster, for one
48. Mature ones
49. Oui in Weehauken
50. Dough tool
52. Bay of Naples isle
54. *Jaws* site
55. ___ the way
56. Lock of hair
57. *The Sun ___ Rises*
58. Iced
59. Not bare
61. Big boom
65. My! A mouse!
67. Tennis shot

★ **Solution on page 307**

Moving

ACROSS

1. He razed his brother
5. No strings attached
9. Titled Turk
14. Lots of curls
15. Croquet spot
16. Moving
17. Fork site
18. Kind words
19. Sound effect for gravity
20. Daycare member
21. Inundated
22. What a shepherd does
23. Ocean vessel
25. She's herself in the comics
27. Despicable dog
28. Large lot
29. Kin of ahem
33. Acts like a fence
36. Good gravy
38. Flusher in a flat
39. Embarrassed
40. Altered
42. ___ aboard!
43. String of flowers
44. Bellhop calls
45. Like an igloo
47. Espouses
49. Hog's home
50. Accomplished
51. Bigot's blight
53. Heckled
57. It holds water
60. Trotsky turndowns
62. "We ___ Family"
63. Beside
64. Watery nook
65. Like king of the mountain
66. Game players
67. Round watchers
68. Fix a room
69. Race part
70. Go through mail
71. Worry

DOWN

1. Wheelbarrows
2. In motion, to Holmes
3. Upset
4. It's east of Eden
5. Bloomer
6. *M*A*S*H* role
7. Merino mamas
8. Veils
9. Alliance writings
10. Taking a siesta
11. Phaser setting
12. ___ quarters
13. Torah holders
21. "We are not ___"
24. Be responsible
26. On a single occasion
28. Flavorful
30. Door sound
31. It might wear thin
32. Informed
33. Woody's son
34. "Drive My Car" interjection
35. Alter an issue
36. Trial handouts
37. River ripples
41. It's hard to see through
46. Crackpot
48. Reason for a steak?
50. Can't stand
52. Teen turmoil
53. Holdout's claim
54. Not now!
55. Slowly dissolve
56. Station
57. It has a big mouth
58. Got down
59. Bee attractor
61. Toy for Tom Smothers
65. Sandy's sound

★ **Solution on page 307**

Pleased as punch

ACROSS

1. Inventor Sikorsky
5. The Big ___
9. Look at the bar
13. Was conveyed
14. Act superior
16. Over the PA
17. Times of note
18. Swine statements
19. It might be rustled
20. ___ *la Douce*
22. Droop
24. Become gray
25. Shot preventer
28. Schedule
30. Hand warmer
31. Rodeo rope
33. Rocks at the bar
34. Lets go
36. Flings
40. Load runner
42. Intended
44. Milne bear
45. Mork's boss
47. Roebuck's partner
49. Startling cry
50. Spread
52. Popular antiseptic
54. It's often split
57. Last name in glass
59. 4th Star Wars word
60. Choose poorly
62. Dawdle
63. Test sites
65. Place for dinner
67. Pleased as punch
71. Missile holder
72. Command the wheel
73. Title Caron film role
74. Once more
75. Firms up
76. Premiere date

DOWN

1. Outrage
2. State leader for short
3. Honorific homage
4. Fail to yield
5. More than an I-ful
6. Crook's cover
7. Abel, to Adam
8. Ties up the phone
9. Horshack's cry
10. That's all I need!
11. Midsized, at the movies
12. Tribal sage
15. Russian rulers
21. Underwater colony
23. No kidding!
25. Cubist's device?
26. Parts of a kit
27. H or O
29. Meal starter
30. Japanese 29 Down
32. Sailing
35. Lose a lap
37. Cook of books
38. Funny in the head
39. Bird in the comics
41. Caucus site
43. Nomads
46. Cloud ___
48. It might have a pull-out
51. Bullseye hunters
53. Like some paints
54. Lightweight wood
55. One more time
56. Honorable
58. Dot on the map
61. Charlie Brown curse
64. Mud worshiper
66. Flower between flowers
68. Edge
69. Part of IPA
70. Ruckus

★ **Solution on page 307**

Some of this and that

1	2	3	■	■	4	5	6	7	8	■	9	10	11	12
13			■	14						■	15			
16			■	17						■	18			
19			20						■	21				
■	■	■	22				■	23	24					
25	26	27			■	28	29					■	■	■
30				■	■	■	31				■	32	33	34
35				36	■	37			■	38	39			
40			■	41	42			■	■	■	43			
■	■	■	44					45	■	46				
47	48	49					■	50	51			■	■	■
52					■	53	54					55	56	57
58				■	59						■	60		
61				■	62						■	63		
64				■	65					■	■	66		

ACROSS

1. Stick out
4. Showed remorse
9. Lose it
13. Some
14. Widget
15. Show TLC
16. Gravestone letters
17. They glow
18. Edges
19. Fulton's folly
21. Basketball maneuver
22. Owl's howl
23. Pages
25. Brother of Moses
28. High point
30. Donkey dialogue
31. Party dip
32. Pamela ___ Martin
35. Subscription suspension
37. Standard finger count
38. Protest against
40. Chicago transits
41. Water ___
43. Mystical one
44. Oddball
46. Behaved
47. Extras
50. Practically unique
52. Sandwich need
53. Early posse person
58. Announcers Edd or Monty
59. Cruise ships
60. Pierre's pal
61. Fail to include
62. In the wrong way
63. Cambridge campus
64. Impetuous
65. Supports
66. Billboards, for instance

DOWN

1. Mason ___
2. Piece
3. Species
4. Some of this and that
5. Uncreative ones
6. Inventor's spark
7. Kirk, to Spock
8. Doctor of Dental Science
9. Play prose
10. Unworldly one
11. Metal garb
12. Undesired companions
14. Evil one
20. Alohas, asea
21. Worked at
24. Ambulance worker, for short
25. Like a can-do person
26. Sea that's a lake
27. Knocks
29. Rotate
32. Vamoose
33. Incite
34. Looked at
36. Correct
37. Italian dessert
39. Host with the most
42. It helps
44. Millionaire's motive
45. Persnickety
46. Decorative
47. Can't stand
48. Gritty situation
49. Slicer sites
51. They emanate
54. ___ thin air
55. Doll's word
56. Between
57. Micromanager's concerns
59. Quincy's home away from home

★ Solution on page 307

I didn't mean it!

ACROSS

1. Salsa server
6. Prickly ___
10. Prepare a gift
14. Trial and ___
15. ___ grease
16. Not gone
17. Slack-jawed
18. Like a wet noodle
19. Crudely copies
20. Captain Morgan's is spiced
21. Questionnaire answer
22. *America's ___ Wanted*
23. Quarantine
26. Prepare to fire
28. Insolent
29. Nature walks
33. TV time
36. Chore
37. Maintain a motor
38. Jeweler's measure
39. Put in the microwave
40. Wheel part
42. Actress Lupino
43. Cyber-savvy one
45. Labored
46. Wanted
48. "Man of the Year" magazine
49. Blueprint abbr.
50. Marker by a road
54. Working model
57. Piano wood
59. It can be pitched
60. Beasts of burden
61. Henpecks
62. I'm ___ get ya
64. Prong
65. 21 Across opposite
66. Leading
67. Kind of poker
68. Holler
69. I didn't mean it!

DOWN

1. Closes in on
2. Dispute
3. Swimmer's woe
4. Bobby-soxer's dance
5. It needs processing
6. Savory sensor
7. One sent away
8. Dole
9. Takes again
10. Pow!
11. Estevez's ___ *Man*
12. Mythic marauder
13. "Can we? Can we? Huh?" person
21. Brief hits
24. Acreage
25. Burst
27. Annoying
29. Patsy
30. ___ at me!
31. Valley girl's "er"
32. *Citizen Kane* prop
33. ___ Row
34. Roe foe
35. Times of note
36. Black ice go-with
39. British finale
41. Study
44. % of Earth's surface that's water
45. Cunning
47. Pressed
48. Tree frou-frou
50. Business bigwig
51. One that has
52. Sense, in an acronym way
53. Smithers, to Mr. Burns
54. Adds speckles
55. Off ramp
56. Diner document
58. Not dressed up
62. Rest stop reason
63. Hammy P.I. response

★ **Solution on page 307**

Chapter 6

Easy Does It

It gets filled out

ACROSS

1. It gets filled out
5. Leftover dish
9. Series for Spitz
13. Adequate
14. Role for Lloyd or Coogan
16. Be a lookout, perhaps
17. Fancy storers
18. Put back to work
19. Madonna option
20. From the side
22. Director Reiner
23. Dead heat
24. Chicken option
25. Defended
28. Breakfast treat
31. Row at a wedding
33. Baby seal
34. Get from a teacher
36. Leisure
39. Psychic's "sight" for short
40. He lived backward
41. The Big ___
43. Small, to a small one
45. Drops in
47. Joplin's forte
48. Phooey!
49. Roulette bet
50. O.J. judge
51. It's just a ___ . . .
53. Storage spot, often
56. Least normal
59. Exclude
60. Evergreen type
61. Drag around
64. Sundae topping
68. Lower digits
70. Good witnesses for Scopes
72. ___ hands
73. *The River's* ___
74. Piano piece
75. Any unabridged dictionary
76. Cozy home
77. Ted Turner topic
78. It's fine for swine

DOWN

1. Ump's call
2. Nature's maraca when dried
3. Soapbox speech
4. Me, to me
5. Stop, Spot
6. Mount St. Helens residue
7. Recipe verb
8. Big wedge
9. When I was a ___
10. Diminish
11. Pitfall for Pauline
12. Rider's mount
14. Easily broken
15. Puzzle on *Concentration*
21. Striped ump
26. They're addressed to the bench
27. Trouble collection
28. Considered
29. ___ crust
30. They make you jumpy
31. Get out of bed
32. Six outs
33. Stroke
35. Andes adventure
37. Herb sample
38. Fill with joy
40. Old tall tales
42. Self respect
44. It's covered by a collar
46. Female Fabergé owner, perhaps
52. NASA missile series
54. Hoop loop
55. What a ticket does
56. Frequently
57. Part of LED
58. ___ of society
62. At the moment of
63. Hereditary unit
64. West Side Story group
65. Golden Calf, for one
66. Red furry monster
67. Osmose
69. Established
71. Stomach

★ **Solution on page 308**

Hear ye, hear ye

ACROSS

1. Navy SEALs and others
6. What Navy SEALs often do
10. Like after-dinner coffee, often
15. Angel in the theater
16. TV award
17. All to no ___
18. Window cover
19. Non-PC snowman item
20. High IQ group acronym
21. Hankering
22. Business handout
24. Actress MacGraw
25. Syllabus starters
27. Candy cover
31. ___ urgency
33. Pacts
35. Bloke
36. ___ nerve
37. Least outdated
40. Place for a booking
41. Branch
44. Broke bread
45. Palindromic vessel
47. Cheap cigar
49. Choir tier
50. Landed-one's lung
51. Surpass
54. Went separate ways
56. Ruler's rod
57. Showy bloom
59. ___ diem
60. A few
61. Cookie canister
64. Hilo hi
67. Bun's spot
69. Hippo's cousin
71. Uses the gym
72. In basket, perhaps
73. Ren and Stimpy
74. Sheer
75. Fresh child's response
76. 39 Down or touch

DOWN

1. Mary Baker ___
2. Local urban legends
3. Tamer than "still life"
4. Best
5. Puts up
6. Copy for marking up
7. In the thick of
8. Mystical pest
9. Tincture
10. Beaver building
11. First lady?
12. Reception munchie
13. Lanes
14. Natural talent
23. It's subjective
26. Uh-uh!
27. Shed tears
28. Frequent flyer's question
29. Listing
30. Snapshot, informally
31. Pac-10 team
32. Been there, done ___
34. Castle
38. Sidestep
39. Aesthetic sense
40. Hear ye, hear ye
41. Turmoil
42. Provoke
43. Mix well
46. Tree ring
48. Mythical meanie
49. GOP member, for short
51. Spotted wildcat
52. Place for two gentlemen
53. Stands for 23 Down
54. Actress Dawber
55. APBs
56. Petty fights
58. Does city work
62. Hostelries
63. You might pay through it
65. Boat, familiarly
66. Seek permission
67. Photo ___
68. Route word
70. Tiller's tool

★ **Solution on page 308**

1	2	3	4	5	■	6	7	8	9	■	10	11	12	13	14
15					■	16				■	17				
18					■	19				■	20				
21			■	22	23			■	■	■	■	24			
■	■	25	26					■	27	28	29	30			
31	32					■	33	34							■
35				■	■	■	■	36					■	■	■
37				38	39	■	40					■	41	42	43
44			■	45		46			■	47		48			
■	■	■	49					■	■	■	■	50			
■	51	52						53	■	54	55				
56							■	57	58					■	■
59			■	■	■	■	■	60				■	61	62	63
64			65	66	■	67	68			■	69	70			
71					■	72				■	73				
74					■	75				■	76				

Gets cozy

ACROSS

1. DINKs have two of them
5. Attire for Aristotle
9. One who's off base, for short
13. Brit's buck
14. Badge
16. Not taped
17. Uppity type
18. Wine whereabout
19. Has 1001 ___!
20. They're snippish
22. Kitchen verb
24. Shocking animal
25. Freddy's street
26. It might be toasted
27. West of Hollywood
29. Did a favor for
33. Any port in a ___
37. Man of many voices
39. Something you might lend
40. *The Scent of Green* ___
42. Fawn
43. Boo-boo's buddy
44. Buttinsky's word
45. Shopper's need
47. Improv drawing
49. Got the award
50. Like horseradish
52. Suit fabric
53. Gets cozy
55. Netting
57. Dear
58. Go for the gold
59. Doc bloc, for short
62. Dick Grayson, for one
66. Scarred from scandal
68. It might be palmed
69. Alehouse
71. NSA concern
72. Put up a picture
73. Award givers, often
74. Journey
75. Kiwanis cousins
76. Fouls up
77. Usher's job

DOWN

1. *Dukes of Hazzard* role
2. Fluid ___
3. Oven verb
4. Uses a hanky
5. Like some underwear
6. Does a mechanic's job
7. Take shape
8. Call to Yorrick
9. Grads
10. Lay's rival
11. CB'ers tail
12. Reduced by
14. Chastise
15. Maneuvered on the court
21. Sordid
23. Francis, for one
28. Center
29. Giant great
30. Crystal-lined cavity
31. Spread ___
32. Like used paint
33. Bear children
34. Resort lake
35. Some tourneys
36. Gate crasher
38. Native American icon
41. Disaffect
43. That hurts!
46. Baby announcement opener
48. Option 3, sometimes
50. Monster movie monster
51. Pays respect
54. They leave little to the imagination
56. DPW concerns
59. Love
60. News group
61. Talented
62. It hurts
63. Santa's snub
64. Field for Fleming
65. Mild-mannered
66. Bambi, for one
67. *Hamlet* has several
70. Midnight blinker, often, for short

★ **Solution on page 308**

Yes, that's what I said

ACROSS

1. Poison ___
4. Impale
8. Tallied
13. Polygraph influencer
14. Question on "Jeopardy"
16. Start some tennis
17. Give permission to
18. Yes, that's what I said
19. Ordinary
20. Pool person
22. Inspirational Buscaglia
24. Not pretty
25. Boat maneuverer
26. Patch
28. ___ patrol
31. Say it like so
35. Mission
36. Stink up the place
37. Rabbit holder?
39. ___ of return
40. Singers
42. Alternative to a check
43. Face shape
44. Superball sound
45. Wine region
46. "___ o' My Heart"
47. "Singin' in the ___"
48. Former somebody
51. Fixed a room
53. Indian instruments
54. However
55. Went for a seat
56. Sink stoppage
59. "___ Works Hard for the Money"
62. Miscue?
66. Levity
68. Go past due
70. Caught ya in the act!
71. Display site
72. Got closer to
73. ___ none
74. Subscribe again
75. River team
76. Sample slightly

DOWN

1. Bad things
2. Hotel room concern
3. Snowy Sasquatch?
4. Curled a lip
5. Russian ruler
6. Gouger
7. ___ pepper
8. Deadly biter
9. Grand
10. Kind of queen
11. Fiendish
12. Fail to permit
14. Fleet
15. City near NYC
21. Crumb
23. Bid
27. Type
28. Less yellow
29. Time without juice
30. Pull back
31. Common driver
32. Monopoly player piece
33. Bar choice number 2?
34. Samples
35. Trim a picture
38. Weed out
41. Trace
42. Beach spot
44. Visible parts to traps
47. *Less Than Perfect* lead actress
49. Plane people
50. Went bug-eyed
52. Past
56. Scorch
57. Use a decoy
58. It may not bode well
60. Farm layer
61. Upper management type
62. Liege
63. Keep ___ on
64. Spiced drink
65. Angelic instrument
67. Like tartare
69. Golf standard

★ **Solution on page 308**

Put away for a rainy day

ACROSS

1. Door ___
5. Lessens
9. Data
13. Slender reed
14. Outcast
16. Soccer score
17. Not even one
18. Navel ___
19. Prominence
20. Seeking an eye for an eye
22. Furrier's wares
24. You there!
25. ___ it or lose it
26. Enjoy a meal
27. It's near Phoenix
29. Maintains
33. Scale
37. Scrap
39. Cheerio grain
40. Places to bust a bronco
42. Subterfuge
43. Type of shirt
44. Flush
45. Flabbergasted
47. Mailroom employee
49. Soup legume
50. Slept loudly
52. Rapper's entourage
53. Epitome
55. Where it is
57. Stool pigeon
58. Superior's title
59. "My country ___ of thee . . . "
62. Flawed reason
66. Heir ___
68. Anthropologist Margaret ___
69. Armed ___
71. A law ___ itself
72. ___ the way
73. Like birthdays
74. Senator's stint
75. Body shops
76. Adds color to
77. Halt!

DOWN

1. Biblical inside man
2. Like the sky
3. Pink Floyd hit
4. Second word of "One Week"
5. Wilde title character
6. Boast
7. Hopper
8. Kitchen herb
9. Light
10. Time for Earp
11. The Flying Fickle Finger of ___
12. Chico's cheers
14. Elegant quality
15. Contrary views
21. Southern soup
23. Pole at a port
28. Media network
29. Crunched muscles
30. Weed tendrils
31. Told things
32. Put away for a rainy day
33. Frequently filled food
34. *Joanie ___ Chachi*
35. Thinktank output
36. A-Team members
38. Ranch visitors?
41. Bless
43. ___ or con
46. What befalls one
48. *Aida,* for one
50. Complication
51. Drives off
54. Weakens
56. Under the influence
59. Dogma
60. Chapter 1, often
61. Percussive dance show
62. Annoying ones
63. ___ of faith
64. ___ lamp
65. Dorm dweller
66. Crop circle size, say
67. Tire troughs
70. Billy ___ Cyrus

★ **Solution on page 308**

Reverence

ACROSS

1. Mortgage
5. Cauldrons
9. Plentiful
14. If all ___ fails . . .
15. Flyboy
16. Add
17. Tourist ID
18. Spacious
19. Redo a team
20. "Did you ___ see a lassie . . . "
21. Toreador's ta-da
22. Miserable
24. Odo portrayer
25. Apartment
26. Quaint hotel
27. Can opener
30. Boulevard
32. Spot
33. Paint concern
34. "Amazing Grace" noun
37. Temp job
39. Ump's cry
42. Play ___
43. Army members
44. Mustard's milieu
45. Type of session
47. Meringue need
48. Observances
50. "___ to Sender"
52. ___ Annie
53. Reverence
55. One who stays
59. Valued stone
60. "Roundabout" group
61. Swine ___
62. ___ of Evil
64. Defense
66. He had a salty spouse
67. Brass metal
68. "Nights in White ___"
70. Push
72. *Born Free* role
73. Baker's cover
74. Loses energy
75. "___ Barrel Polka"
76. Giraffe features
77. Practice for a fight
78. Not the O in OTB, but a good guess

DOWN

1. Part of a Rube Goldberg design
2. Bar fruit
3. Okey-dokey
4. Less distant
5. Broke, as in a law
6. Recuperating from a burn
7. Actor Hanks
8. In fashion
9. Brings into harmony
10. The Red Planet
11. Toy
12. D.A. degree, for short
13. Hurricane center
15. According to Hoyle
23. United
28. Family females
29. Casino actions
31. Female flock member
35. Hurried
36. Fireside ___
38. Caption
39. Go for the plate
40. Not manual
41. Expense
44. Jagged rock
46. Sweatshirt, for one
47. Pass receiver
49. Proverbs
50. Fights back
51. Ways to get there
54. Spider's home
56. Pavilion
57. Sent away
58. Put through the washer
61. Plant life
63. Unpleasant reminders
65. Sausage unit
68. Break a Commandment
69. Best a test
71. ___-hop

★ **Solution on page 308**

Off yonder

ACROSS

1. Have a ___ day!
5. Put out candles
9. Prickly subject
14. Very pale
15. Sweet scent
16. Like Ouija
17. Dancer's bend
18. Ran at Lyme Rock
19. Put ___ for later
20. Tingle
22. Like some books
23. G-man
24. Model sticker
28. Ferocious feline
31. Mixed
34. Mass transit at a park
37. Flipper flopper
38. Collie comment
40. Arsenal stash
41. Kind of suite
43. Comes after fa
44. Treatment locale
45. Turn around
46. Sub command
47. Garden supply
48. Rein in
49. Went offtrack
51. Tunes
54. Parking garage need
55. Corporate types
56. Baseball stat, for short
58. Shutter piece
61. Patrons
67. Scottish garb
69. Hoists across
70. Computer click-on
71. Map extra
72. Overturn
73. Poke
74. Building layer
75. Achieves
76. Has din-din

DOWN

1. Baby respites
2. Bali or Capri
3. Stubble spot
4. "Bette Davis ___"
5. Pigtail
6. Bonkers
7. Touches up
8. Cash cache
9. Maude portrayer
10. Outcome
11. Eye part
12. Page
13. Mr. Brady portrayer
15. Comic Johnson
21. Off yonder
25. Holdings
26. Water ___
27. ___ you kidding?
28. Cheerleader prop
29. Like a bed after getting up
30. Bossy's beckon
31. Landed
32. Without a hitch
33. Mobs
34. Church time
35. Rub off
36. Like satire
39. Took off
42. June honorees
46. Molten shaper
48. Spar
50. Comparable
52. G or R
53. *The Great* ___
56. Unnerves
57. Defeat
58. Slope sliders
59. Dryer gunk
60. Besides
62. Desire
63. Helpful hints
64. Neutral tint
65. Cycle
66. Boundaries
68. Maid's challenge
69. Loving hold

★ **Solution on page 308**

Uncanny ability

ACROSS

1. 10-K's
6. This for that
10. What's in today
13. Not bankrupt
15. Kind of button
17. Kind words
18. "Purple Rain" artist
19. More wise
20. ___ the lifeboats!
21. Freight weight
22. Uncanny ability
24. Like a clod
26. Circulars, for instance
28. Gigs
29. Sandwich in a shell
31. Chai, for one
32. Paige Davis supplies
33. Like the desert
34. Used a stool
35. Less than twice
36. Operatives org., for short
37. ___-be
39. By one's lonesome
43. Sharp taste
45. Fair worker
46. Arnold, for one
47. Calla ___
49. Sound device
51. Whitish stone
52. Tea biscuits
54. Quilting event
55. Had on
56. Sake
57. Dance mate
59. Steamed
60. Writing assignment
61. Scot's topper
64. Baseball's Griffey Jr.
65. Kind of talk
68. Lentil or pea
70. 60 Across class, for short
71. Hotel booking
72. People of note
73. Billy ___ Williams
74. Walked
75. Looks for

DOWN

1. Enchanted
2. It needs a pick
3. Kind of doctor
4. Endless time
5. Gives the heave-ho
6. Bystander
7. Takes a hike
8. ___ not only that . . .
9. B&W film missile
10. Incite
11. Gets used to
12. Unfavorable impressions
14. Principle beliefs
16. Fault finder
23. Passages
25. Dress to the ___
27. Start to doze
28. Hourglass filler
29. Diplomat's necessity
30. Sills selection
32. Plexiglas and others
38. Shameless
40. Well-timed
41. Joe Isuzu, for one
42. Bad pickup maneuver
44. Act superior to
45. Musical symbol
48. Bays
50. Flower features
51. Run a tab
52. Peaceful
53. Exact ___
56. Used a two-wheeler
57. Green cover
58. Nikolai's negatives
62. Running ___
63. Military cafeteria
66. Daily grind
67. Balloon filler
69. How 'bout that?

★**Solution on page 308**

Bestow knowledge

ACROSS

1. Auntie Em, for one
5. Roadie's gear
9. "A" on the radio
13. Evangelist Roberts
14. Is a sore winner
16. Carrot or beet
17. Non-PC ritzy garb
18. Like Johnny One-Note
19. Cuts the lawn
20. Pea place
21. Latin love
22. Asian discipline
24. Iditarod needs
26. Mountain lions
29. Bestow knowledge
33. Perk
35. Lower
37. Standard inning count
38. Washcloth
41. Less like Oscar Madison
42. Play with a pick
43. Darkened
45. Italian ice
47. 54 Across initial skill, perhaps
48. Ollie's partner
49. Sign
51. Nonbeliever
54. She knows things
57. Car type
58. Proclamation
60. Monty Python member
62. Seeped
65. Use a crowbar
66. Rat
69. More stressed
71. Make meringue
72. "Duke of ___"
73. Fire starter
74. Non-PC Halloween costume
75. Imp, perhaps
76. Walrus tooth
77. "This ___ on me!"

DOWN

1. Merry walkabouts
2. Baltimore player
3. Got in, like a plane
4. Fraternal one
5. Palo ___
6. Othello, for one
7. Hook's nemesis
8. Remain
9. Bunker item
10. Ghost writer statement?
11. Less than hoped for
12. UFO occupants, for short
14. Moll's leg
15. Ski spot
21. Trip with a T-bar
23. Hired ___
25. Film that flubs
27. Flambé
28. Type of headache
30. Merlin's went down
31. Calamitous
32. Like chocolate, usually
33. Take to task
34. Sub
36. Some of the wurst places
38. Host Limbaugh
39. Adds a chip
40. Unfriendly look
42. Imitated Icarus, at first
44. Not to be 32 Down
46. Photo finish
50. Forged ahead
52. Little bit
53. Fishing spot
55. Type of diversion
56. Writer
59. r56gs and fd6
61. Look for 59 Down
62. Proposal amounts
63. Onion's kin
64. Make 59 Down
66. Play baccarat
67. ___ of the land
68. Couple keeper
70. Wildebeest
71. *Doctor* ___

★**Solution on page 308**

Exceptional

ACROSS

1. Blasé
6. Big brass
10. Saloon order
14. Barrio buddy
15. Help a charity
17. Runner's goal
18. Prop for Uri Geller
19. Small wheel
20. Desecrate
21. *Seems Like ___ Times*
22. Showed feelings
24. Puts out an APB
26. Tsar's "zip it!"
28. Gift-opening squeals
29. Do farm work
30. Sanitation engineer's verb
32. Marvelous
37. Shows disdain
40. Exceptional
41. Bring in a brigand
43. Ewe, to you
45. Playful bite
46. Scope
48. During business hours
49. Attention calls
51. Smitten
52. Helped the Tin Man
54. Fight interjection
55. Put in line with
58. Bit of wood for Woods
59. Shriekers in *The Princess Bride*
61. Major roadway
62. Hollywood hopefuls
65. Green Gables gal
66. Wane
67. Baccarat request
69. Engineer's plan
73. Early life form
76. Expensive eggs
78. For ___ the marbles
79. *Alice* role
80. Ocean tourist's sight
82. I must bid you ___
84. Put out
85. Harsh
86. G ___
87. Not all
88. Take a breather
89. Does QA work

DOWN

1. Fleece seeker
2. Beyond what's needed
3. Vacuum tube
4. Prima donna's drive
5. Test-taker's ta-da
6. Crown wearer, sometimes
7. ___ I miss my guess . . .
8. Like a bowling ball
9. Gulped a gordita
10. Clever
11. *Their Finest ___*
12. Delete
13. Hamiltons
15. Pillow stain
16. Schwarzenegger flick
23. Like a shrinking violet
25. Not a people person
27. Supreme seat
31. Abby's twin
33. Like a stuffed shirt
34. Gap
35. Hereditary
36. Footnote symbol, sometimes
37. Try to hit skeet
38. Cheats at school
39. Folded food
42. Like some eyes
44. ___ walnut
45. Fresh
47. Some marbles
50. Party job
53. Type of hat
56. Info session
57. Grounds keeper?
60. Macaroni
63. Prepare soda
64. Justice symbol
65. Come about
68. Steer clear of
70. Poker couples
71. Choose
72. Items for Clouseau
73. Actresses Arden and Plumb
74. ___ to self . . .
75. Leading edge?
76. Underground chamber
77. Vessel for the Volga
81. ___ *Alibi*
83. Buck's beau

★ **Solution on page 309**

Cunning

ACROSS

1. Instant
6. Fluffy's feet
10. L.A. team
14. Sell, slangily
16. Tricycle part
17. Be in on the con
18. Turbulent
19. In an unfriendly way
20. Bruce Lee specialty
21. Pull
22. Half a dime
24. Percentage
25. Tire trouble
27. Leather type
29. Blue
30. On fire
32. Locomotive power
34. Colorful singer
36. Oven emanations
40. Longest arm bone
41. Candy goo
45. ___ Cass Elliot
46. Weather forecast
47. Tea leaf alternative
48. Floor cover
49. Pilgrimage
51. Avoided a trial
53. Racer's measure
54. Prestigious
56. Public defenders
58. Mark
61. 41-Across go-with
62. POTUS advisers, for short
65. 62 Across member
67. Bible book
68. Provide
70. Fasten
72. Earnings
75. *Trading Spaces* verb
76. Component
77. Drool
80. Muckamuck
81. Tell item
82. People person
83. Makes a slip
84. Price after the discount
85. Offspring

DOWN

1. Appropriate
2. Divisive word
3. Cyclical process
4. Part of FYI
5. Thanksgiving tuber
6. Eats like a bird
7. Frère's farewells
8. License holder, often
9. Cunning
10. Punjabi prince
11. Rubs against
12. It might be mixed
13. *The Day the Earth* ___ *Still*
15. Like a real spitfire
16. *ET* topic
23. Repeat
24. Tushie
25. Small insect
26. Fung's workplace
28. Arrangement
30. Attraction
31. Tornado shape
33. Kid's cry
34. Security seizures
35. Oh, sugar!
37. Where to coop a sloop
38. Good-luck charm
39. Wise ones
42. 1998 Tony-winning play
43. Shed
44. Like a phoenix
50. Powder holder
51. Dateless, or doe's date
52. Bishop's bailiwick
53. Bar supply
55. Stick in one's ___
57. Save
59. Streetcar name
60. Goes into
62. Chutzpah
63. Scornful smirk
64. Abacus user
66. Munchies at mi casa
69. "I dropped it!"
71. Seating at sermons
72. Hummus holder
73. Frankly state
74. Cat plaything
76. ___ *Joey*
78. Spots in the media
79. Kind of service

★ **Solution on page 309**

Stuck

ACROSS

1. Stuck
6. Go whole ___
9. Lion's share
13. Theatre byways
15. Satisfies
17. World's fair
18. Showy food style
19. ISBN go-with
20. Maturing one
21. Tall tale
22. Part of PRNDL
24. They're in fashion
26. Snaky one
27. Slot machine reward
29. In addition
30. Attached firmly
32. Dig up
36. Doc flock, for short
37. Respect
39. Cherry, for one
41. Sudden
44. Permit
45. *The Last Remake of ___ Geste*
46. The Seven ___
47. Least complex
51. All-night affair
52. "___ on Down the Road"
53. Basketball hoop part
54. Commentary from the stage
56. Cobra kin
57. River giver
60. Little lion
61. Ordinary
63. Heroine player
67. Ole in Oregon
68. Overwhelm
70. Kind of squad
72. Salad item
75. Bossy one
76. Circle of life
77. Approval
78. Society somebodies
81. Pitcher or bowler's goal
84. Egg on
85. Like many stadiums
86. Flying ___
87. Ness specialty
88. Controller's spot
89. Ones like you

DOWN

1. Mistake
2. Field flowers
3. At hand
4. Shade provider
5. Society gal
6. Choice words
7. Baseball slugger
8. Toothpaste form
9. Impressive streaker
10. Yaks, for example
11. Hightailed it
12. "Sixteen ___"
14. Apart
15. Took daddy steps
16. Parlor piece
23. Pirate agreement
25. Wander
27. Gas supplier
28. Student
31. Reason
33. Pulls down
34. Don't ___ on me
35. Lift at sea
38. Ghostbuster goo
40. Union expenses
41. Like Blackbeard, often
42. Monster
43. Grating
45. Payola
48. Vicinity
49. Crab walk
50. Gauche
55. Ride the waves
57. Order
58. Repeated
59. One way to be run
62. Asked for divine help
64. Mongrel
65. Sew genes
66. Quidditch role
69. Lecturer's collection
71. Mooring spots
72. See the town
73. Gumbo ingredient
74. Gift givers
79. John, in an advert
80. Rapscallion
82. Go with the music
83. Want to atone

★ **Solution on page 309**

Pickle pusher

ACROSS

1. Mexican munchie
6. Pickle pusher
10. Green gem
14. Dessert with filling
16. Gave rise to
17. Solar eclipse, perhaps
18. Baby berth
19. Achieves
20. Like some wives
21. Lock leveler
22. Made a turn
24. Any one of a famous trio
25. Sole stud
27. Overbearing one
29. Toweled off
30. Affects for the worse
33. Shattered
35. One exceeding their reach
37. Devotedness
39. For the taking
40. South African concern
44. Pro vote
45. Mean manager's trait
48. Go with the bulls
50. Strong
52. Nylons
53. Kneels to
54. Bookish ones
58. College sideline
60. Rukeyser, for one
61. Lion's spot
62. It might be sworn
65. Kink
66. Poe talker
68. Episode starts, perhaps
70. Judgmental one
73. Improved wine
74. They're notarized
75. With flourish
78. Recuperate
79. Dole out
80. Hint
81. Like some shindigs
82. Place for mail
83. Impressive stories

DOWN

1. Guitar part
2. Hundred ___ Woods
3. Ali, once
4. Owned
5. Bribe
6. Beloved one
7. Crane kin
8. Gets, like a job
9. Monty Python starter
10. Leno plum
11. What sinners make
12. Banish
13. 1 Across or 1 Down
15. Go back
16. Borscht source
23. Bridge hand
24. Some are self-evident
25. Lawsuit
26. Avoid 24 Down
28. Aids an arsonist
30. Questionable
31. Maned mamas
32. Fabric fold
34. It might have seeds
36. It's too good to believe
37. Yearnings
38. Anger
41. Password, for short
42. Parody quality
43. Checks for prints
45. Large monkey
46. *Carmen,* for one
47. ___ *Kids*
49. Robin's place
51. Friend of Harry and Hermione
52. Beatle film
55. Cover
56. Accordance
57. Hoover, for one
58. Not opulent
59. Come up with
61. Movie type
63. Vibrato
64. Greetings!
65. Fling
67. Water ripple
69. Block
70. Carry on
71. Delineate
72. They're to be paid
74. Is in the past
76. Jamaican drink
77. It goes against

★ **Solution on page 309**

Crossword solver

ACROSS

1. Crossword solver
6. Place to relax
10. Blood and tears go-with
15. Provide
17. Nag or crab
18. Princess regalia
19. Go through the clouds
20. Surmounting
21. Return
22. Grand total
23. Hall-of-Famer Williams
25. Ump's call
27. It might be bitter
28. Sailor's workplace
29. Important periods
30. Pitfall
31. Bob's partner
32. Bit of wood
34. Not do so well
35. One used to ducking
37. Freaking out
42. Spiritualism
45. Hawaiian isle
47. Pact partner
48. Stop, stag!
49. Circus cover
52. It can be blown
53. High time?
54. Planting spots
55. They're projected
57. Paint debris
60. Doh man
62. Propeller
63. Confirm
66. WWII flyers, for short
69. They're sometimes put on
71. Tempest
72. Actor Reiner or Lowe
74. Under the weather
75. Grand ___
76. Pub potion
77. Prior to now
78. Palm off
80. Those opposed
82. Private eye
85. *The ___ Amigos*
86. Show appreciation
87. Handymen
88. Full
89. Antlered animals
90. Hot and bothered

DOWN

1. Mighty military men
2. Musical sketches
3. Not vegetable or mineral
4. Rhoda's mom
5. World Wide Web, familiarly
6. Gobs and gobs
7. Bit for a horse
8. Winter's lace
9. Mechanism
10. Church feature
11. Get the prize
12. Bistro patron
13. Fighter's theatre
14. Past due
16. Safe getaways
24. Gain deservedly
26. Ethically okay
29. Like Cruella De Vil
33. Tropical lizard
36. Italy has one that leans
37. Keep mum
38. African adventure
39. Slimy slider
40. Choice word
41. Salon stock
42. Holds
43. Lamb serving
44. Like a hepcat
46. Recipe verb
50. Something unusual
51. Not age-specific
56. Nothing but
58. Drank to
59. Follow
61. Office shape
64. Bowling units
65. Cultured treat
66. Splits
67. Lanai bye-bye
68. Minx
70. Picayune
71. Takes where you intake
73. Overly in charge
79. Do you understand?
81. Shoot the breeze
83. Skipper's sleep spot
84. Banana fan

★ **Solution on page 309**

Be in charge

ACROSS

1. Tiny passageways
6. They're extra at hotels
10. It's threaded
15. Nome homes
17. *Spenser: For* ___
18. Kind of secret
19. She's a graduate
20. All over again
21. Be in charge
22. Plumber's helper
23. Russian spirits
25. Had
26. Band member
28. Play for time
31. Bounty
33. Silicon or Sonoma
37. Go back
38. Was sore
41. Ahab's all-rights
43. Ices
44. Not a fun one
46. Detach
47. No novice
48. Bugs and others
49. Bust support
50. Spock's standouts
52. Remade a manuscript
54. Delivered notes
55. ___ and tired
56. Doctrines
57. Things to bob for
59. Pony pleas
61. Still on the shelf
62. It goes around, but reads back and forth
65. Torme's talent
66. Over what's recommended
70. It's built up
72. Unfilled initials
75. Valve line
76. It might be clogged
77. Bring to mind
80. Fratware
81. Penultimate fairy tale word
82. Swervy skiing
83. It's related
84. Depend
85. Worries

DOWN

1. Hitchcock title start
2. Hard on the eyes
3. Blue's pawprint, for one
4. Singer Lehrer
5. Bart, to Homer
6. Actor Everett or Lowe
7. Text from pens?
8. Halloween option
9. Put in stitches
10. Leisurely walk
11. Plane people
12. Crop helper
13. Bank
14. Meander
16. Thoroughly enjoyed
24. British tome, for short
26. Is indebted to
27. Doggy ___
29. Disinclined
30. *Shane* star
31. Part of a song
32. Keep in place
34. Noun associated with 32 Down
35. Ogle
36. Hankered
37. Learning the ___
38. Covered with lotion
39. Body double
40. Straw poll request
42. Gremlin specialties
45. Greatest
51. Do the bunny hill
52. Cavern effect
53. Musical extras
54. Ad
58. Free spot, for short
60. ___ spoon
61. Function
63. Popeye's love
64. Ward off
66. Mare fare
67. Italy's shape
68. Thus
69. Astronomy object
71. Rather
72. *A* ___ *of Two Cities*
73. Smear
74. Charity collection
76. According to
78. Xmas extra
79. Intrepid, for one

★ **Solution on page 309**

Prized one

ACROSS

1. Verb with "petard"
6. Race units
10. Daddy
14. Gets under one's skin
16. ___ to the fact . . .
18. *The Lion King* villain
19. *Dennis the* ___
20. Understandable
21. Tizzy
22. Blue material
24. Unhealthy engine sounds
26. It isn't pretty
29. Protuberance to a princess
30. ___ ton
31. ___ SEAL
33. Hit
34. Mother's Day month
37. Incubator item
38. Beach party treat
40. Coquet
42. Monsieur
43. It's not intentional
44. Sworn statements
45. Speechless
48. Bugs Bunny addressee
49. Kind of bag
50. Castaway count, including Gilligan
52. Vicinities
54. Aries, for one
57. Eloquent ones
58. Schedules
60. Winter woe
61. Common conjunction
62. The Emerald ___
64. Shredded
65. Now I get it!
66. Prized one
67. Filled with holes
69. Aerials
74. Concert location
75. Plant of '80s decor
76. *Escape from New York* lead role
78. Harmony
82. Henderson's TV hubby
83. Roof parts
84. Like some court documents
85. Works of 57 Across
86. Penny
87. Had a siesta

DOWN

1. Scenery chewer
2. *A Chorus Line* finale
3. No room at the ___
4. Daytime TV fare
5. Moguls
6. Funny in the head
7. Hole punch
8. Pizzas
9. Red fish
10. Surreptitious summons
11. Undesirable spots
12. Couple
13. They might be martial
15. Like many knives
17. There's not much to it
23. Defiant cry
25. Mr. Roarke's cohort
26. Farm females
27. Berra of irony
28. Like an etching
32. Bears' data
33. 100 ___
34. Type of witness
35. Cigar cinder
36. "Owner of a Lonely Heart" group
39. Bond portrayer
41. Have wings
46. Moist
47. ___ *Pulver*
49. Russian empresses
50. Place to relax
51. Long, long period of time
53. Be crazy about
55. It's sore
56. Honey drink
58. Data book
59. More than lures
63. Pick up on
68. Sticker
69. Frizzy hair
70. Necessitate
71. Arbor Day honoree
72. Split ___
73. Stash away
74. Suit part
77. Barbie's guy
79. Wow, Juan
80. State ___
81. Weed killer of old

★**Solution on page 309**

Assortment

ACROSS

1. It's on a spit
6. Luau option
10. Put off
15. Yank like a weed
17. Was in hock
18. Dome home
19. Assortment
20. Queen Anne's ___
21. Something heard
22. Ground material
23. Ham device
25. Approximate
26. Tried for office
27. Distant
28. Kind of jet
30. Bizarre
33. Temple beams
37. Real
39. Stray
41. Congressional first name
43. Wear by nature
45. Fireplace glower
46. It sometimes comes with capers
47. Kind of tide
48. It's hard for a lawyer to pass
49. Brainstorms
52. Used keys
54. Ace
56. Balcony
58. Petty officer
60. Brilliant
62. Like some edges
65. Driver
67. RBI's kin
68. Watch Junior
70. Lament
74. Bamboo-eating bear
76. It goes with feathers
77. Reducing the payroll
78. Dance with a lei
79. Spot
82. From the time of
83. ___ smasher
84. Stir-fries
85. Mrs. Peel's partner
86. Reviewer Siskel
87. Newsroom needs

DOWN

1. Bit of gossip
2. Musical plays
3. Fervid
4. La preceder
5. Low digit
6. Snitched
7. Hang around for
8. ___ your losses
9. "___ on a Grecian Urn"
10. Aspirin verb
11. Concerns of self
12. Chimney ___
13. Longer than I care for
14. Reactor items
16. Mean leader
24. Debate
25. Had the know-how
27. Bit of trivia
29. Thumber's desire
31. Harsh
32. Before the alarm goes off
34. Point
35. Religious leader
36. Pilfer
38. Wacko
40. Blunder
41. Lymph ___
42. Do forcefully
44. Nerd's pal
46. Intoxicated
50. ___ we there yet?
51. Rescued
52. Greenish blue
53. Parceled out
54. *Suddenly Susan* role
55. Colony member
57. Family group
59. Art pieces
61. Public esteem
63. Manor
64. Rang up
66. Eagle feature
69. Lock
70. Type of fish
71. Escape
72. Wartime booby trap
73. On a lone occasion
75. Title
78. Crone
80. Unlikely ballerina
81. Billiard ball

★ **Solution on page 309**

Adorable

ACROSS

1. Go together
5. Kind of room
9. World wielder
14. Have you any ___?
15. Informed
17. Hot stuff!
18. Sydney salutation
19. Soft wool
20. Soldier
21. In vogue
22. Sit in judgment
23. It might be hard to crack
24. Newsboy's wad
25. It might be oral
28. Comparative word
31. The Shah, for one
32. Yearned
35. Purple shade
37. Adorable
40. Sneak from a jigger
42. Avoided the truth, in a game
43. Senate steno
44. Ring count
45. Where to hang your hats
47. Broke a fast
48. Whine
51. Commandment count
52. Lunar event?
54. Perch
55. *When We Were Kings* subject
56. In abundance
58. Sting
59. Old manuscript
61. Skillful
63. Use a Zamboni
64. Surgical necessity
68. Chest filler, perhaps
71. Dolly, for one
73. Tennis tableau
74. Mint need
75. Dodge
77. Appeared
79. Singer Fitzgerald
80. Tall
81. Drastic
82. Careen
83. Frasier's family name
84. Make an impression
85. Puts together

DOWN

1. Right maker, some say
2. The dog on *Frasier*
3. Goes into the air
4. When the sun's up
5. More than a hole in the ground
6. Take in one's arms
7. Suffering
8. Via, briefly
9. Be on stage
10. Mob
11. Maned beast
12. Skin soother
13. Samples a liquid
15. Plane place
16. Snitched
22. Tongue-lashing
26. Like some bathrooms
27. Absolutely nothing
29. Like a bad alibi
30. Whichever
33. Bewitch
34. *Reader's* ___
35. Stickers
36. Almost mocking
38. Horse opera
39. Rival
41. Full of sass
42. Part of a poll
46. Like some jokes
47. Ruckus
49. Crude noisemaker
50. Water rings
53. Absence excuse
56. State head, for short
57. Carol Burnett tugged item
58. Drop out
60. Drop out
62. Drop out
64. Annoy
65. Vegged
66. Serviced a mower
67. Converges on
68. Soft stone
69. Atop
70. Exercise discipline
72. Greedy grower
76. Tinge
78. Tom, Dick, and Harry
79. Actress Gabor

★ **Solution on page 309**

Chapter 7

Take It Easy

Did you forget something?

ACROSS

1. Patronize a casino
4. Auction action
7. They're not good
11. Like some risky behavior
13. Kick out
14. Puts at ease
15. Kevin's Oscar-winning role
16. Lesson leader
17. Support
19. I knew it!
20. Poker 4 Across
22. Swallowed
23. It's between signs
24. Merge
25. Hep, closer to now
28. Sailing
29. Smog sampler, for short
30. Smear, today
31. *Good Will Hunting* site
34. Hop for the Enterprise
36. Be rude in line
38. Hardly a standout
39. Air show extra
41. Did you forget something?
42. Stays
43. Big-jawed comic
44. Slump
45. Strong soap

1	2	3		4	5	6		7	8	9	10
11			12					13			
14								15			
16						17	18				
19				20	21				22		
				23					24		
25	26	27		28							
29				30					31	32	33
34			35				36	37			
38					39	40					
41					42						
43					44				45		

DOWN

1. They make a wake
2. Result
3. Preference
4. It gets in the way
5. Ferocity
6. More than dislikes
7. Moth meal
8. Posse fugitive
9. Digs
10. Kept
12. Dawn, for one
18. One way to mention things
21. *Annie* and *Gigi*
25. Undo
26. Geronimo, for one
27. Actor McGavin
31. Bates, for one
32. Banned material
33. Like Coolidge
35. Its players weigh a lot
37. Unpretty one
40. By

★**Solution on page 310**

11A, 20A, 18D

Hassle

1	2	3	4	■	5	6	7	■	8	9	10
11				■	12			13			
14				■	15						
16				17			■	18			■
■	■	■	19			■	■	■	20		21
22	23	24				25	■	26			
27				■	28		29				
30			■	■	■	31			■	■	■
■	32		33	■	34				35	36	37
38				39			■	40			
41							■	42			
43			■	44			■	45			

ACROSS

1. Chaplin chow
5. Drop down
8. Kind of book
11. Boating berth
12. Beard alterer
14. And not only that
15. With enthusiasm
16. PBS series
18. Hassle
19. Actor Holm or McKellen
20. Accomplished
22. Long job for a plotter
26. I'm outta here!
27. You might pick up on it
28. Atoll features
30. Spinning stat
31. Second Sunday in May honoree
32. Bring along
34. It ruins the ending
38. Aruba neighbor
40. Chivalry, for one
41. Sauce seasoning
42. Sign of a breakout
43. Limiting word
44. Calming count
45. It has heels

DOWN

1. Mailbox fodder
2. Like some hair
3. Excluding
4. Potential turn-ons
5. Undying
6. Long-eared one's comment
7. Humongous
8. It isn't in stereo
9. Hercule Poirot, for one
10. Bellow
13. All U.S. presidents, so far
17. Down
21. Barber art
22. Not close
23. Burst
24. Mail deliverer
25. Satirize
26. Funny
29. It's messy
33. Wiggle
34. Not 35 Down
35. Not 34 Down
36. Charlotte Rae TV role
37. Scuba site
38. Bit of fuzz?
39. Tree climber

★**Solution on page 310**

8D

Savvy about

ACROSS

1. At a time in the past
5. List keepers, for short
8. Speck
11. Call up
12. Plant frame
14. Savvy about
15. Provoked
16. Call back
18. Followed
19. Gall
20. Newhart's third show
22. It's smaller than a queen
26. Food offerings
27. Realm ruler
28. Went bad
30. Giant slugger
31. In support of
32. Farm layer
34. Avoids attention
38. Stupid
40. NHL MVP
41. Videotape stat
42. Shows one's years
43. "Well, ___ a start"
44. Spaceship jettison
45. Off the map

DOWN

1. Nose botherer
2. On cloud ___
3. Broadway hit
4. Hitching quickly
5. Surrounded
6. Poet
7. Robed TV figure of '95
8. Avoid orders
9. Polish remover
10. King or queen
13. Barge bringer
17. Sphere
21. Baby blossomer
22. Fight finale, for short
23. Missing
24. Aides
25. Vandalized
26. Lawman who sounds like a kind of law
29. Reserved, yet open
33. ___ on your life!
34. Wheels of fortune
35. Corporate identity
36. Needs to pay back
37. ___ Point
38. 3-D scan, for short
39. Tuck's partner

★**Solution on page 310**

14A, 22A, 34A, 41A

Go around

ACROSS

1. Like some vines
6. *The ___ Game*
12. Lunar lander
13. Got away from
14. Perk
15. Go around
16. Bush appointee of 2002
17. Busy one
18. Generation ___
19. Toothpaste form
20. Reading spot
21. Bombard
22. Local law
25. Change
29. Seek guidance
32. Dapper fellow
33. Cry about
34. Little boy
35. I will, shortly
36. Here or there
37. Broken apart
39. Played freeze tag
40. Maneuvers
41. More than good
42. Multitudes
43. Artificial

DOWN

1. Unhands
2. Hard worker
3. Ancient
4. Mistake
5. Thus far
6. Flower type
7. Red ender
8. Overhang
9. Maxim
10. Cold spot to not lick
11. Capable
17. Like the good Spock
20. Trial test?
21. Caress
23. Creepy one
24. Knows how
26. Van Gogh work
27. Beat at the buffet
28. Record player
29. Opulent
30. Totaled
31. Type of snake
35. About
36. Tab, for one
38. Big reference, for short
39. Gladys Knight associate

★ **Solution on page 310**

1D, 3D, 30D, 35D

It's off the beaten path

1	2	3	■	4	5	6	7	■	8	9	10
11			12					■	13		
14								■	15		
16				■	17			■	18		
19			■	■	■	20		21			
22			23	■	24				■	■	■
■	■	■	25	26			■	27	28	29	30
31	32	33				■	■	■	34		
35			■	36		37	■	38			
39			■	40			41				
42			■	43							
44			■	45				■	46		

ACROSS

1. Not do so well
4. Fly catchers
8. Pertinent
11. Indy's least favorite place
13. Like boffo Broadway, for short
14. Make P.C.
15. Triage bed
16. Leprechaun land
17. Crow call
18. "The ___ I Love"
19. "Here Comes the ___"
20. Took a breather
22. Party for a stripper
24. Video game where you eat cherries and drop apples
25. Fictional governess
27. Town crier?
31. Not exactly
34. Ciao
35. Ozark eater
36. Poke fun at
38. Fleetwood Mac hit
39. Plus
40. Responsible one
42. Leaves in the water
43. Vegetable soup item
44. Flub up
45. Obey a red light
46. He looks down in the mouth, for short

DOWN

1. Gauge
2. Going nowhere
3. Weather influencer
4. Soaking
5. On a grand scale
6. Out of the ordinary
7. Blotto
8. Broad tie
9. Flat
10. Schlepped
12. Family tree members
21. Blake Edwards movie
23. Catch
24. Handyman
26. Hayseeds
28. Died down
29. It's off the beaten path
30. Wants a lot
31. "___ your name"
32. Proprietor
33. M*A*S*H role
37. Display model
38. Hoagie
41. Gown go-with

★ **Solution on page 310**

11A, 3D, 24A, 31A, 43A, 2D, 24D

Swallow whole

ACROSS

1. Conservative radio host
5. Selma's state, for short
8. Title to scare a teen
11. Tender
12. One way to reign
14. Drinking sound
15. Coated
16. Swallow whole
18. "Fate: unknown," for short
19. Corn holder
20. A few
22. Bee bane
26. Dance pose
27. Recommend
28. Can't stand
30. Staff
31. Type of red wine, for short
32. Plop shot
34. Like some rye
38. Perfect example
40. Humdinger
41. Classy
42. Footnote catchall
43. Paw part
44. Exxon product
45. What I hope this book will do . . .

DOWN

1. ... because it's all the ___
2. Stanford rival
3. Go home for the day
4. Dentist's concern
5. Rest ___ . . .
6. One ___ sum
7. Fossey friend
8. Action pics of the '50s
9. No kidding
10. ___ herrings
13. Collide
17. Kid's game
21. Landlubber's aye
22. Combination
23. Refrain syllables
24. Overlooked
25. Takes back
26. Fred's daughter
29. Driveway material
33. Grocery holder
34. Bette's title film role
35. Sitar kin
36. Airline that can provide kosher meals
37. Uneventful
38. Vim and vigor
39. Kind of order

★**Solution on page 310**

16A, 42A, 9D, 23D, 36D

Essential

1	2	3	4	■	5	6	7	■	8	9	10	11
12				■	13			■	14			
15				■	16			■	17			
18				19				■	20			
■	■	■	■	21				22		■	■	■
23	24	25	26			■	27			28	29	30
31					■	■	■	32				
33					34	■	35					
■	■	■	36			37			■	■	■	■
38	39	40		■	41				42	43	44	45
46				■	47			■	48			
49				■	50			■	51			
52				■	53			■	54			

ACROSS

1. Manner of delivery
5. Forty winks or less
8. Trounce
12. Empassioned
13. Have a due date
14. High quality
15. Magritte of art
16. Bled
17. In the buff
18. Use Morse code
20. Slump
21. All grown up
23. Mike Meyers role
27. ___ the thought!
31. Start of a *Three's Company* hangout
32. Setting
33. Cue
35. Beam
36. Glorifies
38. Smooth
41. Office supplies
46. Part of a bento box
47. Jock's pride
48. Cop in *Alice's Restaurant*
49. Flush
50. Ring around the collar
51. Unadulterated
52. Essential
53. Banned pesticide
54. Halt

DOWN

1. Dessert or juice flavor
2. Surpassing
3. 1492 ship with a tilde
4. Jeannie portrayer
5. Part of SNAFU
6. Expect
7. Unexpressed
8. Nomad
9. Time for photo developing
10. Break apart
11. Slight sound
19. Showed your pearly whites
22. Amend
23. Erving, affectionately
24. ___ Speedwagon
25. Humpty Dumpty, for one
26. 8 Down
28. Non-Republicrat, for short
29. Runaround gal
30. 6th word of "Little Miss Muffet"
34. Jimmy's successor
35. Figures out
37. Like boxers, often
38. Some Feds
39. As it happens
40. Listener's words
42. What some corn does
43. Lie next to
44. Calamitous
45. Look like

★ **Solution on page 310**

14A, 23A, 7D, 23D, 35D, 40D

Times up

ACROSS

1. Popular IT language
5. A fifth of Hamlet
8. Git!
12. Delete
13. ___ *Piano*
14. Mr. Bill's cry
15. Not a red ___
16. Hopper
17. Ferry fare
18. It reacts with a jerk
19. Local board
21. Homeland
23. Quaint spots to stay at
26. Hassled
31. Treats topically
32. Cabbage
33. Out of sight
35. Procession
36. I've had enough!
38. On time
42. Motivating words
46. Toddler's 14 Across
47. Ox-like beast
48. Designation
49. Part of a Greek nonet
50. Direct
51. Hurry
52. That was close!
53. Cure hide
54. Both should be in the water

DOWN

1. High-schooler type
2. Ciao in church
3. Transit for Tarzan
4. Went to
5. Times up
6. Carne go-with
7. Sinew
8. Skyrocket
9. Food for fish
10. Chip in
11. Animated type
20. Captivate
22. Not here
23. Humbug preface
24. Manila Thrilla
25. Dip and rise
27. Discussed
28. Title for Brooks in *Blazing Saddles*
29. "Strange Magic" group
30. Solar eclipse time
34. Candy ingredient
35. Army division
37. More than a hobby
38. Draw out
39. Not a chance
40. Bird perch in *Roxanne*
41. Chomp
43. ___ mia!
44. Love to Luiz
45. Takes down

14A, 23A, 36A, 42A, 46A, 5D, 27D, 39D

★ **Solution on page 310**

Managed

ACROSS

1. ___ Pudding
6. *The Ghost and ___ Muir*
9. Pen man
12. Jazzy Shaw
13. Cooking liquid
14. It's baled
15. Collects
16. Reuters rival, once
17. Hit the buffet
18. Gym floor
19. Tangoer, to Lehrer
22. Toll
24. Calibrate
26. Malt shop order
30. In the past
31. Antiwar one
32. Seer
35. A-one
37. Beautifying
39. Wandering
42. Jazz group, for short
45. Scatter
46. Richards of Texas
47. Drag out
49. 42 Across member
50. Managed
51. Confess
52. Desire
53. Pig's digs
54. Lecturer's collection

DOWN

1. Injure
2. Surface ___
3. They're on the books
4. Former Speaker, to friends
5. Toady
6. Pinky or the Brain
7. Ponzi scheme
8. Kitchen gadget
9. Old drink that's new here
10. Regular food item
11. Tsar's tsk
20. Questionnaire question
21. Kind of collision
23. Flesh tinter
24. Check cacher, for short
25. Biblical pronoun
27. Moving
28. Plastic used in pipes
29. Big foot?
33. Standards
34. *Music Man* instrument
35. James Earl Jones wasn't paid for promoting it
36. Presses for a date
38. Tai's partner
39. Culp classic
40. Raced
41. Champ's cry
43. Sad or smutty
44. Matterhorn's mountains
48. Snake-eyes

22A, 51A, 21D, 36D, 39D, 41D

★ **Solution on page 310**

Blameless

ACROSS

1. Yuletide extra
4. Where to see a 1 Across
8. Smart
12. Noir film of '49
13. Pavarotti piece
14. League
15. Blameless
17. Tie up
18. Like flan
19. Was compelled
21. Light
23. Subsides
26. Cream of ___
31. Leapers with long ears
32. Can we go now?
33. Is nothing ___?
35. Advanced
36. Grow grinders
38. He makes an impression
42. *Good Times* actor
46. Specialist
47. Gotcha
49. Related
50. Told a tall tale
51. Icers united, for short
52. Unfavorable impression
53. Goes down
54. "___ a silly . . . "

DOWN

1. Brickell of song
2. Why the ___ face?
3. Phyllis's hubby
4. Buddy
5. Amphitheaters
6. Drill across the diamond
7. Up-to-the-minute
8. Proficient
9. Dressed
10. Multitude
11. It returns
16. Pearl bailee
20. Lack
22. The euro replaced it
23. Sounds of serenity
24. Meadow comment
25. In-flight turn
27. Check again
28. *The ___ of Pooh*
29. Supplement
30. Baker's loaf
34. New Jersey team
35. *Hill ___ Blues*
37. ___, *Indiana*
38. Hell's bells!
39. Use the microwave
40. Ear-to-ear look
41. Like Madeline, in her group
43. Wordy birdie
44. 7/4 cries
45. Be dejected
48. Show stoppers

19A, 47A

★**Solution on page 311**

Premiere

1	2	3	4	■	5	6	7	8	■	9	10	11
12				■	13				■	14		
15				■	16				■	17		
18				19				■	20			
■	■	■	■	21				22			■	■
23	24	25	26			■	27				28	29
30					■	■	■	31				
32					33	■	34					
■	■	35				36			■	■	■	■
37	38			■	39				40	41	42	43
44			■	45				■	46			
47			■	48				■	49			
50			■	51				■	52			

ACROSS

1. Observed
5. Pack
9. Arctic
12. Bridges in the movies
13. Valid
14. "Little Red Book" author
15. Support
16. Wine type
17. Standard
18. Fork over
20. Glop
21. Distorted
23. Unhappy
27. Like *American Idol*
30. Stage area
31. Outrigger
32. Atkins no-no
34. Parlor piece
35. Conspirator
37. Pointer
39. Reclines
44. 31 Across tool
45. Resides
46. It may come calling
47. Hole filler?
48. Short shot
49. One way to fly
50. ___ *Girls*
51. Childish retort
52. The Babe's sultanate

DOWN

1. Becomes less
2. Uh-huh
3. It isn't hard
4. Pistols at dawn, say
5. Saunter
6. Steelhead
7. Revolutionary, perhaps
8. Minute
9. Cheeky
10. *Misery* star
11. Famous sergeant
19. Premiere
20. Suggest
22. Track competitors
23. "Papa ___ a Rolling Stone"
24. Decide on
25. Deletions
26. Coerce
28. Hart mate
29. How 'bout that?
33. It'll make you raise your voice
34. Handles
36. Get your ___ off me!
37. Santa scolding
38. Spike
40. Low
41. Maintain
42. Fizzy drink
43. Tie
45. Place for a facial

18A, 27A, 39A, 51A, 20D, 34D

★ **Solution on page 311**

Comfortable

ACROSS

1. Monitor
6. Bad hair day hair
9. Reaction location
12. Light beer
13. Time Warner purchaser
14. Where this book was published
15. ___ *the Other Reindeer*
16. Civilization antidote?
18. Rugrat
19. Comfortable
21. Film type with stuntmen
23. A Deadly Sin
27. Reach
29. Discuss
31. *Casablanca* star
32. 5/8/1945
33. Decreased?
35. Parts of Rube Goldberg contraptions
36. Through
37. Devotee
39. Break a promise
41. ___-sync
44. Permanent paint
47. Audience address
49. Rival
50. Old man's place?
51. Cable TV made it unnecessary
52. Male cat or turkey
53. Give one's ___
54. Be fluent in

DOWN

1. Blockage
2. Ring thing
3. Distress
4. Version, for short
5. Dissertation
6. Like a he-man
7. Tea type
8. Clue suspect
9. ___ up the works
10. Manipulate
11. Morsel
17. Have faith in
20. Part of a Tennessee Williams title
22. Part of a Steinbeck title
24. Emphasize in print
25. Luminary
26. Flop for Robin Williams
27. Waterless
28. Edible tuber
30. Gorges oneself
34. Elton John hit
35. Record
38. Personalizing item
40. Actress Lanchester
42. Plan
43. Bonus
44. Rearward
45. Murmur
46. "Losing My Religion" group
48. Dine at night

★ **Solution on page 311**

16A, 19A, 29A, 32A

Get ready

ACROSS

1. Target
6. Sailors' hats
10. Scamp
13. Stand
14. Hero
15. Conjunction
16. Cares for
17. Allocate
18. It holds precious little
19. Gaze at
20. Repeated
22. Agent
23. Jogs
24. Poignant
26. Recant
29. *Giant* star
32. American icon
34. It's for mature audiences
35. Fish dish
36. Left
38. Reedy
39. Bait
40. Cheap spot
42. Twists
43. He pities the fool
45. Mooch
47. Golf hole
50. Marker
51. Droop
52. Salvage
54. Kitt, for one
55. Keen on
56. Bird with long plumes
57. *Chances* ___
58. Disarray
59. Live wires

DOWN

1. Entrance fee
2. Comply with
3. Very well
4. Funny
5. Like some seats
6. Cheapskate
7. Hasta la vista
8. Stir
9. Winter crafts
10. So that
11. Additional
12. Get ready
21. Pigeon patter
23. Raptor digits
25. Embellishes
26. Sprinkle
27. Creep
28. Sacred text
30. All over again
31. Is a yes-man
33. Keepsakes
34. Toadied
37. Duck in a kid's book
41. Surrounded
42. Frankenstein's monster standouts
43. Flaky rock
44. Crowd sound
46. Sulk
47. Alleviate
48. One who logs on
49. Darlings
53. Self-worth

★ Solution on page 311

1A, 32A, 43A, 10D

Look at me!

ACROSS

1. Handed over
5. Futon
9. Handouts
13. Exposed
14. Pandora's box filler
15. Get it dead on
16. Suppressed
18. Sushi fish
19. Pollen
20. Look at me!
22. Admits a mistake
25. Apartheid concern
28. At odds
32. Residue
33. Purpose
34. Purpose
35. ASAP
37. Easy dessert?
38. Dubya's degree
39. Examples
42. Clinch
43. Pit crew member
45. Trail in the Northeast
48. They're often said
52. Foul
53. Disperse
56. Measly
57. Fill-in
58. Chunk in a Greek salad
59. Individuals
60. Postponement
61. Affront

DOWN

1. A large amount
2. Each
3. Down from the top
4. Menu item
5. Susana's snoozer
6. Former
7. Vaccine target
8. Strove
9. Like a peacenik
10. Speak well of
11. Skirt type
12. Venetian blind piece
17. She was Caroline in the City
21. Comedian Knotts or Rickles
23. Santa's sled
24. Where to find reel entertainment
25. Talk like Froggy
26. Nick and Nora's dog
27. Singe
29. Heavy book
30. Napoleon's destination
31. Distribute
36. Tijuana treats
37. Strikes against
40. Beads on the ground
41. Like some comebacks
42. Winter wear
44. Words of unity
45. A secretary might take one
46. Hot place
47. Take on
49. Highlander
50. Brute preceder
51. Char
54. Croc doc
55. Doc flock, initially

★ **Solution on page 311**

16A, 20A, 22A, 2D, 44D, 50D

And so on

ACROSS

1. The ___ game
6. "Mamma Mia!" group
10. And so on
13. Devoured
14. One with top billing, often
15. Keanu role
16. Like a Pisan tower
17. It's usually accepted
18. Mover's vehicle
19. Cab tab
20. Those opposing
22. Telemarketer's device
24. Place
27. Uh-uh
28. Rascals
32. Meringue-like cover
34. Scalpel wielder
37. Italian Riviera resort
39. African wasteland
40. Start of a Poitier title
41. Oozed green, if Vulcan
43. Trip part, or that which trips
44. Introduced
48. Prison term
51. Winter woes
55. Prompt
56. Traumatic experience, for one
57. Like the game, to Holmes
58. Offshoot
59. Eat well
60. Blunder
61. Bull word
62. Watermelon missile
63. Pricy

DOWN

1. Show off a smile
2. After hours
3. Fighting tooth and nail
4. Struggle
5. To charm
6. Li'l Abner creator
7. '90s/'00s collectibles, for short
8. Wet the bird
9. Like some committees
10. Be covetous
11. Squad
12. Reasons against
21. Nag's response
23. *Marvin's* ___
24. Side-of-the-mouth comment
25. Home of the Jazz
26. Melody
29. It's what's for dinner
30. Tiny opening
31. Catch
33. Where mummy sleeps
35. Not new
36. They don't go with the flow
38. Offensive
42. Gave a vulgar look
45. Choice in a flip
46. Rolling Stones hit
47. Yogurt type
48. Rip-off
49. Replacement currency
50. *Finding* ___
52. Rabbit's run
53. Medical amount
54. Tread

★**Solution on page 311**

37A, 44A, 3D, 6D, 9D, 47D

Superior

ACROSS

1. Chewed over
6. Like used goods
10. Dunk
13. Superior
14. Munch
15. Fund for the future, for short
16. Tent peg
17. Film spool
18. Near empty
19. Sweetie
20. Shame
22. Public house
23. Where the lesser cuts are
24. Witchy woman
26. Very hot
29. Meager
32. Has a tab?
34. Given that
35. Between
36. Vernaculars
38. Propel
39. Timidity
40. Recipe amt., for short
42. Poker call
43. Rankle
45. Maximum
47. Columnist Buchwald
50. ___ *in Black*
51. *Rocky Horror* opener
52. Punctually
54. Hubbub
55. Guilty or not guilty
56. Marital concerns
57. . . . and I want it ___!
58. Holler
59. Takes the pressure off

DOWN

1. Go, dog, go
2. Capable of
3. Duration
4. Egad!
5. Salad cover
6. Like a digest
7. Blockade
8. Article
9. Psalms interjection
10. It pays off, they say
11. Flatten
12. Puppet master's victim
21. Alter a window
23. Intermingles
25. Illegal immigrants
26. Slant
27. Provided by yours truly
28. Last option, often
30. Romans preceder
31. Role for Stack or Costner
33. Clearance
34. Family band leader
37. Eurekas
41. Like some juice
42. Drive
43. Somalian model/actress
44. Alter a room
46. Cover a floor
47. Part of a Dead Man's Hand
48. Offensive
49. Title role for Shirley
53. PBS provider

★ **Solution on page 311**

6A, 23A, 42A, 52A, 2D, 27D, 28D, 34D

It doesn't hold water

1	2	3	4	■	5	6	7	8	9	■	10	11	12
13				■	14					■	15		
16				■	17					■	18		
19			■	20				■	21	22			
23			24					■	25			■	■
■	■	■	26				■	■	■	27		28	29
30	31	32					33	■	34				
35					■	36		37					
38				■	■	■	39				■	■	■
■	■	40		41	■	42					43	44	45
46	47				■	48				■	49		
50			■	51	52				■	53			
54			■	55					■	56			
57			■	58					■	59			

ACROSS

1. Biblical idol shape
5. Set sights on
10. In favor of
13. Soother
14. Spread
15. O.J. judge
16. Vegetarian picnic dish
17. Was compelled
18. Pinch
19. Freight weight
20. Star followers
21. Over the norm
23. Universal
25. Builder's need
26. Small songbird
27. Former mayor Giuliani
30. Found the funds for
34. Lamp denizen
35. Substantial
36. Like "death by chocolate"
38. Baja buck
39. Horsey sport
40. Kind of shirt
42. Item for a tree
46. Removes
48. Fruit castaways
49. Jurisprudence
50. Hook's foe
51. It doesn't hold water
53. Traversed
54. Temper
55. *Green* ___
56. Andy's boy
57. Liane Hansen's workplace
58. You'll get a rise out of it
59. I've got a ___ on you

DOWN

1. Fills roles
2. Combo
3. Advances
4. Hardly any
5. Mortified
6. Not real
7. Sawbones
8. Chomp
9. Saliva
10. Tweak
11. Lex Luthor's aide
12. Hitchcock flick
20. Cheerful
22. Tedium
24. Like some sloths
28. Racket
29. However
30. Hi-fi item
31. Charge
32. Clasp
33. Cheats
34. Big dos
37. Challenge
41. English assignment
42. *Carmen* or *Faust*
43. Go away and unite
44. Romanian gymnast
45. Boss ___
46. English
47. Nag
52. Diamonds
53. Dick, on *The Dick Van Dyke Show*

★ **Solution on page 311**

17A, 10D, 24D

Stretch the truth

ACROSS

1. Go on about
5. Grinds
10. Temporary bed
13. Like a buoy
14. Storage site
15. Stretch the truth
16. Depot
17. Spectacles
19. Sharpen
20. Princess protuberance
21. Appearance
22. Go bad
24. "Runaway" singer Shannon
25. Batting cage people
28. *Evening Shade* role
31. Almond liqueur
33. Crafted
35. Artificial luge run material
36. Injured, in a way
38. Linguist's study, for short
39. Money makers
40. Decrease
43. Hurtful
44. Concur
46. Lengthen
47. Doubter's response
51. Reserved
53. Brouhaha
54. Not a nice thing
55. *What's Happening* role
56. Therefore
57. Bill for a soda machine
58. Cleaned
59. Earth heirs

DOWN

1. Reason for aloe
2. Regarding
3. Light element
4. Wall hanging
5. Relationship
6. Ones who must watch out for themselves
7. Acquire illegally
8. Brooch
9. Chew out
10. British jazz songstress
11. Sty cry
12. Bigelow or Tetley products
18. "Calvin and Hobbes" bully
23. Remove a layer
25. Possess
26. Poker continued bid
27. Citrus fruit
29. Swerve
30. Uses an abacus
32. Became conversant
33. Buddy
34. Kind of veto
37. Garb
41. ___ of roses
42. Chicago team
43. Nottingham, for one
44. In addition
45. Increase
48. Party pooper
49. Upper hand
50. Obtained
52. Embroider

★Solution on page 311

47A, 51A, 53A, 2D, 10D, 26D, 32D, 34D

Chapter 8

Easy Come, Easy Go

It's hard to see through

ACROSS

1. Cut class
5. One at the plate
11. Gov. watchdog, for short
14. Mom's mom
15. Fill a lung
16. *Days of ___ Lives*
17. Bohemian
18. Inexpensive
19. Smash into
20. Made fun of
22. Spirited
24. Furrier's item
25. Use a divan
26. Some women
30. Jalopy
33. Axle
36. Go away
38. Shed tears
39. Startled cry
40. Dictionary collection
42. Part of a suit
43. It's hard to see through
45. Attacks
46. "I've been ___!"
47. Spud
49. An American Gladiator
51. Military maildrop
52. Estuary
56. Hit film of '97
59. Hit film of '80
62. *Invasion of the Body Snatchers* prop
63. Lola's verb
65. Jimmy the Greek's forte
66. The hole thing
67. Saw the sights
68. Much
69. Underhanded
70. Casual garb
71. Intelligence

DOWN

1. Goes berserk
2. Gold measure
3. Opening
4. Graft
5. LP player
6. Concerning
7. The other shoe dropping
8. ___ sale
9. Very safe airline
10. Green condiment
11. Smile middle
12. Two-part
13. "You and what ___?"
21. Look into
23. Slant
27. Dance for two
28. Wise about
29. Warning
30. Spelt, for example
31. Sci-fi princess
32. Hurtled
33. Highway access
34. Columbus's state
35. Shameful
37. Yes in the Yucatan
41. Shed items
44. Fasten
48. Drinking tributes
50. Rented
53. Soup server
54. Bequeath
55. Determiners
56. Healthy spots
57. Monk's hood
58. Cat call
59. Impression
60. *New Jack City* actor
61. Beatty flick
64. Scheduled

45A, 68A, 5D, 6D, 9D, 28D, 37D, 50D, 60D

★**Solution on page 312**

It's a long story

ACROSS

1. They're forbidden
6. Asian piece of cookware
9. The Capitol ___
14. Poker bye-bye
15. Part of IOU
16. Demolish
17. For sure
19. Use a soapbox
20. Ratifies
21. Like some eggs or children
23. Trend starter
26. They help clear the air, for short
27. Ali, once
30. Green
32. Shopping site
36. Topper
37. Wind catcher
38. Sock smell
39. Environs
41. They get it
42. It's a long story
43. Terrible ruler
44. Depose
45. *A Different World* actress
46. Charlie Brown's cry
47. Spew out
49. They use a comb
50. Like some diapers
52. More up-to-date
54. Anger or calming scent
58. Soon
62. Go out with
63. Overdone
66. Playful critter
67. Hiatus
68. Become one
69. Deprived
70. *Murder, ___ Wrote*
71. Cone

DOWN

1. French city
2. Portent
3. Writer Ephron
4. NIMBY, for one
5. Liquid or gaseous
6. Took the prize
7. He gives a hoot
8. Ring members?
9. Bend down
10. "Little Earthquakes" singer
11. List ender
12. Bread spread
13. Toboggan kin
18. Library code
22. Fruit slag
24. Relax
25. Encounter
27. Seat
28. It's just a stage
29. Eroded
31. Bennett title word
33. Saw
34. Knave
35. Cafeteria supply
40. Came back with
41. Has a party
48. Lookalike
49. Like an egghead
51. What to put in for this
53. Eventually become
54. Desktop item
55. Be aware of
56. Appealing
57. Caviar
59. Blow off steam
60. Analogy words
61. Cheerleader, often
64. Bleachers cry
65. *The Hairy ___*

★ **Solution on page 312**

1A, 14A, 58A, 10D, 11D, 24D, 29D, 53D, 60D

Obviously!

ACROSS

1. One ___ customer
4. Hilo hi's
10. Number one
14. Hacker
15. ___ walk
16. Canadian baseballer
17. Secretive group, for short
18. Peck
19. Base opposite
20. Cut
22. Teresa's topper
24. Kind of base
25. Stays put
26. Made up
29. Church song
32. Helpful Beach Boy girl
33. Outdoor pusher
34. It has a potential for zest
38. She whistled a happy tune
39. Arms race threat
41. Met number
42. Golly!
43. Obviously!
44. Mean
46. It may talk back
47. ___ pig
48. Native Israeli
52. Stag's mate
53. Inflame
57. Claw
60. Phooey!
61. They're against you
63. Become older
64. *Arsenic and Old* ___
65. Asset
66. *Facts of Life* star
67. Facial betrayers
68. Personal quintet
69. Keep track in Scrabble

DOWN

1. Waiting room verb
2. Way out
3. Comebacks
4. Took over
5. Put down
6. Gambler's initials
7. Centers
8. Woody's son
9. Appear
10. Santa need
11. Lotus rival
12. Church feature
13. Hullabaloos
21. Title role for Mia
23. Receptacle
26. Rugged rock
27. Gasped cry
28. Cohan title noun
29. Uproar
30. Turkey Day tuber
31. He calls the shots
34. Dole
35. *Fame* actress
36. Baseball group
37. Early word
40. Burger holder
45. Stitchless ones
46. Welcome item
48. Creep
49. Group
50. Support
51. They may be sacred
54. Axel paths
55. Trunk item
56. Level
57. Bend at the knees
58. My word!
59. Film critic
62. Seen spots

★ **Solution on page 312**

39A, 13D, 27D, 29D, 31D, 35D

By Jove!

1	2	3	4	■	5	6	7	8	■	9	10	11	12	13
14				■	15				■	16				
17				■	18				■	19				
20			■	21					■	22				
23			24				■	25	26		■	■	■	■
■	■	■	27				■	28			29	30	31	32
33	34	35				■	36			■	37			
38					■	39			■	40				
41				■	42			■	43					
44				45			■	46				■	■	■
■	■	■	■	47			■	48				49	50	51
52	53	54	55		■	56	57				■	58		
59					■	60					■	61		
62					■	63					■	64		
65					■	66					■	67		

ACROSS

1. By Jove!
5. Dust makers
9. Ray Finkel's concern
14. *Animal House* chant
15. Journey
16. Sentient
17. Wallop
18. Oil disaster?
19. ___ of discussion
20. Type of chart
21. Rocket part
22. Chosen
23. Put up
25. Bridge worker's degree
27. Aggravate
28. Retract
33. Smooth
36. Undertake
37. Hot stuff
38. Beat
39. Part of HRH
40. Submitted a ballot
41. Gotcha
42. Writer Fleming
43. Brutal
44. Blessing
46. Horse hair
47. Alias initials
48. You might tickle them
52. They're near the city
56. Pool verb
58. Willard or Ben
59. Vigilant
60. Challenging cry
61. Off the deep end
62. Slow slider
63. Beseech
64. Single
65. John Lennon's "Instant ___!"
66. Noticed
67. Opposes

DOWN

1. Clandestine greeting
2. Like some energy
3. Hanging open
4. It might hang open
5. Like Wayne Manor
6. Video ___
7. A ___ and a prayer
8. They may get demerits
9. Most recent
10. Deserter, for short
11. Superman has a red one
12. ___ the Red
13. It's broken off
21. You might raise one
24. Many things going wrong
26. Sunny time
29. It may have four leaves
30. Velocity
31. Kaput
32. Boggs of baseball
33. Use a jigger
34. Stereotypic Asian response
35. Like shoelaces, often
36. Can material
39. Knew
40. Spite
42. It's hard to get out
43. Relished
45. S. Cal. city
46. It's not really there
49. Farsi speaker
50. Singer of "Hotel California"
51. Delays
52. Lie around
53. Forearm bone
54. Nurture
55. Lip
57. Well ventilated
61. State veep

★**Solution on page 312**

1A, 28A, 41A, 1D, 34D, 39D, 45D

Not even close

ACROSS

1. Old-time dance
4. Misbehave
9. Rodeo rope
14. Loan stat, for short
15. Scoundrel
16. Relative by marriage
17. Prop for Mr. Rogers
19. Cutter
20. Washer cycle
21. They have fancy cavities
22. Passes out
25. Market madness
27. Sculpture middle
28. Baby gear
32. Devoted
34. Not even close
35. Traps item
36. Way to go, for short
37. Royal furs
40. Cannonball path
41. Sign word
43. 35 Across site
44. Covet
46. All ___ go!
48. Learner
49. Walks with confidence
51. Belt sites
52. My, my!
55. It comes out of a slot
57. Puts on
58. Believable
62. Bank
63. Went to pot?
64. Brenda's mom
65. Hill sliders
66. Sheriff's squad
67. Plant

DOWN

1. Gives birth to
2. Make a decision
3. Specialist
4. Like a Swiss Army knife
5. *Three ___ in a Fountain*
6. Boat escorts
7. Theatre escort
8. Preferred
9. Probable
10. Hot and bothered
11. Went for another plate
12. Out of harm's way
13. Needs to repay
18. Writing style
21. Gave an angry look
22. Inceptions
23. Wayne's word
24. They tend to come from above
26. King of comedy
29. Characteristics
30. Where arms may revolve
31. Reception receptors
33. Aftershock, for one
34. Tree near some ski ramps
38. Crow's nest route
39. Reserve
42. Spoken
45. Management
47. Rubs out
50. Pool person
51. Charles is its prince
52. Wise birds
53. Opposite of "sic 'em"
54. Jay's rival
56. They're sown
58. Kind of sheet
59. Carol starter
60. Uniter of sorts
61. Crow's cry

★ **Solution on page 312**

4A, 16A, 52A, 4D, 39D, 60D

Double-crosser

ACROSS

1. Get away from
6. Fountain missile
10. Damsel
14. Quarrel
15. Tortoise's also-ran
16. 1994 NL Manager of the Year
17. Took steps
18. OPEC member
19. Ear part
20. ___ poles
21. Fish lung
23. ___ *Twist*
25. Models in ads, for example
27. Astaire's partner
28. Roman god of love
29. Late show, for short
30. Secure
34. Guarantee
37. It's not refined
38. Sluggish
40. Dastardly dog
41. Comprehends
44. Double-crosser
47. Countdown start, often
48. Order
49. Swell
52. They might be charmed
56. Spotted cat
57. Kind of school
58. Nose-bag nibble
59. Impressive, huh?
60. One who 41 Across
62. Why we cook meat
64. Joanie portrayer
65. Governor Grasso
66. Yakked
67. Ding
68. Be a couch potato
69. Depleted

DOWN

1. Obliterate
2. Seven, perhaps
3. Disentangle
4. ___ *Another Day*
5. Chess finale
6. Moppets
7. Premature
8. Strong-armed lobby, for short
9. High boy?
10. Slanders
11. Hit sitcom of yore
12. Subdued
13. Plaintiffs
22. Like conspirators
24. Shortfall
26. Tail swisher
30. Driver's concern
31. ___ you sure?
32. Adjusted
33. Rookie socialite
34. Garb
35. Feel bad about
36. Go astray
39. Recommendation
42. Putty or tar
43. ___ *the Night*
45. They have a beat
46. Took in
49. Was quite fond
50. Sympathetic response
51. Lucy's crony
52. Leak
53. Nary a soul
54. Raptor digit
55. Temp job
61. "Don't Bring Me Down" group
63. Limit

★ **Solution on page 312**

14A, 25A, 41A, 59A, 62A, 66A, 11D, 22D, 32D, 50D, 53D

Here!

ACROSS

1. Taken in
7. Ali ___
11. Close
15. Cold time
16. Pupil's dread
17. Bad reviews
18. Piggy bank filler
19. Filly's father
20. Chip in
21. Understanding
22. Here!
25. Vacate, varmint
26. *Sesame* ___
29. Rasta locks
31. Shock
33. Deli order
35. Sedate
36. Egg entrees
38. It makes a row
40. David Bowie's model wife
41. Outdoor eatery
45. Pesters
46. Relax
48. Sale offer
50. Bleepable
53. Door word
54. It might clock you
57. Tooth trouble
59. Life's work
60. Zest maker
61. American absorbee
62. Tools for duels
65. Nothing
68. As soon as
70. Indian brew
71. Be a burden
74. Fur
75. Ripped
76. Harmonizes
77. Thought
78. Like some parties
79. Assignments

DOWN

1. Notch
2. It hurts
3. Giant access
4. Injunction
5. *The* ___ *and I*
6. Expand
7. Plagued
8. Federation
9. Exposed
10. Add-on
11. Hot tub
12. Lear jet lean-to
13. Messy
14. Panama biter
23. Start again
24. Walk briskly
27. Laborious
28. Insolent
30. Establish
31. Italian wine region
32. Ruckus
33. Macho ones
34. According to
37. Penny pincher
39. Limits
42. Tea time
43. Costs
44. Picks poorly
47. Top gun
49. Greeley's direction
51. Answering machine sound
52. James ___ Jones
54. Ink sources
55. . . . until it ___ on me
56. Seer
58. ABCs
60. I must be ___
63. Photographed
64. Scarlett's home
66. ___ that a shame?
67. Fewer
69. JFK stat, for short
72. A-Team actor
73. Luau staple

★ **Solution on page 312**

15A, 33A, 33D, 34D, 72D

Yikes!

ACROSS

1. Affect
7. Inundated
12. Late night Leno
15. Shell dweller
16. Bogus
17. It may need deflating
18. Fled to wed
19. Arsonist
20. Yikes!
21. Mythical sorceress
22. Practice
24. Ben Stein's question with "Bueller?"
28. Gat, for one
29. According to ___
32. Bother
33. Time about 2,500 years ago
37. Buddy
38. Canadian country singer
40. Squashed circle
41. Yuck!
42. Struck a ___
43. "(Man) of the Year" magazine
44. BSA groups
46. Pasta topping
47. As easy as ___
48. Toothy look
49. Delegate
51. Bickering
52. Accompanies
54. Alphabetic author Grafton
55. Jersey hoopsters
56. 7/4 cry
57. Under the influence
59. Italian cheese
63. Center
67. Ham's spot, often
68. Hog havens
70. Solar eclipse sight
71. Sandy's sound
72. Pounds the pinball
73. Like poor Johnny One-Note
74. But
75. Git!
76. Go back

DOWN

1. Bullet follower
2. Newbie smuggler
3. Nudge
4. Contented
5. Tidy
6. Turner of channels
7. Pertinent
8. ___ leave
9. Sported
10. Responsible
11. Damsel's cry
12. Heckler's call
13. Continues on
14. Repression
23. Childish response
25. Talk a lot
26. Peculiarity
27. As a minimum
29. Blotch
30. Cinema taboos
31. Cultural
33. Fashionable
34. Fly
35. Ploy
36. Opts for
39. The ___ Formerly Known as Prince
45. Scooby or Shaggy, to the villain
46. Dismal
50. Up-to-the-minute
51. Logrolling preventer
53. Carnivore's entrees
57. Handle
58. Show feelings
59. Donkey syllable
60. Brontë heroine
61. Gone
62. Grain building
64. Test-taker's amen
65. Problem
66. Story
69. Fast plane, for short
70. Jam ingredient

★ **Solution on page 312**

33A, 38A, 51A, 59A, 4D, 10D, 11D, 23D, 27D, 33D, 57D

Vision

ACROSS

1. It may have a tumbler
5. Breaks
10. Hurts, like a toe
15. About
16. Ike's opponent
17. Intense and aggressive
18. Remain
19. Waterworks
20. Golfbag items
21. Grant has one
22. Stuff one's face
23. Crete and Capri
25. Long in the tooth
27. Chaps
28. Not bent
33. Nice nightclubs
37. Rose danger
38. Route around
40. Posted
41. Diminish
42. Deck coat
44. That ship
45. Response to a mouse
46. Facet
48. Put up with
50. Storm
52. Reach
53. Outpouring
54. Caretaker
56. Bazaar kin
58. Bile
59. Swindle
60. Grainy, speckled rock
64. They're playing ___ song!
66. Disgusting, casually
70. Combines
71. Mammoth
73. *Peter Pan* pooch
74. Tell target
75. Usher's milieu
76. Edit down
77. Sneezers
78. Iggy portrayer
79. Goes for

DOWN

1. Not wholesale
2. Not fooled by
3. Study all at once
4. It's typically QWERTY
5. Like much Disney fare
6. Vision
7. Tedious
8. Pitch
9. Diego's definitely
10. *Save the Last Dance* star
11. Oppressors
12. Aware of
13. Twist
14. Lip
24. Bash, biblically
26. Like some paper
28. Directs
29. Menace
30. Neophyte
31. Threw a party
32. Halloween option
33. Puff out
34. Bring back on
35. Jumpy
36. Boulevard
39. Temptations
43. Hoarse
47. Plumed wader
49. Encounter
51. Drop off
55. Comes up
57. Word with a handshake
60. Mulder or Scully
61. It's been seized
62. Heidi's home
63. Mideast airline
64. Approximately
65. Offensive to the eyes
67. Complain
68. Weave
69. Sweet spuds
72. Suffer

★ **Solution on page 312**

15A, 17A, 52A, 56A, 2D, 5D, 12D, 35D, 49D, 60D, 63D, 64D

Discovery

ACROSS

1. It's camp
7. Entree preceder
12. Sort
15. Aviator Earhart
16. Steer clear of
17. Bring to Wapner
18. Summer day temperature
19. Loses the chill
20. Worship the sun
21. Follow
22. Ditches
24. Casual-wear
28. Pitcher Guidry
29. Comedian Buzzi
32. Smacker
33. Unflattering pieces
37. Primates
38. Graduate's threads
40. Source
41. Fury
42. Karate levels
43. Movie effect
44. Sanyo rival
46. Mosquito attacks
47. It's cast
48. Lack of difficulty
49. Beat an incumbent
51. Discovery
52. Lifeboater's hope
54. Contend
55. Stamina, for movies
56. Devouring one
57. Italian dessert
59. Superpower problem
63. Unexcited
67. Sloppy ___
68. First show that got the lead out
70. Group concern
71. Give it your ___
72. Sound the alarm
73. It's a mystery
74. Traffic light color
75. Kind of taste bud
76. Divulges

DOWN

1. Role for Welles
2. Poker cry of anteing
3. Till drawer
4. P.I.s
5. Quotes
6. Allergy for some
7. Baste
8. Pirate cry
9. Try it on a ___
10. Top brass
11. Nasty leader
12. Ratio words
13. Kamehameha commemoration
14. *Daily Planet* byline
23. Do a bloodhound's job
25. Stolen
26. Troubled
27. Spring or fall clock verb
29. Elevated
30. Hoo-ha
31. Wee
33. Shove off
34. Concert carnie
35. Amen, perhaps
36. They go with riders
39. Ace's hideout?
45. Dog cries
46. Summer cottage
50. ___ biscuit
51. Put the pedal to the metal
53. Networks
57. Honkers
58. Type of steak
59. Open, a bit
60. Romeo or Juliet
61. Blend
62. This, for one
64. ___ to riches
65. Ticklish one
66. College veep
69. Tennis call
70. Scatter Torme

★**Solution on page 313**

22A, 24A, 52A, 59A, 76A, 2D, 12D, 26D, 33D, 51D, 58D

Something to keep

ACROSS

1. Go under
5. Revises
11. Stew pod
15. Monopoly need
16. End
17. Shelled out
18. Topic
19. Property
20. Bend
21. Platter
23. Something to keep
24. It helps you make piles
25. Plays the banjo
28. Truant one
30. Popular job of old
32. Cookie cooker
34. Look at
35. Puny pup
36. Verb used with "Iraq" in 2002
38. Player
40. Steers
41. Culmination
44. Really?
45. Idi Amin's area
47. Circle lines
49. Venetian vessel
51. Guitarist's need
52. Place
55. Pot contents
56. Use a Zamboni
58. Uses a mister
60. Responds to the villain
61. Somewhat
62. Acorn's ambition
65. Soft material
66. Strauss of stitchery
67. Boob tube receiver
69. Gal
73. Pony Express delivery
74. Painting tools
75. Off-ramp
76. Bit of data
77. Hold a grudge
78. More than attractive

DOWN

1. Vitamin watchdog, for short
2. Easy balloon filler
3. Sand or salt go-with
4. Precede
5. Bedroom item
6. Fraternity event
7. Hill dweller
8. Cappuccino topper
9. Nobel Peace Prize winner of 1984
10. Medical ethics concern
11. Drawing style
12. Dojo doings
13. Outfielder Henderson
14. Abide by
22. Rugrat
25. Lost one
26. Result of crying uncle
27. Sounds off
29. Anesthetized
31. Eat one's words
32. Best
33. What monitors monitor
37. Musical groups
39. British football
41. Assays essays
42. Personal area
43. They hold water
46. Pops in on
48. Twelve diners
50. Emily Dickinson's hometown
52. Job follower
53. Happy
54. Game show specialty
57. Iraqi resource
59. Leaning
63. Helpful person
64. Party supply
65. Forest frond
68. Teeny
70. Prop in *The Shining*
71. Half a jury
72. Dirty place

★Solution on page 313

16A, 61A, 4D, 10D, 11D, 46D

I'm not kiddin' ya!

ACROSS

1. Westward transports
7. Mister's missiles
12. Place to have a mud bath
15. Like some bands
16. Show site
17. One having a mud bath
18. According to schedule
19. Like some academies
20. *The Naked* ___
21. For fear that
22. It's big down South
24. Sluggish
26. Occur
27. With the most rings
28. It's tossed
32. Wine color
33. Muck
34. Checkout item
36. Swimming woe
40. Government-owned carrier
41. Fix before release
43. Enjoys the ice
44. Really bad
46. Revolutionary instrument
48. ___ of work
49. Aide of a sort
50. Tending to clank
52. Director's call
54. Like the euro, relatively
55. Sign of insobriety
56. Without risk
59. Starts the betting
61. *Star Trek* measure
62. *Star Trek* command
63. Made a picture
67. Fury
68. Forum wear
70. Glacial time
72. Pool tester
73. Pick-me-up
74. Stone-faced one?
75. Termination
76. Accustom
77. I'm not kiddin' ya!

DOWN

1. Eye coverers?
2. Writer Rice
3. Figures out
4. Skip
5. *Platoon* site, for short
6. Villainous mannerism
7. Without the curlicues
8. Sought divine intervention
9. Cleric's title, for short
10. Not digital
11. Bike checker, perhaps
12. Last name in detectives
13. Plumbing
14. 86 or 99
23. Was carried on the waves
25. Cute
26. Happy thought sounds
28. Barber's throwaway
29. Rent again
30. Century plant
31. Musical breaks
35. Driving need
37. Bikini, for one
38. Battlefield cry
39. Gotcha!
42. It helps you break up the day
43. Collection
45. Game with a spinner
47. Less
51. Washboard ___
53. Power player
54. Sore loser's call
56. Ill will
57. Home run king
58. At large
60. Nag's comment
63. Bruce or Laura of acting
64. Fury
65. Conceits
66. Journeyed
69. Serengeti grazer
71. Pigeon talk

★ **Solution on page 313**

15A, 18A, 40A, 70A, 7D, 11D, 54D

Dish it out

ACROSS

1. Lively
6. Bid
11. Farm growth
16. Dish it out
17. Kid's name
18. Discover
19. Guild
20. Make fun of
21. Preserved
22. Cheer
23. Fail to recycle
24. Give
25. Worthless
26. Stride
27. Complete
29. Russian empress
31. Place of origin
35. Not-so-nice places
36. Recedes
37. MADD concern, for short
38. Ran off
40. CNN show
42. Reader of sorts
43. Expected
44. Sorry for your ___
45. Happen
49. Glum
52. Manner
53. Shell food
54. Dry "American Pie" place
55. Temporary security
57. Collected
60. Sports events
61. Thaw
62. Under the influence
64. Ought
67. Kilns
69. Exhaust
70. Boil buster
71. Occurrence
72. Line drawings?
73. Church feature
74. Reach
75. Proclamation
76. They get no respect
77. *Feds* star
78. Bull's-eye wannabes

DOWN

1. Caption
2. Ended
3. Don't take them literally
4. Narrow hole
5. Actor Olin
6. Got
7. Parties
8. Lacking fizz
9. Not at this spot
10. Salinger title word
11. Like Joe
12. Glitter
13. Busy
14. Off one's rocker
15. Comprehended
23. Forfeit
24. *Moose Murders* and *Cutthroat Island*
26. Hold
28. Rail rider of old
30. Garnish
32. Ciao, Chico
33. Patient person
34. Stops working
38. Paranormal
39. Pick up
40. Reminder
41. Ice on the go
42. Matinee idol
43. Visits
46. They form attachments
47. Waited for the call, perhaps
48. Something to click on
49. They're yours to keep
50. Eyes in cartoons
51. Remainder
54. Cries for
56. Big-beaked one
58. It's good for what ails you
59. Be the puppet master
63. Trials
64. Swat
65. Skipper portrayer
66. Aware of
68. Kibosh
69. I did it!
71. Have ___ on one's face
72. Nourished

★ **Solution on page 313**

18A, 21A, 55A, 74A, 2D, 13D, 43D, 66D, 69D

Let 'er rip!

ACROSS

1. Kind of campaign
6. Obsessed one
10. Middle ___
14. Qantas critters
16. Get away from
17. Zola portrayer
18. Let 'er rip!
19. Odin or Thor
20. Kerplunk
21. Common title starter
22. Paint the town red
24. Tuck and others
26. Burger for the grill
28. Start of a Linus poster
30. Like some nights
33. They take your car
34. Tile alternative
36. Ten-speeds
37. Granola bits
38. Deli device
40. Skedaddled
43. Best of ___
45. Take in
46. Tea treat
48. Gloomy
49. Clicker
51. Massive
52. Write-ups of hits
53. Talked to a secretary
57. Intensify
59. Clouseau portrayer
60. They go nowhere
62. Talent
63. Take in
64. Leaves out
66. Chem. or Bio.
69. Clinton opponent
70. Ill-suited
72. Time manager?
75. List entry
76. Wane
77. Moolah
78. Monster home?
79. Final
80. Hangs open

DOWN

1. Revue segment
2. Wool eater
3. Lessen
4. Food preposition
5. Item for a maid
6. Liniment ingredient
7. Tosses
8. Want ___
9. Studly one
10. Realms
11. Coffee style
12. "Yeah, right" sounds
13. Under the influence
15. Bombing run
16. Green emotion
23. Famous last words
25. Those in charge
26. What's written on this page
27. Every
29. Sheriff's verb
30. Ones like Oscar Madison
31. Regal regalia
32. Went to pot?
35. Windows predecessor
36. It walks like a man
39. Raffle drawing
40. Path
41. It may require management
42. Special ___
44. Long curtains
45. Alter
47. Driveway drawer
50. Final
52. Cashes in
54. It ___ fair!
55. Came to an end
56. Kindness, for short
57. Signify
58. They're better than birdies
60. Offed
61. Places to relax
62. ___ a check
65. Ball catcher
66. Phase
67. Arrive
68. Pupil's place
71. Bird watchers, for short?
73. Man's best friend
74. *Mad About You* role

★ **Solution on page 313**

18A, 60A, 77A, 4D, 11D, 23D, 35D, 60D

All clear

ACROSS

1. Shindigs
6. Croat's foe
10. Model wood
15. ___ in debt
16. Hierarchy
17. Breaded meat
18. Garlicky sauce
19. Was conveyed
20. Pen pal?
21. Tropical tuber
22. Pressing need
25. Actress Farrow
26. The perfect place
27. Conditional
30. White as a sheet
32. Like deductions
34. Searched
36. Dogs like Snoopy
39. Cut
40. Deduces
43. It comes back
45. All clear
46. Rainbow, for one
47. Bud's buddy
48. Wilbur's smarter half
50. Manet or Monet
52. Component
53. Rat
55. Brides provide them
57. Nurse's instruction
60. Accesses
61. Not a peep
64. Traffic report
66. The knot?
67. Stickiness
69. Play-___
72. Irritates
75. Word processor button
76. Hit the golf ball
78. ___ walk
79. *Roseanne* role
80. Say
81. Incline
82. Ammo go-with
83. They're in the same boat

DOWN

1. Welcome to the barbie
2. Italian tune
3. Weaving machine
4. It's a bore
5. Brandy server
6. Secure
7. Sensual
8. Try to ring up again
9. It comes from the tap
10. Hot dog holder
11. Cash cache, for short
12. Sure-footed one
13. Take effect
14. Wore away
17. Multiplexes
23. Potential suspect
24. Familiarized
26. Nope
28. Something to shake or break
29. Just vegging
30. They're cast
31. Kind of wrench
33. Concerning
34. Joint
35. In-depth
37. Dessert with filling
38. Beaches
41. The Little Mermaid
42. Edsel, to Henry
44. Inning enders
49. 10 ccs., perhaps
50. Becalm
51. Place for clowns
52. Hold
54. Hold
56. Agitated
58. Can ___
59. Sage's benefit
61. Hit movie of 2002
62. Perfect
63. State aid game
65. Oz forest initial fear
68. Island dance
69. Love to excess
70. Concluded
71. Milady's
73. Have a late snack
74. "All the Things You ___"
77. Travel abbreviation

★**Solution on page 313**

48A, 66A, 72A, 13D, 14D, 26D, 56D

Proceed

ACROSS

1. Serious
6. Singer Stefani
10. Bob
13. Plane people
15. Forest regions
17. He played Quincy's aide
18. Hospital fluid
19. Generic product
20. Eva's mate
21. White weasels
23. Poe's house
25. Driving hatred
28. Yearns
30. Proceed
31. Search
33. Going ___
34. Charlotte's place
36. "The Greatest"
37. Bundle
40. Pester
41. Juiced fruit
43. Improve
45. Not much
47. Form of massage
49. Gregarious review
50. Buddhist monk
51. Hi
52. *Twelve Angry* ___
53. *Pushing* ___
54. Indignation
55. Rotation speed, for short
58. Remaining
59. Restrained
62. Begrudges
64. *Rocky Horror* role
67. Stuck-up ones
69. It's raised during trouble
70. Hopper's spot
72. "Are we ___ Devo?"
73. Swallows
75. Mountain climbers
80. Late lunch time
81. They come and go
82. Belgrade's region
83. McCarthy target
84. Chess cry
85. Distributed

DOWN

1. Dispirit
2. Texas tea
3. Torso encircler
4. 911 acronym
5. It's good for what ails you
6. Put on
7. EEE, for example
8. Walking on ___
9. Dundee denial
10. Recess
11. Option C, perhaps
12. Ones on the go
14. Constricted
15. Bit of kindling
16. Hurt
22. A zebra has one
24. Grill tool
25. Tommy gun sound
26. Form of sculpture
27. Ability
29. Ta-ta
30. Passage
32. *Jurassic Park* critter
35. Custodian of goods
38. "Goody Two Shoes" singer
39. Sells off
42. Comrade
44. Campsite constructs
46. One who knows the steps
47. It might be lost in the market
48. Celestial Seasonings drink
56. Item for the stage
57. Precious ___
58. ___ Miz
60. Like impossible goals
61. Take in
63. Did a crabwalk
64. "To the ___ Born"
65. With nary a soul
66. Like some communities
68. Rip-offs
71. "___ She Lovely?"
74. Branch
76. ___ you sure?
77. Wharton grad, for short
78. Be sick
79. Parked oneself

★Solution on page 313

25A, 30A, 33A, 45A, 70A, 73A, 25D, 48D

Hint

ACROSS

1. Quiet comedian
6. Numbskull
10. Animals at home
14. Frozen food brand
16. Listens to
18. Elliptical
19. Where to watch the show from
20. Annoy
21. Newscaster's need
22. Nose part
23. Percolate
25. Pushed over
27. Conferences
30. Likely endorser
31. Like a fool and his money
33. Tarzan wannabe
36. Rely
38. Book of maps
40. Repent
42. Diminutive
43. Offense
45. Like some scientists
46. Patriotic U.S. symbol
49. Laundering money
51. Hoo-ha
52. A girl's place
54. ___ in a lifetime
55. Gymnast's goal
56. It's sweet
57. Fall guy
60. Avoid court
62. Be like a two-year-old
64. Glimpse
65. Roadside breather
69. Uncle Martin feature
73. You might put them on
74. Since
75. Harbor
76. Hold onto
78. Working
81. Cashier concern
82. Big talker, for short
83. Pooh's pal
84. Jab
85. Black and Red
86. Marsh grass

DOWN

1. Party people
2. Bandleader Shaw
3. Garners
4. Wrestling move
5. Abnormal
6. Camera call
7. Bound
8. Granola grain
9. Curses!
10. Puffy ball
11. Not nice
12. Capture
13. It goes downhill
15. Classify
17. Plumber's dilemma
24. Associates
26. Determined in advance
28. Parsley piece
29. Actor Ziering
32. Spot
33. White rock
34. Bomb procedure
35. Hint
36. Mexican toppers
37. Opened
39. Cambridge carriage
41. Brink
42. Ring around the cellar
44. Echoing bird
47. Pay attention
48. Robin Leach used to show it
50. It goes with Mac
53. Seaver stat
58. Even break
59. 1/6 of an inning
61. Dreaded fly
63. Ye gods!
66. Restaurant request
67. Made eyes at
68. Meter men?
69. Each
70. Forbidden thing
71. Hike
72. Collection
73. Gone fishing
77. Part of a royal flush
79. Herr, in England
80. Grow

★ **Solution on page 313**

14A, 20A, 36A, 46A, 62A, 65A, 58D, 69D, 70D

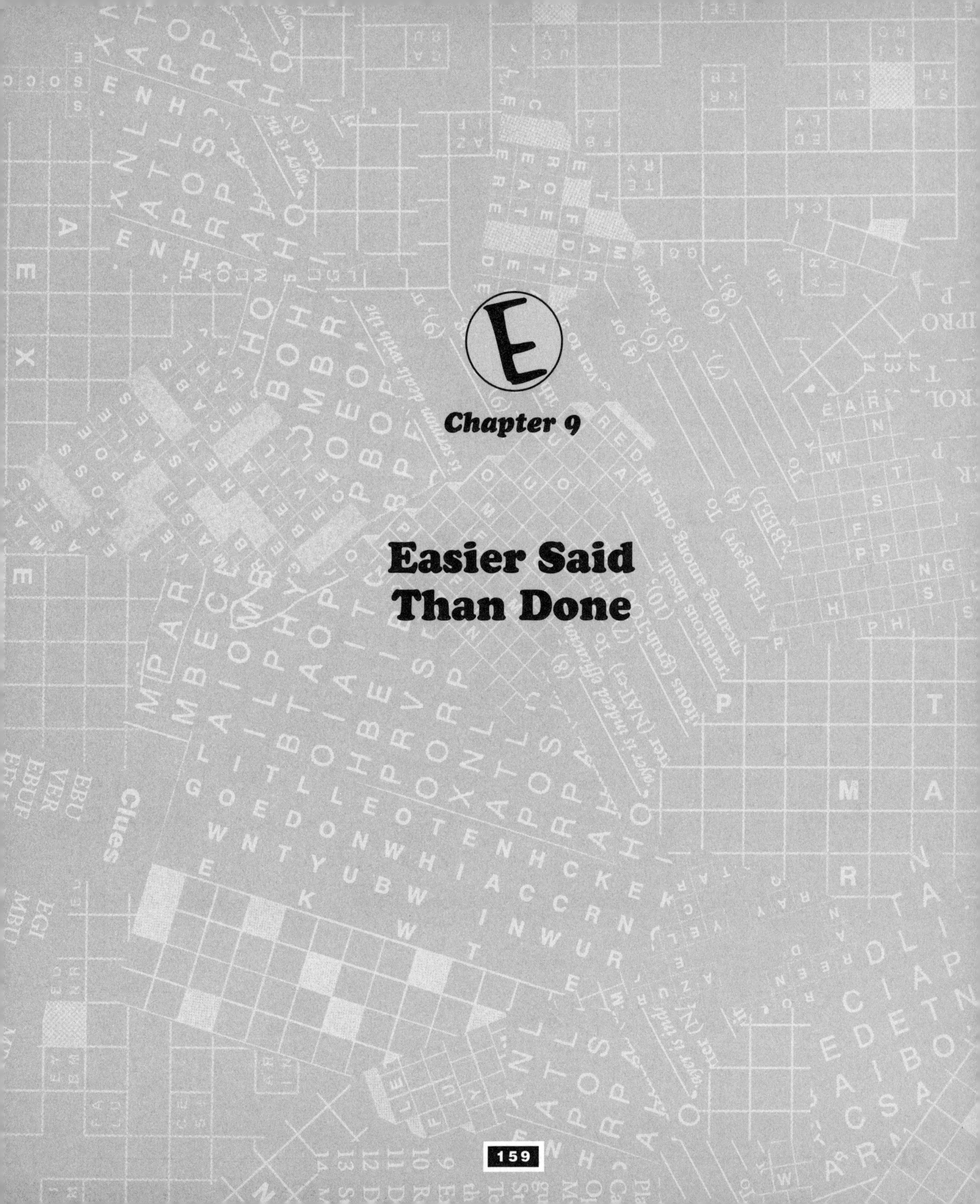

Chapter 9

Easier Said Than Done

Crucial

ACROSS

1. Crucial
4. It might tingle
9. Hammett hound
13. Shirley MacLaine title film role
17. Playwright Levin
18. Domesticated
19. Cel mate
20. Highway sign
21. Nothing
22. Steamed
23. Species
24. Amusement park feature
25. Oh boy!
26. Choke
27. You might get them polished
29. Hacienda
30. Flexible
33. Away from the elements
35. Reaction to a rodent
36. Unjust
38. They get fleeced
40. Trademarked building block
42. Lay off
43. Praise
45. It comes in litres
49. Fireplace tool
51. Experiences
53. Good seller?
54. Choice
56. Olympic cry
57. The Company
58. *Evita* role
61. Removes one's coat
62. Fess up
64. Acquaintance
65. Singular stable snack
66. "Just the Way You ___"
67. Moved around
70. *Psycho* screechers
72. Encourage
73. It's a matter of principle
77. Weather impacter
78. Less ancient
80. It lasts seven days
81. Change things
83. Purges
84. Latino enclave in California
86. Good name for a motivator?
89. Draw out
91. Over there
93. Clinton beleaguerer
95. On no occasion
97. Make it go "vroom"
98. *Models,* ___
101. China setting
102. Helpful one
103. Tradition
105. Tango team
106. Mardi Gras preceder
107. Dancer's aid
108. Troublesome toddler
109. Atypical
110. Capture a 1 Down
111. Misplaces one's trust
112. Strain
113. Charge

DOWN

1. He can go in any direction
2. Part of HOMES
3. Certain securer
4. Dishonor
5. Illustrative story
6. Projector's projection
7. Take down
8. Forbidden fruit site
9. Carbo-concerned doc
10. Dirties
11. It tends to dangle
12. "Is there anything else?"
13. She plays Phoebe's mom on *Friends*
14. Leader who left
15. Do a crabwalk
16. Carnivore's order
28. *Do the Right Thing* actor
29. Did nothing
31. Steamed
32. Go through QA again
34. Bank shot?
36. Cleo's killer
37. The big Red one
39. Alas!
41. Some stocks, for short
44. Mulder's case load
46. Triangular tool
47. *The Grapes of Wrath* extra
48. Meager
50. Those left
52. Caught
53. Altruistic
55. Frying option
58. Shoreline shelter
59. Pelting prediction
60. 007's alma mater
63. Struggling to stay awake
68. Light up
69. Seek water
71. Golfer's concern
74. Oust
75. Alice's boss
76. Rap sheet acronym
79. He takes things back
82. Less large
83. Fascinates
85. British plug
86. Biblical verse
87. In a quandary
88. Befoul
90. Closet material
92. Deliver an address
94. Consultant's concern
96. Contraptionist Goldberg
99. Au naturel
100. A ring might help you break it
102. Homer's dad
104. Half of boxcars

★ Solution on page 314

72A, 77A, 84A, 3D, 39D, 44D, 55D, 74D, 87D

1	2	3	■	4	5	6	7	8	■	9	10	11	12	■	13	14	15	16
17			■	18					■	19				■	20			
21			■	22					■	23				■	24			
25			■	26			■	27	28				■	29				
■	■	30	31				32	■	33				34		■	35		
36	37					■	38	39			■	40			41	■	■	■
42				■	43	44				■	■	■	45			46	47	48
49				50	■	51				52	■	53						
■	■	■	54		55						■	56			■	57		
58	59	60	■	61					■	62	63				■	64		
65			■	66			■	67	68						69	■	■	■
70			71				■	72					■	73		74	75	76
77						■	■	■	78				79	■	80			
■	■	■	81			82	■	83				■	84	85				
86	87	88	■	89			90			■	91	92					■	■
93			94		■	95				96	■	97			■	98	99	100
101				■	102				■	103	104				■	105		
106				■	107				■	108					■	109		
110				■	111				■	112					■	113		

It's almost a sure thing

ACROSS

1. Metric mass
5. "Rock of ___"
9. Runner gp., for short
12. Academy pupil
17. Judge
18. Pro ___
19. Suffer
20. Like blarney
21. Discharge
22. Lumpy fuel
23. Murmur
24. Slightly cold
25. Cloister
27. Prebirthday picture takers, for short
28. Escaped detection
30. Try to go home
31. Afrikaner
33. Asset or debit
34. Battleship call
37. "All right!"
38. Manage
41. '60s dance
43. Do away with
44. Do away with
47. Dershowitz of the defense
48. Five-O farewells
51. Defy
53. Yenta's gift
54. Met
56. Jason's wife
57. "And I Love ___"
59. Uniform
60. Early bird gp., for short
62. They make you 19 Across
64. Soft drink
65. Parked one's self
66. Connection
68. Learning centers
70. Nail holder
72. Medley
74. Type of band
75. Pen
76. Construct
77. Mushroom maker
79. Sumptuous
81. Swinger's setup
83. Sand timer collector on '95 TV
86. With wax, it makes a crayon
87. Simmer
90. Small songbird
91. Spiked
93. Want
95. Author Fleming
96. Word in a triangle
97. Biblical verb
100. Solidify
101. Straitlaced
103. Author Carnegie
104. Wind collectors
105. Stage lover
106. Singer Horne
107. Motivators
108. Bandleader Shaw
109. Fight ender, for short
110. Hipper than hip
111. Parking lot problem

DOWN

1. ___ spoon
2. Gang fight of old
3. Outs
4. Apportioned
5. Jackson Five song
6. It's almost a sure thing
7. In love with
8. Ends the mystery
9. Tempo
10. Garlicky sauce
11. Pull
12. Movies
13. Not damp
14. It might be in the road
15. Sixth sense, for short
16. Biblical pronoun
26. Naval clerk
29. TV Malcolm's at-home brother
32. TV Malcolm's at-home brother
34. '50s fad
35. Rossellini
36. Malleable metal
39. View
40. Disintegrating
42. Label
43. Leg part
45. Military sequence starter
46. Ball balancers
48. Mars counterpart
49. Place to go
50. Paired
52. Punish politically
55. Western
58. Spate
61. Vex
63. "Get lost!"
64. Search carefully
67. Along for the ride
69. Hideous
71. Anti-smog org., for short
72. Sport events
73. Won over
75. Food fish
78. What 71 Down does
80. Insidious insect
82. ___ Crown
83. Species spoiler
84. Snitch
85. Least predictable
88. ___ *Is Enough*
89. Inflict
92. With a little help from my friends
93. Cold-cut cutter
94. Sea saint
97. Jamboree gp., for short
98. Jug handle
99. Vamoose, varmint
102. Could

★ Solution on page 314

54A, 66A, 77A, 81A, 6D, 34D, 50D, 67D, 83D, 84D

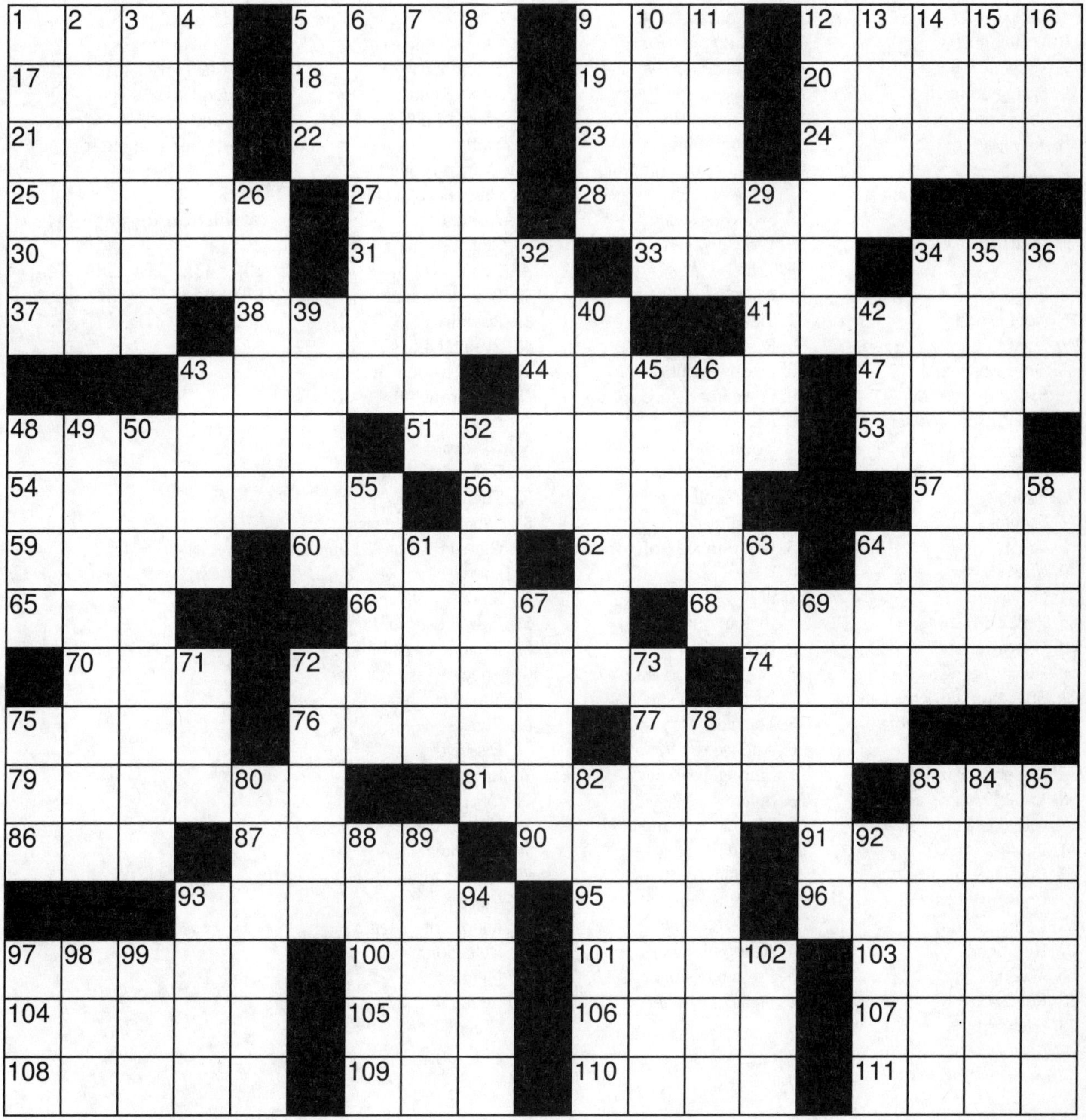

And we're off!

ACROSS

1. Taxi riders
6. Writer Tolstoy
9. Volcanic fallout
12. Spring flower
17. Take pride
18. Yale grad
19. ___ Speedwagon
20. Susan's Emmy role, eventually
21. Basic
23. Wise
25. Steered
26. Not flushed
27. Lucy's cohort
28. Odie's owner
29. Fencing maneuver
30. Giger-influenced sci-fi
31. Rand-McNally publications
32. Fable teller
35. Tributes
37. Spiteful
39. Group
40. Nast's boss?
42. Occupied
46. Parlor drinks?
48. Gathering
50. Deck coating
51. They come to conclusions
53. Former GI, for short
54. Helms's bane
55. Dissect
58. Ernie Kovacs's celebrity wife
61. Impress
62. Russian high-flyer
63. Court exhibits
65. Dandy brandy
67. NFP needs
68. Massage
72. Kent's cohort
73. Intended
74. Triumph for a tyke
75. Spot of land
77. Unbearable waits
80. It's meant for passing
81. Complain
84. Last name in photography . . .
86. . . . and matching first name
88. Swinger's swing
89. Verne's variety
90. Calm
91. It's sticky
94. Ties
96. Release
98. Broadway hit of '77
99. Presenter before a club
100. Rage
101. Clarence, for one
102. Like most films
103. Make a blooper
104. Embarrassed
105. Like one side of a tree

DOWN

1. Pick up on
2. Bar in a car
3. Wanted to do over
4. Nightmarish street
5. Volunteer
6. And we're off!
7. Smiling, probably
8. Smarmy
9. The Little Mermaid
10. Guard
11. Short-fused one
12. Undress
13. Indy's objective
14. Action film extra
15. Pressman's plum
16. Signs of disinterest
22. Menu item near poori and paratha
24. Coop users
29. Track down
30. Surrounded
31. Word bird
32. Workout muscles
33. "Xanadu" band
34. Gardener's supply
36. And so on
38. Business suit add-on
41. Adapt
43. Bracelet's center
44. Look like
45. Eventful times
47. Tribal healers
48. Go through the roof
49. #4 of the Bruins
50. Observed
52. Run of De Mille
53. Tries to win
55. Sancho's sandwich
56. G.I. who's bugged out, for short
57. Storage containers
59. Illegal insecticide
60. Relating to canines
64. They're easily swayed
66. Young singer
67. Pursue
69. Dissolve
70. Brouhaha
71. George's V.P.
73. Help settle
76. Shoe item
78. "It's in my ___"
79. Caught
80. It's out of order
81. Detection
82. Fight site
83. Attempter's admission
85. Greedy one
87. Yom Kippur list element
89. Strip off
90. ___ *Crazy*
91. Cranberry sites
92. Exploits
93. Trust
95. It makes an impression
97. Beatle beau

★ Solution on page 314

23A, 42A, 55A, 58A, 74A, 89A, 94A, 96A, 5D, 6D, 36D, 38D, 41D, 67D, 83D

1	2	3	4	5	■	6	7	8	■	9	10	11	■	12	13	14	15	16
17					■	18			■	19			■	20				
21					22				■	23			24					
25			■	26					■	27					■	28		
■	■	■	29					■	30					■	31			
32	33	34			■	35		36		■	37			38		■	■	■
39				■	■	■	■	40		41			■	42		43	44	45
46				47	■	48	49					■	50					
■	■	■	51		52						■	53			■	54		
55	56	57							■	58	59				60			
61			■	62			■	63	64							■	■	■
65			66			■	67						■	68		69	70	71
72					■	73					■	■	■	■	74			
■	■	■	75		76			■	77		78	79	■	80				
81	82	83		■	84			85		■	86		87			■	■	■
88			■	89					■	90					■	91	92	93
94			95						■	96					97			
98					■	99			■	100			■	101				
102					■	103			■	104			■	105				

Take five

ACROSS

1. Diving platforms
7. A gas guzzler has a low one
10. WWII enlistee
13. Authorize
17. Allocate
18. Operate
19. Pub pint
20. 6/6/44
21. The best of all worlds
22. Spade of literature
23. Files
25. Stanley Cup group, for short
26. Dent
28. Flower part
29. Yes vote
30. Norwegian capital
32. Pantries
35. Jelly ___ Morton
37. Gladstone rival
39. Duos
42. Chow down
45. Take five
47. Alleviates
48. Fictional
50. Trunk
52. Good name for a TV actress?
53. Sprint rival
54. Remote
56. Think tank members
58. "Doggie in the Window" singer
61. Funny in the head
65. Will responder
67. Young goat
68. It alters at the altar
69. "Let me in!" demander
72. Most slight
73. Fight
75. Puts up
77. Mr. T has one
81. Collected leaves
82. Business suit for a knight
83. Yale's locale
85. From the start
87. Frequent flyer
88. Carve
92. Bill
94. Asner role
96. Slumber partier
98. Orange or lime
99. It might be in disguise
101. Apropos
103. Narrate
105. Drench
106. "Weekend Update" show
107. Diamond ___
108. Brought home the bacon
109. Scrawny
110. "The way"
111. Bar cubes
112. Lint sifters

DOWN

1. *Fame* role
2. Swears
3. Ring around the water
4. Split open
5. Whack
6. Slowpokes
7. "___ Love"
8. Spot of assistance
9. Precious rock
10. Trudges through water
11. Loads
12. Leader Chavez
13. Reagan proposal, for short
14. Betterment belief
15. Radar portrayer
16. Wall St. concern, for short
24. Ski spot
27. *Fame* actress
28. Held one
31. Big-tongued one
33. *Gidget* star
34. Raise one's spirits
36. Most recent
38. Troubled
40. Yo-ho-ho drink
41. Espionage agent
42. Disposal site
43. Native Peruvian
44. "True ___"
46. Singer Clapton
47. Go ballistic
49. Pin spots
51. Slurp
55. Compete
56. Tackles
57. Last
59. Nothing sticks to it
60. Pacific isle
62. Danger
63. Minding one's own business
64. Dorm occupant
66. Different
69. *Girl Fight* org.
70. "___ House"
71. Vegetable soup item
74. Rational
76. Sediment
78. Tannery tool
79. Carve wood
80. Welles title role
84. Swerved
86. Band site?
87. ___-Saxon
89. To ___ own self be true
90. Less repulsive
91. Listens to
92. Cooking amt.
93. Baseball brother
95. ___ Karenina
97. Close
100. UFO locale
101. *Girl Fight* gal
102. Shot, for short
104. Show remorse

★Solution on page 314

20A, 42A, 45A, 47A, 58A, 68A, 83A, 5D, 11D, 38D, 47D, 56D, 71D

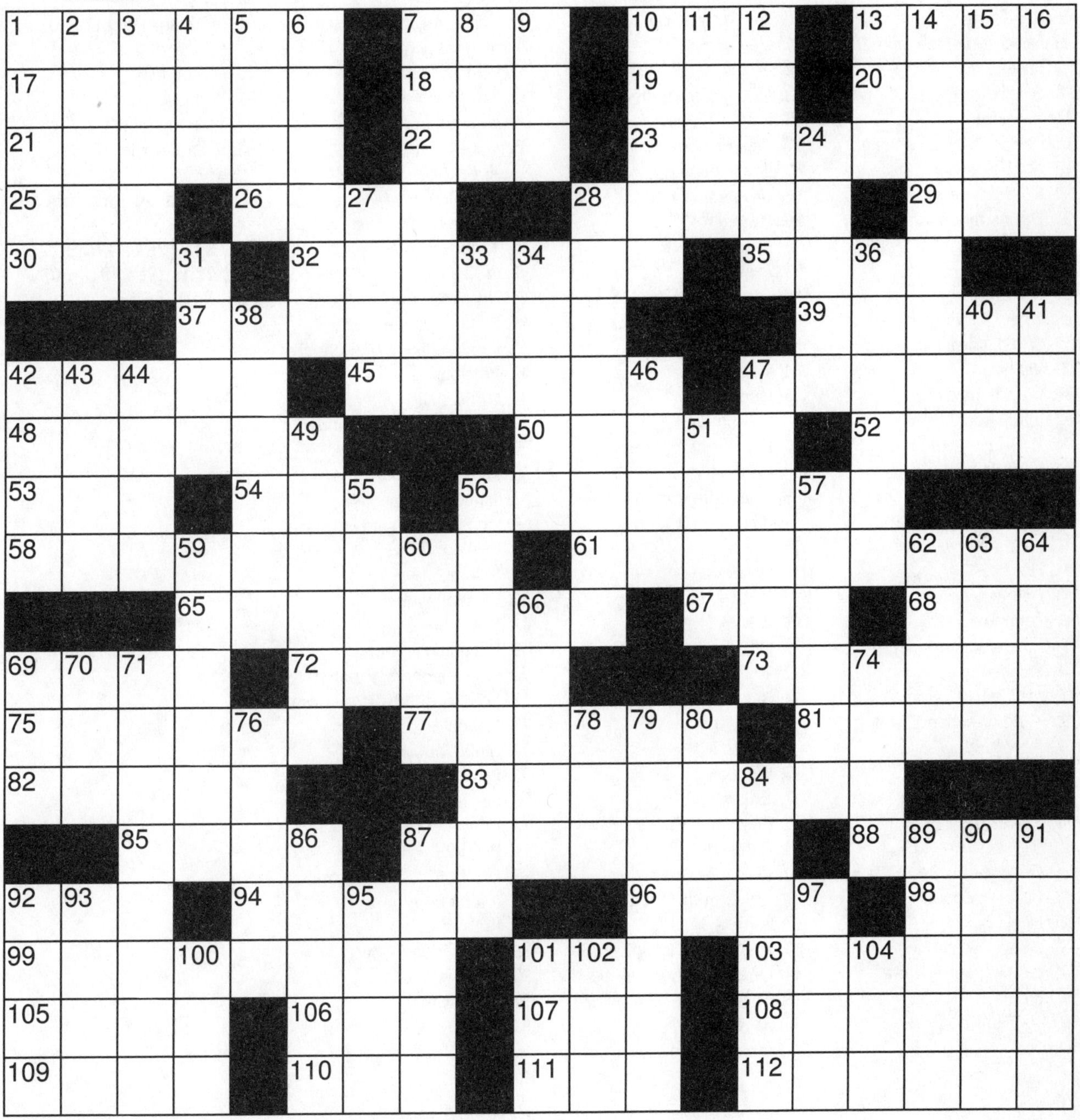

Impulsive

ACROSS

1. Set down
5. Napoleon's new home
9. Fuse units
13. Solicits
17. ___ Lisa
18. Person, place, or thing
19. Actress Taylor
20. Sci-fi princess
21. Doer's motto
22. Whiz
23. Impulsive
24. Dweeb
25. Folger's foe
27. G.E.D. taker
29. Wait on
30. It ends in a cuff
32. Film short
34. Extend
36. Implicates
37. Finance degree, for short
40. Where the cows are
43. Map abbreviation
44. Hot cross ___
45. Call at a hotel
47. Lummox
48. Pina colada topper
50. Smattering
51. Mesopotamia today
53. "The Wasteland" writer
57. Stew holder
58. Urban ___
60. Band offering
61. It goes with "Am not!"
65. "___ Rose"
66. Leftover
68. Novelist Koontz
69. Ike's rival
72. It's worth ten eagles
74. Banking automaton, for short
75. ___ and home
77. Florist's receptacle
80. *Toy Story* villain
81. "___ Bangs"
82. Tree flow-er
83. One in the draft?
85. His and hers
87. Baja or Coney Island
89. Beetle bauble
93. Catcher's catch
96. Panorama
98. Bridge expert?
99. Luau land
100. At what time?
101. Each
103. 99 Across, for one
104. Tiller pullers
105. Quest
106. Danish dam
107. Binds
108. General idea
109. Goes one way or the other
110. Tread
111. Desires

DOWN

1. Off
2. Townie
3. Ridiculous
4. Fuel ferry
5. Extremity
6. Burden
7. Excavate
8. Playwright Chekhov
9. Contender
10. Regal dances
11. China in the round
12. Sample
13. His heroes are self-made
14. One who knows things
15. Chicken ___
16. Salty drink
26. Ward off
28. The Andes go through it
29. Six-year position
31. Give the right
33. Knee-high to a grasshopper
35. Wiggly swimmers
37. *A Few Good* ___
38. Spy's plant
39. Mirror
40. Teri's TV role
41. O.K. survivor
42. Not close up
44. Southern siren
46. Floated, like a bad check
49. Precious
52. OPEC nation
54. Thomas Watson founded it
55. Prevention unit
56. Mint specialist
57. Jamaican treats
59. Houston who sings
62. Bigelow brews
63. Solemn vow
64. Treating words
67. Snack
69. Delighted sounds
70. Mule catchers, for short
71. Spot to hear a story from
73. Mandate
76. Attila cohort
77. Price of the movies
78. Sis, in America
79. Phaser setting
84. Provide
85. Doom for some dinosaurs
86. It ain't common
87. Put on a coat
88. What cops follow
90. Riveting one?
91. Burns's mate
92. Sanctify
93. Air with a bite
94. Show for Henner and Hirsch
95. Is repentant
97. Bondage
100. Which people?
102. Squad provision

★**Solution on page 314**

21A, 32A, 36A, 45A, 53A, 61A, 72A, 101A, 9D, 56D, 64D, 84D, 85D

1	2	3	4	■	5	6	7	8	■	9	10	11	12	■	13	14	15	16
17				■	18				■	19				■	20			
21				■	22				■	23				■	24			
25				26	■	27			28				■	29				
30					31	■	32						33			■	■	■
■	■	■	34			35		■	36						■	37	38	39
40	41	42	■	43			■	44				■	45		46			
47			■	48			49		■	■	■	■	■	50				
51			52	■	53				54	55	56	■	57			■	■	■
58				59		■	60					■	61			62	63	64
■	■	■	65			■	66					67		■	68			
69	70	71			■	■	■	■	■	72				73	■	74		
75					76	■	77	78	79		■	80			■	81		
82			■	83		84				■	85				86	■	■	■
■	■	■	87							88		■	89			90	91	92
93	94	95			■	96						97	■	98				
99				■	100				■	101			102	■	103			
104				■	105				■	106				■	107			
108				■	109				■	110				■	111			

Words to live by

ACROSS

1. Winter wrap
6. Break
9. Bloom County fellow
13. Cushioned comfort
17. Morning delivery
18. Fiscal
20. Class teacher, briefly
21. ___ the law
22. Conjecture
23. Go no further
24. Like washer water
26. *Witchblade* airer
27. Hit French film
29. Spaniel say-so
32. Girl of the ball
33. Michigan city
35. Harvest
37. Private ___
39. True pro
41. Shirt size
43. Sight
45. Highland hat
48. Take a snooze
49. Like much of *The Osbornes*
51. Big name in fruit
52. Fen-phen firers, for short
54. Many-lived ones
55. Words to live by
57. 'allo, Henri
61. Embrace
62. Bear
63. Again!
64. Kind of bonding
65. Car makers, for short
66. Jazz style
67. Lack
70. Hitch hastily
75. Scone go-with
76. Bed liners
77. Shimmered
78. "Walk on the Wild Side" singer
81. Took in
83. It might be strung along
84. Two-master
87. Ill. neighbor
89. Not damp
90. Chicken options
91. "Just as I suspected!"
94. Admit
96. Tears
97. Involved
100. Dracula, for one
104. Purina rival
105. Atypical
106. Boo-boo
107. He gets no respect
108. Assigned bit of work
109. Sticky something
110. Actor Quaid

DOWN

1. Refreshing water
2. He sang about Minnie
3. G.I. address, for short
4. Versions, for short
5. Cigar defender
6. Ekes out a living
7. Pained
8. "The Raven" author
9. A.M.
10. Wannabes, often
11. Smith of the papers
12. ___ *Eleven*
13. Crichton book
14. Dental brand
15. Page number
16. Following
19. "___ on your life!"
25. Judge
28. Tumbler's pad
29. Military supply
30. Folk dance
31. Lessen
34. Late dinner hour
36. ___ à la mode
38. Night
39. Savaged
40. Clothes for a demonstration
42. Ready to do
44. Accountable
45. Loose garment
46. Actor Guinness
47. Go well
49. Ferry taker
50. Statistics
51. Hoover, for one
53. They need to be paid
56. Peg
57. Most accomplished
58. ___ in a while
59. "March Madness" org., for short
60. Scribble
62. Take to court
64. Runs the panel
68. 68 Down
69. Group for young gals, for short
71. Tennis shot
72. Was indebted to
73. Lute-shaped fruit
74. Water wrinkle
77. Fellow
78. Enters the Web
79. "Nice fireworks!"
80. Oust an in
82. Linked
84. Leash
85. The Andes go through it
86. Heavy herbivore, briefly
88. Kitchen gadget
92. Listen up!
93. Tune
94. Letterman rival
95. Role for Myrna
98. It has the Jazz, for short
99. Holdup
101. Big holder
102. Concur
103. Give it a go

★ **Solution on page 314**

33A, 78A, 94A, 6D, 14D, 40D, 42D, 44D, 78D, 82D

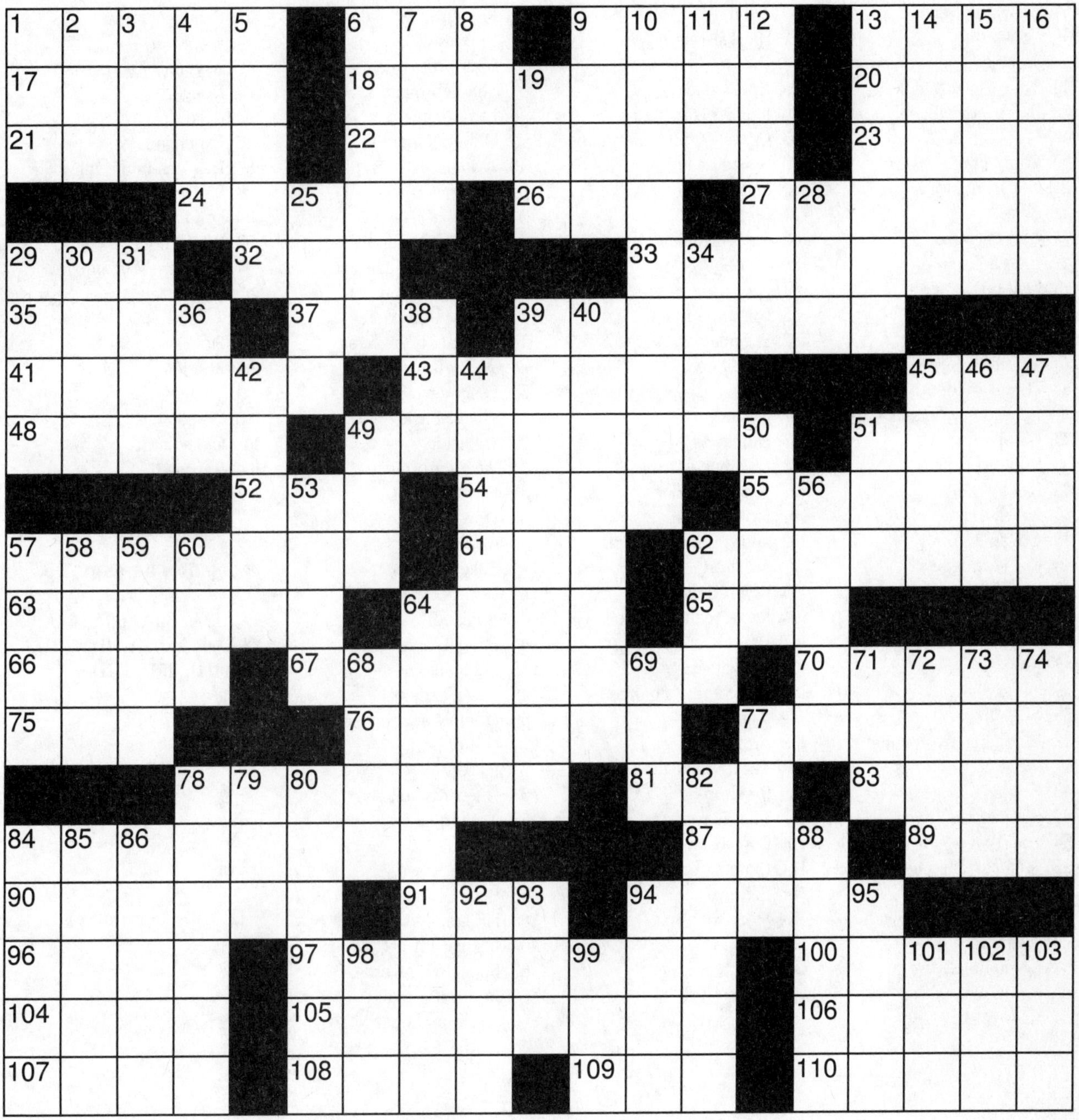

Despicable

ACROSS

1. Ad-writing venture
6. Osaka one
9. Tumble
14. They go with tucks
18. Bruce's daughter
19. Per
20. Camp craft
21. Left's org., for short
22. Beneath
23. ___ *Pinafore*
24. Hill chain
25. Leaf line
26. Counter-shove
27. Diner setting
29. Till fill
30. Flower holders
31. Ringy-dingy person
33. If not
34. Kimono cloth
35. Ball
36. Israeli airline
38. Goose liver
40. Car loan letters
43. Beat for Estefan
46. A couple of bucks
47. Carrier
48. As well
49. Oahu outing
50. ___ *Street*
52. It helps get you going, for short
53. Examine
54. Puts forward
56. Good name for a driver
57. Features of some chairs
59. School coop
60. Diner's road sign with "Get gas"
62. Egyptian veep
63. Proportion
64. Early MRE
66. Tartar studier, for short
69. Thorough
72. Breakfast item
73. Ha!
75. Abel's dad
76. It isn't clear
77. Cry after ringing a triangle
79. Bowie beau
80. Part of L.A.
81. Prepared
82. Top Olympian
83. Throng
84. Fool pitier
85. Dummy's perch
87. Salamander
88. Cruz's cry
89. Drop
91. Onslaught
93. Funniness
98. Revamped
100. Self-centered
101. Frog homes
102. 2nd Amendment gp., for short
103. Revered one
104. Plane seating choice
105. Drag
106. Less at risk
108. *Gong Show*'s dance machine
109. Armada
110. They amuse the troops, for short
111. That is to say . . .
112. Comeback
113. Clothing or item for bed
114. Perceive
115. Store supply

DOWN

1. Disney dog
2. Amassed
3. Decide
4. Precious concealer
5. Ringo's wife
6. Swift brute
7. Shade providers
8. Lama/llama guy
9. Old document
10. Twinges
11. Committed
12. Registers
13. Tommy ___ Jones
14. Kind of engagement
15. Fleming's footwear
16. Bend at the knees
17. Phoenix hoopsters
28. Wager taker, for short
30. Fought
32. Mounteback
33. Set aside
34. Weather protector
37. Part of AWOL
39. Does *Antiques Roadshow* work
41. Bulletin
42. Decays
43. Applaud
44. Fling a king
45. LEM launcher
46. Down-and-out
50. Monthly account summary
51. Full of pep
52. Players
53. Offensive holiday?
55. Not virtual
58. Tirade
61. Did farm work
63. Rotation rate, for short
65. Humphrey successor
66. It's just for show
67. Showdown word
68. Put in the mail
69. Storm preceder
70. Unpleasant emanation
71. Extinct giants
74. Employer
78. Asylum of sorts
81. Dodge
83. ___ car
86. Expunged
87. Degrees in a right angle
88. 83 Down
90. Load carriers
92. Was unwell
94. Bar from Fort Knox
95. Conclude
96. Take the tab
97. Stories
98. Residence
99. Thought
100. Despicable
101. Outlet item
104. Rearward
107. Physicians' affiliation, for short

★Solution on page 315

1A, 19A, 36A, 60A, 64A, 73A, 84A, 98A, 111A, 2D, 7D, 11D, 15D, 34D

1	2	3	4	5		6	7	8		9	10	11	12	13		14	15	16	17
18						19				20						21			
22						23				24						25			
26				27	28					29					30				
31			32						33					34					
			35				36	37				38	39				40	41	42
43	44	45				46							47				48		
49					50					51		52				53			
54				55				56				57			58				
59				60			61					62							
			63						64		65						66	67	68
69	70	71							72				73			74			
75					76				77			78				79			
80				81						82					83				
84				85			86		87					88					
		89	90				91	92				93	94				95	96	97
98	99					100					101						102		
103					104						105				106	107			
108					109						110				111				
112					113						114				115				

Lay it on the line

ACROSS

1. Attack watchers, for short
6. Chew the fat
9. Great one?
14. Weight
18. Iowa commune
19. "___ to Billy Joe"
20. Prohibited
21. Aloud
22. View unlike *Green Acres*
24. Rival
25. Reply to the Little Red Hen
26. Actress Bassett or Lansbury
27. Verse
29. Gulf off Iran
30. Silence
33. Plant
36. Fetid
37. Eats
40. Toe woe
41. Person in "Matchmaker"
43. Compadre
45. Ceasefire
47. Made use of
51. Given entrance
53. Bruce Bannon's weak spots
55. Holy town?
56. Nervous
57. Naysayer
59. Actress Lesley ___ Warren
60. One who gives
62. Eye test
63. Woe is me!
64. Like some R movies
67. Trace
70. Poker "out"
73. Fred Astaire's daughter
74. Same
78. Plan
82. Recent Winter Olympics site
84. Children
85. Galore
86. They buffet buffets
88. Join
90. Available
91. Split
92. Liturgy lecture
94. "Quite impressive!"
95. Group often played in *Muriel's Wedding*
98. Cry for help
100. Vicious fishes
101. Gator kin
102. Nile city
104. Plane place
110. Elevated
111. Fair-colored
113. It's out of whack
116. Actress Falco
117. Deserves and gets
118. Fawn's mom
119. Wonder Woman's alias
120. A Cub Scout might do a good one
121. Bird word
122. Male offspring
123. Modify

DOWN

1. Wine region
2. Sign
3. Pealed
4. Play along
5. Willy Wonka's writer
6. The reader
7. Airing providers
8. Do domestic chores
9. Exorbitant
10. Recycled items
11. Follows
12. Writer Clancy
13. Chest item
14. Sightseer's ride
15. What the nose knows
16. "Church Lady" detection
17. Skulk
23. Diamond Head's site
28. Baby bottle units
31. Golden Rule word
32. Knighted one's title
34. Decide on
35. Times in line
37. Head light?
38. Prayer closing
39. Spot
40. What a beatnik might beat
42. Story mover
44. Lightheaded
46. Lack of difficulty
47. Common carrier
48. Enthusiasm
49. Mrs. Krabapple
50. Gets into
52. X
54. Scramble
57. Photo shop pickup
58. Gremlin
61. Have obligations
63. Vail competitor
64. Crony crowd
65. Racetrack shape
66. Prego rival
68. It isn't pretty
69. Toll road
71. Unit of electricity
72. Hair care lair
74. Fascinated by
75. Slammers
76. Bleeper
77. Early video game
79. Not fooled by
80. State where coffee is often unsampled
81. Tit for tat?
83. Enclosed, via e-mail
85. Multitude
87. Two film roles for Keanu in '03
89. Memorable time
93. Corporate overseers, for short
95. Felt sore
96. White wearer
97. *Key Largo* star
99. Musical accompaniment
100. Hub
103. Queen Boleyn
105. *M*A*S*H* star
106. Ace
107. Pesty insect
108. Bothersome bumps
109. Backside
111. Lay it on the line
112. Bar concern
114. Calf cry
115. Actor Gazzara or Kingsley

★ Solution on page 315

25A, 30A, 51A, 56A, 70A, 78A, 90A, 8D, 47D, 79D

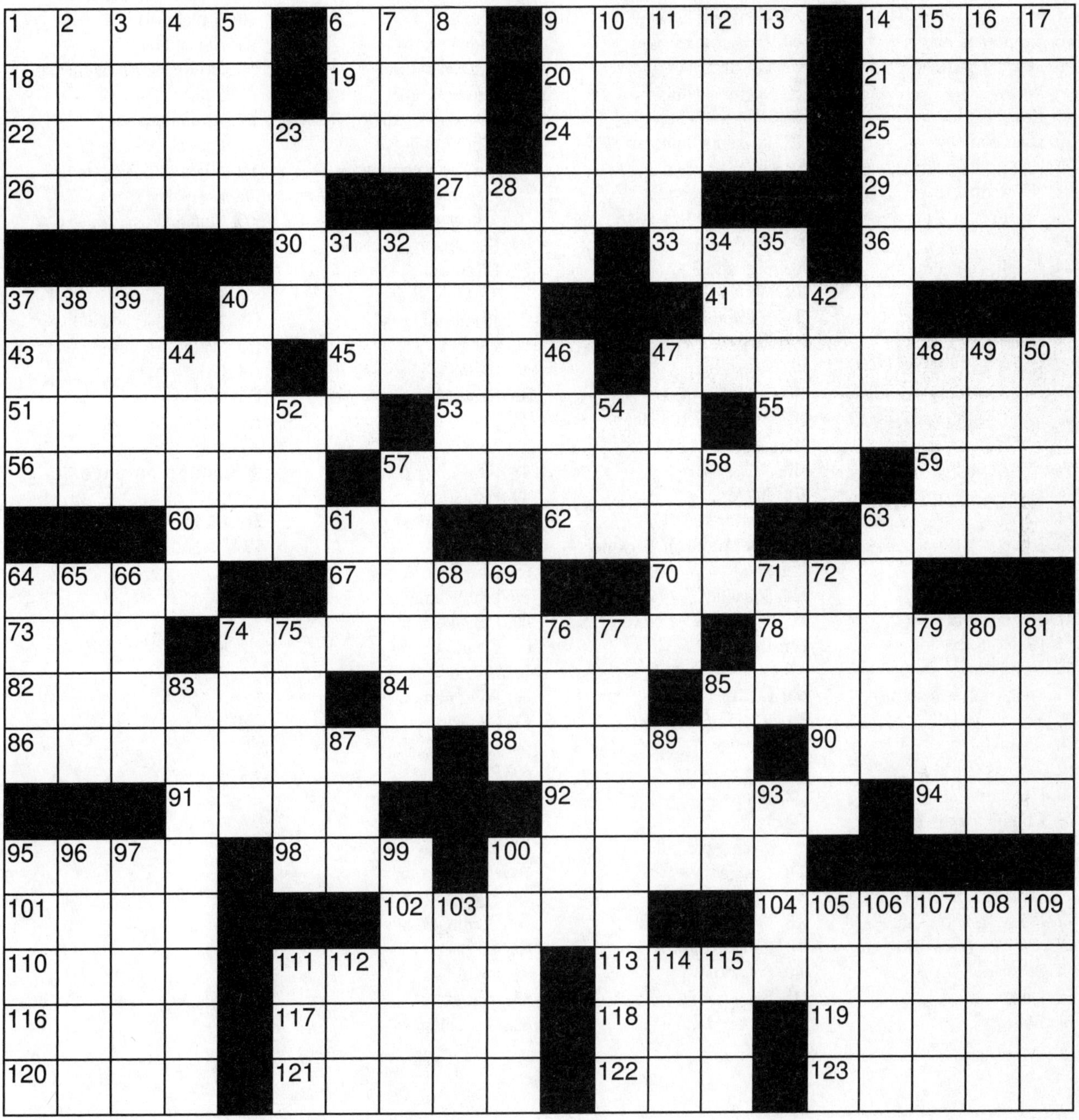

It's nothing, really

ACROSS

1. Mack, for one
6. Supportive one
9. Hockey items
14. Wrong
18. Keys
19. Lake maneuverer
20. The cruelest month
21. "How do I love ___?"
22. Attempts at a scene
23. Do a scene
24. Jungle charger
25. Ike's ex
26. Balki's cousin
28. Dire fate
29. Kirk's arm
31. Steak option
34. Craw or maw
36. Anchors wear them
37. Ham's period
38. Like some skirts
41. In a bit
43. Dollop
44. Like some eyes
45. Zsa Zsa verb
47. Easter roundup
51. Break down
53. Good buddy
54. Walkie-talkie response
56. Secretary skill
58. Shameful
62. Actress Grier
63. Hang ten
65. Cheers for the bullfighter
66. Must
68. Less bland
71. Gran
72. He sang about Alice
73. *The Joy Luck Club* author
74. Secures
77. Detaches
81. Accepts
83. Grower's tool
85. "___ – it is done"
86. "Where have you ___?"
87. Words from Caesar
89. Literary output
91. Role for Nancy
92. It has its highs and lows
94. Simple refrain
96. Potter's need
97. ___ the coop
100. Twirl
102. Skedaddle
104. Weather impacter
106. It's nothing, really
107. Surprise victory
109. Norse veep
110. Campfire treat
112. It may need testing
113. Leak
117. Lotion ingredient
118. Judges
119. Humor
120. The Ayatollah, for one
121. See to
122. Squalid
123. "___ Now or Never"
124. Defunct

DOWN

1. It needs assembly
2. Secretive U.S. org., for short
3. Genre
4. Probe
5. Writing piece
6. Luau entree
7. Off-color
8. Museum piece
9. Early release
10. Supports
11. Superhero's enemy
12. We are family
13. ___ the hogs
14. Got
15. Omelet need
16. Actress Zellweger
17. Age measure
27. Collection, briefly
28. Responsibility
30. Caregiver conglomerate, for short
31. Synonym collector
32. Keenen ___ Wayans
33. Dizzy Gillespie's forte
34. Treasure ships
35. Asian princess
39. Cut
40. Oh my!
42. Corkscrews
44. Real
46. Jar cover
48. Bilks
49. Feta source
50. Beefy battler
52. Part of DJ
55. Like Dick Clark?
57. Like lightning?
59. Delighted
60. Casino city
61. United
64. Fried munchie
67. Plunged
68. Effort
69. Book part
70. About
75. One's ___ in life
76. PBS show
78. *Cats* man
79. They go to the center
80. Commandment word
82. Interlaced
84. Sushi fish
88. Said aloud
89. U.S. alliance
90. Experimental places
93. A place to stay
95. Not often
96. Florida town, or further away
97. Parade entrant
98. Punchbowl dipper
99. It has many layers
101. Holey layer
103. Chilling
105. Tomb raiders?
107. Act or acre
108. Butter servings
111. West of Hollywood
112. MV no-no, for short
114. Livid
115. Solitary
116. Clear

★Solution on page 315

31A, 54A, 66A, 74A, 81A, 87A, 94A, 102A, 104A, 61D, 70D

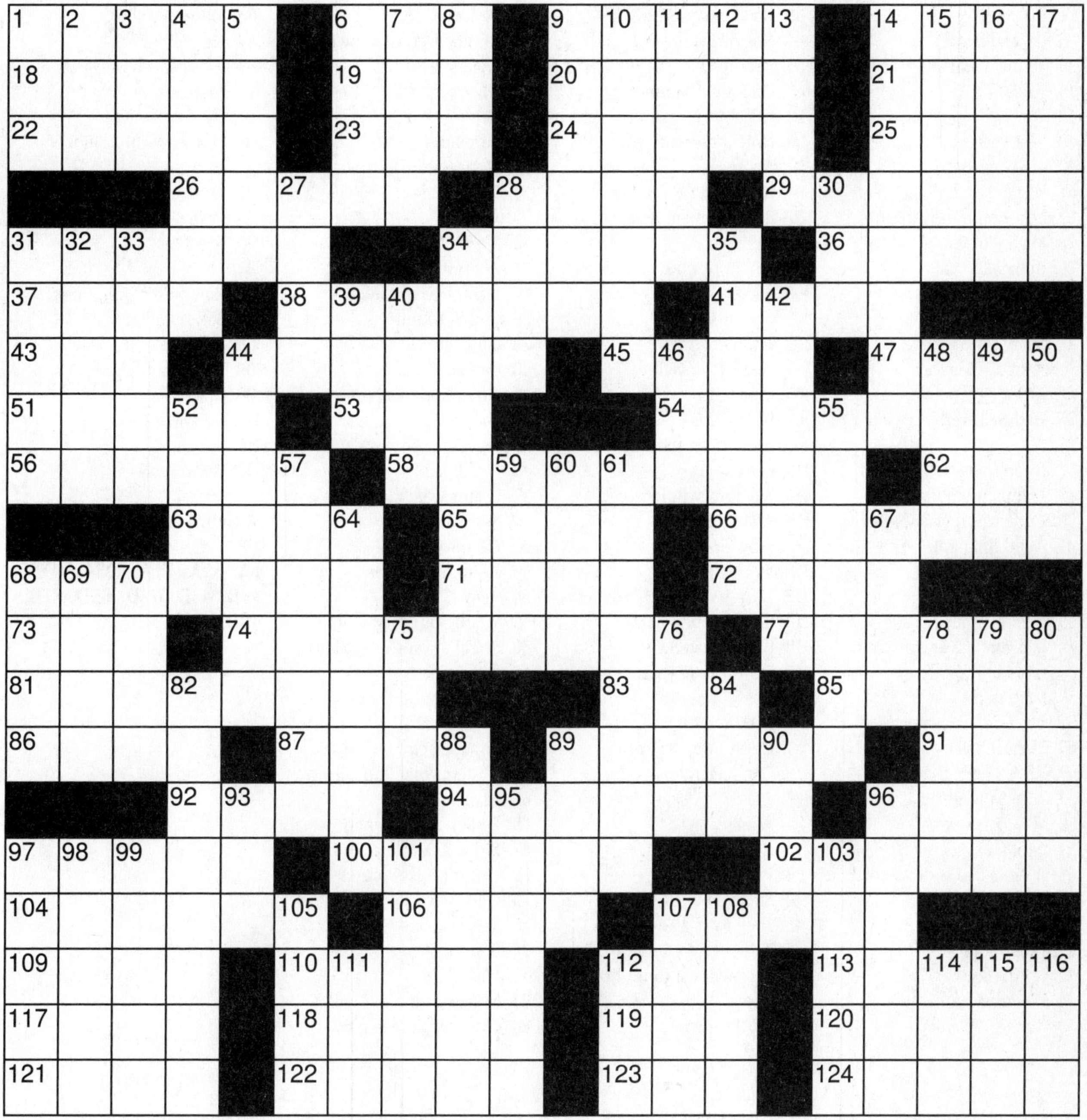

Crazy one

ACROSS

1. Irk
6. Ollie's friend
10. Tennis great
14. Assist
18. Top
19. Misplace
20. Crazy one
21. Wicked
22. Last name in fashion
23. Mighty trees
24. Ruth's TV foil
25. Descartes who was
26. Pluck
28. Ms. go-with, for short
30. Actress Fleming
32. Atom ___
35. Bad S&L verb
36. ___ trip
37. Depressing
38. Plague member
39. *Cat Ballou* Oscar winner
41. Need liniment
42. Tube for playing
44. ___ alarm
45. Recipe amt., for short
48. Mat maneuver, for short
49. Lincoln's spot
50. Sure thing
52. It's a real downer
55. Two-wheeler
57. Add a period
58. Took a load off
59. 55 Across part
61. Graduate degree
64. It feels like a downer
68. Stop at sea
70. Gun
71. Plus more, for short
72. Loan out
74. Place with trees
79. Type of monkey
82. "Send in the Clowns" start
83. News org. since 1958
84. Not divisible by 2
85. Relishes
88. Doubles champion?
89. Conspire in crime
90. Hotels have them
92. Approval
94. Like Christie's murders
97. Barbie's main squeeze
98. Sacrifice
99. It's more than skin deep
100. Social outcast
102. Cereal serving
103. Choice words
104. Hyde Park sight
105. Broadcast
107. Broadcasts
109. Away from the city
113. Leah's son
114. '96 Tony winner
115. A singer or pen pal might drop one
116. Steer clear of
117. *Harper Valley PTA* actress
118. She was born free
119. Bunny material
120. Film role for Sandler

DOWN

1. Get it away from me!
2. Completely
3. Twist ___
4. Significant
5. Agent's cuts
6. Pizza need
7. Stroll
8. How to get an answer
9. Topic for *In Search Of*
10. One with a Nome home
11. Upset
12. All the rage
13. Transporter request
14. Savior
15. Choice before showing fingers
16. Alice portrayer
17. Beg
27. Turns tail
29. They're for the poor
31. Pooh's love
32. Agenda
33. Makes fun of
34. Allergy sound
35. It may need mulch
36. Called to mind
39. Go easy
40. Castle
43. Grammarian's class, for short
45. Fracas
46. ___ milk
47. Critter watchdog, for short
49. Spiced tea
51. Go into
53. Church selection
54. Actor Connery
55. Woolly one's welcome
56. She'll always have Paris with Rick
60. Movie rental format
62. Total control
63. Smart-alecky
64. A steno might take one
65. Somewhat
66. Pantry staple, once
67. Striped purple pool ball
69. Destiny's Child and others
73. Harrow rival
75. Troop group, for short
76. Starchy growth
77. Flip
78. They catch flies
80. Major Japanese city
81. Ditto
86. Manicotti filler
87. Store
88. It doesn't hold water
89. Generally
91. Circular beach
93. Did worse than fidget in church
94. Where Jobs made jobs
95. Revealed
96. Must have
99. Part of an AAA item
101. Carpooler's comment
102. Storage items
103. They go with crafts
106. Brooks of comedy
108. Chit
110. Be sorry for
111. Sum
112. *WKRP* role

★ **Solution on page 315**

1A, 39A, 71A, 103A, 4D, 39D, 45D, 62D, 65D, 81D, 89D, 101D

1 2 3 4 5 6 7 8 9 10 11 12 13 14 15 16 17
18 19 20 21
22 23 24 25
26 27 28 29 30 31
32 33 34 35 36 37
38 39 40
41 42 43 44 45 46 47
48 49 50 51
52 53 54 55 56 57
58 59 60 61 62 63
64 65 66 67 68 69 70
71 72 73 74 75 76 77 78
79 80 81 82 83
84 85 86 87 88 89
90 91 92 93
94 95 96 97 98 99
100 101 102 103
104 105 106 107 108 109 110 111 112
113 114 115 116
117 118 119 120

Where you probably are now

ACROSS

1. Social stain
7. Ring veep
10. Li'l singer
13. Friendly
18. Baby food
19. To not buy this book
20. *Diamonds* ___ *Forever*
21. Where you probably are now
22. Reverse moats
23. Try to beat others
24. Tried to beat others
25. Like some dresses
26. Person of habit
27. It's in Oregon
29. Sea color
31. "Is the corned beef ___?"
32. Speed ___
33. Tubes that get served
35. Frigid
37. Stocking shade
40. Escaped
42. Big frozen chunk
46. Snarls
48. Living attire
49. Greetings
52. *Blazing Saddles* role
53. Escaped
55. Dessert with filling
57. Further
58. Kicked off
59. Expenditure
61. Blushing
62. Baby powder
64. Deal
65. Tempest locales?
68. Jeopardize
71. Went for home
72. Actress Raines
73. Hide ___ hair
74. Ambitious crossword tool
76. Foreign correspondent?
80. It's covered with enamel
83. Rural spot
85. Big wave
86. Actor Davis
87. Singer/politician
88. "Evil Woman" group
90. Auto shop purchase
91. Sob stories
93. Indy's hat
96. Deli counter cry
97. Cunning
98. Weight
100. What bees do
102. Not sharp
105. It's in red wax
107. Uplifting
109. Failing
112. Improved
114. Antagonism
115. Greetings
116. Pass
118. A way in
119. "Weekend Edition" broadcaster
120. Bush or Clinton
121. Scalawags
122. Car option
123. ___ cheese
124. Riddle
125. Saws wood

DOWN

1. Bridge
2. 1984 Peace Prize winner
3. Monopoly player piece
4. Come together
5. Battle
6. Guess
7. Money in
8. ___ go bragh!
9. ___ tag
10. Gold measure
11. *Three Kings* extra
12. Bill of fare
13. Sargasso ___
14. Underdog's voice
15. Lake or canal
16. Spewer in Sicily
17. In the past
28. Gee!
30. Not be so hot
32. He had a big nose
34. *High Sierra* actress
36. Arrived
37. Conclusion preceder
38. Apartment or henhouse
39. ___ of return
41. Casino cube
42. Do like Elvis
43. 100 series class, often
44. Marsh bird
45. Driving needs
47. Talk a blue streak
50. Reviled
51. Tin Man's request
54. It's not in the script
56. Counted to ten
60. Kennel calls
63. Goes up
64. D.C. channel
66. Certain Alaskan
67. Prospector's work
68. Along for the ride
69. Bullwinkle, for one
70. Text
75. Mogul, often
77. Trim
78. NYSE rival
79. Get an IPO
81. Hotline helpers
82. Loaf end
84. Marry
85. Rich cake
89. Flips out
92. Pastrami surrounder
94. Drew
95. 119 Across and 64 Down
98. Curly-haired comedian
99. ___ board
101. Hosiery material
102. Have a hunch
103. Star in *The Birdcage*
104. Dog in *The Thin Man*
106. Rackets
108. Hawaiian port
109. Steed sticker
110. Words of comprehension
111. Untouchable one
113. This changes everything
117. Early tale word

★ Solution on page 315

53A, 74A, 76A, 14D, 34D, 54D, 56D, 68D, 89D, 110D

1 2 3 4 5 6 7 8 9 10 11 12 13 14 15 16 17
18 19 20 21
22 23 24 25
26 27 28 29 30 31
32 33 34 35 36
37 38 39 40 41 42 43 44 45
46 47 48 49 50 51 52
53 54 55 56 57
58 59 60 61
62 63 64 65 66 67
68 69 70 71 72
73 74 75 76 77 78 79
80 81 82 83 84 85
86 87 88 89 90
91 92 93 94 95 96
97 98 99 100 101
102 103 104 105 106 107 108 109 110 111
112 113 114 115 116 117
118 119 120 121
122 123 124 125

Perfect scores

ACROSS

1. Big foot?
4. Seems appropriate
8. Advantage
13. *Life of ___*
18. Body checker, for short
19. Edible pod
20. Kind of bean
21. Popeil's marketing co.
22. Ingenue's dream
24. Musical sounds
25. Whispered greeting
26. It comes back
27. Through
29. Chinese food order
31. Business card abbreviation
32. Dog-eat-dog place
35. Anzac 'allo
37. Gotcha
39. Twisted
41. Ridicule
44. Flyers for HRH, for short
47. Lucy's partner
48. Wee one
51. They go on and on
52. Covering
54. Give the impression
56. Multistored entity
58. Dribble
59. First name in tennis
61. Uneasy
64. Trend watcher's concern
66. Point of view
67. Mohammed founded it
72. Guide
73. Scale
75. Uncooked
77. TV sitcom mom
80. Reenacts
81. "___ Old Black Magic"
85. Test answer
86. Contact people
88. Perfect scores
89. What we hold to be true
91. Lower digit
93. Light line
95. Light line
96. Acela owner
97. Its motto might be "Head down!"
100. Verb for after a power failure
102. Went down
104. Con collection
108. Touch-and-go ward, for short
110. Cross boss
112. Singer Janis
114. Part of SNL
115. Broadway brings it with the funk
117. Detached
119. Army pitchman
122. Mary-Kate or Ashley
123. 17 Down's role
124. Country bumpkin
125. Defense plan of the '80s, for short
126. Dubbed
127. Prepared to propose
128. Childish retort
129. "___ Sir! That's My Baby"

DOWN

1. It's hot and glowing
2. Susan's eventual Emmy soap role
3. "___ Days a Week"
4. Supporting
5. Likeable president
6. Go over
7. H. H. Munro's pen name
8. Competent
9. Armstrong's role on *Moonlighting*
10. Get under one's skin
11. Part of an agenda
12. Opening song in *Shrek*
13. Stork, supposedly
14. Poppycock
15. One way to take things
16. Wile E. Coyote's supplier
17. Carol's mate?
23. Star Trek foe
28. Period
30. Supply at a blood drive
33. "A Bushel ___ a Peck"
34. Mighty salad?
36. Banned crop aid
38. Periods
40. Told an untruth
42. Actress Wallace of *E.T.*
43. Odd way to pick things up, for short
44. Smoothing tools
45. Wore down
46. Area of expertise
49. Pump number
50. Yours might get stolen
51. Lama land
53. Seeger of song
55. Like Hanks as a villain?
57. Batter's swing
60. Social clod
62. Sound system
63. Lowdown
65. Family reunion attendees
68. Right away
69. Oktoberfest order
70. Rock concert venue
71. Needing a bib
74. Birthplace of the Bass-o-Matic, for short
76. Lay into
78. Like Roseanne's National Anthem
79. It counts against you
81. TV filler, for short
82. Edge
83. Do-gooder's pastime
84. Lose energy
87. Yearly
90. London section
92. Epic time
94. Phone company or Roman number
98. Take a powder?
99. Fit
101. Runner's sport
102. Show disinterest
103. Coral reef
105. Namby-pamby
106. Keep away from
107. Leftmost lane avoiders
108. A party to
109. Fizzy drink
111. Cheuse of NPR
113. Feeling
116. I told ya so!
118. Above average
120. An eye is their logo
121. Seinfeld uncle

★ Solution on page 315

22A, 25A, 29A, 32A, 77A, 119A, 128A, 15D, 45D, 78D, 87D, 90D, 108D

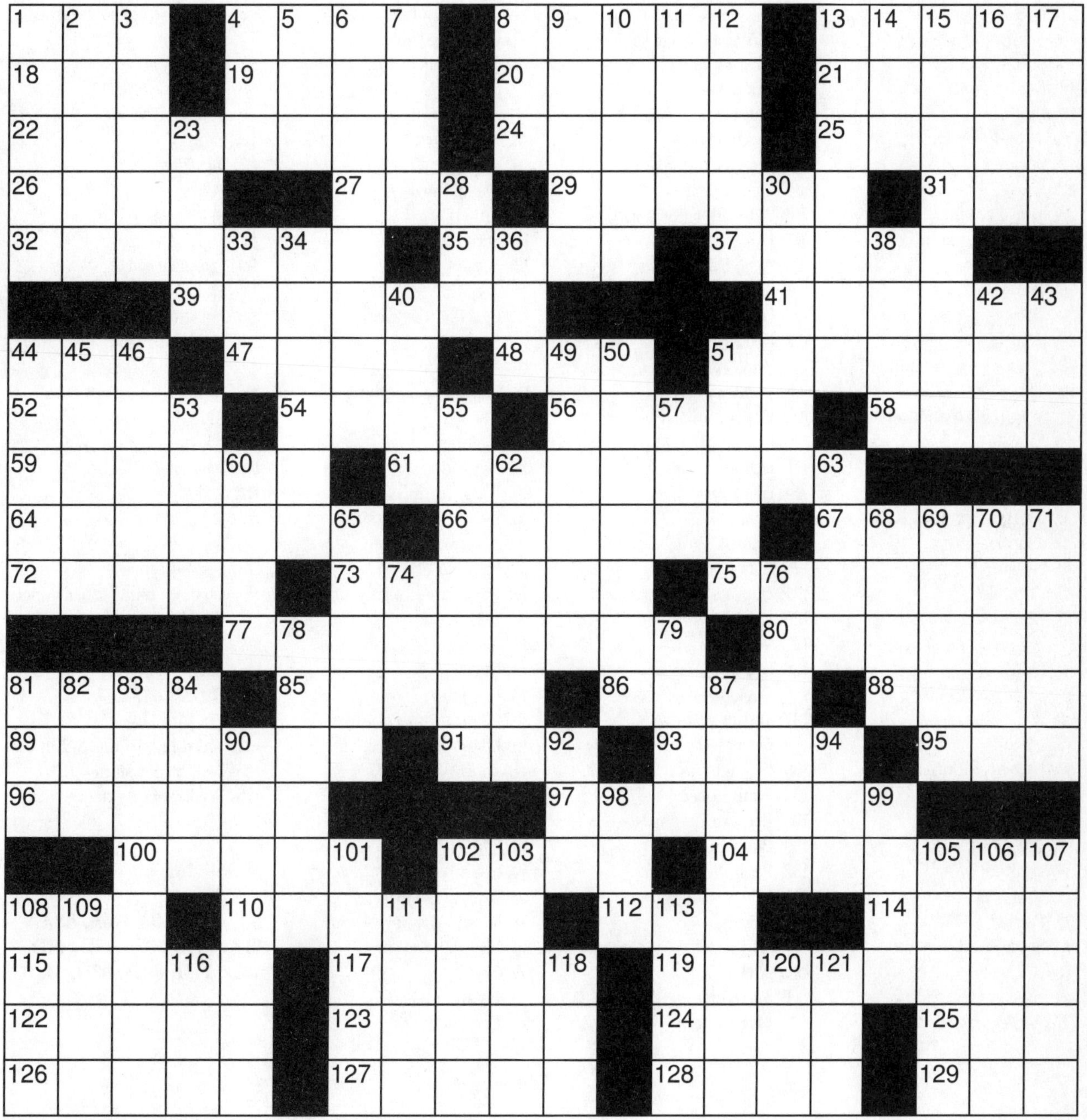

It's too good to be true

ACROSS

1. It grows on ears
5. Ski lift parts
10. Sound aids
14. Edit
19. Brother in baseball
20. It might be kicked
21. Spinner of a sort
22. Enjoy
23. Travel enabler
24. Oversell at summer stock
25. Sarge's dog
26. Took place
27. They take place
29. Bear lair
30. "I Saw ___ Standing There"
31. Volleyball maneuvers
32. Explain
34. Kinda
37. Fewer
38. Like pie, so they say
39. "Surfin' ___"
40. Nervous
42. Compile
45. Rest stop sign
47. Scram, ham
50. Sheds
54. Where Ipanema is
55. Still product
57. Ditch
58. Rhymer of boxing
59. Color
60. Pest
62. Uncomfortable
64. It's unnerving
66. Use a horn
67. Porch
69. Spicy food indicator
71. Bat wood
73. Exploit
74. Actress Irving
76. Hitcher's words
77. ___ salad
81. IRA user, perhaps
84. Olympic site of '52
88. Handle
89. Gather
91. Movie dog
93. Q neighbor, usually
94. One + one =
96. Bill spitter, for short
97. Extra
98. "___ Be There"
99. Like some deals
101. Driver's need
102. I'll be!
103. Wink number
105. Deserve
107. Ella, en ingles
109. Not nearby
111. Go up
114. Like tubers
117. Trial
121. Unbroken
123. Classic car
124. Dubya's deg., for short
126. Hot
127. Vegetation
128. Federal veep
129. Geeky ones
131. Turner of movies
132. Occupied
133. Cigarette group
134. Pond cover
135. Red one?
136. Bjorn Borg, for one
137. Farm workers?
138. *Wings* role
139. Driven

DOWN

1. Surrendered
2. Martini item
3. "I'm sorry" gift
4. They're subtle
5. Graduate project
6. Sound effect in a comic book
7. Dwelling
8. Ceremony
9. Pool people
10. Waikiki welcome
11. Tiny bugs
12. Scour
13. Hit play initials
14. Today!
15. Lorelei portrayer
16. Suggest
17. They blow
18. Slip into something
28. Cheap
31. Stainless ___
33. Age-old
35. It comes in bolts
36. Events with passing
39. Aisle walkers
41. Brought up
42. Put-upon ethnicity after 9/11
43. *Enemy* ___
44. Classy
46. Growth
48. Best at a pie contest
49. Like some stocks, for short
51. Food that may have peanuts
52. "___ is not to . . ."
53. Search for
56. They're sworn
61. Victor Vasarely's genre
63. Farm attraction
65. Sing
68. Freshen
70. Connect with
72. Relieve
75. It's too good to be true
77. Regarding
78. Despicable
79. Lilith portrayer
80. Volleyball cry
82. Tangle
83. Ingratiate
85. Pokey
86. Inflection
87. Sigh; if ___!
90. Chow down
92. Truly
95. As bad as it gets
100. Dragged through the mud
104. Camden Yards nine
106. Swinging single, before Jane
108. It's viewed in a pew
110. Was anxious about
111. Splits
112. Other-side-of-the-aisle person
113. Feed the fire
115. Gasp or faint, for instance
116. Oenophile's souvenirs
117. It gets stowed
118. Blast
119. Rebel of 1917
120. Put into law
122. Third leg, to the Sphinx
125. Wall Street starter
128. Bookkeeper's degree
130. "On a Clear ___"

★Solution on page 316

5A, 34A, 50A, 76A, 88A, 91A, 97A, 99A, 44D, 61D, 70D, 77D, 80D, 92D, 112D

1	2	3	4	■	5	6	7	8	9	■	10	11	12	13	■	14	15	16	17	18
19				■	20					■	21				■	22				
23				■	24					■	25				■	26				
27				28		■	29			■	30			■	31					
32						33		■	34	35				36		■	37			
■	■	■	38				■	39			■	■	40			41		■	■	■
42	43	44			■	45	46		■	47	48	49	■	50				51	52	53
54			■	55	56				■	57			■	58			■	59		
60			61						■	62			63		■	64	65			
66				■	67				68			■	69		70					
■	■	■	71	72		■	73			■	74	75		■	76			■	■	■
77	78	79				80		■	81	82				83		■	84	85	86	87
88					■	89		90			■	91				92				
93			■	94	95		■	96			■	97					■	98		
99			100				■	101			■	102			■	103	104			
■	■	■	105				106	■	■	107	108		■	109	110			■	■	■
111	112	113		■	114			115	116			■	117					118	119	120
121				122		■	123			■	124	125		■	126					
127					■	128				■	129			130		■	131			
132					■	133				■	134					■	135			
136					■	137				■	138					■	139			

It was an accident!

ACROSS

1. Marsupial critter
6. Actor Morita
9. Gordian Knot resolver
14. Confidence games
19. Liver or spleen
20. Like Abner
21. Greek sorceress
22. Okay
23. Hot, in England
24. Nemesis
26. Like some eyes
27. Filled one's tummy
28. Knight club
30. Mare fare, in song
31. "It was an accident!"
33. Upstart
35. Whelp's word
36. Like some lines
40. Unexcited
41. Welles of film
43. Author of "The Tell-Tale Heart"
44. Bruin giant
45. *Rocky* star
48. Piece in the paper
50. Come back
52. Experienced one
53. Hawaiian starch
54. "Why, the very ___!"
56. Hit
58. Batman portrayer
62. They're serious
64. It might get tilled
65. Viewable
66. Tale of Troy, with *The*
68. Slugger's stat
69. Strumpet
72. Longer than long
74. It also rises
76. Lonely Beatle gal
80. "Wink, wink, nudge, nudge" actor
81. "I can't accept that"
82. Silver, for one
84. The Plastic ___ Band
85. *Clueless* catchphrase
88. Less distant
91. Number for Caruso
93. Puts a limit on
96. *Shrek* actress
98. Coalition
99. Tierra ___ Fuego
100. Establishes
102. Standard, briefly
104. Foci
105. Notice
106. Apiece
107. Google rival
109. Piltdown Man, for one
111. *Guys and Dolls* lead
113. War survivor
114. Handbag
118. Topic
120. Absorbed
121. IT pro
122. Big Red
123. Range
126. Slickers
129. Decorate
131. Yellow one's lack
132. Miraculous meal
133. It makes MADD mad, for short
134. Shade
135. Fade away
136. Begin's co-Nobelist
137. Command center
138. Landscaping tool

DOWN

1. Bible of Islam
2. Peddle through speech
3. Resigner of '73
4. Young boy
5. Currently
6. It's really nothing special
7. Station
8. Hospice gift, for short
9. Does muckraking
10. Adored
11. Nice things to say
12. Flutter letters
13. Belafonte refrain
14. Serious invitation
15. Hope holder
16. "I knew it!"
17. Pie material
18. Short
25. Stockpiled
29. G.P.'s gp., for short
32. They offend
34. Computer components, for short
37. Matter for discussion
38. Proofreader's catch
39. Comb user
41. British entry collection, for short
42. Monkee man
43. They avoid straight lines
45. Past a sell-by date
46. Past one's best
47. Past one's boiling point
49. Pocket at a party
51. Bag contents
55. Set out
57. Later!
59. Coil
60. Flyer to JFK
61. Assassin's accessory
63. Area for toning
67. Ming, for one
70. Plus
71. Rod's companion
73. Fissure
75. Place for a piercing
77. Wanderer
78. Suspended
79. Haley work
83. Muck
85. *Our Miss Brooks* actress
86. Later!
87. Spot in the water
89. And so on, for short
90. *Big Night* entree
92. Sticky stuff
94. Banter
95. Cara who was in 79 Down
97. G.I.'s address, for short
101. Grassland
103. Auto body
104. Tell
108. Rad beatnik
110. Vein filler
112. Stamping ground
114. Class clown
115. Between
116. The middle size, at the movies
117. One keeping to themselves
119. Coat of ___
120. Outer layer
123. J. Low org., for short
124. Amber Alert, for one, for short
125. Woody's ex
127. Kind of bond or shoe
128. Fuss
130. Accomplished

★ **Solution on page 316**

22A, 48A, 58A, 85A, 91A, 10D, 13D, 34D, 46D, 57D, 60D, 78D, 86D

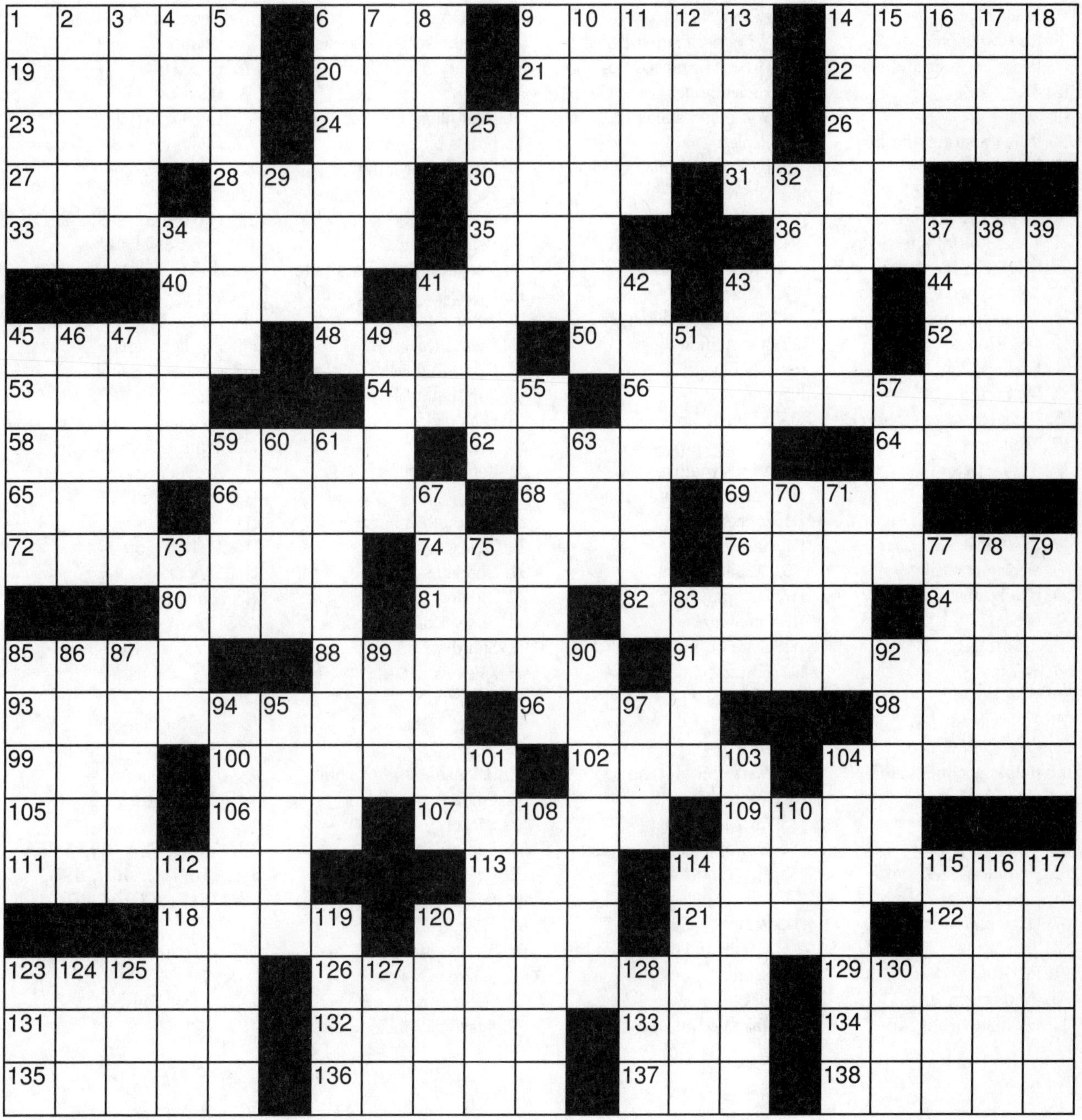

A slippery slope

ACROSS

1. Slacker
6. Be revolutionary
11. Old cars wear and tear
15. Set
19. Set
20. It has a stone and fuzz
21. Bubbly place
22. *Star Trek VI* star
23. Actress Dickinson
24. Tribal font of knowledge
25. Learning aid
27. Tropical wood
29. Where an "Injun" might say "How"
31. Southern larder items
32. Spots on the TV
35. Turner's stat, for short
36. Exchange
38. Andre Young, today
40. Dig up
41. It has rules
44. Capture
48. Madonna role
50. Use Botox
51. Slip-up
54. Art arrayer
55. Well-known
56. Turn down
57. ___ analyst
59. Celebrity Stein
60. Raunchy comic middle moniker
61. To the utmost
63. Yankovic parody
64. Not allow
65. Off the cuff
67. Like some prisons
69. Singular
71. Finesse
73. Commotion
74. It's made from cane
75. Hazard
78. Put together
80. Whopper manufacturers
84. Group for troops, for short
85. Heavy rock
87. You might shift it
88. Pepless
89. La Brea exhibit
90. Church veep
92. Twit
94. Comfort
95. Crude one's lack
97. Destroy
98. Climber's challenge
99. It's nothing new
100. Machinate
102. Ongoing
105. Raggedy doll
106. Center
109. Minds the hits
110. Show signs of boredom
111. Indeed
112. Take on
115. "What a mess!"
117. Like pie
119. Bin item
121. State of India
124. Forum participant
128. Dangers
129. Red item
130. Abu ___
131. Marry but not tarry
132. Try to take off
133. Misses the mark
134. Our nineteenth president
135. Grace portrayer

DOWN

1. Gershwin who knows the score
2. Book nook
3. Take up the rear
4. Ernie's widow
5. 113 Down loaf
6. Freethinker's possession
7. Count on
8. Dire
9. Rink filler
10. Frog's place
11. Coin-flipper in film
12. Popular news adjective since 9/11
13. Beatle byline
14. They're third from the top
15. "Monster Mash" man
16. Actor Epps
17. Geena Davis series
18. Gridiron guys
26. You might blow it
28. Handpick
30. Suitably
32. Item collection
33. Bereft
34. Nude one's lack
36. Tallied
37. Charlotte had one
39. Judging
42. Show fear
43. Stand for art
45. Ark official
46. Pro group
47. Tubes of Italy
49. Anger
52. Bake sale gp. for short
53. Embark
57. Sticker
58. Extreme bargain
62. Fix up
66. Surgeon's request
67. Strain
68. Actress Meara
70. *Survivor* adjective
72. Got a "heads up"
74. Reality TV lack
75. Green actions
76. Hayes of song
77. Olympic relay item
78. Clutch
79. Birds of prey
81. Like some fairs
82. A slippery slope
83. Singer Easton
86. Like
91. Not the ones yonder
93. Coast clobberers
94. Joined together
96. Gale
98. Highly skilled
101. Hooligan's hand
103. Capital of Saudi Arabia
104. Hunky-dory
107. Subdued
108. Tenth U.S. president
112. Ardent
113. Bagel place
114. Gawk at
116. 11/11 honorees
117. Styx classic
118. Clinton opposer
120. Honest one
122. ___ Na Na
123. For example
125. Crowd
126. ___ financing
127. Teacher's org., for short

★ **Solution on page 316**

38A, 63A, 65A, 69A, 115A, 5D, 6D, 12D, 46D, 49D, 53D, 81D, 86D, 104D

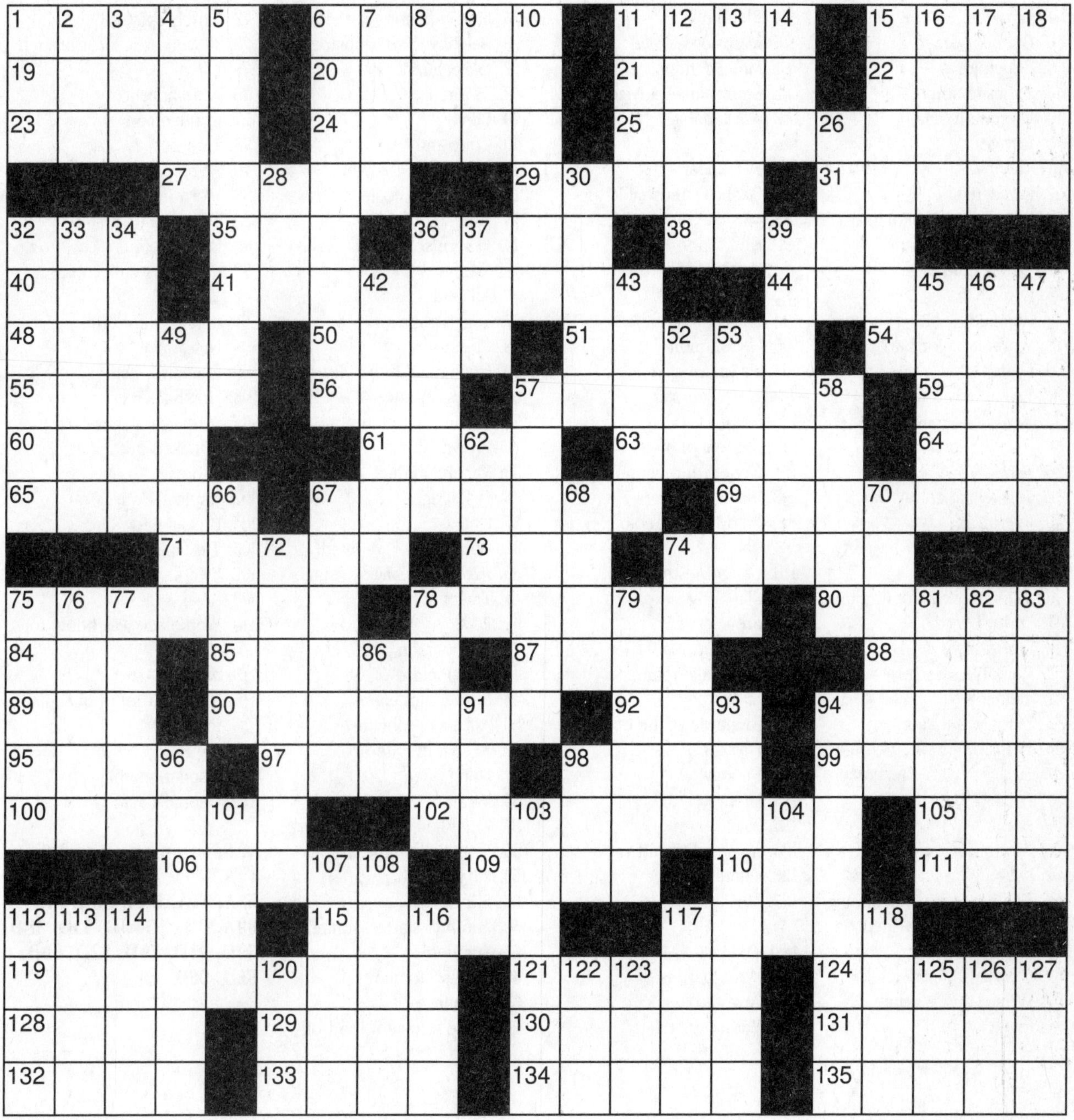

Phooey!

ACROSS

1. Doctrine
6. Bonnet buzzer
9. Bocce items
14. Shocked sounds
19. Hammerin' Hank
20. Private
21. Lie ahead
22. Xerox rival
23. "The ___ of Kilimanjaro"
24. Homer's neighbor
25. Circus employee
26. Overwrite
27. Ridicule
28. Workplace for Larry King
30. Outfit
31. Eulogy, for one
33. Ran
34. Derisive responses
36. Silly
38. Top-selling candy bar
40. Interim
42. Decked out for the party
43. Truly amazed
46. Title guy in a Joplin song
47. To be heard
48. Like doilies
52. Raid, like expense accounts
54. Smoothie maker
56. *West Side Story* heroine
57. Sunlight, to a newspaper
58. Funt's request
60. Pacific
61. Kin, but not by blood
62. Crummy
64. Clinic, actress, or topping
65. *Gilligan's Island* location
66. Ish
67. Grassland for grazing
68. Where things come together
70. Tec
74. Blue line?
76. Many-footed bug
81. Mini-Eden
82. Bear market advice
83. Ark inhabitor
84. Eggy?
85. Sweetheart
86. Hasbro's mushable toy
88. Musical mishmashes
90. Fala food?
91. Very tight
92. Shell rival
94. Soak
95. Uncommon
97. Hawaiian starch
99. *L.A. Law* star
102. Burger serving
103. Musical dramas
107. Nobel's invention
108. Water worker
109. Freddie the freeloader, for one
110. Caught in the act!
111. Slithering slayer
112. Proficient
114. Tara surname
116. They take returns
118. State
120. Richards of the court
121. Drops out
122. Phooey!
123. Grant
124. Jogs
125. It uses dits and dahs
126. Charlie's place
127. Musical pauses

DOWN

1. Wine barrels
2. Arrested
3. Eat away at
4. Stock stat, for short
5. Like captions
6. Beethoven's birthplace
7. Grass guzzler
8. Close
9. Blink
10. Concerned
11. Souvlaki ingredient
12. More than mislead
13. Force
14. Where souvlaki is served
15. Manner
16. Ascend
17. Tough puzzle
18. Casts off
29. Hush-hush group, for short
30. Take a chance
32. Anchor with Murphy Brown
35. Vader's raiders
36. O.J. judge
37. Gnaw
38. Boris Becker, reputedly
39. "Constant Craving" singer
41. Treaty concerns
42. *USA* ___
43. First person
44. Best Picture of '58
45. Boulle film extras
49. Alice's chronicler
50. See ya in Salerno
51. Hang open
53. Mean ones of old
55. Final Four org., for short
56. Dolphins' home
59. Oft-rerun show
63. Stir up
64. Pep talk starter, sometimes
65. Spinner
67. Actress Tomlin
69. Beguile
70. Place to take a load off
71. Passageway
72. Lickety-split
73. Toasting drink for brunch
75. Lift
76. Accomplice
77. Courteous
78. Tied
79. *Happy* ___
80. Word in an ultimatum
82. You might let it
83. Burger topper
87. Computer collection
89. Visit
91. Impressive, huh?
93. Not brazen
96. Franklin's bills
98. Horshack's cry
99. Arrow in a maze
100. Knocked out
101. Pad user
102. Naples and Nassau
104. Breaks into
105. Tie type
106. Ejects
109. Kojak's lack
110. Workplace watchdog, for short
113. Asta or Astro
115. It takes a lot of patients, for short
116. Big Blue
117. Good-for-nothing
119. George's spot

★ Solution on page 316

52A, 61A, 66A, 86A, 97A, 99A, 2D, 5D, 9D, 13D, 38D, 39D, 41D, 59D, 82D, 89D, 91D, 96D

1 2 3 4 5 6 7 8 9 10 11 12 13 14 15 16 17 18
19 20 21 22
23 24 25 26
27 28 29 30 31 32 33
34 35 36 37 38 39
40 41 42
43 44 45 46 47 48 49 50 51
52 53 54 55 56
57 58 59 60 61
62 63 64 65
66 67 68 69
70 71 72 73 74 75 76 77 78 79 80
81 82 83 84
85 86 87 88 89
90 91 92 93 94
95 96 97 98
99 100 101 102 103 104 105 106
107 108 109 110 111
112 113 114 115 116 117 118 119
120 121 122 123
124 125 126 127

Up to the task

ACROSS

1. Gigi and Lili
7. Bookie alternative, for short
10. Fixes clothing
15. Quincy's table
19. Seder participants
20. Chef school, for short
21. Underwater menace
22. Dickens title word
23. Awful
24. Top ___ List
25. Sales on TV
26. Gal Friday
27. Breed
28. Endured
30. ___of-war
31. Eagerness
32. What Putin might put in
34. Beatles' sergeant
36. Slap sound
39. The Shah, for one
41. Baseball's Guidry
43. Copper coin
44. Place to take a soak
47. They get assigned rotations
50. Preceded
52. Furry foot
53. Rental penalties
55. *Little Women* author
56. She had the comm under Kirk
58. Came to pass
59. Wigwams
61. Baby birds?
62. Itch
63. We've been over them before
66. Lobby that brings out the big guns
68. Four Corners state
69. Onslaught
70. Escort
73. Q-Tip, for one
76. Olla, for one
77. Intensify
79. Easy exemplar
82. Where things may get totaled
84. Yoda, to Luke
85. Negev native
87. Oversell the act
88. Spoiled
90. Like this grid, at first
93. Rod Serling's daughter
94. Georgia's neighbor
96. National nestlings, here
97. An original Siamese twin
98. Discontinue
99. Camp aide, for short
101. Hogs
102. Opts for
104. Kittens, or where they go
106. Alliance since 1949
110. Fair worker
113. Ltd. over here
115. Expense
117. Case
118. Like most antiques
119. Psalms interjection
121. Understanding
122. Is of use
124. Main squeeze
125. Marx Brothers title word
126. Designer Claiborne
127. Center
128. *Modern Maturity* org., for short
129. ___ on a true story
130. NOW concern, then
131. Least junior

DOWN

1. Give access to
2. Primitive
3. Investment
4. Support
5. Spring bulb
6. Adventure
7. Sushi fish
8. Bottleneck
9. Talk
10. It settles after activity
11. ___ *a Boy*
12. Mock-up
13. Cat activity
14. Oink joint
15. Desolate
16. Put down
17. Ray of film
18. It may have a head on it
29. Keyed up
31. Misbehave
33. Period
35. Like some oats
37. Had a bawl
38. Army marcher
40. Passes on
42. Must
44. Gush
45. Winter wear
46. Flooded
47. Go out for recess
48. Exceptional
49. Prince William's school
51. What early PCs use
54. Prance
55. Uninterested
57. Eleventh ___
60. Finless fish
61. Key on a word processor
64. Game site
65. Chinese way
66. '60s jacket
67. Go rancid
69. Lie beside
71. Self-worth
72. Oscar-winning title role for Lemmon
73. Fuss
74. Lady
75. Beside
78. Demand
79. Up to the task
80. Author Harte
81. Heels
83. Inadequate
84. Opposite of 74 Down
86. Burns's mate
88. Hot stuff at school
89. Cold-blooded ones
91. Less stale
92. Yours for the taking
95. 66, for example, for short
100. Delight
101. Poem part
102. Conclude
103. Catch
105. *A League of ___ Own*
107. Tolerate
108. Does dirty work
109. Get-go
110. Crisis center of '62
111. Like whale watchers
112. Bring up, or what to bring up
114. Punch-out of contention
116. Malevolent
119. Weep
120. MPG impacters, for short
123. Insert

★ Solution on page 316

21A, 28A, 50A, 53A, 70A, 1D, 8D, 12D, 31D, 92D, 102D

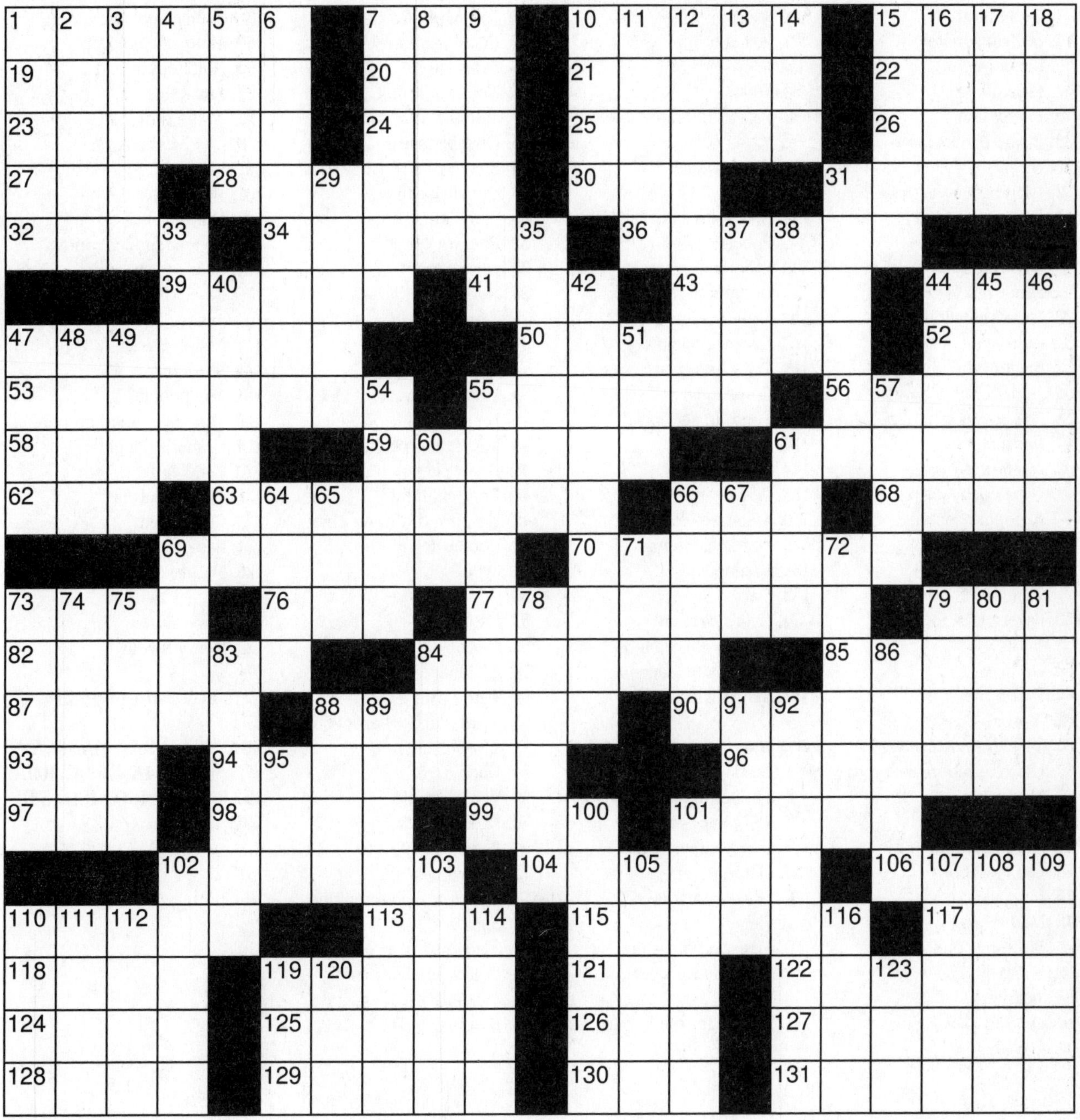

Hustle

ACROSS

1. Expression
6. Sicilian spouter
10. Londoner
14. Pie nut
19. Expression
20. Inside picture
21. Hustle
22. Island off Venezuela
23. Carbo-load food
24. Schedule
26. Supreme ruler
27. Semester, for one
29. Steak selection
31. Cider gal
32. Singer Etheridge
36. Jenny Lind, for one
38. Pay attention
41. Cart haulers
42. Awareness
44. *Get Shorty* actress
47. Account accessor
49. *Where the Boys* ___
50. Innovative
51. Yalie
52. Levels
55. Locks
56. Holders
60. Saves
62. 2 proof
65. Very domestic water
66. Old map abbreviation
67. Must
69. Handling
71. American Indian tribe
75. Get a 100 on
76. Surprised
78. Marble
79. Sleeping soundly?
82. Football cry
83. Admirer
84. Lie back
86. *Days of Wine and Roses* actress
91. Writer Ferber or Millay
93. Sully
94. Trust
96. Person of habit
97. Yoga position
99. Encompasses
100. Did
102. Oscar, for one
106. Principles
108. Panorama
109. "It ends here"
110. Front occurrences
112. Discover again
114. Cry when el toro loses
115. Component
118. Come in second
119. Big strings
122. Metal fastener
125. Cease, at sea
130. Nice farewell
131. Words to Brutus
132. Luxurious
133. Place
134. Lightly brown
135. It might get signed
136. Not in attendance
137. *Aida* setting

DOWN

1. Gremlin
2. Thriller of '49
3. "___ Impossible"
4. Cooperstown legend
5. Outdoor pools
6. One-day actors
7. Fit
8. *Miss Saigon* setting
9. Yellowbeard's yes
10. Pigtail
11. A speeder might burn it
12. Air taxi destination
13. ___ Might Be Giants
14. Cooking spray
15. Screw up
16. Noah's ark units
17. Stomachs
18. Olympic site
25. Shade provider
28. Demitasse filler
30. Early lunch time
32. Role for Heston
33. Ousted one
34. Not on the take
35. Place to stay
36. See a movie
37. What fun!
39. Frustration
40. Feel sorry for oneself
43. Meter, approximately
45. Establishes
46. The real deal
48. He played a news chief
53. Cookie seller
54. Type
55. ___ *Doubtfire*
57. List ender
58. Measure
59. Hightailed it
61. Agree with
63. Ideal place where a snake spoke
64. Duds
68. Work hard for
70. Reduce
71. It may be hard to crack
72. Crikey!
73. *Death in Venice* author
74. Sign up
77. Shuttle planes
80. Upton Sinclair novel
81. Picks up
85. Respect
87. It ain't hard
88. Passage place?
89. More adorable
90. Notorious
92. Sax range
95. At the time of
98. ___ *Miss Brooks*
101. Night
102. Winter vehicle
103. Holy site?
104. Bedelia of kids' books
105. Bursts forth
106. Level
107. Award
111. Native Alaskan
113. Move out
116. Oily people?
117. They may need crunching
118. Homer's daughter
120. Bandleader Brown
121. Please leave
123. CFO, often
124. Base
126. Not do much of anything
127. At ___ rate
128. Have dinner
129. Hanoi holiday

★ **Solution on page 316**

20A, 26A, 29A, 44A, 60A, 67A, 86A, 94A, 100A, 109A, 122A, 131A, 46D, 48D, 53D, 57D, 102D

1 2 3 4 5 6 7 8 9 10 11 12 13 14 15 16 17 18
19 20 21 22
23 24 25 26
27 28 29 30 31
32 33 34 35 36 37 38 39 40
41 42 43 44 45 46
47 48 49 50
51 52 53 54 55 56 57 58 59
60 61 62 63 64 65
66 67 68 69 70
71 72 73 74 75 76 77
78 79 80 81 82
83 84 85 86 87 88 89 90
91 92 93 94 95 96
97 98 99 100 101
102 103 104 105 106 107 108
109 110 111 112 113
114 115 116 117 118
119 120 121 122 123 124 125 126 127 128 129
130 131 132 133
134 135 136 137

Chapter 10

Common Denominators

The riddle

1	2	3	4	■	5	6	7	8	9	■	10	11	12	13
14				■	15					■	16			
17				18						19				
■	■	■	20					■	■	21				
22	23	24					■	25	26			■	■	■
27						■	28					29	30	31
32					■	33					■	34		
35				■	36					■	37			
38			■	39					■	40				
41			42					■	43					
■	■	■	44				■	45						
46	47	48			■	■	49					■	■	■
50					51	52						53	54	55
56				■	57					■	58			
59				■	60					■	61			

ACROSS

1. Deliver
5. Guarantee
10. Crepe cookers
14. Subtlety
15. Where the Heat rule
16. Got it!
17. Start of riddle
20. Unlike a 98-lb. weakling
21. Leaning
22. Structurally strengthened
25. Refrain from working?
27. Call returns
28. Popular honeymoon spot
32. Checks
33. Must
34. Emulate Jack Frost
35. Of course!
36. Middle of riddle
37. Needle
38. Troop support gp.
39. They try to pull you in
40. Fighter field
41. Boz and Saki
43. Already fixed
44. Indie's irkers
45. Crispy candy
46. Prepares to recycle
49. *Northern Exposure* walk-on role?
50. End of riddle
56. Tony-winning title role of 2000
57. Tony-winning title role of 1977
58. Noah's scout
59. High time?
60. Made a cake
61. Piece of cake

DOWN

1. Noticed
2. I missed that!
3. Keogh kin
4. "Ain't That a Shame" singer
5. Campfire treats
6. Handle
7. Effortless
8. G.P.'s gp.
9. Periphery
10. Western prop
11. Wine region
12. Famous moonwalker, to friends
13. Shakers or Quakers
18. *Ishtar* settings
19. Bronco-busting call
22. Flub
23. Point the finger at
24. Stone of Hollywood
25. Lots
26. Hooked on
28. *Airport* actress
29. Reason for martial law
30. Son on *The Jeffersons*
31. New news
33. Long-eared hoppers
36. Waste manager
37. Feigns
39. Rider's rope
40. Come about
42. Lane of Hollywood
43. Made doubtlessly clear
45. *Casablanca* star
46. Getz of jazz
47. The Buckeye State
48. Modernize, perhaps
49. Shalhoub title role
51. Deli order or bill
52. Stranded evidence, for short
53. Funnyman Knotts or Rickles
54. Caviar
55. Sales ___

★ **Solution on page 317**

The answer

ACROSS

1. Sugar unit
5. Famous
10. Deplaned
14. "Back in the USSR" acronym
15. Disco club name phrase
16. Philosopher Descartes
17. Boot accessory
18. Start of answer
20. Richter scale event
22. It's just for show
23. It gets you down
25. Singer Loeb
27. They march on March 17
31. Assassinates
33. Shoot!
36. Actress Wallace of *E.T.*
37. V. C. Andrews locale
38. Fan's fave
39. Persuade
40. Middle of answer
43. Individually
46. Slips into
47. Upticks
51. Plant
52. Split
53. Writing purchase
54. Gandhi, for one
56. Biblical victim
58. Winner takes ___
59. Keep lookout
62. Radiant
64. End of answer
68. Not fooled by
71. "If I ___ a Rich Man"
72. *You Only Live Twice* extra
73. Verve
74. Elizabeth Taylor collection
75. Choice words
76. Curb or eave

DOWN

1. Trucker items, for short
2. Diamond expert
3. Flower set or scent
4. Unbleached linen shade
5. Lapped item
6. Rubbernecks
7. Nail holder
8. Zoinks!
9. Portion
10. Suit you don't want pressed
11. Grazer's grassland
12. These words, essentially
13. Driving aid
19. Let out
21. Brady maid
23. Dye casters, for short
24. Fate
26. They're attached
28. Sworn oath
29. Expanse
30. It's cast
32. Ninny
34. Rocks the boat?
35. Baba of legend
38. Privy to
39. Smart
41. Fitting tribute
42. Warble
43. Waste in a tray
44. Luau staple
45. Have
48. Had
49. Unagi fish
50. Sandler's start, for short
52. "___ Tuesday"
53. Squeegee guy, often
55. Goes through with it
57. *Deliverance* item
60. Sicilian spewer
61. Like some pizza crust
63. Slime
64. Meadow maven
65. Irritate
66. Before, before
67. Pacers' st.
69. Kid's game
70. Torero bravo

★ **Solution on page 317**

Fab Four by Three

ACROSS

1. Dogie detainer
7. Dogpatch drawer
11. Close to the ground
14. Actress Silverstone
15. Locale
16. Troop's address, for short
17. Beatles single
20. Car park, in the States
21. Imbibe
22. Capture
25. Green condiment
28. Banjo's place
29. Bring together
31. Suffer
33. Combine
34. Well-disciplined
36. Did review work
38. Beatle single
43. Upright
44. Charm
45. Arachnid's abode
48. They take the pot, for short
49. Due
50. *Beverly Hills Cop* lead role
52. Fire-breathing critter
56. Trinity's guy
57. Rainy place, to 'iggins
59. Lamb's lament
60. Beatles single
68. Conclude
69. Squabbling
70. "Wouldn't that be great?"
71. Mouth M.D.'s degree
72. Takes steps
73. Testified

DOWN

1. Luxurious place?
2. Reminiscent of
3. Cause for saying "darn it"
4. Bartender's question
5. It's highly breathable
6. Waylay
7. Desert life
8. The Bible details it in cubits
9. Where flock folk are
10. Best bud
11. Equatorial gal
12. Launched
13. Succeeded
18. Media merger org., for short
19. Rankle
22. Bee-like?
23. Chip in a chip
24. Delivery room call
25. Log
26. Swedish import
27. Blackjack request
30. Scrabble piece
32. Trust
35. Suit material
36. It's well-worn
37. Tie
39. Role in *The Lion King*
40. 23 Down words
41. ___ of the above
42. Cogito ___ sum
45. Fresh from the dryer
46. Use up
47. Possession of most of ZZ Top
51. Stretch the truth
53. Facilitates felonies
54. ___ pedal
55. Sworn statements
58. ESPN topic, briefly
61. Like NASDAQ trades, for short
62. Cambridge campus, for short
63. Desirable
64. Superfund folk
65. Establish
66. It's no ___
67. Acquiesce agreement

★**Solution on page 317**

Tic-Tac-Toe

1	2	3	■	4	5	6	■	7	8	9	■	10	11	12
13			■	14			■	15			■	16		
17			■	18			■	19			■	20		
21			22		■	23	24				25			
26				■	27			■	28			■	■	■
■	■	■	29	30		■	31	32		■	33	34	35	36
37	38	39				40			■	41				
42			■	43			■	44	45		■	46		
47			48		■	49	50				51			
52				■	53			■	54			■	■	■
■	■	■	55	56		■	57	58		■	59	60	61	62
63	64	65				66			■	67				
68			■	69			■	70	71		■	72		
73			■	74			■	75			■	76		
77			■	78			■	79			■	80		

ACROSS

1. Looked after a lad
4. Medic
7. Caribou cousin
10. Symbol of messiness
13. Mogul's deg.
14. *Quincy, M.E.* actor
15. Sign of summer
16. Detergent ingredient
17. PC people
18. Bank automaton
19. Kingston Trio hit
20. Alias acronym
21. Hitchcock film
23. Say "Less!" to "More!"?
26. Plus more than I care to say, for short
27. Just ducky
28. Admirer
29. Isle starch
31. Arena adjutant
33. Removed from the "tag sale" box
37. What you have when you have a cow?
41. Sequence
42. Pertinent
43. Gender
44. Inspiration for Velcro
46. Snookums
47. *The Purple Rose of* ___
49. Miskey?
52. If not
53. Junior, to Senior
54. Cause for license suspension, briefly
55. Experienced one
57. *Blame It on* ___
59. Wine valley
63. Home-wrecking appliance?
67. Lurk
68. Guarantee
69. List starter
70. Personal library
72. La Brea goo
73. Raggedy one
74. Convened
75. Debtor's letters
76. John ___ Lennon
77. Senate support
78. Hit letters
79. He was attached at the hip
80. ___ Remo

DOWN

1. Bump off, biblically
2. Church veep
3. Buccaneers' home
4. *Being John Malkovich* actress
5. Giant giant
6. ___ platter
7. Kevin Clash, on *Sesame Street*
8. Excuse
9. Qantas mascot
10. Balkan native
11. Toddler
12. Tree ring
22. Food for Fido
24. Pod at the market
25. Like an old well?
27. Gal Friday
30. Approximately
32. Exile isle
34. Say again
35. Thud in the water
36. Sawbucks
37. Knight's weapon
38. Fiery gem
39. Elevator inventor
40. Big fair
41. Black bird
45. Fix a mess
48. Bank seizure
50. Concerning
51. Sty cry
53. Oklahoman
56. Hotel request
58. Film in need of distribution
60. 48 Downs, often
61. Original intention
62. Ohio city
63. My word!
64. *Star Trek*'s Roddenberry
65. Actress Olin
66. Nix from the top
67. Comfortable
71. Practically forever

★ **Solution on page 317**

Clothes encounters

ACROSS

1. Tears to pieces
6. Buck
10. Christiania, now
14. 1966 hit song/movie
15. Role for Myrna
16. Train for the ring
17. Casual attire for the movies?
19. Abandon
20. Ship parts
21. George Bailey ran one
22. It's a life saver, for short
25. Discernment
26. Packs
27. Slightest
29. Fabricated fabric
32. Indignation
33. Met melody
34. The Promised Land
36. Thinks over
38. Fab Four do
39. He had a word for that
42. Parish head
44. Rose Bowl letters
45. Overly
47. Standing up
49. 666 is his number
50. Stuck
52. Olive output
54. Soup sphere
55. Tribal sage
56. Use the OED
59. Overindulge
60. Leggings for bed?
64. Kid's pinned item
65. Racetrack shape
66. Becomes bored
67. Newsboy's wad
68. It may speak wonders
69. All-nighter's omission

DOWN

1. Blitz-busting flyboys, for short
2. Politico Segal
3. Superbowl org., for short
4. Decreases in likelihood
5. Six-line stanza
6. Boring film
7. Shredded
8. They might be industrial
9. It's pumped
10. 14 Across got Caine his first
11. Consumer's topper?
12. Donkey Kong device
13. Dare's ending
18. You there!
21. Sub detector
22. Silent one
23. Llama land
24. Conductor's suit item?
26. Darlin'
28. Store sign
30. Item a squirrel squirrels away
31. Go on and on
35. High quality
37. Hunt
38. Homer's barkeep
40. Loosen
41. Ciao
43. It's set off
45. Linked
46. Due back
48. Make squiggles
49. Dulls
51. Cinema deliveries
53. Mamie's hubby
56. Igneous rock source
57. Not by shot
58. Spector of music
60. Picked up
61. It's pretty raw
62. Get it?
63. Clairvoyant's claim, for short

★ **Solution on page 317**

Fruity folk

ACROSS

1. ___ the music
5. Main artery
10. Iowa city
14. Concept
15. Drops in temperature
16. Vamp of silents
17. Vocal quality
18. Fruity rocker
20. Golfbag accessory
21. Porgy's gal
22. Actress Barkin or Burstyn
23. Low-budget UFO
25. *NFL 2Night* channel
28. It means trouble
29. Hammett hound
31. Joe Tynan portrayer
33. Persian, today
36. One way to fly
38. You ___?
42. Fruity baseballer
45. Shot that's shot
46. Kitten's comment
47. Available
48. All cleaned up
50. Kind of exercise
52. Student stat
55. Barker?
57. Zoning concern
61. Funny Sherman
63. 55 Across growth
65. Film with slow poison
66. Fruity singer
69. Shady trees
70. Clan warfare
71. Old instruments
72. Collect
73. Mary Baker ___
74. Bottomless pit
75. Seasons

DOWN

1. Porn, to some
2. Later in Le Havre
3. Star
4. Use a club car
5. Tolerate
6. Impressed crowd cries
7. Waken
8. Hospice specialty
9. Inquire
10. First victim
11. *227* star
12. Miscalculated
13. Abstain
19. Reach down
21. *Fawlty Towers* manager
24. A hole in the ground
26. Take-home pay
27. Farm vehicle
30. Observant
32. Exhibition halls
33. Eddie Cantor's wife
34. Make a dent
35. Weapon
37. Hockey great
39. Beholder's eyeful
40. 35 Down defenders
41. Rip-off
43. Fight
44. Like a 41 Down
49. Peak in Sicily
51. Think about nothing else
52. Screw-up
53. Worked at
54. To the audience
56. Gas needle reading
58. Didn't do much of anything
59. Wanderer
60. Tries to draw air
62. Aunt Bee's call
64. Rahs for Raul
67. Resembling
68. Pint of ale place
69. Period of note

★**Solution on page 317**

Who goes there?

1	2	3	4	5		6	7	8		9	10	11	12	13
14						15				16				
17						18			19					
				20	21				22					
23	24	25	26		27		28	29			30	31	32	33
34				35								36		
37							38		39		40			
			41			42		43		44				
45	46	47			48		49		50			51	52	53
54						55		56						
57			58		59						60			
			61	62				63		64				
65	66	67				68	69			70	71	72	73	74
75						76				77				
78						79				80				

ACROSS

1. Fight site
6. It comes and goes
9. Bewildered
14. ___ carpet
15. Promissory note
16. Collection of spectators
17. Ring around of coral
18. Where whales bail
20. Take advantage of
22. Waterborne wiggler
23. Pueblo art community
27. Event's need to get known
30. Like populous lines
34. Shop supports
36. Hope, for one
37. Seafood medley
38. "I don't know that name"
40. Annoying tyke
41. Lose prose
43. Ruth's *Laugh-In* partner
45. Each
48. Turner of a rebellion
50. Respectful
54. And not
55. Church position
57. First choice
59. Mixed ___
60. Go through the roof
61. Wanted poster acronym
63. It may be used as evidence
65. Pub
70. Seamy
75. Lariat
76. Tuneful Tillis
77. Use a lectern
78. Grillmaster's garb
79. Be nosy
80. Fund

DOWN

1. Physician's flock
2. Stool pigeon
3. Power-hungry motivator
4. Nothing at all
5. It fights for rights
6. They may be used as evidence
7. Time-Warner purchaser
8. Couple
9. It doesn't feel good
10. Bridge underling?
11. Three before do
12. Dolly, for one
13. Sandwich men have them
19. Intriguing place?
21. Reason to carry the damsel in distress
23. Recipe amt.
24. Tourist attraction discount provider
25. Be in arrears
26. Trudge and tote
28. Shylock, notably
29. Precautionary folk
31. ___ *American Cousin*
32. Not the FBI or the CIA, but the other one
33. Obtained
35. Past the sell date
39. Annie, notably
40. Quasimodo cry
42. Fastening strip
44. ". . . Toto ___?"
45. Word before the 44 Across quote
46. Luau starch
47. Ball
49. Slugger Williams
51. Words that alter at the altar
52. Social affair
53. Give Enron a "buy"
56. ___ accepted
58. Took care of
59. Head Red
62. *Star Trek II* villain
64. Burn queller
65. It's uplifting
66. Rend
67. Lent item
68. Diamond expert
69. Rev. talk
71. Spittoon kin
72. Totally awesome
73. Asian on TV in '95
74. Lawn beads

★ **Solution on page 317**

Go figure

ACROSS

1. Gig
4. Not a straight line
7. Have the rights to
10. Brit ship init.
13. Pie ___ mode
14. Banana eater
15. Blow away
16. Upton Sinclair novel
17. Where to get away from it all?
21. Lift up
22. Take more than a peek
23. Hand holder
26. Letters, or letter's contents
28. Win the whole series
29. Tick off
30. Army address
31. Irving of acting
33. Like some wines
34. Women's mag., familiarly
36. Frighten
38. Place to chill out?
44. Previous
45. Was laid up
46. Young fellow
49. He wrote *Octopussy*
50. Horde member
52. Keep going!
53. Sign of spring
55. Privy to
57. Hi from Hogan
58. Scraping the ceiling
59. Monty Python title role
61. Lord Nelson's last stand?
68. Swallow
69. Innocent one
70. It counts against you
71. Bump's place?
72. Hwy.
73. Athena's pet
74. Mendel's concern
75. Driver's bane

DOWN

1. Pugilist's punch
2. Barcelona bravo
3. Get in the way
4. Klee, Gauguin, or Cézanne
5. News flash
6. Tidy up
7. It strokes
8. Doughboy event, briefly
9. A national association for teachers and students
10. Kept for oneself
11. *The Crucible* playwright
12. Starting to drop off
18. Coincided
19. Cowboy's nickname
20. This instant!
23. Flaky stone
24. Anemic's lack
25. You might ace it
27. Soft stone
28. Like pitas
30. Ad cat
32. Buddy
35. Pictorial of sorts
36. Balloon filler
37. Scan, of sorts
39. The Company
40. Singer Braxton or Tenille
41. Attired
42. Russian river
43. Vortex
46. Part of LDS
47. Landing spot of old
48. Expand
50. Just awful
51. Togetherness
54. Wee one
56. Gp. for Wizards and Magic
57. Jungle charger
60. Water color
62. Hoo-ha
63. Almost empty
64. Toothpaste option
65. Hit show of the '80s
66. Pooh pal
67. Pod for Mork

★ **Solution on page 317**

Front and back

ACROSS

1. Journey
7. Not fooled by
11. Needle hole
14. Freezer
15. Whack
16. Benediction bench
17. Mode of transferring property
20. ___ Vegas
21. Wily
22. Good name for a thief
23. Hill folk
25. She played Sidra
28. Follow
32. Eavesdrop
35. Stocking slit
36. Singers
39. It's like a vase
40. Avoid at all costs
41. Partygoer count
45. It isn't safe
46. It isn't good
47. Tumbler of sorts
48. It needs refinement
49. Wolf cryer
52. They're unbelievable
54. Fabergé egg owner, perhaps
55. Green in the movies
59. "It's no ___!"
61. Dim one
63. Make one go agape
64. Be OK with the opposition
70. Butter serving
71. London section
72. Got out
73. Ta-da, to Tomas
74. Cold weather forecast
75. Rifle parts

DOWN

1. Comfy casa
2. "My bonnie lies over the ___ . . ."
3. It's uplifting
4. Washboard ___
5. Who ___ there?
6. Kowtows to
7. Strange
8. Here ___ there
9. Wedding cake section
10. Like rentals
11. They might help clear the air
12. Uh-huh
13. Meadow mama
18. Tsar's har-har
19. Drop
24. Like Teflon
26. News organization
27. Business abbrev.
29. Hidden humor
30. Cone head?
31. Input
33. Rub the wrong way
34. A place to stay
36. Modern computer component
37. In need of a shave
38. Arrival
40. They have shafts
42. It's piercing
43. Exactly
44. Bridge specialist, for short
49. Approximate
50. Gift givers
51. Spring bouquet
53. Paint choice
56. Third rock from the sun
57. Canary comment
58. Pays attention to
60. *A Yank at* ___
62. Airport cry
64. Military destination, for short
65. ___ Friday
66. Way to go, for short
67. Think you're clever, eh?
68. *Leave It to Beaver* actor
69. Musician's job

★**Solution on page 317**

Horsing around

ACROSS

1. Pull one's leg
6. Like a he-man
11. Spot of goodness
14. Moving
15. Poker exit call
16. Hit
17. Nile port
18. It isn't pleasant
20. Egyptian veep
21. Show on Nickelodeon
23. One-named model
24. Spotted food item
28. Heartfelt fondness
31. Puts up a fight
35. Go back
36. Hindu separatist
37. Wee one
38. Mideast flyer
39. "That proves it"
40. Peel
41. Peachy
42. Make an oath, say
44. Piece of luggage
46. Administer an oath, say
48. He puts up with a lot of bull
49. Best man's chore, often
51. Drop
54. Irish New Ager
55. Best
58. Crucial
62. Good job!
64. Freddy's street
65. Unwise
66. *The ___ Limits*
67. Helms's bane
68. You might throw it in
69. Long

DOWN

1. Diplomat's skill
2. Jacob's twin
3. Working hard
4. Title film role for Sidney
5. Forming a rut
6. Just a ___!
7. Pedro's pal
8. Machine part
9. What was that again?
10. Cooperstown name
11. Stroller on the telly
12. Poet Teasdale
13. Sermon stopper
19. Itsy-bitsy
22. "___ you have found her . . ."
24. Lose a sunburn, in a way
25. Soft cheese
26. Get it away!
27. Bat wood
28. Regions
29. Not on deck
30. It might be coiled
32. Serious
33. Trunk
34. They might be rustled
36. Patronize Elias Howe
39. Seeger piece
40. Amuse oneself
42. Good name for a crafty one?
43. Through
44. Fluctuate
45. Good going, mac!
47. Movie dog
48. Fireplace shelf
50. Tubes for dinner
51. Willing to share
52. Nephew or uncle
53. Title film role for Shirley
55. Ciao
56. In excess of
57. Extreme eye candy
59. College by the Charles
60. Beatle beau
61. Car makers?
63. Lament

★Solution on page 318

Thrice-heard songs

ACROSS

1. Chill in the air
4. What the cast has
9. Striped shooter
14. Type of sandwich
15. Curaçao neighbor
16. Role on "What's Happening?"
17. *Meet Me in St. Louis* song
20. Prepare to be shot
21. Obviously
22. Maude portrayer
23. Heeded
26. Sailor's cap
27. Quenching sound
28. Large deer
29. Shepherd boy of opera
32. Thin food
33. The East
35. The Greatest
36. John, to Elton John
37. S Club 7 song (or Don Henley lyric)
43. Debt color
44. PBS funders
45. Require
46. Stand for art
49. They're not important
51. '80s defense plan
52. They're black and white, traditionally
53. Hole goal
54. Turned over
56. Boise's st.
57. Cine choice
58. New currency that's prospered
60. Elvis and Jay-Z song
66. They have it both ways
67. Untrue
68. Hotline call
69. It's black, traditionally
70. A long time
71. Clean supporters

DOWN

1. Peacock co.
2. ___ *Fly Away*
3. School gp.
4. Eastern temple
5. Trajectories
6. Govern
7. Late filler, for short
8. Foot displayer
9. Part of the foot
10. Thicken
11. Like fertile land
12. Car need
13. Put into operation
18. "All Things Considered" airer
19. It keeps your ears from popping
23. Leader
24. She was born free
25. Analogous
26. King novel
27. Pun response
30. They'd restrain spirited folk
31. Like
32. Food fish
34. Surveyor's units
36. Angle
38. Food fish
39. Corporate bigwig
40. Untouchable one
41. Give up
42. Hone
46. It's a mystery
47. Sound signals
48. Not quite roars
49. Soothe
50. Big upswings
53. Luau fare
55. Luau fare
57. I'm tryin' to talk to ya!
58. Governor Grasso
59. Pre-1991 map acronym
61. Chrysler's Iacocca
62. Actress Dawn Chong
63. Driving abbrev.
64. ___ service
65. Comfortable setting

★ **Solution on page 318**

Aye, Aye, Captain

ACROSS

1. Code crackers, for short
4. Samuel's mentor
7. Top gun
10. IRS action, for short
13. Drum holder
14. Bled
15. Cleaning item
16. Kimono closer
17. 40 Across activity
20. Milne marsupial
21. Recipe abbr.
22. Historical martyr
23. Amount for the squeamish
24. It's bid in Canada
27. Recently
29. Curious
32. TV host Linkletter
33. Mideast flyer
34. Psychedelic shirt
36. Baseballer who gets outs
40. Vacation spot, often
41. Couples' cruiser
42. Dame ___
43. Asian mushroom
46. Broth bringers
48. *Fame* star
49. Sample a smoothie
50. She's out standing in her field
51. Shapeless one
54. Dramatic musical
56. Burden
57. Thai delicacy
59. Gemini folk
63. Evictor's demand
64. Extreme yen?
67. Hit from *A Chorus Line*
68. 50 Across observation
69. What happened next?
70. Hollywood wife of Davis
71. Fireside chatter, familiarly
72. ___ ideas?
73. Cloner's need
74. Home of Mr. Bill, for short

DOWN

1. *Aliens* tot
2. 9-3 maker
3. Part of BA
4. Muff up
5. Lots of "Deck the Halls"
6. Printer type
7. Domingo ditty
8. Custard-filled dessert
9. It hatches
10. It comes from the heart
11. Wartime transport
12. Part of LED
18. Whitman resigned from it
19. Acronym that stands for something
23. ___ forces
25. When the sun's out
26. Annoyance
28. Like the Beatles, they say
29. Lex Luthor's henchman
30. Cable alternative
31. The wurst place
33. One with an ornate head topper
35. Got the plane ready
36. Live and breathe
37. In wait
38. More than suspected
39. No trouble at all
41. Alias abbr.
44. You might pick it up
45. Title adjective with 1,001
46. Fabrication
47. CPA's busy mo.
49. Caterer's or bookie's concern
51. Standoffish
52. Diamond center
53. *Shane* or *High Noon*
54. Mighty tree
55. Actress Lesley ___ Warren
58. Acceptable
60. Annexes
61. Spotted
62. Feat using feet
64. Dr. J's operating org.
65. Comfortable place
66. Mont. neighbor

★ **Solution on page 318**

Twofer

ACROSS

1. Received
4. Like a snake
9. First in a series
14. Nairobi Trio member
15. Learner
16. Like a seedless apple
17. 6' 1" "sexy" leading man of film
20. Apprentice
21. Capture
22. Poker holding
23. Wise one
26. Show sleepiness
30. Saying
32. Actress Wray
33. Newscaster Murrow
37. Scammed
39. Not a whit
40. TV laugh-getter of old, whose hit show started on radio
43. Stride
44. This gal
45. Vacation homes
46. Select
47. Tuffet
49. Egg holder
51. Active one
52. ___ due
56. Saloon
58. Omission
61. Soulful British singer
66. Curvy
67. Settler's vehicle
68. Slag yielder
69. Westminster, for one
70. Choose the lesser of two evils?
71. By now

DOWN

1. Wayne's co-host
2. *Aida* or *Carmen*
3. Stetson wearer, often
4. Ollie's partner
5. Fix completely
6. Idle
7. Living loop
8. Definitely
9. Facial standout
10. Towering
11. Take it like a ___
12. More distant 44 Across
13. Tack on
18. Stashed
19. Small bill
24. 51 Down, for one
25. Soccer structure
27. Run ___ of
28. Would you like to
29. Kiev kiboshes
30. Medical charter, for short
31. Nice things to say
33. Incite
34. Hang
35. Time spent on hold
36. Put-on
38. "Whip It" group
39. Gridiron gp.
41. Stereotypical Asian assent
42. It's nothing, really
48. Part of ROY G. BIV
50. Clifford's pal
51. Famous hoopster
52. Inky flower
53. Rattle
54. Soccer cry
55. Credo
57. Barney's bucolic boss
59. Allied group
60. Posted
61. Eventful time
62. Tennis ploy
63. Butter holder
64. Be outstanding
65. Kubrick CPU

★ **Solution on page 318**

Don't mention the war

ACROSS

1. Hog wild?
5. Judgmental one
9. Actress Garbo
14. Marie Wilson role
15. Bugle song
16. Vegetates
17. Calm singer?
20. John ___
21. Actor Sharif
22. Voluminous volume, for short
23. Macaroni
25. Give one's ___
27. Pup's cry
31. Enjoy these clues
32. Clay, today
34. Morpheus was his mentor
35. Cluster in some cereals
38. Memorable nights
39. The reader
40. Calm request for entry
45. Had existed
46. Get better
47. She married an *X-Files* star
48. Wall hanging, perhaps
49. Lots of time
50. It might take you in
54. It makes snow go
56. Hwy.
58. Grand ___ Island
60. Enmity
62. Dinner freebie
64. Longtime space station
65. Calm prize ceremony
70. Used a beeper
71. Gone fishing, perhaps
72. Opulent
73. Olympic hero of '36
74. Perry White's call
75. Film dog for a Greek guy

DOWN

1. Auction action faction member
2. Jim Palmer, for one
3. Tiny being
4. Got the heck out
5. Cuts off
6. Chinese cabbage
7. Grand Ole place
8. Eagle makers, for short
9. ___ club
10. Roddy Piper's adjective
11. *Civil Wars* role
12. Nurse's gift
13. "___ away!"
18. Right this minute
19. Do repo work
24. Stink
26. Slow flow
28. "Only Time" artist
29. Sparrer Spinks
30. Fretful look
33. Gotcha
36. Yearn
37. Proof
38. It can glow in the dark
40. Trade
41. James ___ Jones
42. Regarding
43. Catch one's breath
44. Headstrong
51. Bit parts
52. Between
53. Comedienne Warfield
55. Swell
57. Burn rubber?
58. Talk like a kid
59. According to
61. Beatty film
63. Forthright
65. Military address, briefly
66. What crows crow
67. Yearly count
68. Gab
69. CFO, often

★**Solution on page 318**

Kids' characters invented for this puzzle #1

1	2	3	4	5	■	6	7	8	9	■	10	11	12	13
14					■	15				■	16			
17					■	18				19				
20				■	21			■	■	22				
23				24				25	26			■	■	■
■	■	■	■	27			■	28			■	29	30	31
32	33	34	35		■	■	36			■	37			
38					39	40				41				
42				■	43			■	■	44				
45			■	46			■	47	48		■	■	■	■
■	■	■	49				50				51	52	53	54
55	56	57			■	■	58			■	59			
60					61	62			■	63				
64				■	65				■	66				
67				■	68				■	69				

ACROSS

1. Lightweight wood
6. Make art
10. Do deck work
14. War fear
15. Habitat
16. Do farm work
17. They're seen in *American Gothic*
18. Albuquerque sight
20. Scheme
21. Gambler's haven
22. Equip
23. Gal from the washer?
27. Oscar Madison's room
28. Seer's sight, for short
29. Singer Secada
32. Have a fit
36. I don't think so
37. Stay in a funk
38. Sharp fellow?
42. Use a plane
43. Lend a hand
44. Citrus slag
45. Animator Avery
46. Hound harrumph
47. Critical hospital spot, for short
49. Loud guy?
55. Restrained
58. Hire
59. Abraham's grandson
60. Vaudeville yukker
63. Spanish hero
64. Adored one
65. Throat filler
66. Detached
67. Hitchcock classic
68. Big-jawed comic
69. They go on and on

DOWN

1. Colorful fabric
2. Wait
3. Hermit
4. Kind of campaign
5. Belly muscles
6. Unrefined
7. Clan
8. Jet-setter, perhaps
9. Wart-nosed one
10. Get up
11. Coil
12. Ray of film
13. Went like the wind
19. Gather
21. Giant manager of the '40s
24. Culp/Cosby classic
25. Rachel's sister
26. Workplace watchdog, for short
29. Singer Lennon
30. Aired essay
31. Trawler gear
32. Be a lookout
33. Mine shaft, essentially
34. Dangerous dino
35. Ornate holder
36. Homer's neighbor
37. Sprint rival
39. Emma's TV replacement
40. Sound system
41. Accurate
46. *Sweet Liberty* actor
47. We're on!
48. Eva's mate
49. The Good Book
50. Grammarian's no-no
51. Greetings
52. Award named for a secretary's uncle
53. Worker's request
54. Some art pieces
55. Commotion
56. Commotion
57. Each
61. Org. with tight ends
62. *Where the Wild Things* ___
63. Recede

★ **Solution on page 318**

Oh no, not again!

1	2	3	■	4	5	6	7	■	8	9	10	11
12			■	13				■	14			
15			16					17				
18				■	■	19			■	20		
■	■	21		22	23	■	24		25	■	■	■
26	27		■	28		29	■	30		31	32	33
34			35				36					
37					■	38			■	39		
■	■	■	40		41	■	42		43		■	■
44	45	46	■	47		48	■	■	49		50	51
52			53				54	55				
56				■	57				■	58		
59				■	60				■	61		

ACROSS

1. Pussycat's playmate
4. What's the big ___?
8. Speed ___
12. It's just dawned on me!
13. GI at a univ.
14. Oberlin's state
15. *Concentration* plan
18. Start of a long Stallone title
19. ___ tub
20. Fashion line
21. Dwarf's refrain
24. UK ref.
26. Three-faced one
28. Flabbergast
30. Tree sap
34. Rudeness
37. 86 or 99
38. New co. aider, for short
39. Rap sheet acronym
40. G-man group
42. Golfer's tool or site
44. Tarzan's pal
47. Freud's find
49. Tether
52. Auditor's ahas
56. Quahog or littleneck
57. French female
58. Salesman, briefly
59. Distressed one's call
60. Kindled
61. Judgment ___

DOWN

1. Doesn't have both ___ in the water
2. Make more edgy?
3. *Rent* inspiration
4. Ruiner of many former stars, for short
5. Wingdings
6. Make an impression
7. Possible response to a cat
8. Athlete's pride
9. I don't think so
10. It was green in a King title
11. It might be ABAB
16. Info outlet, for short
17. Like the fiery phoenix
22. Less slow
23. Cries of pain
25. Scout group
26. Quite a time
27. Not even move
29. Mommy has three
31. Coast
32. Rub the wrong way
33. Covert operators, for short
35. Business org.
36. Easiness symbol
41. Ford's predecessor
43. Coffee container
44. St. Louis has a notable one
45. Soccer celeb
46. Plus more
48. 1952 Olympic host
50. Response to a court tort
51. Catch sight of
53. "Safe" cracker
54. Variety
55. Well!

★**Solution on page 318**

All-American

ACROSS

1. Nuns take them
5. To pieces
10. Model MacPherson
14. Monumental
15. *West Side Story* song
16. Still life object
17. Group encountered by Holmes
20. Fred's sister
21. Set
22. Mrs. Dole's org.
23. Street on *Peyton Place*
25. Lucy's co-star
26. Camp aide
27. Med. amt.
30. In
32. Attempts to pass
33. Wine barrel flavoring
34. Two charcoal lumps, perhaps
35. Behind
37. Disease fighters
43. Irving Berlin honoree
44. Group that votes together
45. Stick in the water
46. Special agent
49. Oktoberfest drink
50. Imbecile
51. Inning ender
52. Its password was "Mickey Mouse"
54. The shoe width of Sasquatch
56. Deli option
57. Hangman line
58. Toothy look
62. Judging group
67. Letterman rival
68. Bed and breakfast
69. "Sweet 16" org.
70. Idyllic spot
71. *M*A*S*H* locale
72. Willy Wonka writer

DOWN

1. *Alice* role
2. It's near the back of the front section
3. Like 49 Down
4. Lug
5. Koop gp.
6. ___ thai
7. "___ You Lonesome Tonight"
8. Like Ruffles potato chips
9. ___ *of the Unexpected*
10. Gasahol encouragers, for short
11. Multigenerational one
12. Metcalf of *Roseanne*
13. Assembles
18. Shocking creature
19. Inventor Whitney
24. Perhaps
25. Don't follow orders
27. Request of AAA
28. Yuck
29. Go through the snow
31. Sportscaster Allen
32. Devoured
34. That scared me!
35. Worship
36. They issue Stern warnings
38. Soldier material
39. Good job, gaucho
40. John, to Ringo
41. Male tyke
42. Sign of success, for short
46. Turkey talk
47. Like some cider
48. Harmonize
49. "The Old ___" (*Chitty Chitty Bang Bang* song)
50. More than request
52. Patriotic gp.
53. Beverage
55. Second sight, for short
59. Atahualpa, for one
60. Reuben's mom
61. Jets to Jerusalem
63. Time spent on hold?
64. Sticker
65. "You're Still the ___"
66. Bobby Inman once headed it, for short

★ **Solution on page 318**

Chapter 11

They All Scream Themes

Kids' characters invented for this puzzle #2

ACROSS

1. Spending limit
4. Amorphous entity
10. Humid
14. Forehead marker once a year
15. Paths
16. Greengrocer's pod
17. O in Oahu
18. Furry guy
20. Bird of prey
22. Webcam operator
23. Merchant mariner
24. Yom Tov yakker
29. Tote
32. Ultimate objects
35. "Chances ___"
36. Mend
38. "Fatha" Hines
39. Deceased
41. Sealy rival
42. Spicy ___ roll
43. Broker Boesky
44. Specialties
46. *Pushing* ___
47. Like some snakes
49. Cut into
51. Knobby joint
52. *Norma* ___
53. Milne's first name
56. Scarab
59. Guy with depth
63. Tide rival
65. Rick's love
66. Not quite
67. Dogie command
68. Adelaide 'allo
69. Chaps
70. Court

DOWN

1. 51 Across neighbor
2. Sailing
3. Gassy guy
4. Mailman?
5. Respond like Lurch
6. Amscray!
7. Words to Brutus
8. Plunks down a wager
9. Tennis pro
10. Homer's "Why'd I do that?"
11. Pen name initials
12. Hospital checker, for short
13. ___ for the course
19. Hits the wrong key
21. Slugger Ripken
25. Use the black market
26. Guy who goes below the belt
27. Mac of comedy
28. Moreau's spot
29. Stimulus response
30. Afraid
31. Herby sauce
32. Cab patronizers
33. Lovely Beatle gal
34. Steamed
37. Land of Incas
40. Bomb dropper
45. Chase scene locales
48. Respond to the sun
50. Bub to a beatnik
54. Obsessed sailor
55. Jodie Foster film
56. Make reservations
57. Ultimatum word
58. Part of HOMES
59. Insult
60. Ancient
61. Olympics chant
62. Wellness gp.
64. Digested

★ **Solution on page 318**

Some kind of mix-up

ACROSS

1. Kind of chart
4. Highlander
8. Shocked
14. Catapult trajectory
15. Jason's ship
16. Pasta piece
17. Feather go-with
18. ANOINT
20. Young pigeons
22. Kid deliverer
23. Woolly female
24. Browbeat
27. Staleness
28. Check for prints
31. Fancy-schmancy
34. Kato Kaelin was a witness before him
35. It gets taken in an office
37. Ferocious
41. ENTAILS
44. Fresh
45. Listen up!
46. Drink like a cat
47. Like slim pickings
49. Sacred song
50. Use a scissors
53. Relax, men
56. Work a hide
57. Puz. counterpart
59. *Gilligan's Island* inhabitant
63. LORE
67. Deli loaf
68. Hit French film
69. Nod neighbor
70. 1040 people
71. Climber's spikes
72. Tugboat tasks
73. Personal

DOWN

1. Light touches
2. Invasion site of 2003
3. It's neutral
4. *Ninotchka* star
5. Came up
6. Quiche need
7. Bud's best bud in comedy
8. Actress Heche
9. Feta source
10. Burning
11. See ya at the Seine
12. Loses speed
13. CIA director, at press time
19. Flush
21. Step up to the challenge
25. It wasn't built in a day
26. Knit
27. Earth heirs
28. Part of CD
29. Where Hatch hatched
30. Seafood, or snack for Chaplin
32. At a distance
33. Clock sound
35. Football's Ditka
36. "Orinoco Flow" singer
38. Trust
39. Prep at the last minute
40. Athlete's channel owned by Disney
42. Fill-in
43. Exceptional
48. Big do
49. Coop layer
50. Subway hold
51. Wolf of literature
52. Cove
54. He resigned in '73
55. Lettered metal, usually
57. English
58. Cries for Charo
60. Tennis racket part
61. Rochester's beloved
62. Others
64. "Twilight" gp.
65. Nonetheless
66. Altar avowal

★**Solution on page 319**

Double-header headlines on 2000 politics

ACROSS

1. Part of DJ
5. They're annoying
10. Tadpole who's all grown up
14. Fictional detective's dog
15. Fictional detective
16. Dance with a 21 Down
17. Letter opener
18. Russian post filled
20. *Just Shoot Me* star
22. Least silly
23. Part of a Greek salad
26. Giant hitter
27. Rd.
28. GOP order, perhaps
33. Ga. neighbor
34. Asian holiday
35. Opening word
39. Kind of closet
42. Singer Shannon
44. Goliath slayer
45. He fishes around
47. What you get for getting home
49. "You're Still the ___"
50. Dem. complaint, perhaps
54. Pipe type, for short
57. Shooting plan that got shot down, for short
58. Droplet
59. Carnivore's entrees
62. They're excessive
66. Recount headline
69. Kind of medicine
70. Nothing, to a tennis player
71. Tipster Tripp
72. Give a sly eye
73. TV talker of old
74. It goes up
75. Become one

DOWN

1. *My Two* ___
2. Yo comprendo
3. By oneself
4. Wine amount
5. Cleo's killer
6. Computer brain, for short
7. Hair mussers
8. Reviser of histories, perhaps
9. Law makers
10. Dull sound
11. ___ space
12. The first people to be invited
13. *Inferno* or *Gremlins* creator
19. What Mr. T did to the fool
21. Ring around of posies?
24. Blaster, for short
25. Getting on in years
28. Festive event
29. *Chocolat* actress
30. Lurch's verb
31. SNL alumna
32. Top secret org.
36. Promise
37. Diminutive
38. Tree of knowledge locale
40. December temp job
41. Wrestling hold
43. Breather
46. Purchase for a car
48. Where you might see a blitz, for short
51. Ad-lib
52. Record
53. Blossoming
54. Song for Sunday
55. Pep
56. Desire
60. Told a 64 Down tale
61. Rational
63. Desire
64. Lanky
65. *Citizen Kane* prop
67. Actress Lupino
68. Tour of duty locale, for some

★ **Solution on page 319**

All caught up

ACROSS

1. Politico Alexander
6. Sudie portrayer
10. Miser's concern
14. One of the ABC islands
15. Put it another way
17. Salinger work
19. Timely time
20. Ref. set
21. Knight's title
22. Wicker material
25. Pigeonhole
29. Take
30. Be in the tub
34. Dagnabbit
35. Base
37. Croat, for one
39. Grand ___ Opry
40. Improvised
45. *Six Feet Under* airer
46. Neighborhood
47. So that's your game!
48. Seaside saint
50. Norms
52. Spin doctor's surgical work
56. Serengeti striped one
58. ___ *Jones*
60. Sham
62. According
63. Long March veep
64. Get sick
70. Aided enormously
71. Bizarre
72. Normal
73. Alice's odist
74. *Roxanne* supply

DOWN

1. They tie one on
2. Perch for pairs
3. Adapt, in an extreme way
4. *All My Children* airer
5. College cry
6. It gets to you
7. Not moist
8. Dashed
9. Crumb carriers
10. Religious one
11. Stick that's wide at the bottom
12. Slob's digs
13. Eagle aid
16. Boot top place
18. Multiple eras
23. One, on a scale of one to ten
24. Oahu outta-here
26. Gator kin
27. 24 Down dance
28. Place with fig leaves
31. $6M Steve's boss
32. Styled like
33. Clouseau's cohort
36. Devastate a record
38. TV censor
40. Name start for a fancy restaurant
41. Competent
42. Pyramid, essentially
43. Octopus's home
44. Castle, so they say
49. Future detector
51. Tends
53. Hard shells
54. Defensive role
55. Eats away at
57. Desire
59. Mohawked actor
61. I think I did good!
62. Babe's Bunyan
64. *60 Minutes* airer
65. Drivers' gp.
66. Man's material, in Oz
67. And not
68. Desire
69. Corp. veep

★ **Solution on page 319**

Going to extremes

1	2	3	4	5	■	6	7	8	9	■	10	11	12	13
14					■	15				■	16			
17					18					■	19			
20				■	21			■	22	23				
24			■	25			■	26				■	■	■
■	■	■	27				28					29	30	31
32	33	34			■	■	35				■	36		
37				■	38	39				■	40			
41			■	42				■	■	43				
44			45					46	47			■	■	■
■	■	■	48				■	49			■	50	51	52
53	54	55				■	56			■	57			
58				■	59	60				61				
62				■	63				■	64				
65				■	66				■	67				

ACROSS

1. Hooligan
6. Diploma recipient
10. Need at a T-bar
14. Creepy
15. ___ Marlene
16. Hooked on
17. Tallest water drop on Earth
19. Lack
20. Germinator
21. Two before "ignition"
22. Filmdom
24. Rocker Nugent
25. Batter's swing
26. Rollers in a game
27. Largest body of fresh water on Earth
32. Confounded
35. Bombard
36. Ewing's group, for short
37. Accurate
38. Action flick sequence
40. Related
41. Anointed substance
42. Like the Kalahari
43. Topple
44. Highest spot on Earth
48. Foreshadow
49. Al Capp's drink
50. Stalk growth
53. They squirt 29 Down
56. Lorne Michaels show, for short
57. My treat
58. Space
59. Lowest spot on Earth
62. Desert dweller, often
63. Best-selling astrologer
64. Rational
65. ___ *Make a Deal*
66. Optimistic
67. News makers

DOWN

1. Hooligan
2. She played Nurse Betty
3. Goaded
4. Even-steven
5. Muscular fish
6. Look
7. Aggravate
8. Every
9. Adherant
10. One in need of confession
11. Dummy's perch, often
12. Supermarket purchase
13. Fizzy water
18. Yogi suggests you take it
23. *Ricochet* rapper
25. Driving org.
26. Union fees
27. F. ___ Bailey
28. Hammett hero
29. See 53 Across
30. Play award
31. Rotten review
32. Mighty mite
33. Ernie Kovacs's "The Nairobi ___"
34. *Star Trek* helmsman
38. Debtee
39. Rash item
40. Suitable
42. Astride
43. Application
45. Cold War threats
46. Was exhausted
47. *Vogue* rival
50. Follow
51. Prayer closings
52. Peruses
53. Aloud
54. Center
55. Precisely
56. Bodies of water
57. Stench
60. Dr.'s gp.
61. Vicious biter

★ **Solution on page 319**

Card game enders

ACROSS

1. November's gem
6. George Bush once led it
9. Floats through the air
14. Spicy sauce
15. Follow through
16. Lazy one
17. Sheepish statement
18. Head honcho
20. Caesar who slayed them
22. Peter Parker's ammo unit
23. Opera heroine
27. Sawyer of the news
30. Lighten
34. MIT setting
36. Traffic ticket option
37. Felt green?
38. Squeamish response
40. Goad
41. Off
43. Water entrances
45. No prob
48. Seal a Cinch-Sak
50. Medical meting
54. Take in
55. Picker's aid
57. Astounds
59. Lamp filler
60. Chuck Barris item
61. Where to go in England
63. Whichever
65. Logroller, of sorts
70. UFO odor?
75. Burst forth
76. Gp. In *The Crying Game*
77. Quite a while
78. Reason to visit a body shop
79. Wife
80. Easily available

DOWN

1. Slot filler
2. Texas tea
3. "The Gold Bug" author
4. Resembling
5. Undesirable spots
6. Funt's adjective
7. 50 Across follow-up site, briefly
8. Money disp.
9. ___ cutter
10. Casa clay
11. Common ailment
12. Piggy count
13. Full house acronym
19. Baa ma
21. Ta-da!
23. *Stroker* ___
24. "Jesse" singer
25. Plate distributor, for short
26. Bear with
28. Ripen
29. Basic essential
31. Mo. for fools
32. Go limp
33. Laser sensor
35. Classic car
39. Yarn lover
40. Employing
42. No more Mr. ___ Guy!
44. ___ tem
45. ". . . a ___ of troubles and by opposing . . ."
46. They do body work, for short
47. 66, for one, briefly
49. Baby New Year kidnapper
51. Before now
52. Card game cry
53. Essayist's class, for short
56. Beauty prizes
58. Verb in Washington signs
59. Yucky glop
62. Decides
64. Tommy Smothers's prop
65. Supplied
66. Bile
67. Do like Logan
68. Li'l singer
69. Go astray
71. Buddhist sect
72. Bit for one with a bit
73. Heston headed it, for short
74. Zener card skill

★**Solution on page 319**

Sean Connery flicks

ACROSS

1. Common complaint
4. Relaxing place
7. Apple alternative
10. Uppermost
13. Musical sense
14. Laugh track collection
15. Dawn, for instance
16. Resentment
17. Sean Connery film of '96
20. Gullet
21. Sing part of "Hocus Pocus" by Focus
22. Author output
24. Frolic
27. Answers in *Jeopardy*
29. Intriguing place
30. Cry against the bull
31. Cinematic style
35. Bookie's numbers
37. Spring-time sound
40. Stack from the bank
41. Amistad, for one
42. Phrase
43. Rephrase
44. Shell food
45. Raises a stink
46. Aerial replacer
47. Avoided lumps
49. ___ Don
50. Gallery givers, for short
51. Fool
55. Ruthless ruler
56. Midday break
59. Vital vessel
61. Sleeve
62. Sean Connery film of '65
67. Doc flock, for short
68. 49 Across, in Spanish
69. It's important to me
70. Pool breaker
71. Outlaw
72. Spud bud
73. Place for cars
74. Embarrassed one's face cover

DOWN

1. Joined together
2. Boathouse item
3. The end of an ___
4. Vamoose
5. Bamboo biter
6. *Angela's* ___
7. Rhoda's mom
8. Feel the ___!
9. Soul deliverer
10. Sean Connery film of '81
11. Aloud
12. Where the plate gets passed
18. Trick
19. He's got a lot on his mind
23. Put the kibosh on
24. Perches
25. The usual
26. Sean Connery film of '92
28. Paint protector
32. 7/4 cries
33. She entertains
34. Bible book without the G-word
36. Plant missiles
37. Piece of land
38. Dorm denizens
39. Paint choice
48. Baby toy
52. Fleming who wrote of M and Q
53. ___ T
54. Ragu rival
55. Cola choice
56. Volvo rival
57. Marie Wilson's friendly role
58. Yoo-hoo on the blue
60. Hurry
63. Apply
64. Poker or tennis term
65. Shlep
66. Chair part

★ **Solution on page 319**

Song clips

ACROSS

1. Secure
6. Brush brand
11. Electrical unit
14. Rock ___
15. ___ bear
16. Durocher of baseball
17. Disco era classic
19. It's not meant to be broken
20. Apple aimer
21. Go to
23. Jacket fabric
27. Canal of song
28. Will we ___ know?
29. They call the shots
32. Style
34. Setting for *The Crucible*
36. Chanced upon
38. Utmost
39. Ranch alternative
41. Cook's qty.
44. Parlor piece or empire
46. Loathe
48. "This just in" item
50. Gender determiner
52. Not-so-wordy one
53. Cool!
54. Reese's TV costar
56. It goes against the norm
59. Right this second!
61. Athena's consort
62. Classic oldie song
68. Flower art
69. Hi to a 68 Across wearer
70. Jet set
71. Yearning
72. The Tick's mighty cry
73. Seeing red

DOWN

1. ___ Alamos
2. Clever
3. ___ service
4. Wail
5. Duvalier's domain, once
6. October sparkler
7. Class list
8. Ryan's *Love Story* costar
9. It dribbles down a cone
10. Maverick of baseball
11. *Oklahoma!* song
12. Blue *Yellow Submarine* extra
13. Minor flurry
18. Rex's sleuth
22. Three-ring container
23. It's near Phoenix
24. Almost circular
25. Conway Twitty song
26. "We Three Kings of Orient ___"
30. Big Ben buggy
31. Dieter's entree
32. She played the title role of Rosemary
33. Siamese teacher
35. Fly catcher
37. One of a 1492 trio
40. ___ the line
42. Between none and all
43. Quarry
45. *Little Man* ___
47. Yuppie's car
48. Base
49. ___ baseball
51. Five years after Gary U.S. Bonds's birthday
55. Alternate
57. Restful places
58. Hound's howl
59. Arty NYC zone
60. Counterfeit catcher, for short
63. Muck
64. Actor Wallach
65. Be suffering
66. Byway, briefly
67. Bill's film pal

★ **Solution on page 319**

Severe cutbacks

ACROSS

1. Hannibal Smith's group
6. Make eyes at
10. Attire
14. Ivana's replacer
15. Change
16. Follow
17. Story about a gal with personality
20. Vampire author
21. It's binding
22. Aardvark appetizer
23. Puts the metal to the metal
24. Bit of wind
28. Mouth
30. I doubt it
31. Military group
35. Horse or bean
37. Story about a swordsman
41. 57 Down
42. Speak highly of
43. *X-Files* extras
44. Dire
48. Bar
51. Smart actor
54. "Boola Boola" student
55. A Mouseketeer
57. Run
58. Story about a builder
62. Lupe's love
63. Clip
64. Dunne or Papas of acting
65. Mob bosses
66. Rake's hangout
67. Perspiration portals

DOWN

1. Acela owner
2. Hummus ingredient
3. Fabricates
4. It heals the burn
5. Riddle of the Sphinx answer
6. Refuse
7. Secreter
8. *Star Wars* maven
9. Big wig
10. Fetching lad
11. Honest one
12. ___ your engine
13. Tourney freebie
18. Come out
19. Not the latest
23. Partial bikini adjective of song
25. Ben Stiller's mom
26. 40 Down
27. Hammer holder
29. Trudge
32. Rapscallion
33. Shrine name starter
34. Homeland Defense org.
35. Burrito buyers
36. Bullet follower
37. Amish pronoun
38. Red ___
39. Near, Middle, or Far place
40. 26 Down
45. It goes on when it goes off
46. *Taxi* role
47. Potato chip features, sometimes
49. Unpleasant emanations
50. Mythical piper
51. Koran veep
52. Clean a sidewalk
53. Threw in
56. Telemarketers, perhaps
57. 41 Across
58. Tiny bit
59. Physician's alliance, for short
60. Kidnapper in a Rudolph special
61. It may be glossed over

★**Solution on page 319**

She went that-a-way

ACROSS

1. Bandleader Arnaz
5. Quiz answer
10. Event for the RAF
14. Big show
15. Agent Ness
16. Go no further!
17. Blow one's top
18. Pale purple
19. Grills
20. She went downhill
23. Tick off
24. Six-legged lifter
25. Customize
29. Interjection of the Bible
31. Enter
32. Garden site
33. Night driver's bane
35. Preamble's second word
36. She went *Under the Tuscan Sun*
40. Gambler's prize
43. Assurance
44. Lots of money
48. Morale
50. Flat hat
51. "Relax"
52. It helps shape
54. Physician flock
55. She went to TV and movies
59. Rhymed word for Rudolph
62. Mental picture
63. Now, and I mean it!
64. Jellystone resident
65. Manchester moola
66. List of eats
67. Part of an REM, Marcel's, or Pink Floyd hit title
68. Condition
69. Previous

DOWN

1. Can't stand
2. Past due
3. Dot
4. Kirk's birthplace
5. Criminal
6. Like a Pisan tower
7. Sprightly song
8. Fly high
9. And so on
10. Classic poser
11. Is no longer
12. Kind
13. Monty Python opener
21. Feh!
22. Gobbled up
26. Portion
27. How pretty!
28. Hwy.
30. What happened next?
31. Desalinization slag
33. Wildebeests
34. Musician Paul
37. Presumptuous greeting
38. Blood lines
39. Meadow mama
40. Free pitch, for short
41. Decide on
42. Bolo, for one
45. Large Asian lake
46. Humiliates
47. Remain
49. Collect
50. 39 Down comment
52. Disrespecter
53. Actress Witherspoon
56. Porn
57. Lithe Lipinski
58. Glower
59. Rope-climbing place
60. Pub pit stop
61. Arrogance

★**Solution on page 319**

Foreign-born all-Americans

1	2	3	■	4	5	6	■	7	8	9	■	10	11	12
13			■	14			■	15			■	16		
17			■	18			19				20			
21			■	■	22			■	23			■	■	■
24			25	26				27				28	29	■
■	■	■	30				■	31			■	32		33
34	35	36				■	37					38		
39			■	■	■	40			■	■	■	41		
42			■	43	44			■	45	46	47			
48			■	49			■	50				■	■	■
■	51		52				53					54	55	56
■	■	■	57			■	58			■	■	59		
60	61	62				63				64	■	65		
66			■	67			■	68			■	69		
70			■	71			■	72			■	73		

ACROSS

1. Buddy
4. By way of
7. Police alert, for short
10. Rocks at a bar
13. Mined-over matter
14. "The One I Love" group
15. Which person?
16. Place down
17. Gusher gush
18. All-American athlete from Norway
21. *The Ice Storm* director
22. Juliette Low org.
23. Fireplace remains
24. All-American scientist from Germany
30. Impressed reactions
31. Shoe for a wide box
32. Overly
34. *WKRP* role
37. *Charlie's Angels* actress
38. Lay down the lawn
39. Discoverer's cry
40. War survivor
41. Beatle beau
42. Naughty
43. Bickering
45. Snug neckwear
48. Hit sign
49. Rile up
50. Kind of duck
51. All-American industrialist from Scotland
57. Actor Aldridge
58. O.J. judge
59. The sun, for instance
60. All-American writer from England
65. Tango necessity
66. Heated event
67. Sticky stuff
68. Just out
69. British container
70. Wasabi wampum
71. Termination
72. "Just the Way You ___"
73. Some

DOWN

1. Wampum
2. The Little Mermaid
3. Star
4. Indy's quest
5. Drawn-out
6. Tickles one's funny bone
7. Floor
8. Worded
9. Given a leg up
10. Species
11. American 69 Across
12. Spotter
19. First name in skating
20. *Evita* role
25. Geologic time unit
26. Glass of Hollywood
27. Peachy keen
28. Calming words
29. Herman's Hermits leader
33. Stinky scent
34. Pugilist ploys
35. Tara family name
36. Wore
37. Tennis call
40. Opinion
43. Big concern post-9/11
44. Federal crime
45. Quincy, for one
46. Snookums
47. Countdown number
50. Charo, for instance
52. Unclear
53. Group with operatives
54. *She's ___ Have It*
55. Mr. Noodle portrayer
56. "___ and Ivory"
60. Stab
61. Work on the plot
62. Possess
63. Veggie unit
64. Farm female

★ **Solution on page 320**

Throw in the towel

1	2	3	4	5	■	6	7	8	9	■	10	11	12	13
14					■	15				■	16			
17					■	18				■	19			
■	■	20			■	21				22	■	23		
24	25				■	■	■	26			■	27		
28					29	30	31				32			■
33			■	■	34			■	■	35				■
■	■	■	36	37				38	39			■	■	■
■	40	41			■	■	42			■	■	43	44	45
■	46				47	48				49	50			
51			■	52			■	■	■	53				
54			■	55			56	57	■	58			■	■
59			60	■	61				■	62			63	64
65				■	66				■	67				
68				■	69				■	70				

ACROSS

1. Follow
6. Shopping spot
10. Paul Bunyan's pet
14. "Rabbit food"
15. Walkie-talkie ender
16. Part of DAG
17. Cultured gem
18. Singer Stubbs
19. Steady look
20. Place to get away from it all
21. Snow bank
23. Slam into
24. Respond to reveille
26. Inventor Whitney
27. Mother's Day's month
28. Start of riddle
33. Bond author Fleming
34. Presently
35. They go with lasses
36. Middle of riddle
40. Bohemian
42. Comedian Aykroyd
43. Asian ___
46. End of riddle
51. Cunning
52. Expert
53. Ally McBeal's roomie
54. Crooner Cole
55. Go by thumb
58. First name in pet detectives
59. Wimbledon winner
61. Quite a party
62. Old hat
65. Disaster recovery gp.
66. Persia, today
67. Come after
68. World power of old
69. The Big Apple's finest
70. Jobs in computers

DOWN

1. Kitchen meas.
2. Tommy Chong's daughter
3. One with a Nome home
4. Flying transport of legend
5. Canadian country singer
6. Form former
7. Swear up and down
8. Go over
9. Hodgepodge dessert
10. Halloweener's accessory
11. Like some houses
12. Marketplaces
13. Rival
22. It's on the cover
24. "Over There" time, for short
25. Snoop's cry
29. Abolish
30. First 60% of the answer
31. Alfred Nobel, for one
32. Paved substance
36. Had lunch
37. Water being of myth
38. Skater Babilonia
39. Blast it
40. Reference books
41. Beats
43. Smooth one's art
44. Kathie ___ Gifford
45. Put to work
47. Humble beginnings
48. Phone type
49. Window accessories
50. Take back
51. Mistake
56. Show appreciation
57. Shadow puppet
60. Musician's asset
63. Car/truck hybrid
64. Having a lot of sole

★**Solution on page 320**

Hits of 1968

ACROSS

1. Vocal jazz style
5. It gets in hot water
11. Success
14. Autobahn auto
15. Invader of Gaul
16. Bat wood
17. It begins "Drop your silver . . ."
20. Decline health-wise
21. ___ Tech
22. Six-year job
23. 5 Down
25. Corny
26. Water wagglers
29. Heap
31. Toot one's own horn
34. *Seinfeld* role
36. Took cover
39. Steppenwolf song
42. Fictional first baseman
43. Yearn
44. Excuse me, in Sussex
45. Totally absorbed
46. Bit of data
48. Weigh station queue
51. Religion
55. Grocery option, for paying or bagging
58. Cum.
60. Helms's focus
61. Troggs song that became Mary Tyler Moore's theme
64. Badly copy
65. Reservation sites
66. ___ spumante
67. ___ Years After
68. Acceptance votes
69. Celebration

DOWN

1. Long stories
2. Nobelist of 1903
3. Dancing-Fred's sister
4. Make a knot
5. 23 Across
6. List ender
7. 24-7 banker
8. Lobster eater's aids
9. Sun worshiper's salve
10. Hand worth throwing down
11. West Indies republic
12. Childish retort
13. "All done!"
18. Final Four org.
19. Hard to come by
24. Booboo's buddy
27. Summary
28. Biased opinion
29. Plumbing
30. Doin' nothin'
31. Autobahn auto
32. Yay!
33. Back when
35. Holy chest
36. Greetings
37. Wyo. neighbor
38. *L. A. Law* actress
40. Cher's child
41. Funny Rudner
45. Hilltop
47. Way off yonder
48. Squashing sound
49. Avoid a big wedding
50. Expert
52. "Occupied"
53. They're staked
54. Past one's limit
56. Listener's comment
57. Head toppers
58. Happiness
59. It gets you in
62. French article
63. Fumbler

★ **Solution on page 320**

Sides reversed is

ACROSS

1. You might need to watch yours
5. Free ___
11. One who is all thumbs
14. Heavens to Betsy!
15. Loose cannon
16. One who knows their way around
17. Ring leader?
20. Break even
21. Run in neutral
22. Drop
23. Organize
25. Venezuela's capital
28. Enterprising start
30. Stain
33. Supremo
34. Insecticide that threatened the bald eagle
37. Routes that have deteriorated
42. Past
43. Dash
44. Genie's home
45. Art's places
49. Early show
52. Puff up
56. Unseen *Will and Grace* ex
57. Performances
58. Fancy holder
59. Dieting, perhaps
64. Cereal grain
65. Cutesy call
66. Famous last words
67. Slophouse?
68. Bed liners?
69. Shortly, in business

DOWN

1. In a way
2. *A League of ___ Own*
3. Set foot in
4. Luau item
5. Erasure mark
6. Way to keep your eyes
7. Business letter abbr.
8. Star on *The Facts of Life*
9. Critical patient's site, for short
10. 18 Down + 1
11. Visual
12. Battle ground
13. Road splits
18. 10 Down–1
19. "Old chap" preceder, often
24. Piedmont city
25. Condo kin
26. Actress Bancroft
27. Lively dance
29. Its outsiders are said to be from "away"
30. "Be prepared" gp.
31. Trek part
32. John ___ Lennon
34. Means of ID
35. "___ Bones"
36. Chef's qty.
38. "The corned beef, is it ___?"
39. *Allure* rival
40. Part of IPA
41. Rick's old flame
45. Cotton-picking devices
46. Parish veep
47. Emcee openers
48. Otherwise
49. PC language
50. Bothered
51. Yum!
53. Corrodes
54. Actress Garbo
55. Eventually become
57. Tennis pro
60. Cyclops feature
61. Steiger or Serling of entertainment
62. Garment
63. Vast amount

★ **Solution on page 320**

No grade school

ACROSS

1. Like some eyes
6. Carnivore's preference
10. Strike
14. Lost
15. As well
16. Was a passenger
17. Musician with no grade school
20. At least one
21. Take a load off
22. Party
24. Vault
28. Actor/director with no grade school
34. Shake up
35. Broadside
36. Mystique
37. Neckwear
38. Controls
40. Detailed drawing
41. Give it a go
43. Nonprescription med.
44. Recovers from racing
46. Industrialist with no grade school
50. Separate
51. Top-class
52. Balance out
56. Adam, to Alan
59. Showman with no grade school
65. "Understood"
66. Otis's adventure pal
67. A sight for sore eyes
68. "Diamonds and Rust" singer
69. Billfold items
70. Pelt

DOWN

1. Southern California
2. 007's school
3. Pale as a ghost
4. Thief set
5. Jabber
6. Rum drink
7. Glamour mag
8. The biggest continent
9. Bests
10. Good show sign
11. Ted's TV boss
12. Pitches
13. Mini missile
18. Arsenio's last name
19. Actress Ward
22. Long fish
23. Weapon
25. Cleanup crew, for short
26. Grads
27. Skull and crossbones guy
28. Scrubs
29. Coif
30. Author Jong
31. Soup holder
32. British ship intials
33. Baby's breaks
34. Tynan's portrayer
38. Fight
39. Yada-yada-yada
42. Do incorrectly
44. Write
45. Time period
47. Italian erupter
48. Proportions
49. Xmas song
53. A red little monster
54. Enter
55. Competent
56. Just okay
57. Valhalla host
58. CFO's concern, perhaps
59. Chest protector
60. Olympics chant
61. Price
62. *That '70s Show* role
63. Spanish article
64. Fellow, to a beatnik

★**Solution on page 320**

Children's classics

ACROSS

1. Lear rival
7. Confront
11. Era rival
14. Director's call
15. Pianist Hines
16. In the past
17. Margaret Wise Brown story
20. Piglet's mom
21. Cancel
22. Delivery item
23. Inspirator of 1 Down
26. Place for an IPO
27. Yucatan native
30. Goal
31. Tennis tourney
34. Black History month
41. Ludwig Bemelmans tale
43. Fancy cake topper
44. ___ *Bedelia*
45. SCTV kin
47. *A River ___ Through It*
48. It blows
52. Fall guys
55. Sign up
57. Moll's feature
58. Security call, for short
61. Jean de Brunhoff book
65. Nose-to-nose outcome
66. Clannad member
67. Catty one
68. Reach a decision
69. Taboo look
70. Reduced a sentence

DOWN

1. It was inspired by 23 Across
2. It's repeated
3. Thick soup
4. Peppermint Patty, to Marcie
5. Bait and switch
6. Gun-getting gal
7. Not many
8. Bond rating
9. *Tales from the ___*
10. Exile isle
11. Decorated
12. Blue Moon Det. Agcy. secretary
13. Star of *Young Frankenstein* and *Everybody Loves Raymond*
18. Car bar
19. Coffee holder
23. Candle
24. Blaze
25. Kind words
27. Fall flowers
28. Right away!
29. *Star Wars* sage
32. Fancy-antlered one
33. Absolutely nothing
35. Sports ___
36. Dream marker, briefly
37. Mac people
38. Left-wing gp.
39. Desecrate
40. Pro votes
42. Egg site
46. Symbol
48. Reach
49. Nerdy
50. Winter forecast
51. High notes
52. Rock
53. Mistake
54. Implant
56. Dance instruction
58. Somewhat
59. It might be cracked
60. Raised
62. Catcher's place
63. Have a gabfest
64. "The greatest"

★**Solution on page 320**

Dr. Seuss classics

ACROSS

1. Headliner
5. Food for a jungle carnivore
9. Version
14. Isn't bad
15. Skeleton item
16. Magazine work
17. Dr. Seuss classic
20. Emulate Betsy Ross
21. Oft-lent item
22. Lecturer's lectern
23. Fizzy drink
26. River ripple
27. Follow
30. Accept
32. Taste bud sense
33. Sand ___
34. It yields something valuable
37. Dr. Seuss classic
42. Keebler worker
43. Author Uris
44. Sharp
45. Revises to screenplay
47. Touchy aurophile
48. *Rocky Horror* role
51. Treaty contingency, perhaps
53. It changed the way we watch TV
55. Joplin piece
56. Styled like
59. Dr. Seuss classic
63. Biblical verb
64. Bird feature
65. *E.T.* prop
66. Chip at
67. Slow boats
68. "Got it!" item

DOWN

1. Has give
2. Weary
3. All over again
4. Hwy.
5. Beg
6. Little scamp
7. Fabergé item
8. Absolutely!
9. SMERSH head
10. Blush
11. Plant pest
12. Fake
13. Classic rock opera
18. Sign gas
19. Show up
23. Type
24. Edison's collection
25. Gumbo pod
27. U.S. Open champ of '68
28. Neato!
29. Territory
31. HQ
34. Carried a debt
35. Flightless bird
36. It's like forever
38. Past one's youth
39. Clean up
40. Silver lining
41. Related
45. Was a big fan of
46. Run naked
47. One of them brought myrrh
48. Form of influence
49. Look up
50. Pedro's pal
52. Supports
54. London gallery
56. Battery fluid
57. Leia's rescuer
58. On the water
60. Filler program, for short
61. That girl
62. Batter's stat

★ **Solution on page 320**

Chapter 12

Clueless Crosswords

Fill 'Er Up 1

3 LETTERS
ABS
ACE
ART
ATE
AWE
CAP
DRY
EBB
EEL
EGO
ERA
EWE
ICY
LEI
MOP
OAT
PIC
RED
ROD
ROT
RUE
RUG
SAD
SHE
SUN
TEE
TEN
TUG
VEG
YES

4 LETTERS
AGER
EDGE
ISN'T
MEET
OGRE
REAR
STAR
VARY

5 LETTERS
ENTER
ORBIT
RULED
STATE
STOUT
TILDE
ZESTY

6 LETTERS
ASSURE
AUNTIE
CRISPY
DEVOTE
EASILY
ESTATE
HEATED
PECANS
STOOGE
UNSEAT
VENEER
WINDOW

7 LETTERS
ODYSSEY

8 LETTERS
PINTSIZE
SYNOPSIS

9 LETTERS
BARRACUDA
INCAPABLE

★ **Solution on page 320**

Fill 'Er Up 2

3 LETTERS
ACT
AGO
AHA
AND
AXE
BIT
BRA
EAR
EAT
INN
MAP
MAT
OAR
OIL
ONE
PIE
PRO
PUT
RIM
RIP
ROW
SEE
TAN

4 LETTERS
ALOE
AMEN
ATOP
CHAI
EGOS
ERGO
EYED
FARE
FETA
GALA
GLEE
IDEA
MADE
MESA
NINE
NIPS
ODOR
PERT
RAVE
RISE
SAME
SEMI
SINS
STAB
STEW
SWAM
TAXI
THEM
UNTO
WEPT

5 LETTERS
AGAPE
AGILE
AMBLE
ELDER
GALES
MANIA
NOTED
PEARL
PLUMP
PRIME
SPOOF
STOLE
STUNT
TABBY
TIGER
TITLE

6 LETTERS
AMULET
EMBLEM
FELINE
IMPALE
NARROW
PROMPT
STUPID
WALNUT

7 LETTERS
PICCOLO

8 LETTERS
ATTRACTS
MIDNIGHT

9 LETTERS
CALIBRATE
OVERRULED

★ **Solution on page 320**

Fill 'Er Up 3

3 LETTERS

ADO
AFT
ALE
AMP
ARE
BAA
BEG
CAN
CAW
DEN
DUG
ELF
ELK
END
EON
ERA
EWE
FEZ
GAL
GYP
HAS
HEN
HER
ICE
ILL
INN
IRE
JOT
LEI
LOX
LUG
MAR
MOW
NIX
ODE
OHO
OLE
ONE
ORE
OWL
OWN
PLY
RUE
SEE
SHE
SKI
SOL
TOE
TOP
TWO
VAN
VOW
WEE
WHO
YEN

4 LETTERS

BIBS
ERGO
FELL
GENE
HOST
IRON
JOIN
KNEE
LUAU
NAPE
QUIT
RARE
SEAT
SOAK
TALE
VETO
WEEP
ZOOM

5 LETTERS

AFOUL
ALGAE
ALLOW
APTLY
JELLY
LEASE
MAJOR
OLIVE
OMITS
SELAH
SENSE
TENET
TYPED
VINYL
VISTA
WEARS

6 LETTERS

AROMAS
RELATE
RETIRE
SALMON

9 LETTERS

FREQUENCY

★Solution on page 321

Fill 'Er Up 4

3 LETTERS
AFT
ALL
APE
ARE
DRY
EEK
ELF
FAB
FUN
HOE
ICY
ILL
ITS
KEG
LAY
LEG
NAP
OAF
OIL
OOH
REV
RID
SAW
SEA
SOL
STY
TIE
TRY
UGH
VIE
ZAP
ZED

4 LETTERS
ACES
AGER
ANTS
AQUA
ARCS
ARIA
ARTS
AVID
CHAI
CLAW
DEAL
DELI
EARL
EDGE
ERRS
EVES
GEAR
IDEA
JADE
KEYS
LAVA
MAZE
MEAT
NEST
ONCE
OPEN
PERT
PHEW
PLAN
PSST
QUIT
RACE
RAJA
RIDE
RUNG
SLIT
SMUT
TIDE
UNDO
VAST
VIOL
VISA

5 LETTERS
AIOLI
ASTIR
BURRO
FENCE
FLEAS
GNOME
IDLER
LEAST
PESKY
REMIX
SLASH
SLEEK
SLEPT
TRUCE
UNION
VILLA

6 LETTERS
BRONZE
BUGLES
COERCE
DELUXE
ENVIED
FAILED
KEEPER
SEWERS
TWELVE
WAITER

7 LETTERS
AREAWAY
LARDERS
NEGATED

8 LETTERS
ANCESTOR
PREVIEWS

9 LETTERS
ANOMALIES

★ **Solution on page 321**

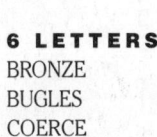

Fill 'Er Up 5

3 LETTERS
AGO
AID
AIR
ALE
AMP
AND
ANY
BYE
DIE
EAT
EGO
EWE
FOG
FOR
GOO
HEY
ILK
LOT
LUG
MAC
MET
NOW
ODD
ODE
OOH
ORE
OWN
RED
SUE
TEA
TOM
VEX
WEE
ZIT

4 LETTERS
AREA
DEED
ELSE
GAZE
IDEA
MAMA
NEXT
OMIT
OPTS
QUIP
SODA
WOVE

5 LETTERS
ABETS
BATTY
CUSHY
DRANK
HARSH
HORSE
HOSTS
JADED
JUMBO
NANAS
OUTDO
UNDER
WINKS
YOUTH

6 LETTERS
BARRED
SQUIBS

7 LETTERS
APRICOT
LIKENED

8 LETTERS
COMMUTER
NARRATOR

★ Solution on page 321

Fill 'Er Up 6

3 LETTERS
ADO
DON
EAR
EGO
ERA
EWE
FAD
GAS
GEM
HOW
IRE
JIG
LIE
RAN
USE
WAS
WHO
YES

4 LETTERS
ACRE
ADDS
ANTE
ARKS
AWLS
AXLE
BLAH
CZAR
DAZE
DEED
EDGE
FIAT
GEAR
HATE
HOOK
ICON
MERE
NANA
OAKS
OWES
OWLS
PREY
QUAD
QUIT
SALE
STAT
TEST
TOOL
TUTU
UNDO
UPON
WHAM
WHOA
WOES

5 LETTERS
AROMA
CLERK
EGRET
EJECT
ELDER
EXPEL
GNASH
HOLEY
INEPT
ISLET
LEVEE
NEWER
ORGAN
PSALM
RADIO
RELAY
SLOPE
STOOL
TENTS
TIARA
TWINE
UNCUT

6 LETTERS
BIASES
DELETE
MORTAR
RAVENS
SLIGHT
TAUNTS

7 LETTERS
ENCORES
SEDATED

8 LETTERS
ANCIENTS
TRESTLES

★ **Solution on page 321**

Fill 'Er Up 7

3 LETTERS
ADO
APE
BYE
DOG
EEL
END
EYE
FIT
GAS
GOO
ILK
ITS
OLD
RAN
RAW
RYE
SEE
TAB
TIE
WAD

4 LETTERS
AKIN
BOOT
BUSH
CLAD
DRIP
FACT
IDEA
IDOL
NEED
NERD
NETS
ODOR
ONTO
PLIE
SIGH
SING
SPOT
STIR
TOLL
VENT
VISA
YETI

5 LETTERS
ALLOY
AMISS
ATTIC
DIODE
ELATE
ELDER
ENTER
ERODE
HORSE
IRATE
KNEAD
LAPEL
LEDGE
MEDAL
OPERA
SATIN
SLEET
STORY
TANGO
TONES

6 LETTERS
ARTIST
CRITIC
GORGES
ONIONS
OTTERS
PISTOL
TEASER
VIRILE

7 LETTERS
SETTLER
SLANDER

8 LETTERS
ARACHNID
SCEPTERS

9 LETTERS
CONCEALER
ENVISIONS
GROCERIES
UNDERTAKE

★ **Solution on page 321**

Chapter 13

Theme Party

Food, wonderful food 1

1	2	3	4	■	5	6	7	8	■	9	10	11
12				■	13				■	14		
15				■	16				■	17		
■	■	■	18	19		■	■	20	21			
22	23	24			■	25	26				■	■
27			■	28	29			■	30		31	32
33			■	34				35	■	36		
37			38	■	39				■	40		
■	■	41		42			■	43	44			
45	46				■	■	47			■	■	■
48			■	49	50	51		■	52	53	54	55
56			■	57				■	58			
59			■	60				■	61			

ACROSS

1. Dutch cheese
5. Brewer's yeast
9. Absorb, like gravy
12. Part of IPA
13. Recipe words
14. Another part of IPA
15. Italian cooking style?
16. Broil
17. Food school, for short
18. Recipe abbr.
20. Hungry-Man rival
22. Soy sauce
25. Red wine also called Shiraz
27. Way more than 18 Across
28. ___ Moco (a burger with a fried egg, rice, and brown gravy)
30. Spirit sometimes used in tapenade
33. Sushi tuna, often
34. Dos Equis, for one
36. Strong Brazilian coffee
37. Jicama or horseradish
39. ___ trout
40. Place often having a quaint restaurant
41. Frequent detail for Chinese food
43. Stovetop
45. Epicure's pride
47. Where to skim from
48. Sushi squid
49. A lubricating liquid
52. ___ apple
56. Sushi fish
57. Their tails are used in soup
58. Common fruit shape
59. Tea ___
60. More than merely dip
61. Keg tapper

DOWN

1. Farm spray watchdog
2. Indian legume or dish
3. ___ purpose flour
4. Like some beans
5. Food fish
6. Fruity drink
7. Advised quantities, for short
8. Seder spice
9. Artificial sweetener
10. Aglio e ___
11. Fruit shaped like a light bulb
19. The "meat" of onion or garlic
21. ___ prik (hot sauce)
22. ___ fruit
23. Hostess product
24. Seasoning from a shaker
25. One without much meat
26. ___ Imperial apple
29. Seasons a pan, perhaps
31. Flan mold
32. Ice cream holder
35. UK candy bar
38. A "short shot" of a beverage
42. Red Bordeaux wine
44. Chef's garb
45. Bow ___ (farfalle)
46. Caribbean fruit resembling a peach
47. Loosely cover meat
50. Kitchen gadget manufacturer
51. Black-eyed or goober ___
53. Caviar, for instance
54. ___ Tai (drink)
55. Shape for some kitchens

★ **Solution on page 321**

Food, wonderful food 2

1	2	3	■	4	5	6	7	■	■	8	9	10
11			■	12				13	■	14		
15			16						■	17		
■	■	■	18			■	■	19	20			
21	22	23			■	24	25			■	■	■
26			■	27	28			■	29	30	31	32
33			34	■	35			■	36			
37				■	38			39	■	40		
■	■	■	41	42			■	43	44			
45	46	47			■	■	48			■	■	■
49			■	50	51	52				53	54	55
56			■	57					■	58		
59			■	■	60				■	61		

ACROSS

1. Italian wine standard
4. Dutch cheese type
8. Cola, casually
11. Beating and folding add this
12. Where to coat with egg and bread crumbs, fry, and season with Parmesan
14. Food pesticide regulator
15. Diner "special"
17. Cooking vessel
18. French for "garlic"
19. Campfire treat
21. Rub clean
24. ___ spumante
26. Anago or unagi
27. Waffle brand
29. Mexican dough
33. Trans fatty ___
35. Chef Rachael ___
36. ___ *Chef* (Japanese head-to-head cooking show)
37. *Mostly Martha* adoptee
38. Spanish grapes
40. Pistachio or macadamia
41. Cannoli or manicotti
43. Pub on *Murphy Brown*
45. Had a fine meal
48. Milk, at a diner
49. Italian for "goose"
50. Another name for muttonfish
56. Tasty mushroom
57. Chinese takeout disclaimer, often
58. Summer refresher
59. Cookie selling gp.
60. Beef Wellington or mayonnaise honoree, originally
61. Recipe unit for whale chowder?

DOWN

1. Type of flounder
2. Sesame or olive product
3. French or Italian vineyard
4. Kind of apple
5. Type of seasoning
6. Recipe preposition
7. Place setting, perhaps
8. Hard-skinned fruit
9. ___ ayam (Indonesian chicken in coconut milk)
10. French mixture served with bread
13. Bird's ___ soup
16. ___-de-vie
20. "La Bohème" lead, who has no money for food
21. Cook en papillote
22. Another name for a chickpea
23. *Chocolat* actress
24. Tequila base
25. ___ bean milk
28. Food, casually
30. Souvlaki ingredient
31. ___ food
32. They can be covered in chocolate and eaten
34. Middle Eastern fruit
39. ___ cake
42. Thick Japanese noodle
44. ___ sack (grain bag)
45. One step up from 1 Across
46. Italian desserts
47. California wine region
48. Completely cover
51. Haddock's family
52. Aussie delicacy
53. Common cereal grain
54. Japanese veggie similar to fennel
55. Arm count for calamari

★**Solution on page 321**

Food, wonderful food 3

1	2	3	■	4	5	6	7	■	■	8	9	10
11			■	12				13	■	14		
15			16						■	17		
■	■	■	18			■	■	19	20			
21	22	23		■	24	25	26			■	■	■
27			■	■	■	28				29	30	31
32			33	■	34			■	35			
36				37			■	■	■	38		
■	■	■	39				40	■	41			
42	43	44			■	■	45	46		■	■	■
47			■	48	49	50				51	52	53
54			■	55					■	56		
57			■	■	58				■	59		

ACROSS

1. Chili ___ carne
4. *Iron Chef* faction
8. ___-in-one method
11. Japanese sea urchin
12. Wine region of Spain
14. ___ Tai (drink)
15. Tangy stew, low on sauce
17. Chili ___
18. Salmon ___
19. ___ pudding
21. What braided cheese resembles
24. Really enjoy what you eat
27. 12 Across growth
28. ___ greens
32. U.S. wine industry overseers, for short
34. French for garlic
35. ___ d' oliva
36. Dutch liqueur
38. Sugar units, for short
39. A Greek cheese
41. Wine quantity
42. ___ Mayer
45. Sliced pepper shape
47. Kind of tea
48. Pink snapper
54. ___ chocolate
55. Dish unlike "drunken chicken"?
56. ___ pla (Thai fish dish)
57. Had food
58. Preps the cake
59. ___ Maria

DOWN

1. Demitasse, for one
2. Number of cells in yeast
3. Less than a nosh
4. Sandwich cookie
5. Root beer maker
6. Where meringue tends to be placed
7. Spanish for garlic
8. Famous cookie man
9. Cafe au ___
10. Asparagus and garlic, technically
13. ___ brose (Scottish drink)
16. Vert-___ (greenish herb sauce)
20. He sang about someone's restaurant
21. Griller's prides
22. Shape of some serving plates
23. Spanish duck
25. ___ di Pepe (small soup pasta)
26. ___-au-vent
29. Preposition in an Italian cookbook
30. Grilled specialty
31. A spoonful of sugar?
33. Greek salad ingredient
34. What whipping adds
37. Popular Greek dish
40. Pear-shaped fruit
41. Kind of mushroom
42. Japanese tea
43. What a chaser follows
44. Actress Blanchett, of the film short *Bangers*
46. Corn units
49. Luau fare
50. Malaysian dessert
51. Crunchy chocolate-covered item
52. Tom ga ___ (Thai soup)
53. ___-ebi (sweet shrimp)

★ **Solution on page 321**

Food, wonderful food 4

1	2	3	■	4	5	6	7	■	8	9	10	11
12			■	13				■	14			
15			16					■	17			
■	■	■	18			■	19	20		■	■	■
■	21	22		■	23	24			■	25	26	27
28				29	■	30			■	31		
32			■	33	34				■	35		
36			■	37			■	38	39			
40			■	41			42	■	43			■
■	■	■	44			■	45	46		■	■	■
47	48	49		■	50	51				52	53	54
55				■	56				■	57		
58				■	59				■	60		

ACROSS

1. Baste
4. Breakfast brand
8. Trendy appetizer
12. Bulb used in France
13. Croaker or kingfish
14. Indian spinach sauce
15. When to eat a basic square
17. To squeeze through a pastry tube
18. Actor Holm of *Big Night*
19. Amt. in rice bags
21. Linzer torte ingredient
23. Venison's source
25. Thousand-year-old egg coating
28. Zaatar ingredient
30. Had food
31. Kung ___ chicken
32. In the style of
33. Toll ___ cookie
35. Daiquiri base
36. Where cranberries grow
37. Thousand Year ___ Egg
38. Table ___ (menu)
40. Farm spray regulator
41. Not go bad
43. Pits in an avocado
44. ___ Equis
45. Cornstalk growth
47. In the Zone Diet, it's a carbo and protein block
50. Recent food concern
55. Arincini or kofta shape
56. Give meat a chance to rejuice near the surface after cooking
57. Chorizo spice
58. Drinking cheer
59. Citrus drinks
60. Little bite

DOWN

1. Nuoc ___ (Vietnamese fish sauce)
2. Goose
3. Nam ___ (Thai fish sauce)
4. Food additive for removing heavy metals
5. Put through the mill
6. It's made from chicle
7. Egg dishes
8. Recipe amts.
9. Yellowfin
10. Baby food
11. Improve wine
16. ___ bean
20. Wine grape's heritage
21. Mint ___
22. Microwave oven maker
24. ___-vie
25. Chef's attire
26. Quickly cook
27. ___ cooking
28. Like mussels before a red tide
29. Mango squash
34. P&G fat substitute
39. ___ d'oeuvre
42. ___ pudding
44. Flat, as a drink
46. Chocolate-covered ___
47. Cooking qty.
48. Wine barrel flavoring
49. "Kiss my grits!" gal
51. Cabernet or shiraz
52. Butterfly, basically
53. Spanish mackerel, in Japan
54. Dot or ice

★ **Solution on page 321**

Food, wonderful food 5

1	2	3	■	4	5	6	7	■	8	9	10	11
12			■	13				■	14			
15			■	16				■	17			
18			19		■	20		21		■	■	■
■	■	■	22		23		■	24		25	26	27
28	29	30		■	31		32		■	33		
34				35		■	36		37			
38			■	39		40		■	41			
42			43		■	44		45		■	■	■
■	■	■	46		47		■	48		49	50	51
52	53	54		■	55		56		■	57		
58				■	59				■	60		
61				■	62				■	63		

ACROSS

1. Food for a baby
4. Crispy cookie
8. Form of shortening
12. Grey snapper
13. Sandwich in a shell
14. Aglio e ___
15. Head of Alice's restaurant
16. ___ pit BBQ
17. General ___ Chicken
18. Julia Child's NPR cohort
20. Loose papillote
22. Host Carmichael of *Calling All Cooks*
24. British candy bars
28. Abuse alcohol
31. Japanese tea
33. Deviled eggs, for instance
34. One way to cut
36. ___ crackers
38. Butter serving
39. Sushi go-with
41. Tuna ___
42. Half of a Japanese stew
44. Pita's ethnicity
46. Top-of-the-line avocado
48. A la ___ (Russian-style)
52. Brut, for one
55. *Iron Chef* group
57. Unlike a squab or capon
58. *Chocolat* actress
59. Squeeze juice from
60. ___ sticker
61. Strongly flavored drink
62. Soft cheese
63. DDT banners

DOWN

1. Cryovac need
2. Red tropical fruit
3. Fruit pomace
4. Cherry pit
5. Cover with sauce without hiding the food's shape
6. Vinegary
7. Corn ___ (type of bread)
8. Monkfish
9. *Happy Days* diner
10. Harsh Brazilian coffee flavor
11. ___ Equis
19. Bakery worker
21. Type of Indian bread
23. Soda
25. ___ Beauty apple
26. Quennelle shape
27. Common seasoning
28. Recipe qtys.
29. Moonfish
30. Middle Eastern or Greek bread
32. Angel ___ pasta
35. Tijuana water
37. Fruit that looks like a plum, but tastes like an orange
40. Bacon serving
43. Drug used in a drink
45. Popular seaweed for salad
47. ___ apple
49. Filled tortilla dish
50. Unimpressive food
51. Safe food additive for metal protection
52. Corn serving
53. Preposition in a cookbook
54. Coq au ___
56. Mai ___

★ **Solution on page 322**

Food, wonderful food 6

1	2	3	4	■	5	6	7	8	■	9	10	11
12				■	13				■	14		
15				■	16				■	17		
■	■	■	18	19			■	20	21			
22	23	24				■	25			■	■	■
26			■	27		28		■	29	30	31	32
33			■	■	34			■	■	35		
36			37	■	38			39	■	40		
■	■	■	41	42		■	43		44			
45	46	47			■	48				■	■	■
49			■	50	51			■	52	53	54	55
56			■	57				■	58			
59			■	60				■	61			

ACROSS

1. Ropa viejo base
5. Another name for porgy
9. Sop
12. ___ Curaçao
13. Laughable dessert?
14. Type of beer, for short
15. Italian for seed, as in "___ di melone"
16. Italian oil
17. Fondue ___
18. Dessert, or flavor
20. French wine region
22. Russian food (variant spelling)
25. Goose
26. Albarino wine base
27. Cake decorater
29. Surf and ___
33. A dry red wine, briefly
34. Japanese prawn
35. ___-au-vent
36. Bread spread
38. ___ pao chicken
40. When preceding "mode," with ice cream on top
41. Macaroni shape
43. Martini with a white onion, not an olive
45. Food for Caesar?
48. Bill of fare
49. ___-cook
50. Water, in Mexico
52. Much-maligned canned hash
56. Roadside hotel, often with dining
57. Shaper used in cooking
58. Healthy drink, from pop-culture sprouting seeds
59. ___ Maria
60. Filet of ___
61. He played the villain in *Big Night*

DOWN

1. Briefly, scrod's always less than three of these
2. Ginger ___
3. German beer since 1492
4. 22 Across base
5. Dessert usually with a fruit topping
6. Young male farm worker?
7. Yam
8. Indian bread
9. Japanese soup
10. ___-faced sandwich
11. It's put in a 57 Across
19. Bluefin cousin
21. ___ pint (Scottish drink)
22. Osso ___
23. Egg's shape, approximately
24. Broccoli ___
25. Citrus drink
28. Bird eaten Down Under
30. Spanish wine need
31. Chewy candy brand name
32. Traditionally, a custard dessert
37. Edible tuber
39. Sloe ___ fizz
42. Dutch cheeses
44. Anheuser-___
45. Revolving skewer for roasting
46. Buffalo
47. Actress Olin of *Chocolat*
48. Heat and spice, like cider
51. Moo ___ gai pan
53. Asian beef noodle soup
54. Aioli need
55. Nuoc___

★**Solution on page 322**

Bible crossword 1

ACROSS

1. "in the days when the judges ___": Ruth 1:1
6. "he had ___ himself with a new garment": 1 Kings 11:29
10. "A ___ answer turneth away wrath": Proverbs 15:1
14. "And Moses said, I will now turn ___": Exodus 3:3
15. "talents of silver to ___ them chariots": 1 Chron. 19:6
16. Biblical weed
17. "and the garment, and the ___ of gold": Joshua 7:24
18. About whom was said "Am I my brother's keeper?"
19. "out of the ___ furnace, even out of Egypt": Deu. 4:20
20. "comfort yourselves together, and ___ one another": The. 5:11
22. "bore his ear through with an ___": Exodus 21:6
24. "and he ___ his birthright unto Jacob": Gen. 25:33
27. "took away the locusts, and cast them into the Red ___": Exodus 10:19
28. "The young lions roared upon him, and ___": Jer. 2:15
32. "Stand in ___, and sin not": Psalms 4:4
33. "buried in a good ___ age": Gen. 15:15
34. "when ___ began to multiply": Gen. 6:1
35. "Give ___, O ye heavens, and I will speak": Deu. 32:1
36. "Yet will I bring one ___ more upon Pharaoh": Exodus 11:11
38. "Why is thy spirit so ___, that thou eatest no bread?": 1 Kings 21:5
39. "Nineveh, and the ___ Rehoboth": Gen. 10:11
40. "when she lay down, ___ when she arose": Gen. 19:35
41. "And Jacob ___ pottage": Gen. 25:29
42. "Whereas thou ___ been forsaken": Isaiah 60:15
43. "And Samuel told him every ___": 1 Samuel 3:18
45. "And she fastened it with the ___": Judges 16:14
46. "but the talk of the lips tendeth only to ___": Pro. 14:23
49. "even as a ___ gathereth her chickens": Matt. 23:37
50. Fowl's place
51. "___ that it was good": Gen. 1:18
52. "ye tithe mint and ___": Luke 11:42
53. "stringed instruments and ___": Psalms 150:4
55. "shut the doors, and ___ them": Neh. 7:3
56. "he hath ___ his bow": Psalms 7:12
57. "That which groweth of ___ own accord": Lev. 25:5
58. "And Noah builded an ___ unto the LORD": Gen. 8:20
60. "Therefore I will ___ and howl": Micah 1:8
63. "the land of Nod, on the ___ of Eden": Gen. 4:16
65. "that it may give seed to the ___": Isaiah 55:10
69. "for all their sins ___ a year": Lev. 16:34
70. "Who told ___ that thou were naked?": Gen. 3:11
71. "they look and ___ upon me": Psalms 22:17
72. "And Saul ___ David from that day and forward": 1 Samuel 18:9
73. "and Rachel travailed, and she had ___ labor": Gen. 35:16
74. "came and ___ them into the pot": 2 Kings 4:39

DOWN

1. "for the ___ flesh is unclean": Lev. 13:15
2. "neither shall ye ___ enchantment": Lev. 19:26
3. "took a chest, and bored a hole in the ___": 2 Kings 12:9
4. "sharp as a two-___ sword": Psalms 149:6
5. "What ___ is this that ye have done?": Gen. 44:15
6. "and they be ___ in their minds": 2 Samuel 17:8
7. "Persia, Ethiopia, and ___ with them": Eze. 38:5
8. "These ___ the three sons of Noah": Gen. 9:19
9. "I made haste, and ___ not": Psalms 119:60
10. "Stand ___, and I will hear what the LORD": Num. 9:8
11. "And all that handle the ___, the mariners": Eze. 27:29
12. "going to and ___ in the earth ": Job 1:7
13. Commandment count
21. "And the inhabitant of this ___ shall say in that day": Isaiah 20:6
23. "maimed, or having a ___": Lev. 22:22
24. "The trees . . . are full of ___": Psalms 104:16
25. "the screech ___ also shall rest there": Isaiah 34:14
26. "___ upon the top of his staff": Heb. 11:21
29. "they had no ___ so much as to eat": Mark 6:31
30. "But of the tree . . . thou shalt not ___ of it": Gen. 2:17
31. "called the ___ land Earth": Gen. 1:10
33. "Let us make man in ___ image": Gen. 1:26
34. "Surely oppression maketh a wise man ___": Ecc. 7:7
37. "which he had ___ in the land of Canaan": Gen. 36:6
38. "And Abraham said, My ___will provide himself a lamb": Gen. 22:8
39. "My punishment is greater than I ___ bear": Gen. 4:13
41. "The nobleman saith unto him, ___, come down ere my child die": John 4:49
42. "___ thee two tables of stone": Exodus 34:1
43. "___ dwelt in Sodom": Gen. 14:12
44. "Then Bathsheba bowed with ___ face to the earth": 1 Kings 1:31
45. "any that ___ against the wall": 1 Samuel 25:22
46. "Thou shalt ___ it in pieces": Lev. 2:6
47. "___ now, I pray thee, to meet her": 2 Kings 4:26
48. "And he stayed ___ another seven days": Gen. 8:10
50. "Go to the ___, thou sluggard": Pro. 6:6
51. "savour, wherewithal shall it be ___?": Matt. 5:13
54. "What ___ thee that thou fleddest?": Psalms 114:5
55. "fellows of the ___ sort": Acts 17:5
56. "and pour out the ___": Judges 6:20
59. "until an ___ head was sold": 2 Kings 6:25
60. "___ unto us!": 1 Samuel 4:8
61. "lest ___ find him should kill him": Gen. 4:15
62. "___, and wherein the snow is hid": Job 6:16
64. " ___, our eye hath seen it": Psalms 35:21
66. "The LORD is a man of ___": Exodus 15:3
67. "and how long will it be ___ they believe me": Num. 14:11
68. "His eyes shall be ___ with wine": Gen. 49:12

★ **Solution on page 322**

1	2	3	4	5	■	6	7	8	9	■	10	11	12	13
14					■	15				■	16			
17					■	18				■	19			
■	■	■	20		21			■	22	23		■	■	■
24	25	26		■	27			■	28			29	30	31
32			■	33			■	34			■	35		
36			37			■	38			■	39			
■	■	40			■	41			■	42			■	■
43	44			■	45			■	46				47	48
49			■	50			■	51			■	52		
53			54			■	55			■	56			
■	■	■	57			■	58			59		■	■	■
60	61	62		■	63	64			■	65		66	67	68
69				■	70				■	71				
72				■	73				■	74				

Bible crossword 2

ACROSS

1. "there he ___ the man whom he had formed": Gen. 2:8
4. "___ not the poor, because he is poor": Pro. 22:22
7. "___ gave me of the fruit, and I did eat": Gen. 3:6
10. "Thou shalt ___ them, and the wind": Isaiah 41:16
13. "he planteth an ___, and the rain doth nourish it": Isaiah 44:14
14. "Stand in ___, and sin not": Psalms 4:4
15. "with ___ and ink ": 3 John 1:13
16. "I am old and stricken in ___": Joshua 23:1
17. "the days of ___ and mourning for Moses": Deu. 34:8
19. "of the garden thou mayest freely ___": Gen. 2:16
20. "as a thread of ___ is broken": Judges 16:9
21. "he took ___ of his ribs": Gen. 2:21
22. "And ___ upon a stately bed": Eze. 23:41
24. "Of the oaks . . . they made thine ___": Eze. 27:6
27. "thou shalt ___ up the tabernacle": Exodus 26:30
29. "The paper ___ by the brooks": Isaiah 19:7
32. "And Moses ___ all the words of the LORD": Exodus 24:4
34. "he made the stars ___": Gen. 1:16
36. "stayed in ___ for a season": Acts 19:22
37. "___ there be light": Gen. 1:3
38. "The rings, and ___ jewels": Isaiah 3:21
40. "The hills ___ like wax": Psalms 97:5
42. "write him a ___ of this law": Deu. 17:18
43. "Haman sought to destroy all the ___": Esther 3:6
44. "and didst ___ thyself even unto hell": Isaiah 57:9
47. "___ a man or woman, that they die": Exodus 21:28
48. "over the ___, and divide it": Exo. 14:16
51. "make your heaven as ___, and your earth as brass": Gen. 4:22
52. "unto ___, the end of all flesh": Gen. 6:13
54. "he hath ___ falsely": Lev. 6:5
56. "Let the earth bring forth ___": Gen. 1:11
58. "they did ___ the breastplate": Exodus 39:21
60. "which ___ him ten thousand talents": Matt. 18:24
61. "___ waters are sweet": Pro. 9:17
63. ___, tooth for tooth": Exodus 21:24
65. "adultery, in the very ___": John 8:4
67. "have given a ___ for an harlot": Joel 3:3
68. "thou ___ thyself in cedar?": Jer. 22:15
72. "the priest's ___from the people": Deu. 18:3
73. "And Adam called his wife's name ___": Gen. 3:20
74. "I saw Absalom hanged in an ___": 2 Samuel 18:10
75. "And if a man ___ not in wait": Exodus 22:16
76. "the ___ number of them": Num. 3:48
77. "rams' skins dyed ___": Exodus 25:5
78. "the wheat and the ___": Exodus 9:32
79. "there was no room for them in the ___": Luke 2:7

DOWN

1. "the ___ of the lion": 1 Samuel 17:37
2. "the prophets . . . that ___ their tongues": Jer. 23:31
3. The Bible's second word
4. "___ upon the earth forty days": Gen. 7:4
5. "make restitution unto the ___ thereof": Exodus 22:12
6. "to ___ I am ashamed": Luke 16:3
7. "swords or ___": 1 Samuel 13:19
8. "in the ___ of the day": Gen. 18:1
9. "to ___ into Egypt": Gen. 12:11
10. "and slew the ___ of them": Psalms 78:31
11. "they were lost three days ___": 1 Samuel 9:20
12. "Now there arose up a ___ king over Egypt": Exodus 1:8
18. "on the upper door ___ of the houses": Exodus 12:7
22. "the price of his ___": Lev. 25:50
23. "a book . . . with seven ___": Rev. 5:1
24. "the ___, and the night hawk": Lev. 11:16
25. "Great that ___ not clean": Gen. 7:2
26. "the name of the wicked shall ___": Pro. 10:7
28. "words ___ to be understood": 1 Cor. 14:9
30. "eatest thereof thou shalt surely ___": Gen. 2:17
31. "Why is thy countenance ___": Neh. 2:2
33. Seth's son
35. "Take a pot and an ___ full of manna": Exodus 16:33
39. "the earth ___ her mouth, and swallow them up": Num. 16:30
41. "thy ___ and thy she goats": Gen. 31:38
42. "___ thou lift up thy voice": Job 38:34
43. Book after Luke
44. "___ a pit for your friend": Job 6:27
45. "a people that do ___ in their heart": Psalms 95:10
46. "ye have ___ against me": Eze. 35:13
47. "He that by usury and unjust ___": Pro. 28:8
48. "they plow iniquity, and ___ wickedness": Job 4:8
49. "How long will it be ___ ye make an end of words?": Job 18:2
50. Eighth word of the Bible
53. "thou hast ___ my voice": Gen. 22:18
55. "there come two ___ more hereafter": Rev. 9:12
57. "___, just, holy, temperate": Titus 1:8
59. "Thou shalt not ___ to offer": Exodus 22:29
62. "thou shalt ___ thy neighbor as thyself": Lev. 19:34
64. "And he took a ___ of oxen": Samuel 11:7
65. "Why make ye this ___, and weep?": Mark 5:39
66. "and cheweth the ___": Lev. 11:3
68. Rom. follower
69. "And Samuel arose and went to ___": 1 Samuel 3:6
70. "because their ___ is very grievous": Gen. 18:20
71. Commandment count

★ **Solution on page 322**

1	2	3	■	4	5	6	■	7	8	9	■	10	11	12
13			■	14			■	15			■	16		
17			18				■	19			■	20		
■	■	■	21			■	22				23		■	■
24	25	26		■	27	28			■	29			30	31
32				33	■	34			35	■	36			
37			■	38	39			■	40	41				
■	■	■	42				■	43				■	■	■
44	45	46				■	47				■	48	49	50
51				■	52	53			■	54	55			
56				57	■	58			59	■	60			
■	■	61			62			■	63	64		■	■	■
65	66		■	67			■	68				69	70	71
72			■	73			■	74			■	75		
76			■	77			■	78			■	79		

Bible crossword 3

ACROSS

1. "came the ___ and the hoary frost": Job 38:29
4. "and saith, ___, I am warm": Isaiah 44:16
7. "of ___ own accord": Lev. 25:5
10. "ye shall eat the ___ of the land": Gen. 45:18
13. "And he said, ___; but thou didst laugh": Gen. 18:15
14. "They ___ my path": Job 30:13
15. "dip the ___ of his finger in water": Luke 16:24
16. "he planteth an ___": Isaiah 44:14
17. "unto a people that thou ___ not": Ruth 2:11
19. "and ___ me from my sin": Psalms 51:2
21. "Go to the ___ . . . consider her ways and be wise": Pro. 6:6
22. "with the ___ of his cart": Isaiah 28:28
23. "whereupon the house ___": Judges 16:26
27. "spread over it a ___ wholly of blue": Num. 4:6
31. "the two side ___ with the blood": Exodus 12:22
32. "whose top may ___ unto heaven": Gen. 11:4
35. "let it rest and ___ still": Exodus 23:11
36. "plowing with twelve ___ of oxen": 1 Kings 19:19
37. "they that ___ the pen of the writer": Judges 5:14
38. "the ___ of lions": Daniel 6:19
39. "all the men are ___ which sought thy life": Exodus 4:19
41. "thou shalt ___ them in pieces": Psalms 2:9
43. "___ is me": Psalms 120:5
46. "I ___ the people . . . none of the sons of Levi": Ezra 8:15
48. "offered sacrifice unto the ___": Acts 7:41
52. "birds of the ___ have nests": Luke 9:58
53. "the name of the ___ was Leah": Gen. 29:16
54. "Like a ___ or swallow": Isaiah 38:14
55. "let me ___ and gather after the reapers": Ruth 2:7
57. "which is highly ___ among men": Luke 16:15
59. "and ___ with thy foot": Eze. 6:11
62. Hath, nonbiblically
63. "I would ___ my life": Job 9:21
66. "hardly ___ and angry": Isaiah 8:21
70. "standeth in ___ of thy word": Psalms 119:161
71. "every thing . . . in the earth shall ___": Gen. 6:17
72. "We ___ all one man's son": Gen. 42:11
73. "a nourisher of thine old ___": Ruth 4:15
74. "and they hated him ___ the more": Gen. 37:5
75. "Ye shall not ___ of it": Gen. 3:3
76. "And the first came out ___ Esau": Gen. 25:25
77. "and a ___ of cedar beams": 1 Kings 6:36

DOWN

1. "wrote them with ___ in the book": Jer. 36:18
2. "dream, and there is none that ___ interpret it": Gen. 41:15
3. "mine ___ shall no more see good": Job 7:7
4. "and he shall make ___ for the harm": Lev. 5:16
5. "unleavened bread . . . out of the land of Egypt in ___": Deu. 16:3
6. "Where ___ thou?": Gen. 3:9
7. "with the scab, and with the ___": Deu. 28:27
8. "take thee a ___, and lay it": Eze. 4:1
9. "I answer him with your ___": Job 32:14
10. "A dry wind . . . not to ___, nor to cleanse": Jer. 4:11
11. "the jawbone of an ___": Judges 15:16
12. Sixth word of the Bible
18. "And when they ___ wine": John 2:3
20. "and over ___ the earth": Gen. 1:26
22. "in the day ___ they were created": Gen. 5:2
23. "And Moses sent to ___ out": Num. 21:32
24. "Is any thing ___ hard for the LORD?": Gen. 18:14
25. "___ thy father, and he will show thee": Deu. 32:7
26. "they ___ in thy market": Eze. 27:17
28. "and bare Abraham a son in his ___ age": Gen. 21:2
29. "and ___ them about thy neck": Pro. 6:21
30. "a ___ doth gather her brood": Luke 13:34
33. "___ poison is under their lips": Psalms 140:3
34. "was ___ . . . as a cloak": Isaiah 59:17
37. "the ___ shall come down upon them": Exodus 9:19
40. "for it was now ___": Acts 4:3
42. "givest thy gifts . . . and ___ them": Eze. 16:33
43. "and ___ his head": Jer. 18:16
44. " ___ for the light": Exodus 35:28
45. "and ___ the lamp . . . went out": 1 Samuel 3:3
47. "widows shall not ___": Job 27:15
49. "take the ___ with the young": Deu. 22:6
50. "and they shall be ___ flesh": Gen. 2:24
51. "which had ___ me in the right way": Gen. 24:48
54. "the thunder and hail ___": Exodus 9:33
56. "the hole of the ___": Isaiah 11:8
58. "wherein ___ is life": Gen. 1:30
60. "the Jews which were of ___": Acts 21:27
61. "And the servant ran to ___ her": Gen. 24:17
63. "and called the light ___": Gen. 1:5
64. "be cow, or ___": Lev. 22:28
65. "And the LORD ___ a mark upon Cain": Gen. 4:15
66. "And the middle ___ . . . of the boards": Exodus 26:28
67. "Give ___, O ye heavens": Deu. 32:1
68. "would have repented long ___": Matt. 11:21
69. "in the morning the ___ lay round": Exodus 16:13

★ **Solution on page 322**

1	2	3	■	4	5	6	■	7	8	9	■	10	11	12
13			■	14			■	15			■	16		
17			18				■	19			20			
■	■	■	21			■	22					■	■	■
23	24	25				26		■	■	27		28	29	30
31					■	32		33	34		■	35		
36				■	37						■	38		
■	■	■	39	40			■	41			42	■	■	■
43	44	45	■	46			47			■	48	49	50	51
52			■	53					■	54				
55			56		■	■	57		58					
■	■	■	59		60	61		■	62			■	■	■
63	64	65					■	66				67	68	69
70			■	71			■	72			■	73		
74			■	75			■	76			■	77		

Bible crossword 4

ACROSS

1. "their round ___": Isaiah 3:18
6. "I did ___ them as the mire": 2 Samuel 22:43
11. "the hole of the ___": Isaiah 11:8
14. "a land of oil ___, and honey": Deu. 8:8
15. "or famine . . . or ___, or sword?": Romans 8:35
16. "___ and all manner of herbs": Luke 11:42
17. "much ___ than thy father": Job 15:10
18. "his feet and ___ bones": Acts 3:7
19. "And Pharaoh commanded his ___": Gen. 12:20
20. "hath no ___; it is ready to burst": Job 32:19
22. "my couch shall ___ my complaints": Job 7:13
24. "Neither do men light . . . and put it under a ___": Matt. 5:15
28. "and the LORD hath blessed me ___ my coming": Gen. 30:30
31. "that I came into ___": Acts 20:18
32. " ___ like morsels: who can stand his cold?": Psalms 147:17
35. "My name is ___, for we are many": Mark 5:9
36. "The thoughts . . . ___ only to plenteousness": Pro. 21:5
37. "And it is a ___ thing that the king requireth": Daniel 2:11
39. "followed ___ after them into the battle": 1 Samuel 14:22
40. Villainous Judean king
41. "My righteousness I hold ___": Job 27:6
45. "the dragons and the ___": Isaiah 43:20
46. The first man
50. "Let him ___ evil": 1 Peter 3:11
52. "And ___ indeed she is my sister": Gen. 20:12
54. "ye shall ___ up early": Gen. 19:2
55. "one ___ by one cherub": Eze. 10:9
56. "thou ___ thereof shalt surely die": Gen. 2:17
58. "unto wizards that ___, and that mutter": Isaiah 8:19
60. "___ praise to the LORD": Judges 5:3
62. "were strong and ___ for war": 2 Kings 24:16
64. "and make ___ upon the hearth": Gen. 18:6
66. "that he is not ___ of": Matt. 24:50
71. "That these made ___ with . . . Sodom": Gen. 14:2
72. "And others had ___ of cruel mockings": Heb. 11:36
73. "the ___ of these words": Gen. 43:7
74. "one little ___ lamb": 2 Samuel 12:3
75. "gave the ___, and caused them to understand": Neh. 8:8
76. "to ___ into Egypt": Gen. 12:11

DOWN

1. "upon the great ___ of the right foot": Exodus 29:20
2. "Love worketh no ___ to his neighbour": Romans 13:10
3. " ___ them out of the hand of the wicked": Psalms 82:4
4. The first woman
5. "Let my people go, that they may ___ me": Exodus 8:1
6. "Goliath . . . whose height was six cubits and a ___": 1 Samuel 17:4
7. "pitched his ___": Gen. 12:8
8. "two of every sort . . . into the ___": Gen. 6:19
9. "compel thee to go a ___": Matt. 5:41
10. "If it ___ the king": Esther 1:19
11. "escaped into the land of ___": Isaiah 37:38
12. "will ___ thee at the law": Matt. 5:40
13. "the ___ of the scribes": Jer. 8:8
21. Samuel's mentor
23. "all the merryhearted do ___": Isaiah 24:7
24. "And the stork and the ___": Lev. 11:19
25. "teach the children of Judah the ___ of the bow": 2 Samuel 1:18
26. "what is my ___, that thou . . . pursued after me?" Gen. 31:36
27. "was barren; she ___ no child": Gen. 11:30
29. Book before Gal.
30. "at the ___ of forty days": Gen. 8:6
33. "the cock ___": Matt. 26:74
34. "thou shalt rise ___": Judges 9:33
35. "the LORD ___ me to": Gen. 24:27
38. "Cain ___ up against Abel his brother": Gen. 4:8
40. "___ dreadful is this place!": Gen. 28:17
41. "being ___ in number": Gen. 34:30
42. "he planteth an ___": Isaiah 44:14
43. "the king shall hold out the golden ___": Esther 4:11
44. "for ___ have I seen righteous before me": Gen. 7:1
46. "thou ___ cursed above all cattle": Gen. 3:14
47. "the serpent said . . . Ye shall not surely ___": Gen. 3:4
48. "and set them upon an ___": Exodus 4:20
49. "And when all the kings were ___ together": Joshua 11:5
51. "but for the ___ sake": Matt. 24:22
53. "Abram had dwelt ___ years in the land of Canaan": Gen. 16:3
57. "an ___, and an amethyst": Exodus 28:19
59. "and ___ her nails": Deu. 21:12
60. "of the waters called he ___": Gen. 1:10
61. "ye inhabitants of the ___": Isaiah 23:6
62. "stand in ___ of him": Psalms 33:8
63. "the ___ of the bear": 1 Samuel 17:37
65. "if any of his ___ come to redeem it": Lev. 25:25
67. "having a ___, or scurvy": Lev. 22:22
68. "Go to the ___, thou sluggard": Pro. 6:6
69. "like a ___ or young hart": Song of Solomon 2:9
70. "Do they not ___ that devise evil?": Pro. 14:22

★ **Solution on page 322**

1	2	3	4	5	■	6	7	8	9	10	■	11	12	13
14					■	15					■	16		
17					■	18					■	19		
■	■	■	■	20	21			■	22		23		■	■
24	25	26	27			■	■	■	■	28			29	30
31				■	32	33	34	■	35					
36				■	■	37		38		■	39			
■	■	■	■	■	40					■	■	■	■	■
41	42	43	44	■	45				■	■	46	47	48	49
50				51		■	52		53	■	54			
55					■	■	■	■	56	57				
■	■	58			59	■	60	61			■	■	■	■
62	63		■	64		65			■	66	67	68	69	70
71			■	72					■	73				
74			■	75					■	76				

Bible crossword 5

ACROSS

1. "For thou ___ cast me into the deep": Jonah 2:3
6. "my couch shall ___ my complaints": Job 7:13
10. "the women ___ hangings for the grove": 2 Kings 23:7
14. "If he hath wronged thee, or ___ thee": Phi. 1:18
15. "ivory, and ___, and peacocks": 1 Kings 10:22
16. "and ___ they tell him of her": Mark 1:30
17. "the ___ of these words": Exodus 34:27
18. "he ___ on the ground": John 9:6
19. "which are ashamed of thy ___ way": Eze. 16:27
20. "with the ___ of our lives because of the sword": Lam. 5:9
22. "And ___ flesh died that moved upon the earth": Gen. 7:21
24. "___ there went up a mist from the earth": Gen. 2:6
27. "for the ___ of her foot": Gen. 8:9
28. "is a vanity ___ to and fro": Pro. 21:6
32. "planteth an ___": Isaiah 44:14
33. "The ___ appeareth, and the tender grass": Pro. 27:25
34. "make bare the ___": Isaiah 47:2
35. "I ___ the pride of Judah": Jer. 13:9
36. "the shipmen ___ that they drew near": Acts 27:27
38. "And the earth ___ without form": Gen. 1:2
39. "If . . . in Sodom fifty righteous within the ___": Gen. 18:26
40. "by way of the ___ sea": Num. 14:25
41. "Honor ___ father and . . . mother": Exodus 20:12
42. "seven ___ kine": Gen. 41:20
43. Prayer closer
45. "a ___ . . . and sold a girl": Joel 3:3
46. "lo, the ___ and the flesh came upon them": Eze. 37:8
49. "at this time ___ in the next year": Gen. 17:21
50. "for the fly . . . and for the ___": Isaiah 7:18
51. "ye shall not go very ___ away": Exodus 8:28
52. "The trees of the LORD are full of ___": Psalms 104:16
53. "Rachel had ___ the images that were her father's": Gen. 31:19
55. "___ evil beast hath devoured": Gen. 37:20
56. "Let us search and ___ our ways": Lam. 3:40
57. "shall die in the flower of their ___": 1 Samuel 2:33
58. "men ___ in unawares": Jude 1:4
60. "Have they not ___?": Judges 5:30
63. Man of the garden
65. "put themselves in ___ to fight": Judges 20:20
69. "let them ___ dominion over . . . the sea": Gen. 1:26
70. "a ___, and lay it": Eze. 4:1
71. "and the ___ was heard afar off": Ezra 3:13
72. "Leah was tender ___; but Rachel was beautiful": Gen. 29:17
73. "when Moses ___ up his hand": Exodus 17:11
74. "The river . . . ___ them away": Judges 5:21

DOWN

1. "when the sun waxed ___, it melted": Exodus 16:21
2. "let all . . . the world stand in ___ of him": Psalms 33:8
3. "ye have made it a ___ of thieves": Matt. 21:13
4. "it shall ___ the noses of the passengers": Eze. 39:11
5. "Gideon ___ wheat by the winepress": Judges 6:11
6. "the sin which doth so ___ beset us": Heb. 12:1
7. The forbidden fruit, in theory
8. "Pharaoh's chariots . . . cast into the ___": Exodus 15:4
9. "I will settle you after your old ___": Eze. 36:11
10. "if the plague be in the ___ of the house": Lev. 14:37
11. "And the whole earth was of ___ language": Gen. 11:1
12. "if thou shalt forbear to ___": Deu. 23:22
13. "lie down at the ___ of the heap of corn": Ruth 3:7
21. "have ye made a ___ to day?": 1 Samuel 27:10
23. Oil vessel, in Leviticus
24. "could not be eaten, they were so ___": Jer. 24:2
25. "the law is good, if a man ___ it lawfully": 1 Tim. 1:8
26. "thou shalt not add ___, nor diminish from it": Deu. 12:32
29. "but if well, why ___ thou me?": John 18:23
30. "This is the bread . . . given you to ___": Exodus 16:15
31. "let the ___ land appear: and it was so": Gen. 1:9
34. "and ___ thine hand upon him": Num. 27:18
37. "But the ___ of Sodom were wicked": Gen. 13:13
38. "___ is thy countenance fallen?": Gen. 4:6
39. "if a man ___ number the dust of the earth": Gen. 13:16
41. "upon the great ___ of his right foot": Lev. 14:25
42. "and the ___, all the vessels therein": Exodus 27:3
43. "that thine ox and thine ___ may rest": Exodus 23:12
44. "the LORD ___ him, and sought to kill him": Exodus 4:24
45. "heaven above, and upon the earth ___": Deu. 4:39
46. "and received in the ___ year an hundredfold": Gen. 26:12
47. "go forth to ___ in Israel": Num. 1:3
48. "two men to ___ secretly": Joshua 2:1
50. "therefore shall he ___ in harvest, and have nothing": Pro. 20:4
51. "And the LORD ___ man of the dust": Gen. 2:7
54. "they that bare burdens, with those that are ___": Neh. 4:17
55. "the ___ is healed, he is clean": Lev. 13:37
59. "Doth he . . . ? I ___ not.": Luke 17:9
60. "but if it be a daughter, then ___ shall live": Exodus 1:16
61. "let me go and ___ my vow": 2 Samuel 15:7
62. The mother of all living
64. "He that smitest a man, so that he ___": Exodus 21:12
66. "the . . . barley and the ___": Isaiah 28:25
67. "the hole of the ___": Isaiah 11:8
68. "because thou art ___ alive": Gen. 46:30

★ **Solution on page 322**

1	2	3	4	5	■	6	7	8	9	■	10	11	12	13
14					■	15				■	16			
17					■	18				■	19			
■	■	■	20		21			■	22	23		■	■	■
24	25	26	■	27				■	28			29	30	31
32			■	33			■	34			■	35		
36			37			■	38			■	39			
■	■	40			■	41			■	42			■	■
43	44			■	45			■	46				47	48
49			■	50			■	51			■	52		
53			54			■	55				■	56		
■	■	■	57			■	58				59	■	■	■
60	61	62		■	63	64			■	65		66	67	68
69				■	70				■	71				
72				■	73				■	74				

Bible crossword 6

ACROSS

1. "the ___ of the lion": 1 Samuel 17:37
4. "the ___ of the robe": Exodus 28:34
7. "take an ___, and thrust it through": Deu. 15:17
10. "In the evening ___ went": Esther 2:14
13. "come down ___ my children die": John 4:49
14. "Why make ye this ___, and weep?": Mark 5:39
15. "which is the salt ___": Gen. 14:3
16. "And Joseph made it a ___ over . . . Egypt": Gen. 47:26
17. "And thorns . . . ___ and brambles": Isaiah 34:13
19. "and put ___ into the garden of Eden": Gen. 2:15
20. "Thine ___ shall not pity him": Deu. 19:13
21. "the LORD shall ___ their strength": Isaiah 40:31
23. "And Adam ___ names to all cattle": Gen. 2:20
25. Jacob's twin
28. "___ thou hast not hated": Eze. 35:6
30. "___, and peacocks": 2 Chr. 9:21
33. "A wise man feareth . . . but the fool ___": Pro. 14:16
36. "Take a ___, and put . . . manna therein": Exodus 16:33
37. "Rejoice ye in that day, and ___ for joy": Luke 6:23
38. "the wheat and the ___" (modern spelling): Exodus 9:32
39. "A foreigner and a ___ servant": Exodus 12:45
41. "And the flood was ___ days upon the earth": Gen. 7:17
42. "open thine hand ___": Deu. 15:8
43. "and saw the place ___ off": Gen. 22:4
45. "And Noah ___ to be a husbandman": Gen. 9:20
48. "this day I have___ my vows": Pro. 7:14
50. Eve, originally
53. "___, my lord, I beseech thee": Num. 12:11
54. "when all the men of ___ were consumed and dead": Deu. 2:16
55. "Moreover thou shalt not . . . to ___ thyself with her": Lev. 18:20
57. "cast them out as the ___ in the streets": Psalms 18:42
58. "they had sung an ___": Mark 14:26
60. "an ___ soul shall suffer hunger": Pro. 19:15
61. "they did ___ it with an omer": Exodus 16:18
63. "put our money in our ___": Gen. 43:22
66. "standeth in ___ of thy word": Psalms 119:161
68. "I will not take ___ thing that is thine": Gen. 14:23
70. "the ___, and the wimples, and the . . . pins": Isaiah 3:22
74. "a ___ gathereth her chickens": Matt. 23:37
75. "the ___, and wherein the snow": Job 6:16
76. Despite a big role, her name appears only twice in Genesis
77. "boughs of a great ___": 2 Samuel 18:9
78. "Go to the ___, thou sluggard": Pro. 6:6
79. "___ the earth bring forth the living": Gen. 1:24
80. "wringed the ___ out of the fleece": Judges 6:38
81. "Examine me . . . ___ my reins and my heart": Psalms 26:2

DOWN

1. "my tongue is the ___ of a ready writer": Psalms 45:1
2. "but the hands ___ the hands of Esau": Gen. 27:22
3. "___ with the dew of heaven": Daniel 4:15
4. "lest he ___ thee to the judge": Luke 12:58
5. "in ___, and there he put the man": Gen. 2:8
6. Exodus leader
7. "cypress . . . oak . . . ___": Isaiah 44:14
8. "A just ___ and balance are the LORD's": Pro. 16:11
9. "___ sabachthani . . . why hast thou forsaken me?": Mark 15:34
10. "What meanest thou, O ___? arise": Jonah: 1:6
11. "the ___ is withered away, the grass faileth": Isaiah 15:6
12. "one little ___ lamb": 2 Samuel 12:3
18. "If ye be ___ men": Gen. 42:19
22. "will ___ away tears": Isaiah 25:8
24. "the mighty men of ___": Joshua 1:14
25. "Do not ___, my beloved brethren": James 1:16
26. "___, I pray thee, thou art my sister": Gen. 12:13
27. "his eyes were set by reason of his ___": 1 Kings 14:4
29. "Consecrate yourselves ___ to the LORD": Exodus 32:29
31. "thou shalt ___ the herb of the field": Gen. 3:18
32. "that went to ___ out the land": Judges 18:17
34. "beat the gold into ___ plates": Exodus 39:3
35. "because I was naked, and I ___ myself": Gen. 3:10
40. "he will ___ him to his face": Deu. 7:10
41. "Strangers shall ___ away": 2 Samuel 22:46
42. "And I will make your cities ___": Lev. 26:31
44. "Jacob ___ the . . . flocks": Gen. 30:36
45. "either good or ___": Gen. 31:29
46. Biblical judge and high priest
47. "like an hairy ___; and they called his name Esau": Gen. 25:25
49. "For the ___ of the wicked shall be broken": Psalms 37:17
50. "I will ___ you of their bondage": Exodus 6:6
51. "it went ___ with Moses for their sakes": Psalms 106:32
52. "for the fly . . . and for the ___": Isaiah 7:18
54. "from ___ he was taken": Gen. 3:23
56. "with a stone, or with his ___": Exodus 21:18
59. "Moses . . . his sons were ___ of the tribe of Levi": 1 Chr. 23:14
62. "and take it by the ___": Exodus 4:4
64. "The five kings are found hid in a ___": Joshua 10:17
65. "they ___ they were naked": Gen. 3:7
66. "___, our eye hath seen it": Psalms 35:21
67. "having a ___, or scurvy": Lev. 22:22
69. "___ his days shall be an hundred": Gen. 6:3
71. His wife became seasoned
72. "Hear, O ye kings; give ___, O ye princes": Judges 5:3
73. "the stars of the ___": Heb. 11:12

★ **Solution on page 322**

1	2	3	■	4	5	6	■	7	8	9	■	10	11	12
13			■	14			■	15			■	16		
17			18				■	19			■	20		
■	■	■	21				22	■	23		24		■	■
25	26	27		■	■	28		29		■	30		31	32
33				34	35	■	36			■	37			
38			■	39		40			■	41				
■	■	■	42				■	43	44			■	■	■
45	46	47			■	48	49				■	50	51	52
53				■	54			■	55		56			
57				■	58			59	■	■	60			
■	■	61		62		■	63		64	65		■	■	■
66	67		■	68		69	■	70				71	72	73
74			■	75			■	76			■	77		
78			■	79			■	80			■	81		

TV/film crossword 1

ACROSS

1. Elizabeth ___ of *Lone Star*
5. Morales of *NYPD Blue*
9. TV host Zahn
14. TV's Hutch
15. Blair Brown role
16. Director Welles
17. 1999 role for Jodie
18. Ingrid's *Casablanca* role
19. Comic actor Arnold
20. TV's *Nick at* ___
22. *Quincy* actor
23. *Private Parts* star
26. Admired actor
29. Actor Epps
33. Jed Clampett portrayer
34. Andy Kaufman role on *Taxi*
36. ___ *Million B.C.*
37. *Little Man* ___ (Foster film)
38. *A* ___ *Is Born*
39. *Henry and June* role
40. Actor Byrnes
42. Actress Olivia d'
43. TV cousin of '60s TV
45. Late-night TV fare since 1975: abbr.
47. Setting for *The Drew Carey Show*
49. Wagner role
52. Duvall, in *Popeye*
53. Sorkin of *The West Wing*
55. TV actress Fellows
56. Norm's order, on *Cheers*
58. '60s film canine
59. Star's rep
60. Extra NFL periods
62. Early 007 film
64. *Absolutely Fabulous* role
67. Falco of *The Sopranos*
69. Actress Falana
73. Actor Thatcher
74. Actress Rowlands
75. *I Dream of Jeannie* star
76. *Boys Don't Cry* star
77. Grandpa Walton portrayer
78. Daphne ___ (*Frasier* role)

DOWN

1. Unpaid TV spot
2. Baby New Year kidnapper
3. Role for Whoopi or Sally Field
4. TV voice of Fred Flintstone
5. Alter a film
6. Actress Moon Frye
7. TV's lifeblood
8. Rhoda's TV mom
9. Actress Markie ___
10. *Star Wars* android's first name, informally
11. 1996 Summer Olympics host
12. First name in horror films
13. Director Lee
21. *Newhart* setting
22. TV panelist Chase
23. Actor's milieu
24. Unfilled, on a TV sched.
25. Getty of *The Golden Girls*
27. Film set on a sub
28. Director Preminger
30. Rapid succession of images, in a movie
31. *Star Wars: The Phantom Menace* boy
32. Stimpy's TV pal
35. Actress Meyers
41. Film noir classic
42. Puts on TV
44. German film about a clay statue: 1920
45. 1981 Julie Andrews film
46. TV's Science Guy Bill
48. Actor Lukas ___
50. Kurosawa's *King Lear*
51. Cable TV choice
54. 1987 Kim Basinger film
55. *Cadillac* ___ (Williams movie)
57. De Niro film of '98
61. James Garner film
63. ___ *Window* (Hitchcock film)
64. Dolls based on a film
65. He played the other Cleaver son
66. *Mad About You* role
67. Mork's pod
68. *Gidget* star
70. *Star Trek: Deep Space Nine* role
71. *Titanic* star's nickname
72. Actress Miller

★**Solution on page 322**

1	2	3	4	■	5	6	7	8	■	9	10	11	12	13
14				■	15				■	16				
17				■	18				■	19				
■	■	■	20	21			■	■	22			■	■	■
23	24	25			■	26	27	28		■	29	30	31	32
33					■	34				35	■	36		
37				■	■	■	38				■	39		
■	■	40		41	■	42			■	43	44		■	■
45	46		■	47	48			■	■	■	49		50	51
52			■	53				54	■	55				
56			57	■	58				■	59				
■	■	■	60	61		■	■	62	63			■	■	■
64	65	66			■	67	68			■	69	70	71	72
73					■	74				■	75			
76					■	77				■	78			

TV/film crossword 2

ACROSS

1. *Top* ___ (Astaire film)
4. Actor Vigoda
7. Actress Peeples
10. *Malcolm X* director
13. ___ *Flew Over the Cuckoo's Nest*
14. Actress Wray
15. TV's Byrnes
16. Another role for the guy who played Twiki
17. Late-night TV fare since 1975: abbr.
18. Jim Carrey role
19. War drama of 1981
21. Show on TV
24. Actress Chlumsky
25. Actor Benicio ___ Toro
26. *The Maltese Falcon* actress
30. *21 Jump Street* role
33. ___ *Weapon* (Gibson/Glover film)
35. Director Van Sant
38. 1985 film ___ *Dancing!*
40. Actress Anne
41. Actor Carney
42. What Carol Burnett tugs
43. Gregory Hines film
45. Actress Grey
46. Old movie studio
47. *Chances* ___
48. Sigourney Weaver film
50. Actress Mamie Van ___
52. *Cadillac* ___ (Williams movie)
53. ___ *Knowledge* (Nichols film)
55. Actor on *ER*
56. *Exodus* actor
57. Certain movie planet resident
59. *Frasier* actress Gilpin
62. Actress Eggar
67. Home state in a Reese Witherspoon movie of '02
71. Movie studio
72. Actor Ziering
73. *Green Acres* role
74. Director Lars ___ Trier (*Dancer in the Dark*)
75. *Anything* ___ *Love*
76. *The 5,000 Fingers of* ___ (Dr. Seuss movie)
77. Ben in the film *Ben*
78. Actress Irving
79. Meyers of *Kate & Allie*
80. Dolls based on a film

DOWN

1. Leno or Letterman
2. Actress Heche
3. *To* ___ *the Truth*
4. ___ *in the Crowd* (1957 film)
5. Bogart costar
6. ___ *of Laura Mars*
7. Actor Beatty
8. Actress Lupino
9. TV "clutter"
10. Bert Lahr role
11. *A Yank at* ___
12. ___ Plum, *Little House on the Prairie* role
20. *Cheers* setting
22. What Herman might do at work on *Herman's Head*
23. *Soap* surname
27. Actress Reed (*Major Dad*)
28. Movie plantation
29. Charlie Chan's portrayer
30. Mr. T's TV group
31. *Only the Lonely* actress
32. Actress Black
34. *Star Wars* group
35. TV personality Moore
36. Jaleel White cameo role that took over the series
37. *Platoon* director
39. *Step by Step* actress Keanan
44. Actor Rickman
49. Sonny Shroyer role
51. *Throw Momma from the Train* role
54. Dorothy of "Road" pictures
56. Movie starring Smith and Jones, briefly
58. Actress LuPone
59. Former *Tonight Show* host
60. Actress Joyce of *Roc*
61. He often played bad guys who flipped coins
63. Star of *Dark Angel*
64. Sub thriller *Crimson* ___
65. Wagner role
66. Them, in *Them!*
68. Burt's TV wife in *Evening Shade*
69. *Mr.* ___ (Keaton film)
70. ___ *Which Way But Loose*

★**Solution on page 323**

1	2	3	■	4	5	6	■	7	8	9	■	10	11	12
13			■	14			■	15			■	16		
17			■	18			■	19			20			
21			22				23	■	■	■	24			
■	■	■	25			■	26	27	28	29		■	■	■
30	31	32		■	33	34					■	35	36	37
38				39	■	40					■	41		
42			■	43	44		■	45			■	46		
47			■	48			49		■	50	51			
52			■	53					54	■	55			
■	■	■	56					■	57	58		■	■	■
59	60	61		■	■	■	62	63				64	65	66
67				68	69	70	■	71			■	72		
73			■	74			■	75			■	76		
77			■	78			■	79			■	80		

TV/film crossword 3

ACROSS

1. TV host Serling
4. Extra Superbowl periods, for short
7. Chihuahua who sounds like Lorre
10. Pivotal Jedi role
13. Nickname on TV's *Wings*
14. Movie studio
15. Actress Plumb
16. Horror actor Chaney
17. High-pitched *Addams Family* role
18. Director Miller
19. Clarinet, in *Peter and the Wolf*
20. Dr. Seuss movie role
21. Keanu, in *The Matrix*
22. TV hostess White
24. Frequent TV Xmas show host
25. *Basic Instinct* star
27. Afternoon talk show host
30. Emmy role for Susan, finally
33. Michael Caine film of '64
37. Actor Jannings
40. 1943 Bogart film
42. Rene Auberjonois role
43. Actor Hurt
45. Surname at 1313 Mockingbird Lane
47. *Diamonds ___ Forever*
48. *Wuthering Heights* actress
50. Actress Suvari
51. 1987 Kim Basinger film
53. Davis of *Do the Right Thing*
55. Actress Reese
57. Silent films actress
61. Carla on *Cheers*
64. Splices film
67. Show on TV
68. Special effect for Spock
69. Sean Penn film ___ *Sam*
71. Newman's *Exodus* role
72. Old movie studio
73. Actor Wallach
74. TV spot filler
75. George Burns role
76. ___ *to Midnight* (Bronson film)
77. Actor Majors
78. Movie site or TV unit
79. ___ *Day at a Time*
80. *48* ___ (Murphy/Nolte flick)

DOWN

1. *Casablanca* star
2. TV's Bradford kids e.g.
3. Last name in droids, informally
4. Director Stone
5. When tripled, a WWII film
6. Ollie's costar
7. Episode starter, often
8. Actress Gabor
9. Sandra Bullock film, with *The*
10. Raspy-voiced actor Ray
11. George Wendt, on *Cheers*
12. Goldblum/Pfeiffer flick ___ *the Night*
23. Wyle of *ER*
24. 1996 role for Antonio
26. *Gimme a Break* star Carter
28. *Nick at Nite* features
29. Alda of *M*A*S*H*
31. She played TV George's wife
32. *It ___ From Outer Space*
34. Weekly ritual on *Survivor*
35. *Harper Valley P.T.A.* star
36. *You've Got Mail* director Ephron
37. Actor McGregor
38. Actress Sorvino
39. TV spy show ___ *Three Lives*
41. *Good Times* actor
44. Actress Skye
46. Hoskins, in *Hook*
49. Word in a Hope-Crosby film title
52. Brenda and Rhoda's mom
54. TV's ___ *Edition*
56. *Melvin and Howard* star
58. Wayne's co-host
59. *Star Trek: The Next Generation* role
60. Von Bulow portrayer
61. Spool for film
62. He played the Skipper
63. *That thing you do!* setting
65. 1995 Kenneth Branagh role
66. 1982 Disney film
69. ___ *a Wonderful Life*
70. Vigoda of *Barney Miller*

★**Solution on page 323**

1	2	3	■	4	5	6	■	7	8	9	■	10	11	12
13			■	14			■	15			■	16		
17			■	18			■	19			■	20		
21			■	22			23		■	■	24			
25			26		■	■	27		28	29		■	■	■
■	■	■	30		31	32		■	33			34	35	36
37	38	39		■	40			41			■	42		
43				44			■	45			46			
47			■	48			49			■	50			
51			52			■	53			54		■	■	■
■	■	■	55			56		■	■	57		58	59	60
61	62	63		■	■	64		65	66		■	67		
68			■	69	70		■	71			■	72		
73			■	74			■	75			■	76		
77			■	78			■	79			■	80		

TV/film crossword 4

ACROSS

1. Actor Davis
4. ___ *Girl Friday* (Cary Grant film)
7. Actor Byrnes
10. Actress Ryan
13. ___ *About Eve*
14. *Star Wars: The Phantom Menace* boy
15. *The Thin Man* actress
16. TV's Mrs. Morgenstern
17. Actress Farrow
18. *Sister* ___
19. Kilmer who played Batman
20. *Henry and June* role
21. TV's *Green* ___
23. TV series that often uses DNA testing in its plots
25. *Our Miss Brooks* star
27. Actor Connery
28. *Cousin* ___
30. *Frasier* star
32. Hemsley's TV sitcom
36. Previews, as a film
39. Director Peckinpah
41. "You ___ There"
42. *American Idol* host Abdul
43. *Enchanted* ___
45. TV's ___ *a Living*
46. TV's *L.A.* ___
49. TV's *Diff'rent* ___
51. TV's *Empty* ___
53. Midler film
55. Tim Robbins, in *The Shawshank Redemption*
57. Hot Lips Houlihan, on TV
61. Salma Hayek film
64. Actor Olin
65. Actress Dana
66. Actress Ullmann
67. *The Facts of Life* star
69. Former TV Tarzan
71. ___ *Don't Leave* (Lange film)
72. Three-faced woman of film
73. Where to see Joe Isuzu
74. He'd say, "What EEZ it?"
75. *Howards* ___ (Hopkins film)
76. *The* ___ *We Were*
77. *Top* ___ (Astaire film)
78. PBS TV chef
79. *Mrs. Miniver* actor

DOWN

1. ___ *Family*
2. *Brady Bunch* role
3. Actress Bow
4. He played the hero in *Mars Attacks!*
5. TV's *Models* ___
6. TV laughfests
7. High-flying group of film
8. Edmond O'Brien film
9. Actor McDermott
10. *A Beautiful* ___
11. Ernie's TV partner
12. *The Journey of Natty* ___ ('85 film)
22. Georgia of *The Mary Tyler Moore Show*
24. *The* ___ *of All Fears*
26. Actor in *The Crying Game*
28. TV's *Yan* ___ *Cook*
29. *Mad About You* role
31. ___ *People*
33. Actor Hamill
34. *That Thing You Do!* setting
35. Dick Van Patten role in *Mama*
36. TV's ___ *City*
37. Actress Blanchett
38. Tim ___ of *Star Trek: Voyager*
40. Actress Winningham
44. Mario Van Peebles film
47. TV network
48. *The* ___ *Link*
49. Stage setting
50. ___ *Sting*
52. Actor Danson
54. Certain movie planet resident
56. Actress Bernhardt
58. *What* ___ *Want*
59. Cara of *Fame*
60. Cronyn's frequent costar
61. *One* ___ *Over the Cuckoo's Nest*
62. Actress Maria ___
63. *Who's the Boss?* actress
65. Actress Redgrave
68. Holly Hunter, in *The Piano*
70. She played Caroline on TV

★**Solution on page 323**

1	2	3	■	4	5	6	■	7	8	9	■	10	11	12
13			■	14			■	15			■	16		
17			■	18			■	19			■	20		
21			22		■	23	24		■	25	26			
27				■	28				29			■	■	■
■	■	■	30	31						■	32	33	34	35
36	37	38					■	39		40	■	41		
42					■	■	■	■	■	43	44			
45			■	46	47	48	■	49	50					
51			52	■	53		54					■	■	■
■	■	■	55	56						■	57	58	59	60
61	62	63			■	64			■	65				
66			■	67	68		■	69	70		■	71		
72			■	73			■	74			■	75		
76			■	77			■	78			■	79		

TV/film crossword 5

ACROSS

1. TV talk show host Lake
6. *Rio Lobo* actor
10. Hagman costar
14. Actor Phillips of *Benson*
15. TV talk host
16. *Damn Yankees* role
17. *Dead ___ Society*
18. *Leaving Las Vegas* star
19. Actor Pickens
20. Actress Louise
22. TV's *The ___ Maxwell Story*
24. Edit a foreign film
27. Actress Lamour
30. Movie computer
33. She played Wheezy
35. Actress Cannon
36. *___ Pirates*
37. *Wings* role
38. Roger or Jessica Rabbit
40. *Gremlins* director
42. *Remote Control* host
44. '56 role for Peck
46. Parker Stevenson TV show
49. Sean Connery's first outing as Bond
51. Cleopatra portrayer in '17
55. Actor Mineo
56. Pearl, of TV's *Pearl*
58. *National Velvet* star
60. *Star Wars: The Phantom Menace* boy
61. Marilyn's role in *Gentlemen Prefer Blondes*
63. Cable TV choice
64. Pay-Per-___
66. Obi-Wan portrayer
68. *You've Got ___*
70. *Good Will Hunting* director Gus Van ___
73. DeVito's *Taxi* role
77. Animated Xmas special actor
78. Actor Estrada
79. Cobb portrayal
80. Steed's partner after Emma
81. Sofer of *General Hospital*
82. He played Chan

DOWN

1. Actor's agt.
2. *Quincy* actor
3. *Evita* role
4. Actor William of *Carrie*
5. TV's ___ *Edition*
6. *MacGyver* actor
7. He played an *X-Files* villain
8. *Crouching Tiger, Hidden Dragon* director Lee
9. Hit show for Brandy
10. Movie lioness
11. Ace Ventura's first quarry
12. Actor Mintz
13. *Platoon* setting
21. *48 HRS* costar with Murphy
23. Actress Carter
24. ___ *Hard* (Willis film)
25. *Monk* airer
26. Archie Bunker's place
28. Rene Auberjonois role
29. 1979 Alda role
31. Play a role
32. Actor Tommy ___ Jones
34. Film monster of 1958 and 1988
39. TV's *Law and ___*
41. *ER* role
43. Mr. Television
45. Brolin/Sellecca TV show
46. "The Bicentennial Minute," for instance
47. Kurosawa epic film
48. Noted Richard III portrayer
50. Thomas Chong's actress daughter
52. Model/actress Carol ___
53. Actor Glass of *Barney Miller*
54. Lily's costar in *The Late Show*
57. TV's *Doogie ___, M.D.*
59. *Do the Right Thing* actor
62. Simka's hubby
65. Role for Ingrid
67. ___ *Hand Luke* (Newman film)
68. *Good Will Hunting* setting
69. Actress Gardner
71. *Butterflies ___ Free*
72. *Henry and June* role
74. John's *Pulp Fiction* costar
75. *Big Night* villain actor Holm
76. Reynolds film, with *The*

★**Solution on page 323**

1	2	3	4	5		6	7	8	9		10	11	12	13
14						15					16			
17						18					19			
			20		21				22	23				
24	25	26		27			28	29				30	31	32
33			34				35					36		
37					38	39				40	41			
			42	43				44	45					
46	47	48				49	50				51	52	53	54
55				56	57				58	59				
60				61				62				63		
		64	65					66			67			
68	69				70	71	72			73		74	75	76
77					78					79				
80					81					82				

TV/film crossword 6

ACROSS

1. Trixie Norton portrayer
5. ___ *Magnolias* (Sally Field film)
10. ___ *Set*
14. *That Thing You Do!* setting
15. *The Quiet Man* star
16. Race in *The Time Machine*
17. Serial role for Harrison
18. Actor Cheech
19. Oscar role for Spacek
20. Actress Carrere
21. TV's *You* ___ *Your Life*
22. *The Day the Earth Stood Still* actress
24. *Sun Valley Serenade* star
26. *On the Waterfront* director
30. Actor Julia
33. Paul Newman role of '60
35. Actor Wallach
36. Phoebe on *Friends*
39. Role in *The Honeymooners*
41. Actress Tyler
42. Susan Hayward film
43. Previews, as a film
44. Actress Wallace of *E.T.*
45. *Henry and June* role
46. Vampire portrayer of film
47. *The Journey of Natty* ___ ('85 film)
48. Actress Wiggins of *It's a Living*
49. TV's ___ *Hudson Street*
50. Role for Raquel
52. Actor Terence ___
54. Director Kurosawa
58. Movie pooch
61. Actress Wray
63. Actor O'Herlihy
64. *Frank's Place* star
67. *Enchanted* ___
69. TV's *My Two* ___
70. Film ape
71. Actress Bailey
72. *WKRP*'s setting
73. ___ *We Were Kings*
74. *Silk Stalkings* actor
75. Actress Soleil ___ Frye

DOWN

1. Actor Carradine
2. *My Three Sons* role
3. Actor Quinn
4. *Mrs. Miniver* actor
5. ___ *Like It Hot*
6. Disney's ___ *Darn Cat*
7. *Blue Velvet* find
8. Actress Moran of *Happy Days*
9. Actor Nathan ___
10. Actress Reese
11. Former TV Tarzan
12. TV's *Island* ___
13. *Next of* ___ (Swayze film)
21. *Maude* star Arthur
23. Claude of TV
25. *Mad About You* role
27. Actress Rubinstein of *Poltergeist*
28. *X-Files* extra
29. Phileas Fogg portrayer
31. ___ *Buck*
32. *Blade* cast member, Traci
33. Group led by Hannibal
34. Actor Cox
36. Parador and Freedonia
37. Kurosawa film, with *The*
38. Oscar role of '47
40. *Logan's Run* role (TV show)
43. Daytime TV dramas
47. *Double Dare* goo
51. Actor Walston
53. Manicurist in TV ads
55. *My Own Private* ___ (1991 film)
56. *Talk* ___
57. Williams of *Happy Days*
59. Record a TV program
60. *Greystoke* extras
61. *Backdraft* F/X
62. TV's ___ *Fair*
64. Old movie studio
65. Baby New Year kidnapper
66. TV's *Models* ___
68. Ben, in the film *Ben*
69. Actor DeLuise

★**Solution on page 323**

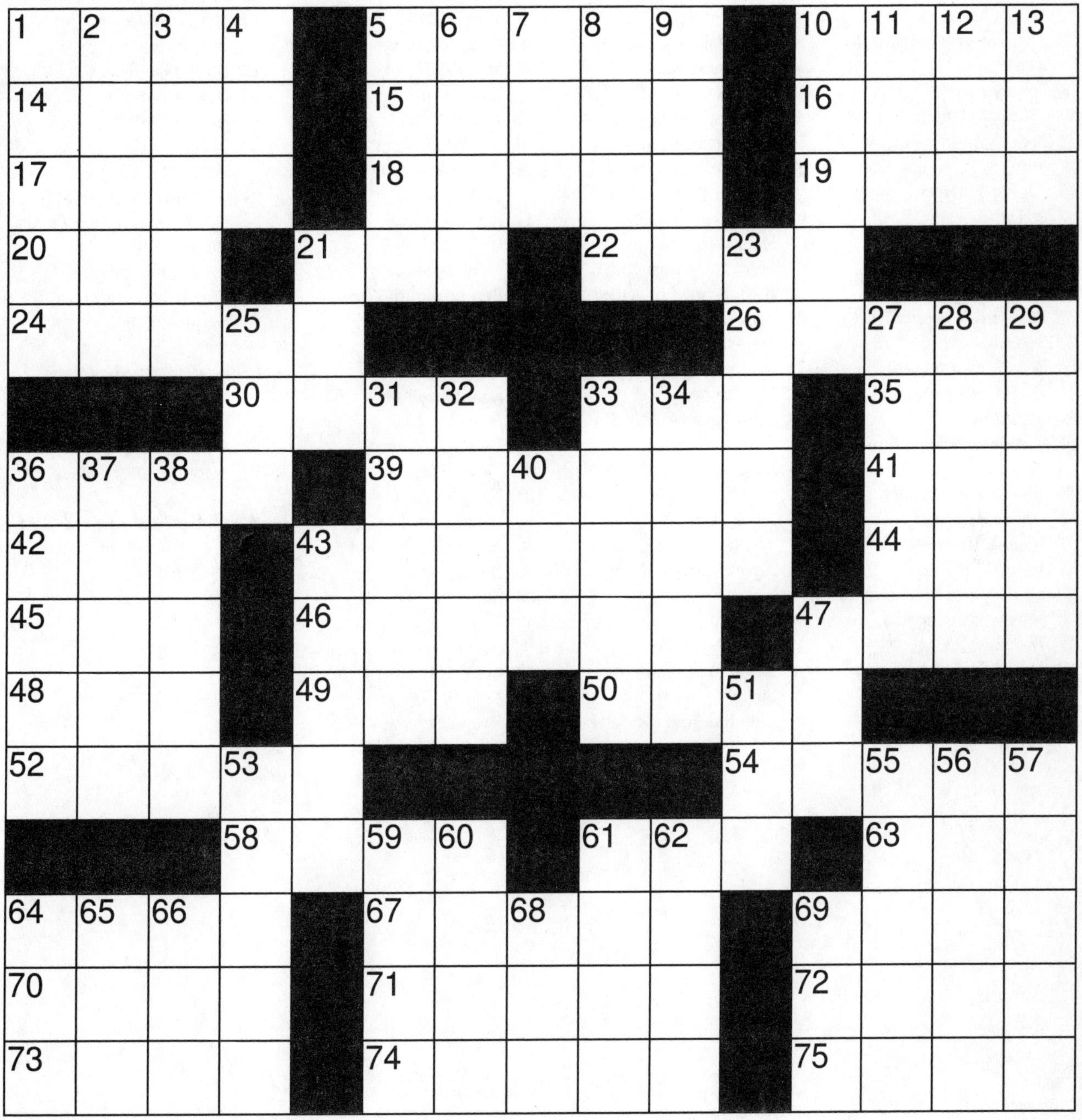

TV/film crossword 7

ACROSS

1. Actor Shepard
4. She played Rosemary in a movie
7. Freddy's street in film
10. TV host Fleming
13. Space constable of TV
14. Indy's original quest
15. Former Enterprise security officer
16. "Who killed me?" film
17. Actress Woods
18. Indy film, for short
20. Respond in *Jeopardy*!
21. See 54 Down
23. Bette Midler title role
24. Ron Howard role
25. Actor Quinn
27. ___ *Peak* (Pierce Brosnan movie)
29. 1987 Beatty/Hoffman film
32. Actress Skye
33. *Michael Collins* actor
34. Actor Corin
37. Garbo's *The Kidd* costar
41. Actress Winningham
43. *The First ___ Club*
45. A teletubby, phonetically
46. Actor Braugher
48. Andy Kaufman role on *Taxi*
50. Actor Palillo
51. *Roxanne* effect
53. Golda's portrayer in 1982
55. *Taxi* or *Seinfeld* role
58. Film background
60. *Truth or ___* (Madonna film)
61. *WKRP's* Flytrap
63. Filmmaker Coen
67. *Top ___* (Cruise film)
68. *Roman Holiday* actress
70. Actress Olivia d'___
71. Actress Meyers
72. *Star Wars: The Phantom Menace* boy
73. Actor Chaney, Jr.
74. Fish portrayer
75. *Norma ___* (Sally Field movie)
76. Actor Davis
77. *TV Guide* abbr.
78. Actor Viscuso of *Soap*

DOWN

1. TV's *My Three ___*
2. Actor West, Arkin, or Sandler
3. Title film role for Bette
4. Uncle Martin, for one
5. *Mad About You* role
6. Director Kurosawa
7. *Minority Report* special F/X
8. '60s TV Western
9. ___ *Doubtfire*
10. Turn a book into a film, e.g.
11. Actress Perez
12. *It ___ a Thief*
19. Actor Ameche
22. Ben in the film *Ben*
24. *Paper Moon* star
26. Actress Barrymore
28. Actress Sheridan
29. Role for Shirley in '63
30. Actor Penn
31. TV's ___ *Copy*
32. *Ricochet* costar
35. *The Green ___* (Hanks film)
36. Actress Marie Saint
38. *Tootsie* actress
39. Carefree sci-fi race
40. *The New ___* (Ullmann film)
42. Comic Kovacs of *The Nairobi Trio*
44. *SNL* scene
47. Baby New Year kidnapper
49. Special effect item for 4 Down
52. *Porgy and Bess* role
54. Don Adams TV comedy, with 21 Across
55. Candice's dad
56. Innes of *ER*
57. Corbin's *L.A. Law* role
58. Movie starring Smith and Jones, briefly
59. Certain film fare
62. Cast-of-thousands film
64. He played the title role in *Witness*
65. Band featured in *Muriel's Wedding*
66. Director Coward
68. Awful actor
69. Actor Lowe or Reiner

★**Solution on page 323**

1	2	3	■	4	5	6	■	7	8	9	■	10	11	12
13			■	14			■	15			■	16		
17			■	18			19				■	20		
21			22		■	23				■	24			
■	■	■	25		26			■	27	28				
29	30	31				■	■	32				■	■	■
33			■	34		35	36		■	37		38	39	40
41			42	■	43				44	■	45			
46				47	■	48				49	■	50		
■	■	■	51		52		■	■	53		54			
55	56	57				■	58	59				■	■	■
60				■	61	62			■	63		64	65	66
67			■	68					69		■	70		
71			■	72			■	73			■	74		
75			■	76			■	77			■	78		

TV/film crossword 8

ACROSS

1. *A Few Good* ___
4. Lupino of *High Sierra*
7. Dangerous quarry for Indy
10. TV's *Models* ___
13. ___ *Got a Secret*
14. Director Van Sant
15. *Gidget* star
16. ___ *to Midnight* (Bronson film)
17. Where the Flintstones live
19. *Office Space* actress
21. Fictional planet of TV
22. *Enemy of the* ___
23. TV's ___ *12*
26. Hoskins, in *Hook*
28. *Big* star
32. Stubing's ship
34. Actress Fisher of *Mannix*
35. *The Commish* actor
36. *In the Line of Fire* actress
38. *SCTV* star
39. ___ *Man* (cult film of '84)
40. Anjelica's husband in a '91 film
42. Slim Pickens, in *Dr. Strangelove*
45. *Jurassic Park* star
47. Perform a role
50. 2001 title role for Dame Judi
51. 1991 Sally Field film
53. Actor MacLeod
55. Actor Florek of *L.A. Law*
56. *That Thing You Do!* setting
57. *My Cousin Vinny* actress
59. Portrayer of Clouseau's boss
61. *General Hospital* actress
64. *The English* ___
68. Actress McClanahan
69. TV's Koppel
70. *Star Wars,* to a Bonzo costar
71. Actress Ruymen
72. Cable TV choice
73. Dolls based on a film
74. Movie preceders
75. Stimpy's TV pal

DOWN

1. Movie starring Smith and Jones, briefly
2. TV actress Plumb
3. ___ *and Stacey* (TV show)
4. Marty Feldman film role
5. Marx Brothers movie
6. Respond in *Jeopardy!*
7. ___ *with Judy* ('48 film)
8. Sofer of *Coupling*
9. Actor Carradine
10. Hairy role
11. Role in *The Matrix*
12. Larry King's TV home
18. *Gladiator* setting
20. *Under Siege* actor
22. Movie workplaces
23. ___ *about Eve*
24. Cooper role of 1941
25. Actress Gardner
27. Actress Marsha ___
29. Actress Grey
30. *The Karate* ___
31. Actor Stallone, to friends
33. TV's Maverick
37. Film company
38. *I Spy* star
39. Spanish-speaking muppet
41. *Shane* star
42. Star of *Babe*
43. *Mad About You* role
44. Actress Ullmann
46. Morales of *La Bamba*
47. Show on TV
48. TV series where DNA is often tested
49. ___ *Mummy*
52. Patrick's *Ghost* co-star
54. *Lorenzo's Oil* star
55. Cooper or Sandler role
58. ___ *Joe Black*
60. Ned Beatty, in *Superman*
61. TV host Linkletter
62. Sally Field TV role
63. Bullock film, with *The*
64. Unpaid TV ad: Abbr.
65. Ferengi special effect
66. TV's *Science Guy* Bill
67. *Grand Ole Opry* airer

★**Solution on page 323**

1	2	3	■	4	5	6	■	7	8	9	■	10	11	12
13			■	14			■	15			■	16		
17			18				■	19			20			
■	■	■	21			■	22					■	■	■
23	24	25		■	26	27			■	28		29	30	31
32				33				■	■	■	34			
35			■	36				37	■	38				
■	■	■	39				■	40	41			■	■	■
42	43	44			■	45	46				■	47	48	49
50				■	■	■	51				52			
53				54	■	55				■	56			
■	■	■	57		58			■	59	60		■	■	■
61	62	63					■	64				65	66	67
68			■	69			■	70			■	71		
72			■	73			■	74			■	75		

Chapter 14

Just Being Silly

The I's have it 1

1	2	3	4	5	■	6	7	8	9	■	10	11	12	13
14					■	15				■	16			
17					■	18				■	19			
20			■	21	22				■	23				
■	■	■	24			■	■	25	26			■	■	■
27	28	29		■	30	31	32	■	33			34	35	36
37				■	■	38		39			■	40		
41				■	42					■	43			
44			■	45					■	■	46			
47			48			■	49		50	■	51			
■	■	■	52			53	■	■	54	55		■	■	■
56	57	58			■	59	60	61			■	62	63	64
65				■	66				■	67	68			
69				■	70				■	71				
72				■	73				■	74				

ACROSS

1. Slip
6. Swing
10. Sting
14. Twirling
15. Clip
16. Fix
17. Skirmish
18. Flight bd. listings
19. Bits
20. Dig in
21. Wrists
23. Ski sticks
24. JFK listing
25. Dip
27. Kill
30. .001 inch
33. Pitch in
37. Knitting rib
38. Filmic 007
40. ___-fi
41. Limits
42. *Micki &* ___ (film)
43. Split
44. Scrimp
45. Insist
46. Split
47. Split
49. Till
51. This: Sp.
52. Chills
54. Ship's hdg.
56. Tilt
59. Sing
62. Tint
65. Rip
66. ___ *Night*
67. Insipid
69. British pic digs
70. Split
71. Risk
72. Mimic
73. Bid first
74. Hits

DOWN

1. Limping
2. District
3. Hit
4. Visit
5. Pick
6. Fight
7. Twist
8. Stinging
9. Right!
10. Digs
11. Twist
12. "Vissi d'___"
13. Plight
22. Mil. bigwig
23. Sit
24. Iris districts
26. Pink
27. Whisk
28. Sri ___
29. Birch's kin
31. "Wish ___, wish . . ."
32. Nit
34. British ___
35. Whiff
36. Link
39. Whiff
42. Did
43. Drifting
45. Schism
48. Kindling
50. This: Sp.
53. GI's bills
55. Clips
56. Sp. miss
57. Spring
58. Kick in
60. Drift
61. Sign
62. ___-kiri
63. GI gp.
64. Fish dish
66. Siding with
68. Mint

★ **Solution on page 323**

The I's have it 2

ACROSS

1. Binding
6. Flight bit
11. Wind dir.
14. Pigs
15. NL/MVP in 1971
16. ___ king
17. Sprinkling
18. Chips in
19. Pitch
20. Thrills
22. Fix
24. Fight
27. Limit
28. Drinks
29. .001 inch
30. Jiff
31. Mid pt.
32. Ill will
34. First st.
35. Birds
39. Miff
40. Flirt with
41. 40 winks
42. TV's Thing
43. Nigh night?
44. *High*___ (1941 film)
45. Imprint
47. Gin mill
48. Twit
49. Mild
52. Filch
53. Driving sticks
54. Shill
55. Pink tip
57. Ditch
58. Flight bit
60. "___ kidding!"
64. Whirlwind
65. Did
66. Impish
67. Thirst
68. Chirps
69. Swill

DOWN

1. JFK sight
2. ___-night
3. ___ Tin Tin
4. Miff
5. Rind
6. Still
7. Fit
8. Skills
9. Ill will
10. Mind
11. Thin
12. Spin
13. Districts
21. Pints
23. Spirits
24. Hit
25. 1492 ship
26. 1979 sci-fi hit
28. SCTV kin
30. Dim ___
31. Biz bigwig
33. Miff
34. Kingpin
36. Brink
37. Chilling
38. Mini fights
40. Dripping
41. Knight
43. Ship's dir.
44. Dispirits
46. Trick
47. Diving ___
49. Mist
50. Skirt
51. Snitch
52. Slink
53. Fish
55. This: Sp.
56. Blinking things
59. It clinks in drinks
61. NM sighting
62. Split
63. Slim printing widths

★**Solution on page 323**

The I's have it 3

ACROSS

1. Drips
6. Limit
9. Limp
13. Chilling
14. Mining find
15. District
16. Thrill
17. With child
19. Witch
21. Night
22. Gig bit
23. Bits
26. Mind
29. "Twilight" gp.
30. Wit
31. Bright fish
35. Stir
36. SCTV kin
37. Frights with IV + IV limbs
39. Fit within
41. Hit
42. Grim
43. Sp. miss
44. Hits
45. Till
46. Twirl
49. JFK sights
50. Liq.
53. Whip
54. Split
56. Picnic dish
59. Bits
63. *High* ___
64. Ship's dir.
65. Rib-tickling
66. Flight listings
67. Didn't stir
68. Drift

DOWN

1. Mini
2. Thin fish
3. RBI's kin
4. Gists
5. "___ pin, pick . . . "
6. Filch
7. Pinch
8. Stir
9. Kid
10. Miffs
11. Trifling
12. ___ *Midnight*
18. Mil. bigwig
20. ___ Prix
23. Inst. VIPs
24. Birch's kin
25. Lift
27. Wright wing
28. Child
30. Ship's dir.
32. Sits
33. Split
34. Skins
37. Mix flick
38. 1 in. = 2.54 ___
40. Pitch
41. Snitch
44. ___ split
47. Fifth qtrs.
48. Fibs
49. Drink
50. Zits
51. Winnings
52. Dimwit
55. Chips in
57. Thin printing widths
58. Dripping
60. High hill
61. ___ king
62. Slick

★**Solution on page 324**

A lot 1

ACROSS

1. Baja rahs
5. Stamps
10. Pts. and qts.
14. Cap-___
15. Trash
16. Sand
17. Jazz fans
18. "Halt, salt!"
19. Blvds. and rds.
20. Map abbr.
21. Plan part
22. Tarzan's pal
24. "Walk Away ___"
26. Warms
30. Small flap
32. Las Palmas cash
35. RSVP part
36. Cash back
39. Latch ___
40. Jazz gp.
41. Track path
42. Bad lad's grab
44. Bawl
45. Ran
46. Charlatan
47. Warns
49. Chang and ___
50. Aardvark snacks
51. Garland
52. Harsh
54. Warmth
58. Flap
60. Nana
63. ___ Baba
64. Smart
67. Hallway
69. Dash
70. 24-karat
71. Gap
72. Staffs
73. Marsh grass
74. ADAs and TAs
75. Flank

DOWN

1. AMPAS award
2. Strand
3. Had
4. Grad. class
5. Bat a gnat
6. Mansard part
7. Stat
8. AF ranks
9. ___ trap
10. Match
11. *D.C. Cab* star
12. Draw
13. AL and WA
21. Pants part
23. "Rats!"
25. Catchall abbr.
27. *MTM*'s Grant
28. Lama's land
29. Smacks
31. Start
32. Standard and ___
33. Naval grad
34. Snatch
36. Play parts
37. Match
38. Pass
43. ___ bran
44. Small dam
46. Catch
48. Slant
53. Ran a 10K
55. ___ Lama
56. Chan man
57. Wash
59. *Man ___ Mancha*
60. Scams
61. Nap
62. Mars
64. Y class
65. Cast
66. Wrath
68. 1948 pact
69. 911 abbr.

★ **Solution on page 324**

A lot 2

ACROSS

1. *M*A*S*H* man
6. Tacks
11. Papa
14. ___ branch
15. ___ *Days*
16. Walkway hazard
17. Catch a catnap
18. Staff
19. Brand-___
20. Whack
21. NAACP part
23. Mad
25. Spasms
26. Chap
28. Sarcasm
31. Grad. class
32. Pts. and qts.
36. Map
37. S.A. mammals
39. Sway
40. Altar garb.
41. Wk. day
42. TNT part
43. Yarn
45. Chan man
47. Brash
48. Saw
49. Atlas chart
50. Tara clan
52. Draft
54. Pack away
55. Alma ___
58. Tall spar
59. Path
62. Tarzan's pal
63. Gnaws
66. "___ Dawn"
68. AF ranks
69. Llama land
70. *Law &* ___
71. D-Day craft
72. Bad
73. Clasp

DOWN

1. ___ Hashanah
2. "That's ___ ask!"
3. Fast
4. Map abbr.
5. Darn
6. Gall
7. ___ *Man*
8. Attach
9. Fall flat
10. "Alas"
11. Bad mark
12. Yarn
13. Damp
22. Plan part
24. At hand
25. Shark part
26. Sap
27. Naval abbr.
28. Rash
29. Calm
30. Waylay
31. Fracas
33. Cab tab
34. Land
35. Mask parts
38. G sharp
44. Bank
45. Mantra chants
46. Dabs
47. Cat's hand
51. Ballpark snack
53. ___ sprawl
54. Brash
55. Plaza
56. Small flats
57. Assay
58. Track ___
59. *M*A*S*H* star Alan ___
60. Map abbrs.
61. Nag
64. ___ flash
65. QB's stats
67. Stray

★ **Solution on page 324**

A lot 3

ACROSS

1. Map abbr.
4. NFL half
7. NY's La Scala
10. That man's
13. Small mark
14. HS class
15. Half and half
16. Aardvark's snack
17. Wraps
19. RR abbr.
20. Fat farm
21. ___ Hashanah
22. Swat
23. "Pshaw!"
24. Say
27. Play
29. Chap
30. Half-and-half half
32. Want-ad abbr.
33. Mad
34. Jack-tars
36. Pranks
40. Chasm
41. Ka ___, HI
42. ___ Lanka
43. Latch ___
45. Dads
47. Catch
48. TV brand
50. Dallas sch.
51. Cal ___
52. Sham
56. Bags
58. Grassland
59. Had a snack
60. Mast
61. Mantra chants
62. ___ Na Na
63. Manhattan park
67. Cravat
68. Bard's always
69. Santa ___, CA
70. Malaga rah
71. AL and WA
72. Grad. class
73. NFL stats
74. Lay an ___

DOWN

1. Want ___
2. Altar act
3. LAX abbr.
4. Can't stand
5. Galas
6. Blackjack
7. Mr. Dayan
8. Attracts
9. ___ alla Scala
10. "___ manana"
11. Data
12. Say
18. At bay
24. La Paz pal
25. That's a wrap
26. Had a nap
27. Fall back
28. Dr.'s graph
31. Tra-___
35. Band
37. TV's Grant
38. Charm
39. Says "Alas!"
44. Scrap
45. Black cat
46. Hang
47. Draw back
49. Halts
52. Cabals
53. Pay
54. Allays
55. Chars
57. Grandmas
60. "Amscray!"
64. Shad ___
65. Math. branch
66. Pants part

★ **Solution on page 324**

4-letter words 1

1	2	3	■	4	5	6	■	7	8	9	■	10	11	12
13			■	14			■	15			■	16		
17			■	18			■	19			■	20		
21			■	22			23	■	24		25			
26			27		■	28		29				■	■	■
■	■	■	30		31	■	32			■	33	34	35	36
37	38	39		■	40	41			■	■	■	42		
43				■	44				45	■	46			
47			■	■	■	48				■	49			
50			51	■	52			■	53	54		■	■	■
■	■	■	55	56				57	■	58		59	60	61
62	63	64				■	65		66		■	67		
68			■	69		70	■	71			■	72		
73			■	74			■	75			■	76		
77			■	78			■	79			■	80		

ACROSS

1. Rate
4. Test
7. Limb
10. Chum
13. Tree
14. Joey
15. Copy
16. Time
17. Fuss
18. Deer
19. Hole
20. Feat
21. Pair
22. Lack
24. Hate
26. Step
28. Duds
30. Tint
32. Haul
33. Veto
37. Nail
40. Soil
42. Pair
43. Grub
44. Flub
46. Blab
47. Past
48. Slog
49. Drag
50. Note
52. Dear
53. Mold
55. Cask
58. Mean
62. Meal
65. Pact
67. Guys
68. Rage
69. Beak
71. Live
72. Rear
73. Spot
74. Hire
75. Pose
76. Thou
77. Iota
78. Rent
79. Owns
80. Flub

DOWN

1. Dine
2. Bush
3. Gush
4. Chic
5. Part
6. Rube
7. Lick
8. Coda
9. Fare
10. Turf
11. Bend
12. Slow
23. Blew
25. Pose
27. Sums
29. Soft
31. Fade
34. Plan
35. Find
36. Laze
37. Grin
38. Fury
39. Iota
41. Drop
45. Rosy
46. Next
51. Sash
52. Laud
54. Keys
56. Void
57. Rein
59. Icon
60. Stay
61. Join
62. Duke
63. Zone
64. Cane
66. Solo
70. Ante

★ **Solution on page 324**

4-letter words 2

1	2	3	■	4	5	6	■	7	8	9	■	10	11	12
13			■	14			■	15			■	16		
17			■	18			■	19			■	20		
21			22			■	23				■	24		
■	■	■	25			26			■	27	28			
29	30	31		■	32			■	33			■	■	■
34			■	■	■	35		36		■	37	38	39	40
41			42	■	43					■	44			
45				■	46				■	■	■	47		
■	■	■	48	49		■	50		51	■	52			
53	54	55			■	56				57		■	■	■
58			■	59	60			■	61			62	63	64
65			■	66			■	67			■	68		
69			■	70			■	71			■	72		
73			■	74			■	75			■	76		

ACROSS

1. Olla
4. Heir
7. Tyke
10. Ammo
13. Grow
14. Whiz
15. Whiz
16. Bend
17. Sick
18. Help
19. Case
20. Mead
21. Tell
23. Fogy
24. Flee
25. Give
27. Jobs
29. Flub
32. Tilt
33. Darn
34. Peak
35. Huge
37. East
41. Fibs
43. Bash
44. Tale
45. Tops
46. Atop
47. Twit
48. Chat
50. Vase
52. Rest
53. Jeer
56. Oily
58. Chop
59. Pink
61. Coat
65. Bled
66. Time
67. Live
68. Dusk
69. Hire
70. Vice
71. Bunk
72. Bind
73. Plot
74. Held
75. Pair
76. Deer

DOWN

1. Duet
2. Gawk
3. Blab
4. Rash
5. East
6. Doze
7. Work
8. Tart
9. Mean
10. Orbs
11. Snap
12. Cons
22. Bark
23. Exit
26. Sofa
28. Gone
29. Ball
30. Hash
31. Ajar
33. Dump
36. Save
38. Epic
39. Flag
40. Cost
42. Esne
43. Snap
49. Anew
51. Thin
52. Spot
53. Bush
54. Quit
55. Held
56. Thou
57. Tend
60. Song
62. Bash
63. Base
64. Fume
67. Feat

★ **Solution on page 324**

4-letter words 3

ACROSS
1. Dads
6. Jets
10. Over
14. Keen
15. Each
16. Hick
17. Mend
18. Pump
19. Smug
20. Rest
22. Yeas
24. Deem
28. Roue
30. Bend
33. Done
34. Kiln
36. Redo
38. Hart
39. Doze
40. Thin
41. Pubs
43. Moth
45. Over
48. Ergo
50. Bobs
54. Dido
55. Glow
56. Jerk
57. Scan
58. Glen
60. Fake
62. Spin
64. Slow
66. Mark
68. Peak
70. Ring
75. Chow
76. Grow
77. Cuts
78. Help
79. Chow
80. Hits

DOWN
1. Norm
2. Stun
3. Dads
4. Live
5. Main
6. Defy
7. Orbs
8. Also
9. Talk
10. Coax
11. Beat
12. Sash
13. Beak
21. Deck
23. Long
24. Wand
25. Dusk
26. Thou
27. Come
29. Horn
31. Ruby
32. Bawl
35. Pure
37. Shed
42. Gall
44. Dull
45. Whiz
46. Howl
47. Work
49. Pale
51. Have
52. Cube
53. Dump
59. Warn
61. Gobs
63. Once
65. Cans
66. Deep
67. Taxi
69. Tart
71. Rare
72. Time
73. Mesh
74. Dolt

★ **Solution on page 324**

O sole me O 1

ACROSS

1. Schnoz
5. Not on ___ (nohow)
10. Honcho
14. Jot
15. Pools
16. Condo
17. Cork
18. 86 or 99
19. Colt's mom
20. Not so loco
22. Scolds
24. Not old
25. Gowns
27. Drops g
29. Not gross
32. "___ No Hooks"
33. Coll. hotshot
34. Book boo-boos
36. ___ or no
37. ___ browns
41. Brown
42. Oolong
43. Cowboys vs. broncos sport
44. Proof word
45. Combo
46. ___ of proof
47. Smooth
49. Color
50. NNW opp.
51. Lot
54. Door: Fr.
56. Common vow
57. Tots' pops
59. Vows
63. Toll
65. Wood
67. Slow flow
68. To boot
69. Sport swords
70. Hot doll of '96
71. Cloy
72. Common ___
73. Notch

DOWN

1. Short snorts
2. Mrs. Oop
3. Floor
4. Hot to trot
5. Doc bloc, for short
6. M.D. or D.D.S.
7. 'Hoods
8. Torn
9. Honors
10. Hobo
11. ___ on
12. "No ___, Bob!"
13. Broods
21. 1 or 66
23. ___-mo
26. Troop grp.
28. Gods' blood
29. Loch ___
30. Proof word
31. ___ *Colors*
33. "C'mon, ___ sport!"
35. Topmost floor
36. Not ___!
38. Tots
39. Spots
40. Strop
42. Bo's no.
43. Cost
45. Comforts
46. Sot's spot
48. Stop color
49. Throws
51. Corncobs
52. Ms. St. Johns
53. Cook
54. Von ___
55. Comforts
58. Lowdown
60. Bow pro
61. Blood: comb. form
62. Blotch
64. Fort ___, NJ
66. WNW opp.

★ **Solution on page 324**

O sole me O 2

ACROSS

1. Confronts
6. Cops gp. who got pot
9. On to
14. Grown
15. Gross
16. Cohort of Doc
17. Boom box
18. Show growth
19. Throng
20. ___ Scott
22. Got 100 on
24. Toots
27. Cowboy's prod
28. Not good
31. Props for Woods
32. Soft knock
34. Scold
36. Know-how
37. Stop on ___
39. Scoop
40. Boor
42. Roth
43. $1,000,000, for short
44. Po'boy
45. Slosh
47. Do wrong
49. Hollow
51. Oolong ___
52. To ___
53. Mork's cohorts
54. Controls to row
56. Hot spot
58. To boot
59. Howl
60. Food shops
63. Long, long ___
65. Brow crown
69. Solo
70. Month for Moms
71. Mork's boss
72. *Go Down* ___
73. ___ - mo
74. Condor condos

DOWN

1. So ___, so good
2. Tooth doctor's org.
3. Cow chow
4. Drops g
5. Shop
6. Two
7. Pod for Mork
8. Lots
9. Hold
10. Knock on ___
11. Fool's mo.
12. Bloodshot
13. CBS logo
21. Como ___
23. 27, to 3
24. Stop, for short
25. 2 proof
26. Slows
27. Ghosts
28. Cotton cloth
29. Workshop
30. FDR or JFK
33. Go for ___
35. Hoop loop
38. Boy
41. John ___
44. Scoot
45. Don Knotts or Rob Morrow
46. Stow
48. Not gross
50. Loops of doom
52. Shoot for
55. Lots
57. John of rock
58. Hog's word
59. Toy
60. Block
61. '70s rock gp.
62. ___ Lobos
64. 128 oz.
66. Fool
67. Bosh!
68. Sol.

★**Solution on page 324**

O sole me O 3

ACROSS

1. RR stop
4. Ott of sport
7. CCC sponsor
10. ___ loss for words
13. Droop
14. Bon ___
15. ___ *Lobo*
16. ___ room
17. Nonstop
19. Photo ___
20. Botch
21. Tho'
22. Knock off
24. "___ boy!"
27. Sol.
30. Throws
31. Word
32. Knock
33. Croc doc
34. Spots
35. Root rot
37. ___ prof.
41. Mork's cohorts
42. Top off
43. Golf norm
44. Words from Mr. Moto
46. Monk
48. Cloy
49. Ho chow
51. Opp. of WSW
52. Solo for Scotto
53. Dock
56. Slop spot
57. Stoop
58. Stood
59. Scot's "not"
61. *Rob* ___
62. Tooth org.
65. Snood
69. WNW opp.
70. Shoot down
71. Offshoot
72. Rd. or st.
73. Short for Long: 1931-35
74. Spot
75. Mormons
76. "___ Clown"

DOWN

1. NNW opp.
2. Do knot work
3. Grow old
4. Locks
5. Flow forth
6. Short, for short
7. '60s do
8. Scoop
9. Rod
10. 'Hoods
11. Short on words
12. Lots of lots
18. Lots
23. Como ___?
24. Lost
25. Prongs
26. Long lock
28. Rock bottom
29. Sort
30. Flood control org.
36. Stood for
38. Room to ___
39. "___ Doll"
40. Plod
45. Work
46. Conform
47. Fox
48. Sword
50. Lots
53. Confronts
54. Worn
55. Top pro
60. Shoots for
63. Do or ___
64. Chop
65. Mr. Holbrook
66. Cop
67. 12/24 or 12/31
68. Oolong

★**Solution on page 325**

Behead before entry 1

ACROSS

1. Antlered one
4. Fungus-to-be
8. Defleece
12. Steak order
13. Whiz kid
14. She played That Girl
15. Wiener wrap
16. Instant
17. Flathead, for one
18. Defeated
20. Plant stem
22. Comic Johnson
24. Time for eggs
28. Beast of burden
31. Festive events
34. Stable parent
35. Styx hit
36. Parsley portions
37. Radar image
38. Church closer
39. Infernal one?
40. Double agents
41. Joiner of sorts?
43. Poet St. Vincent Millay
45. Weird Al Yankovic parody
48. Peter, of Peter, Paul, and Mary
52. Uses one's wings
55. Grim
57. Doll word
58. Actress Foster
59. Location
60. Surgery souvenir
61. Thought
62. Like a post-9/11 coalition?
63. Repair

DOWN

1. Tent peg
2. *West Side Story* song
3. Villainous sort in *The Matrix*
4. Race
5. Bread unit
6. Wander aimlessly
7. African nation
8. Hits hard
9. German gent
10. Wan
11. Sweaty place
19. Miles of *Psycho*
21. Half full/half empty item
23. Absorb knowledge
25. Hooch maker
26. Spooky
27. Gets ready
28. Accuse
29. Tower site
30. Improve
32. Dart about
33. Locked up
36. Dizzying designs
40. Fly like an eagle
42. Ridiculed
44. Performed like an adder
46. Consumer's woes
47. Beg, borrow, or ___
49. Dinner saying
50. Lady
51. Prize
52. Baseball brother
53. Cash rolls
54. Mayberry lad
56. Defense against a knight or mugger

★ **Solution on page 325**

Behead before entry 2

ACROSS

1. Calf parent
5. Grouchy one
9. Ornery kid
12. Knitted
13. Another you
14. Chewed item for a dog
15. Baker's need
16. Somalia's neighbor
17. Dame ___
18. Prissy sort
20. Holler
22. Ones that got away
25. Houston is north of it
26. Put on
27. Flower part
30. Assert as true
34. Coin side
35. Mingo of *Daniel Boone*
37. Kaplan who was Kotter
38. Sanctify
40. Comprehend
41. Party pooper
42. Attorney's exam
44. Short journeys
46. ___ arena
49. Sparkle
51. Verdi opera
52. Messy places
54. Ring around the water
58. Depth of beauty?
59. Fable ending
60. Uncanny
61. Earth inheritors
62. Actress Dunne or Cara
63. Kind

DOWN

1. Old woman's home
2. Slow flow
3. Pub quaffs
4. Guard
5. Placed like Napoleon
6. Tea treat
7. Outrageous
8. Gap
9. Wear away
10. Letter whirler
11. Rising water?
19. Welded
21. Cornfield cawer
22. Take another base
23. Prop up
24. Merchandise
25. Teen film of 2003
28. Beginning
29. Dalai ___
31. Pine
32. Common practice
33. Gets ready, briefly
36. Political airer
39. Hey, you!
43. Preacher
45. Bowling uh-oh
46. Bandleader Jones
47. Nell portrayer
48. Blunt
49. Laundered
50. Something to walk down
53. Drastic
55. Apple slag
56. Ballet bend
57. *Citizen Kane* prop

★ **Solution on page 325**

Behead before entry 3

ACROSS

1. Ballot component of 2000
4. Pinkish hue
8. Wander
12. Designer Wang
13. Trunk item
14. Complain
15. Controls
16. Wise ones
17. Lama land
18. Less distant
20. Right this minute!
22. Ore yield
25. Say a sermon
29. Say
32. Workmate of Lois and Jimmy
34. "___cadabra" (Steve Miller song)
35. Xmas trees, often
36. Cargo hold cargo
37. Vegetarian's no-no
38. Narrow cut
39. Joined
40. They might be read
41. Ascertains
43. Bridge guard
45. Hostess treat
47. More just
51. Wide
54. Patriot Allen
57. Lot in life
58. Do a crabwalk
59. Something to not leave unturned
60. Picture
61. Spies use them
62. Ball attire
63. Curve in the road

DOWN

1. Turner
2. Monte ___
3. 2nd or 6th president
4. Jasper Johns forte
5. Lug
6. Without clothing
7. *Cagney & Lacey* actress
8. Charlie Brown shirt design
9. Tot's spot
10. Dracula's garb
11. Vladimir's veto
19. Cheat at hide and seek
21. Grades
23. Villa rooms
24. *Heathers* or *Sheena* star
26. Noisy place in the Bible
27. Get lost!
28. Shoots the breeze
29. Valdez event
30. Strange
31. Runner's meal
33. Words to live by
36. Infatuation
40. French Sudan, today
42. Battery terminals
44. Smooth operator's devices?
46. Gambling game
48. Title role for Brett Butler
49. Reveal
50. Fashion
51. Threesome
52. *Sweeney* ___
53. Block of hay
55. What an angel backs
56. *Doctor Faustus* author

★ **Solution on page 325**

8 sounds good to me 1

ACROSS

1. Prison inmate
4. Oily bait
8. Demonstrate
12. Large primate
13. Estimate
14. Monsieur's pate
15. Date
16. Sartre's state
17. Prefix for room or date
18. Provide with a trait
20. Frau's mate
22. Bath or Margate
24. State
28. Calculate
31. Dominate
34. What tree rings indicate
35. Medit. state
36. Reprobate
37. Was a candidate
38. Fabricate
39. Pour ___: exaggerate
40. Pontificate
41. Coolidge's running mate
43. Sympathy's mate
45. One who does anticipate
48. Accumulate
52. Emanate
55. Laminate
57. Thriller remade in '88
58. Tolerate
59. Hearty's mate
60. Jackie's mate
61. First-rate
62. Muscat's state
63. With 10 Down, a Giant great

DOWN

1. Crate
2. Initiate
3. Necessitate
4. Group at Watergate
5. It might cover your pate
6. Arches National Park's state
7. Allocate
8. Initiate
9. Rooster's mate
10. Giant great
11. Not so great
19. Operate
21. Inconsiderate
23. Carry ___ of weight
25. Fictional estate
26. First governor of the 49th state
27. Flat rate
28. Gold-plate
29. Where to find Kuwait
30. Gained weight
32. It might deflate
33. Uncle's mate
36. Levitate
40. Ewe's mate
42. Adlai's running mate
44. Gone from one's plate
46. Imitate
47. Perambulate
49. Eve's mate
50. Irate
51. Navigate
52. LAX guesstimate
53. Star in *Head of State*
54. Mamie's mate
56. So. state

★ **Solution on page 325**

8 sounds good to me 2

ACROSS

1. Eliminate
4. Lie in wait
8. Bryce Canyon's state
12. Che's mate
13. Where to find Kuwait
14. Fictional estate
15. Long, long wait
16. Flat rate?
17. Decorate
18. Oscillate
20. Splicing candidate
22. Shark bait
24. Create
28. Soft silicate
31. Pedro's eight
34. Start to dominate
35. In a frenzied state
36. Place to rejuvenate
37. Anagram of "sate"
38. Safety or straight
39. Chirac's state
40. Set straight
41. Create
43. Shearing candidate
45. Reagan's Secretary of State
48. Portrait
52. Imitate
55. Roy's range mate
57. Exterminate
58. They aviate
59. Krogh of Watergate
60. What tree rings indicate
61. Pieces of acetate
62. Disseminate
63. Storage crate

DOWN

1. They pollinate
2. State
3. Rajah's mate
4. Great
5. Manipulate
6. Syndicate
7. Allie's roommate
8. State
9. He probably knows good bait
10. Jackie's mate
11. Hardly an Oscar candidate
19. Strait
21. Lieut.'s subordinate
23. Like one who'd hesitate
25. One who does imitate
26. Herr's mate
27. Monsieur's pate
28. Evidence at Watergate
29. Mideast potentate
30. The ___ Star State
32. One who does calculate
33. Abominate
37. Originate
39. JFK guesstimate
42. Game where you try to mate
44. Manipulate
46. Caesar's fateful date
47. Calculate
49. He might have a date
50. Best picture of '58
51. Blissful state
52. Star in *Head of State*
53. Surface on which to skate
54. First name of a baseball great
56. Prevaricate

★**Solution on page 325**

Appendix A

Glossary

#: Crosswords are called by the number of rows and columns they have, which tend to be the same in the crossword world (a newspaper's daily puzzle is usually a 15, and a newspaper's Sunday crossword is usually a 21; almost always a square puzzle and an odd number).

American-style: See **construction.**

anagram: Rearranging letters to spell something else; occasionally used in a theme

British-style: See **construction.**

byline: A constructor credit.

cheater: A black square that maintains word count, making the grid easier to fill in.

construction/constructor: In an American-style crossword, a constructor constructs using the art of construction. For British-style crosswords, setters set crossword puzzles. British-style puzzles DO NOT have cross-checking, and the clues have a straight half and a cryptic half (there are about a half dozen different styles of acceptable cryptic form).

cross-checking: Having all white boxes used in both across and down entries, so that you can check a square against valid entries going in both directions.

crossword: The first crossword, created by Arthur Wynn, appeared in the December 21, 1913, edition of *New York World.* Word squares go back at least to early Rome.

crosswordese: Words that you rarely encounter outside the crossword world.

cruciverbalism: The art/science of crosswords.

cruciverbalist: Crossword constructor.

entry: An across or down answer.

fill: The entries stuffed into a grid.

grid: A crossword's black/white square pattern.

interconnectedness: Grid quality where black squares don't chop the puzzle into separate pieces.

isle of white: Cut-off part of a grid that is not interconnected.

knothole: A square that's hard to break open, because you have no clue about the across and down entries crossing there.

Margaret Farrar: The world's first crossword editor (for the *New York Times*); she laid down the first ground rules, giving legitimacy to the field.

mirror-symmetry: The feature of a grid where if you chop it in half, then spin it around on its center, it'll match up.

Monday: Traditionally, an easy crossword in a daily newspaper.

new wave: A construction style where entries go beyond your typical dictionary and atlas (more pop culture, arts, business names, IT terms, very recent news, and clues apropos for Jeopardy and Trivial Pursuit).

open: A dense concentration of white squares in a grid.

palindrome: Something that is the same spelled forward and backward; occasionally used in a theme or clue.

partial: A fill-in-the-blank where multiple words go in the blank.

patch: A minor grid rework.

Ray Hamel: Keeper of a great crossword reference list at *www.primate.wisc.edu/people/hamel/cp.html*

Saturday: Traditionally, a tough-as-nails crossword in a daily newspaper; a Monday would be the easy puzzle.

Scrabble: A word game where one can stack across and down words, forming a crude crossword puzzle. When I was a kid, I would jot down good open areas.

square: A box in a grid.

stacking: Putting long answers side by side.

Stephen Sondheim: Lyricist credited for popularizing cryptic crosswords in the U.S.

sticky: Adjective describing a square or section that's hard to break open.

tag: A clue about an entry's form, such as ": 2 wds." or ": Fr." or ": var."

teardown: A major grid rework.

theme: Common concept that runs throughout a puzzle's long entries or even the whole puzzle; such a puzzle is said to be themed.

Tom Swifty: Swapping the initial consonant sounds/blends on the starts of words; occasionally used in a theme.

Unch: Short for "unchecked letter" (see *cross-checking*).

Will Shortz: Current *New York Times* crossword editor (who added bylines and made the puzzles more new wave), host of NPR's "The Puzzler Presents," and someone who actually got a college degree in enigmatology (the study of puzzles).

Will Weng: Former *New York Times* crossword editor.

word count: The number of entries in a grid; some publishers specify word count limits.

word square: A crossword variant (dating back at least to ancient Rome) where the downs and acrosses are the same. It may be well advised to attempt making these before tackling the construction of a whole puzzle. An example of a word square is as follows:

S T A R T
T A B O O
A B O U T
R O U G E
T O T E M

Appendix B

Puzzle Answers

page 2 • **Where the deer and the antelope play**

page 3 • **We've been over these before**

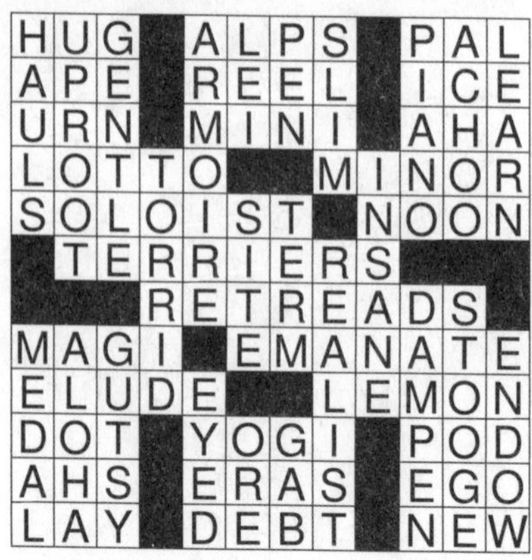

page 4 • **From D.C. to California**

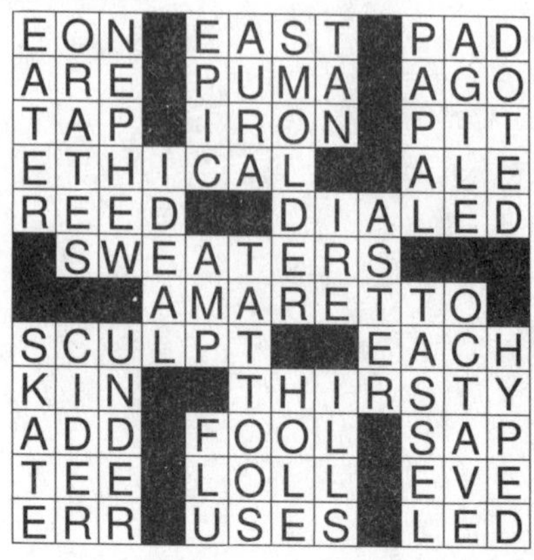

page 5 • **Lack of difficulty**

page 6 • **World that can be whirled**

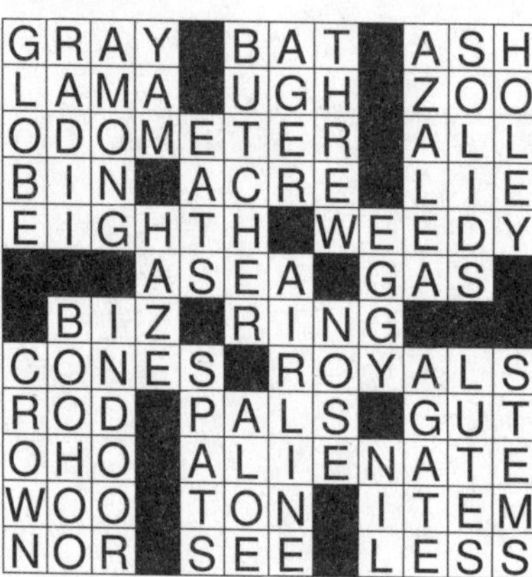

page 7 • **Words of praise**

page 8 • **Infatuated**

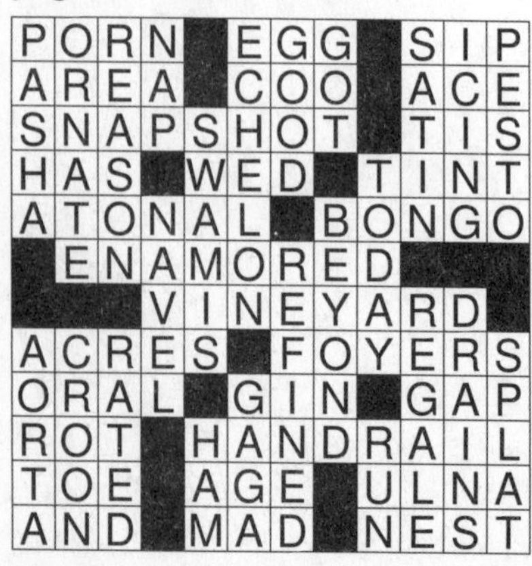

page 9 • **Dagnabbit!**

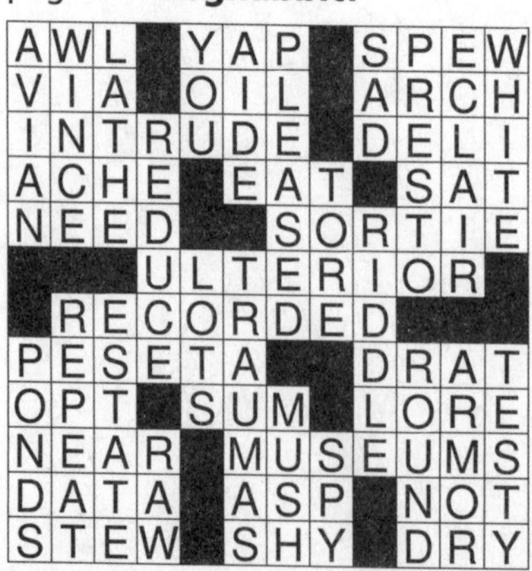

page 10 • **Apprehend**

page 11 • **Suspicion**

A	R	M	Y	■	S	P	A	■	P	O	O	R
B	E	A	U	■	L	I	D	■	L	O	B	E
L	A	M	P	■	E	G	O	■	U	P	O	N
E	L	A	P	S	E	■	R	I	N	S	E	D
■	■	■	I	N	K	L	I	N	G	■	■	■
P	U	R	E	E	■	E	N	T	E	R	E	D
O	R	E	■	A	D	A	G	E	■	A	Y	E
I	N	V	O	K	E	S	■	R	E	N	E	W
■	■	■	P	E	R	T	A	I	N	■	■	■
C	A	M	E	R	A	■	S	M	A	C	K	S
O	V	E	N	■	I	R	K	■	M	A	N	E
P	I	L	L	■	L	Y	E	■	E	V	E	N
E	D	D	Y	■	S	E	W	■	L	E	W	D

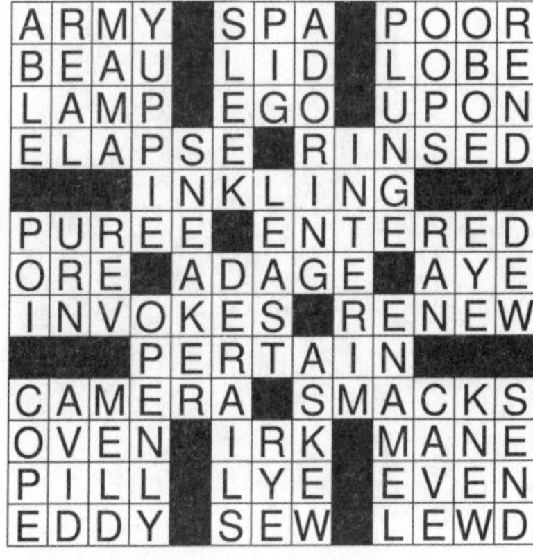

page 12 • **More than just a job**

S	O	R	D	I	D	■	■	B	L	E	A	T
I	G	U	A	N	A	■	C	O	E	R	C	E
F	L	I	M	S	Y	■	O	R	I	G	I	N
T	E	N	S	E	■	S	O	N	■	O	D	D
■	■	■	■	T	I	N	K	E	R	■	■	■
H	E	R	B	■	N	E	W	■	A	N	T	E
E	V	I	L	■	T	E	A	■	R	A	I	N
M	E	M	O	■	E	R	R	■	E	Y	E	D
■	■	■	C	A	R	E	E	R	■	■	■	■
P	A	T	■	F	A	D	■	H	E	A	V	E
A	T	O	M	I	C	■	P	I	L	L	O	W
Y	O	G	U	R	T	■	I	N	M	A	T	E
S	P	A	D	E	■	■	T	O	S	S	E	S

page 13 • **Search for gold**

C	R	A	M	■	U	R	G	E	■	P	I	P
H	O	L	E	■	S	E	A	L	■	E	R	A
O	A	T	S	■	H	A	R	K	■	S	O	L
P	R	O	S	P	E	C	T	■	L	O	N	E
■	■	■	■	A	R	T	E	R	Y	■	■	■
A	L	T	A	R	S	■	R	E	R	E	A	D
P	E	A	R	S	■	■	■	T	I	A	R	A
E	D	G	I	E	R	■	S	A	C	R	E	D
■	■	■	S	C	A	M	P	I	■	■	■	■
A	C	N	E	■	V	I	O	L	A	T	E	D
M	O	O	■	P	I	N	K	■	C	H	A	I
M	A	P	■	O	N	C	E	■	H	E	R	S
O	L	E	■	T	E	E	N	■	Y	E	N	S

page 14 • **Shine**

L	I	S	P	■	V	A	M	P	■	R	A	G
U	N	T	O	■	A	L	O	E	■	A	L	L
S	H	E	D	■	L	I	N	E	■	B	I	O
T	A	R	■	P	E	T	A	L	■	B	A	A
E	L	I	C	I	T	■	R	E	S	I	S	T
R	E	L	I	C	■	E	C	R	U	■	■	■
■	D	E	N	■	D	O	H	■	G	A	B	■
■	■	■	C	L	A	N	■	T	A	I	L	S
S	A	S	H	A	Y	■	B	A	R	R	E	N
E	L	M	■	S	T	E	E	P	■	B	E	E
A	G	O	■	H	I	D	E	■	T	A	P	E
M	A	T	■	E	M	I	T	■	U	S	E	R
S	E	E	■	S	E	T	S	■	B	E	D	S

page 15 • **Flashy**

K	A	R	A	T	■	■	■	P	L	A	N	S
I	R	I	S	E	S	■	L	E	A	G	U	E
T	I	N	S	E	L	■	O	R	N	A	T	E
E	D	G	E	■	O	R	A	T	E	■	■	■
■	■	■	R	O	B	O	T	■	S	L	A	P
C	A	C	T	I	■	A	H	A	■	A	X	E
O	H	O	■	N	O	S	E	S	■	I	L	L
R	O	D	■	K	I	T	■	E	G	R	E	T
N	Y	E	T	■	L	E	G	A	L	■	■	■
■	■	■	W	E	I	R	D	■	A	T	O	M
A	S	P	I	R	E	■	A	R	M	A	D	A
B	U	R	S	A	R	■	Y	E	O	M	E	N
S	P	O	T	S	■	■	■	P	R	E	S	S

page 16 • **Blossom**

A	F	L	A	M	E	■	■	T	R	I	A	L
F	L	O	W	E	R	■	C	R	I	N	G	E
R	E	B	A	T	E	■	L	I	C	K	E	D
O	W	E	R	■	C	R	O	O	K	■	■	■
■	■	■	D	A	T	E	D	■	E	C	H	O
A	H	S	■	W	E	D	■	S	Y	R	U	P
S	E	A	■	A	D	U	L	T	■	A	L	E
P	R	I	C	Y	■	C	O	O	■	B	A	N
S	O	L	O	■	M	E	O	W	S	■	■	■
■	■	■	F	L	A	S	K	■	P	A	S	S
L	O	A	F	E	R	■	I	C	I	C	L	E
O	U	T	E	A	T	■	N	A	R	R	O	W
B	R	E	E	D	■	■	G	R	E	E	T	S

page 17 • **Right now!**

H	A	L	E	■	S	T	I	R	■	B	O	O
A	R	I	A	■	A	I	D	E	■	Y	A	P
T	E	N	S	■	D	R	O	P	P	E	R	S
E	A	T	E	R	■	A	L	S	O	■	■	■
■	■	■	■	A	D	D	S	■	K	I	W	I
S	U	N	■	I	R	E	■	S	E	D	A	N
C	R	A	N	N	Y	■	P	A	R	E	N	T
A	N	N	O	Y	■	B	I	G	■	A	D	O
T	S	A	R	■	T	R	E	E	■	■	■	■
■	■	■	T	A	R	O	■	R	E	A	C	H
H	I	G	H	L	A	N	D	■	A	U	R	A
A	C	E	■	M	I	C	A	■	S	T	A	T
S	E	T	■	S	N	O	B	■	T	O	W	S

page 18 • **Honor**

A	R	F	■	B	A	T	H	■	S	C	U	M
G	E	E	■	A	C	H	E	■	H	O	P	E
A	F	L	U	T	T	E	R	■	O	A	R	S
P	U	L	P	■	■	■	■	■	P	R	O	S
E	G	O	S	■	S	U	M	O	■	S	O	Y
■	E	W	E	■	P	R	O	P	H	E	T	■
■	■	■	T	R	I	B	U	T	E	■	■	■
■	P	E	S	E	T	A	S	■	A	R	M	■
G	E	M	■	D	E	N	Y	■	T	E	A	S
L	A	P	S	■	■	■	■	■	E	L	S	E
U	N	I	T	■	L	I	C	O	R	I	C	E
E	U	R	O	■	A	V	O	W	■	C	O	D
S	T	E	P	■	B	Y	T	E	■	S	T	Y

page 19 • **Wily**

B	L	A	B	■	F	O	R	E	■	A	F	T
R	O	P	E	■	O	B	E	Y	■	T	R	Y
A	C	E	S	■	R	O	S	E	■	T	I	P
S	A	M	E	■	F	E	E	■	B	A	S	E
S	T	A	T	U	E	■	T	R	U	C	K	S
Y	E	N	■	N	I	L	■	A	S	H	Y	■
■	■	■	■	I	T	E	M	S	■	■	■	■
■	M	O	L	T	■	G	A	P	■	S	I	P
P	A	P	A	Y	A	■	D	Y	N	A	M	O
A	N	E	W	■	I	N	N	■	A	L	P	S
N	U	N	■	T	R	U	E	■	C	O	O	S
G	A	L	■	W	E	D	S	■	H	O	S	E
S	L	Y	■	O	R	E	S	■	O	N	E	S

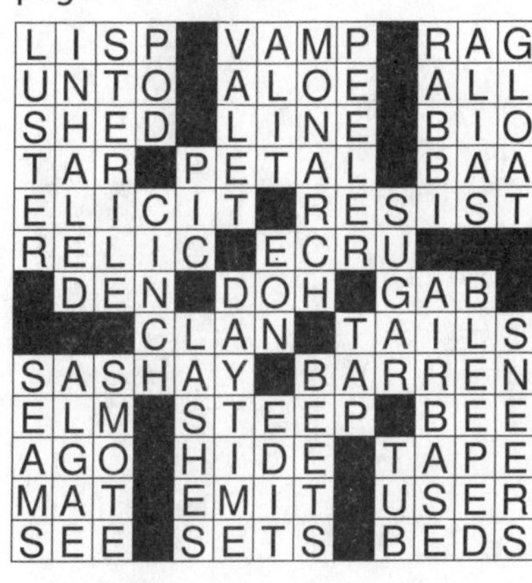

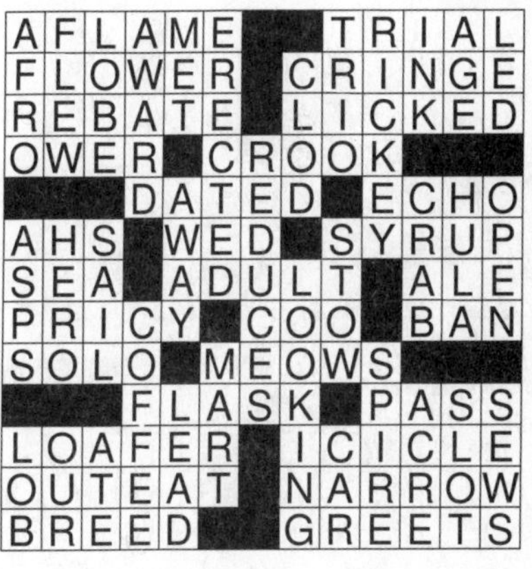

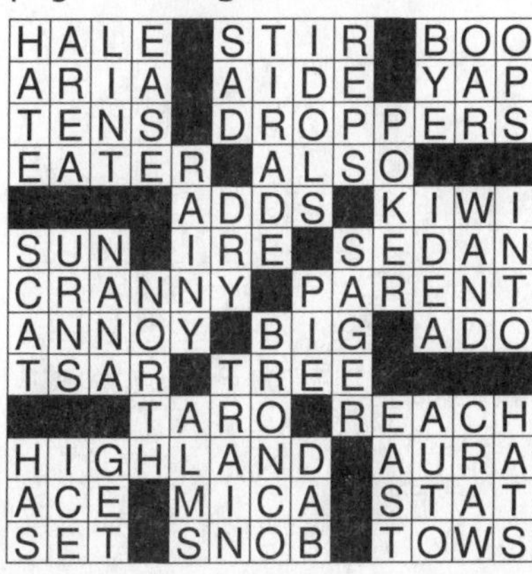

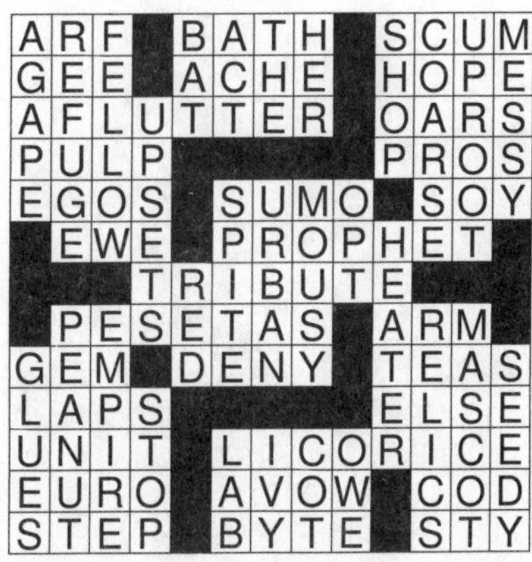

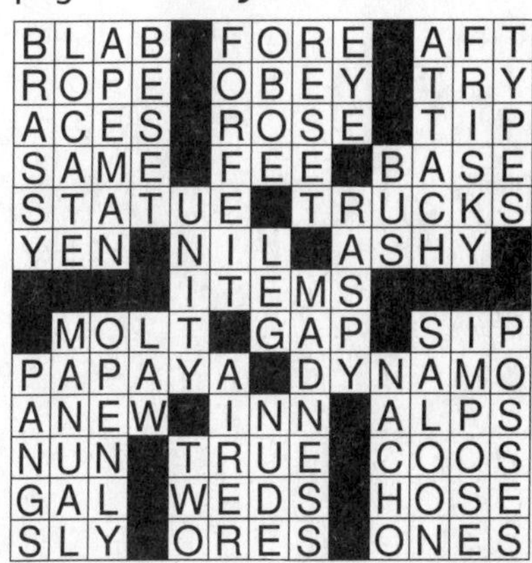

page 22 • **Getting closer**

GUSH MOSS ARCH
ANTE ONTO VILE
IDOL LEAF EGAD
TOPPLE GAINING
PEA NUDGE
AWARDS BAKE
WAG EARLY EBB
LYE REGAL DUE
BADE YOGURT
BEAUT ARC
LEDGERS STEALS
ORAL INFO ATOP
WIPE BILL SEAR
NETS SPUD EDDY

page 23 • **So be it!**

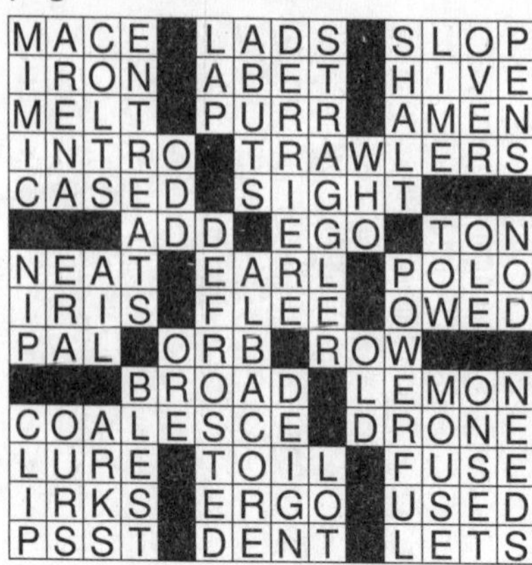

page 24 • **Hey!**

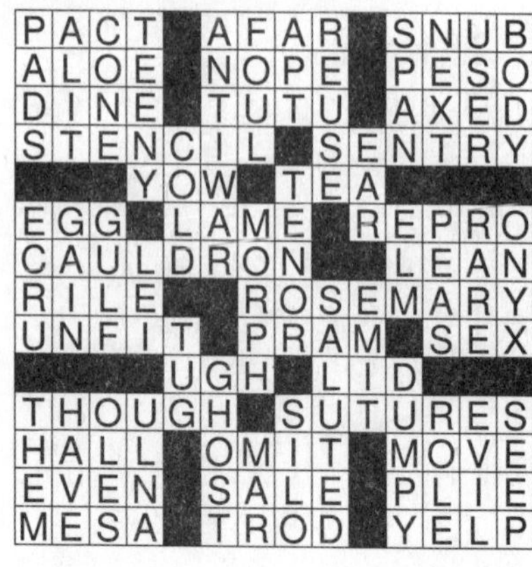

page 25 • **Gain knowledge**

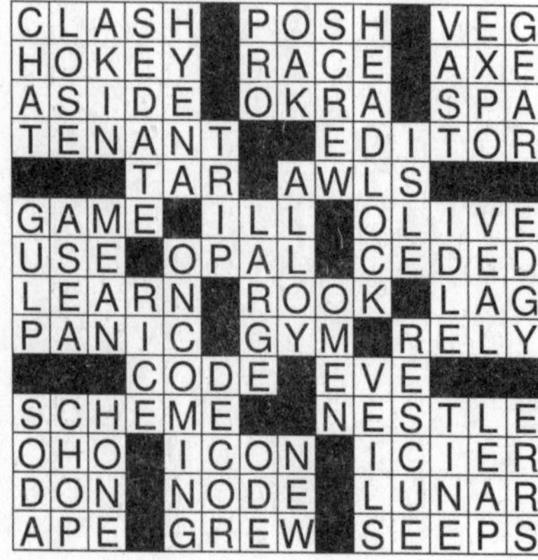

page 26 • **I would, would I?**

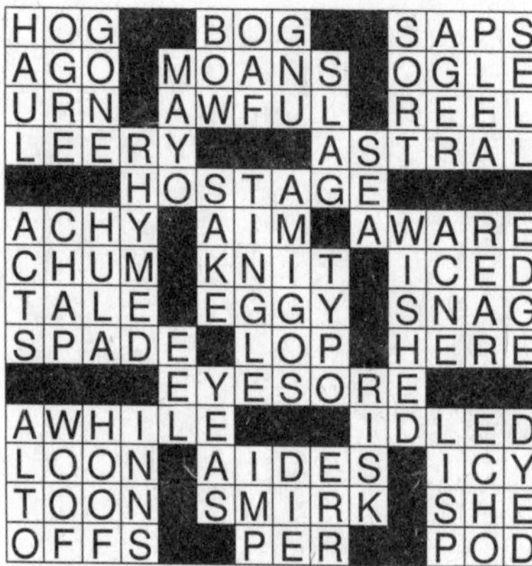

page 27 • **Legitimate**

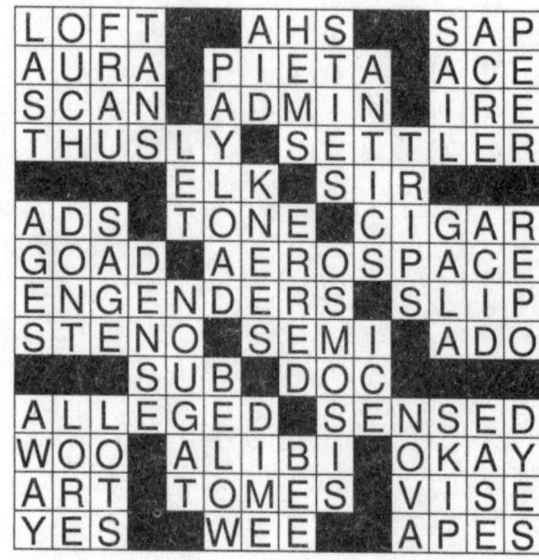

page 28 • **Balderdash**

page 29 • **Grand tale**

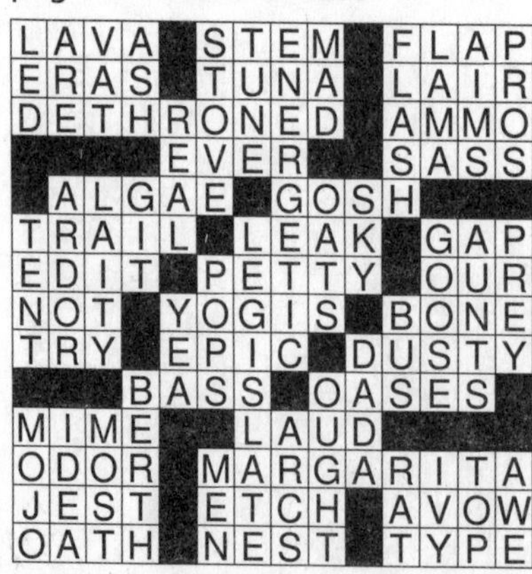

page 30 • **Overwhelmed**

page 31 • With sprinkles

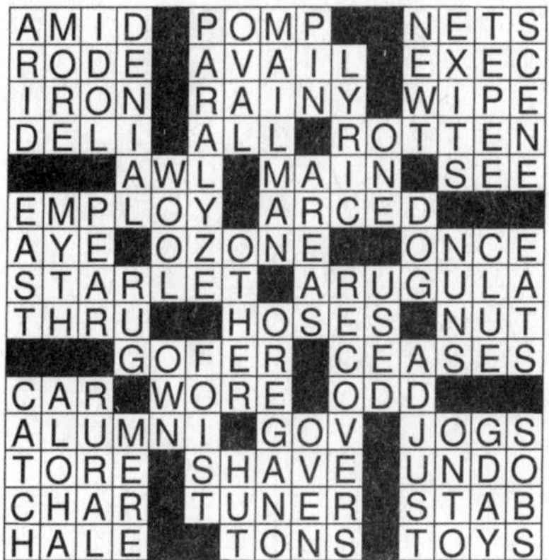

AMID POMP NETS
RODE AVAIL EXEC
IRON RAINY WIPE
DELI ALL ROTTEN
AWL MAIN SEE
EMPLOY ARCED
AYE OZONE ONCE
STARLET ARUGULA
THRU HOSES NUT
GOFER CEASES
CAR WORE ODD
ALUMNI GOV JOGS
TORE SHAVE UNDO
CHAR TUNER STAB
HALE TONS TOYS

page 32 • I like that!

SHOP SEW MOTH
LAME SEVEN EURO
IRIS ELATE DROP
DETOURED WRISTS
NICE BAA
KISMET SIGNIFY
DUTIES GEE MOO
ADEPT VET STARK
MOM AIL LEAGUE
ESSENCE TANDEM
MAC TOPS
STROBE ROSEMARY
TAUT SLATE ALOE
URGE SIDED TILL
BOSS BED STEP

page 33 • Go up and down

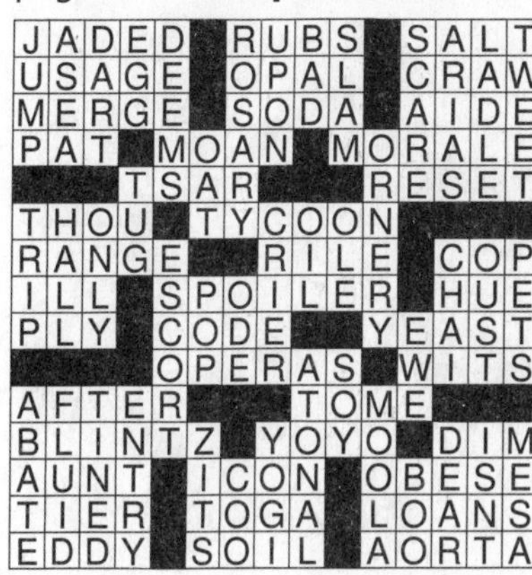

JADED RUBS SALT
USAGE OPAL CRAW
MERGE SODA AIDE
PAT MOAN MORALE
TSAR RESET
THOU TYCOON
RANGE RILE COP
ILL SPOILER HUE
PLY CODE YEAST
OPERAS WITS
AFTER TOME
BLINTZ YOYO DIM
AUNT ICON OBESE
TIER TOGA LOANS
EDDY SOIL AORTA

page 34 • Hurrah

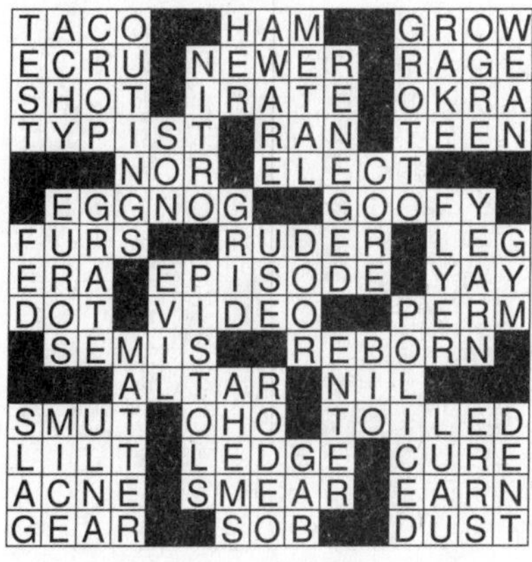

TACO HAM GROW
ECRU NEWER RAGE
SHOT IRATE OKRA
TYPIST RAN TEEN
NOR ELECT
EGGNOG GOOFY
FURS RUDER LEG
ERA EPISODE YAY
DOT VIDEO PERM
SEMIS REBORN
ALTAR NIL
SMUT OHO TOILED
LILT LEDGE CURE
ACNE SMEAR EARN
GEAR SOB DUST

page 35 • Gets all gussied up

SALSA EDGE STAG
UPEND NOON COME
MESAS TUBA ROOT
PSST ORB BLANKS
CARAT LOW
SCHLEP REPLICA
SHEETS RID COD
KIDDO YAP THIRD
IRE GEM PREENS
TEDIOUS DREARY
DUE TRIED
ADMITS HAG LIFE
CIAO SPEW SIREN
HARM EARL INKED
ELKS DYES NESTS

page 36 • I hated this movie

PASS ARCH CARE
ATOP CAROM OVER
REDO RHINO GOGO
ORE BETS WAD
POKE TUSSLE
PLAYER SMOCK
RUT FULLY HITCH
AMEN MOUNT DIRE
MERIT TRAIN MAR
CRISP NATIVE
POLKAS NODE
ALE PLEA PAN
GIVE EXUDE GAPS
EVEN TATER UNIT
REED MONK EDGY

page 37 • Fuss and bother

ABHOR TWAS CHAT
SLOPE RIDE LOGO
HURTS ATOM ABET
YEN ITCH IGNORE
EDIT ANY
PIXELS HAPPEN
CANINE JAR LAID
AVAST WAS FIVER
TENT FEW FLEECY
DESIRE COARSE
LAP ACTS
KABUKI TRIM BIZ
ERAS LYRE ABODE
LINE TEES TOOLS
PADS YAKS EGRET

page 38 • Eccentric

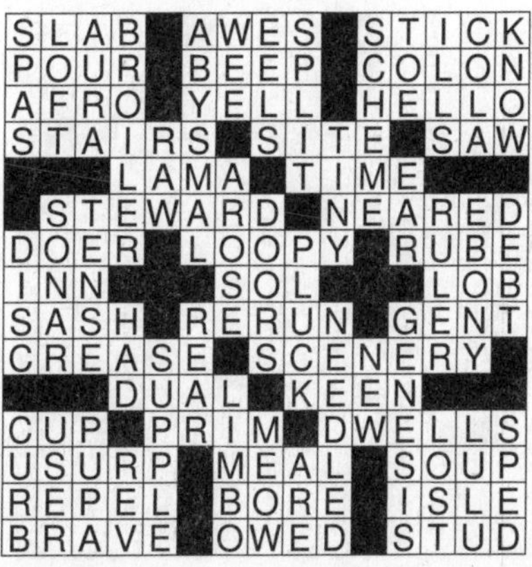

SLAB AWES STICK
POUR BEEP COLON
AFRO YELL HELLO
STAIRS SITE SAW
LAMA TIME
STEWARD NEARED
DOER LOOPY RUBE
INN SOL LOB
SASH RERUN GENT
CREASE SCENERY
DUAL KEEN
CUP PRIM DWELLS
USURP MEAL SOUP
REPEL BORE ISLE
BRAVE OWED STUD

page 39 • We are family

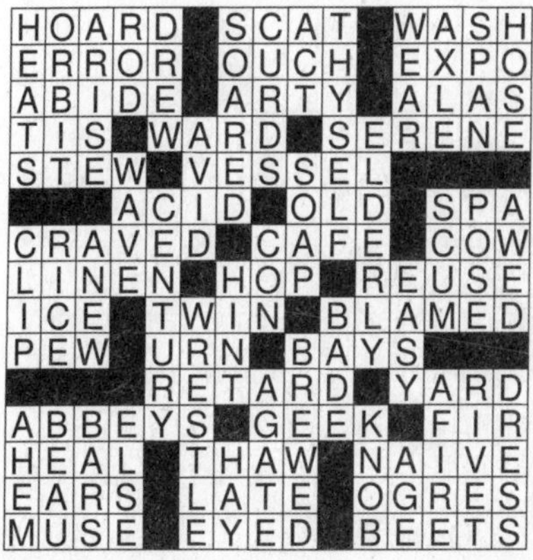

HOARD SCAT WASH
ERROR OUCH EXPO
ABIDE ARTY ALAS
TIS WARD SERENE
STEW VESSEL
ACID OLD SPA
CRAVED CAFE COW
LINEN HOP REUSE
ICE TWIN BLAMED
PEW URN BAYS
RETARD YARD
ABBEYS GEEK FIR
HEAL THAW NAIVE
EARS LATE OGRES
MUSE EYED BEETS

page 42 • **Intrude**

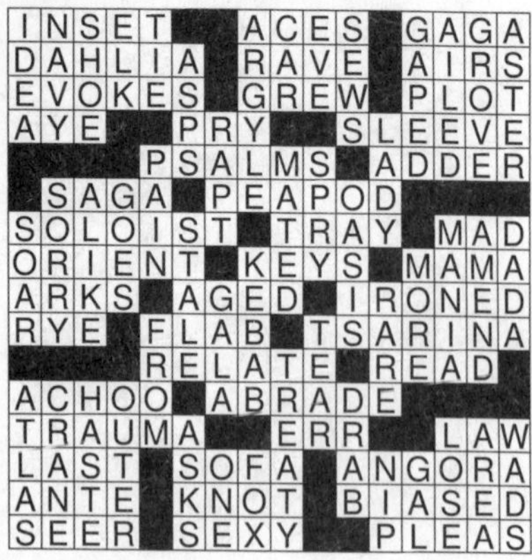

page 43 • **Phooey!**

page 44 • **Hot spot**

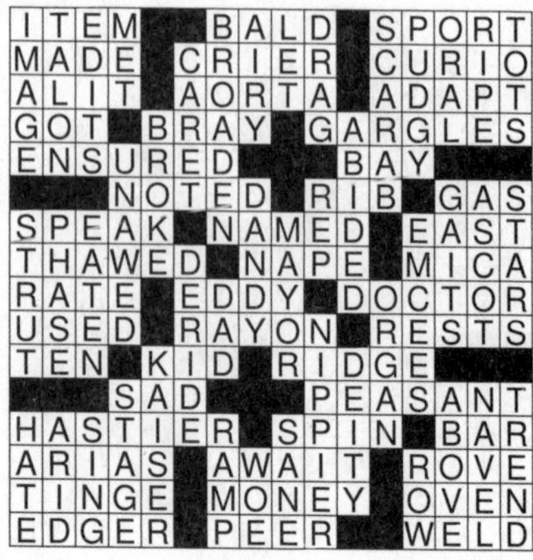

page 45 • **It's mindless**

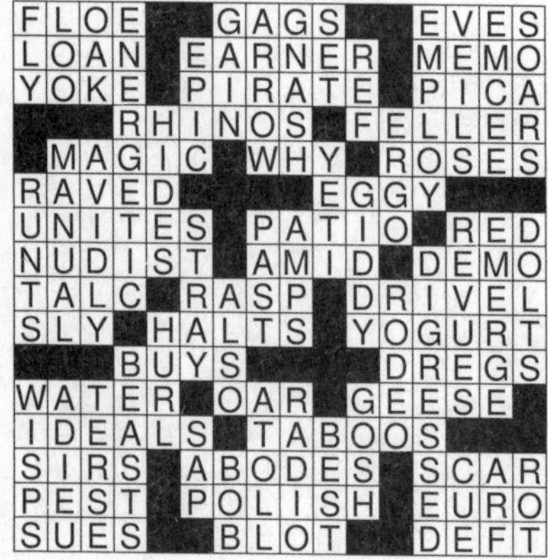

page 46 • **What a relief!**

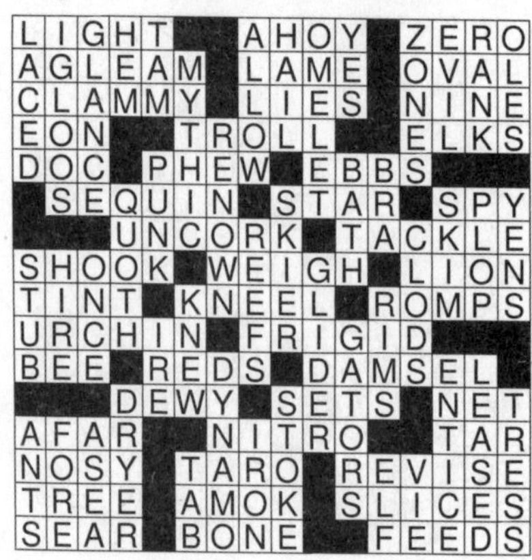

page 47 • **Help out**

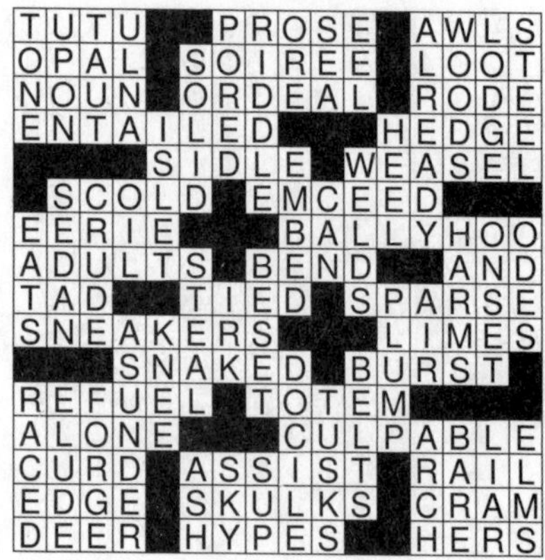

page 48 • **It may be golden**

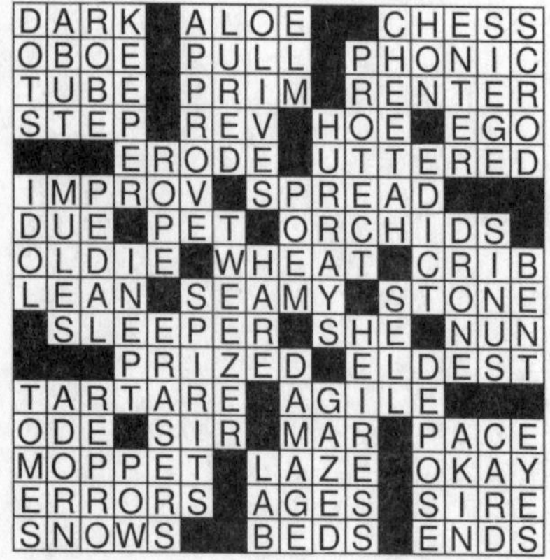

page 49 • **This instant!**

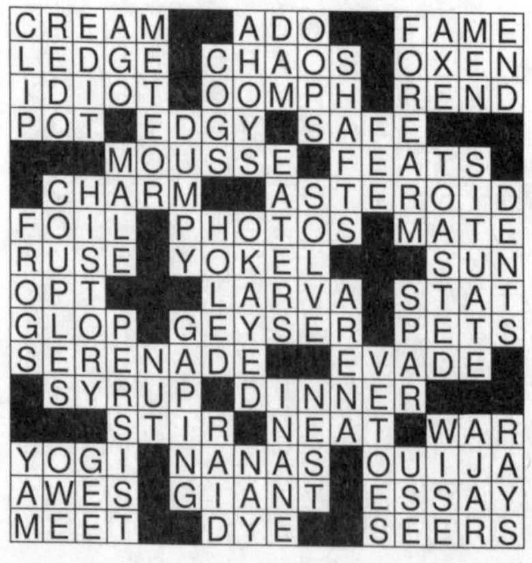

page 50 • **Skedaddle!**

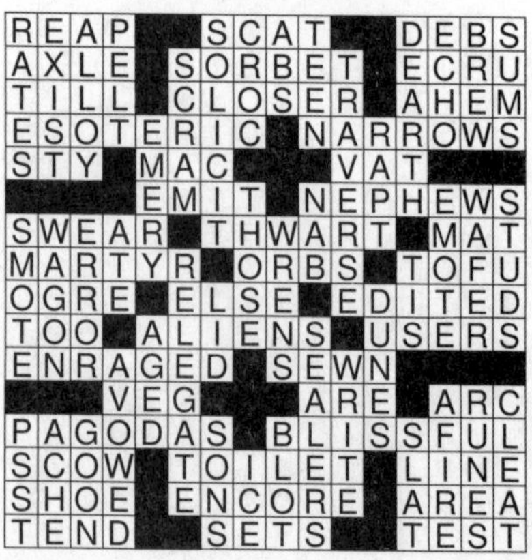

page 51 • **Life story**

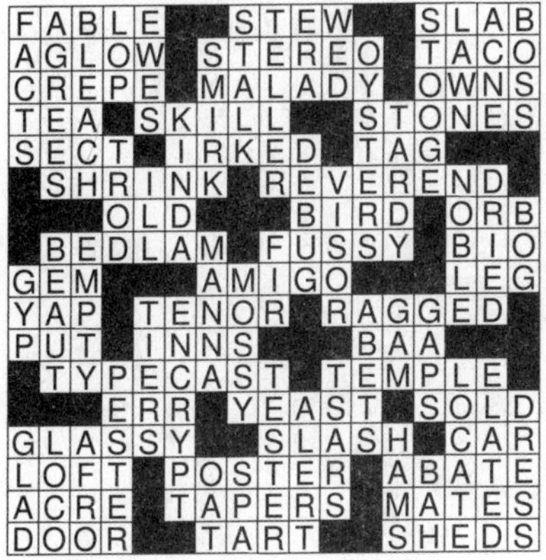

page 52 • **There oughta be one**

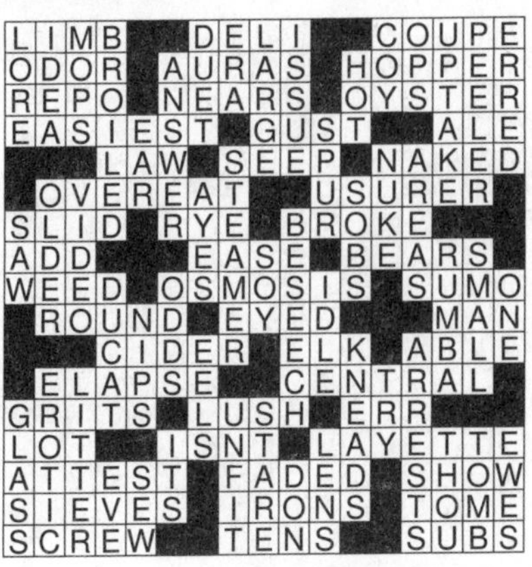

page 53 • **Local star**

page 54 • **Value**

page 55 • **Slivered side**

page 56 • **Up for discussion**

page 57 • **Once more**

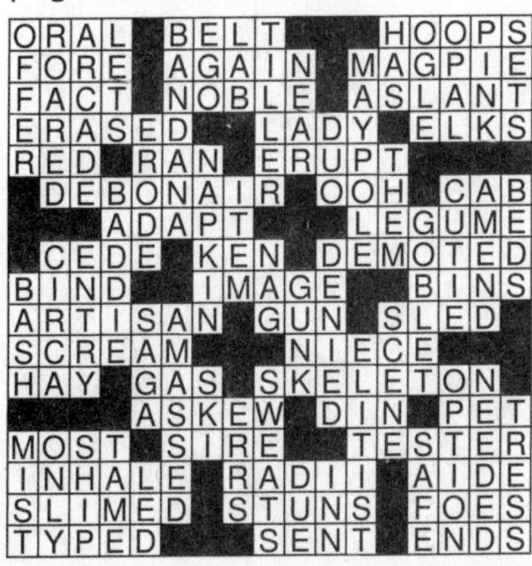

page 58 • **Push over**

page 59 • **Excellence**

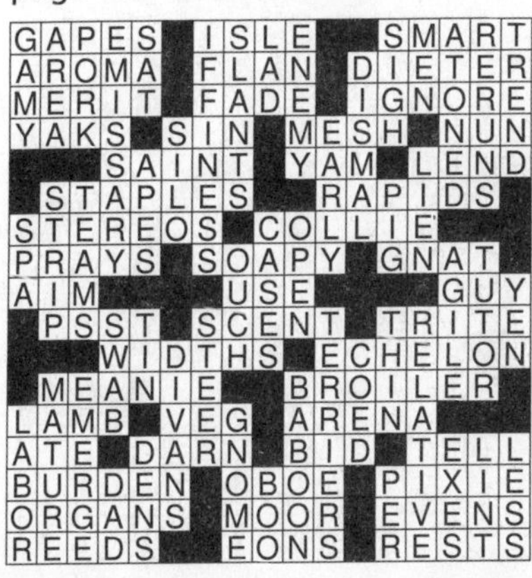

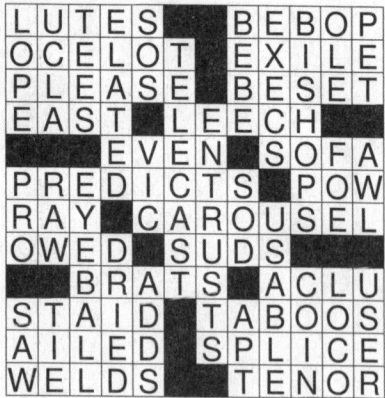

page 62 • **Calm**

L	U	T	E	S	■	■	B	E	B	O	P
O	C	E	L	O	T	■	E	X	I	L	E
P	L	E	A	S	E	■	B	E	S	E	T
E	A	S	T	■	L	E	E	C	H	■	■
■	■	■	E	V	E	N	■	S	O	F	A
P	R	E	D	I	C	T	S	■	P	O	W
R	A	Y	■	C	A	R	O	U	S	E	L
O	W	E	D	■	S	U	D	S	■	■	■
■	■	B	R	A	T	S	■	A	C	L	U
S	T	A	I	D	■	T	A	B	O	O	S
A	I	L	E	D	■	S	P	L	I	C	E
W	E	L	D	S	■	■	T	E	N	O	R

page 63 • **What fun!**

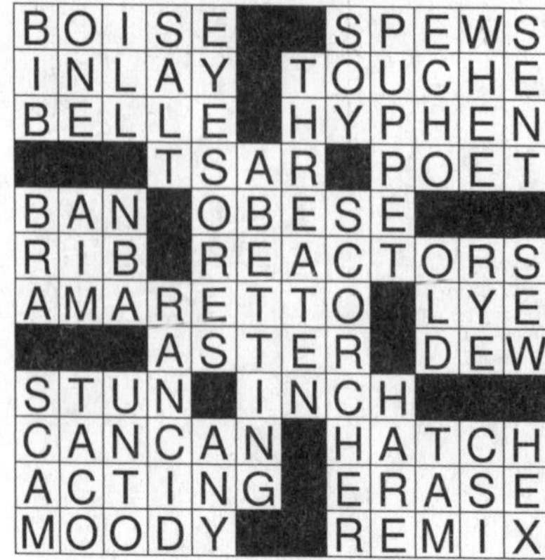

B	O	I	S	E	■	■	S	P	E	W	S
I	N	L	A	Y	■	T	O	U	C	H	E
B	E	L	L	E	■	H	Y	P	H	E	N
■	■	■	T	S	A	R	■	P	O	E	T
B	A	N	■	O	B	E	S	E	■	■	■
R	I	B	■	R	E	A	C	T	O	R	S
A	M	A	R	E	T	T	O	■	L	Y	E
■	■	■	A	S	T	E	R	■	D	E	W
S	T	U	N	■	I	N	C	H	■	■	■
C	A	N	C	A	N	■	H	A	T	C	H
A	C	T	I	N	G	■	E	R	A	S	E
M	O	O	D	Y	■	■	R	E	M	I	X

page 64 • **Success**

C	O	S	T	■	H	A	G	■	P	E	P
R	O	P	E	■	A	L	I	■	L	E	O
E	D	I	T	■	B	I	N	D	E	R	S
E	L	F	■	H	I	T	■	W	A	I	T
D	E	F	E	A	T	■	S	A	T	E	S
■	S	Y	M	P	A	T	H	Y	■	■	■
■	■	■	O	P	T	I	O	N	A	L	■
A	M	I	T	Y	■	N	E	E	D	E	D
H	E	R	E	■	A	I	D	■	M	A	R
E	R	A	S	U	R	E	■	T	I	R	E
A	C	T	■	H	I	S	■	U	R	N	S
D	Y	E	■	F	A	T	■	T	E	S	S

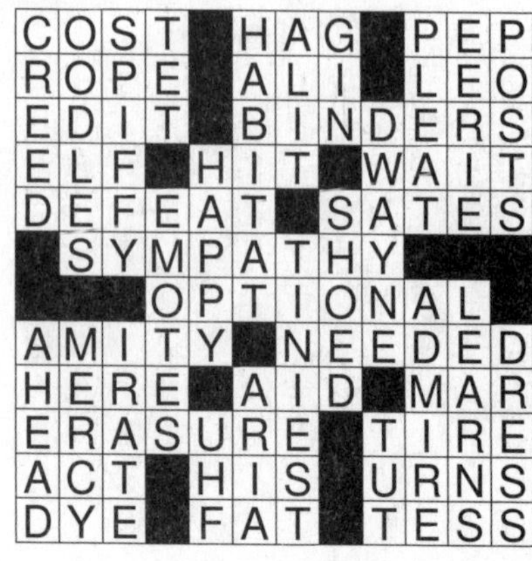

page 65 • **Stay in the game**

O	P	A	L	■	A	R	M	■	A	F	T
S	O	R	E	■	H	U	B	■	M	O	O
C	U	R	T	■	S	E	A	P	O	R	T
A	R	I	S	E	■	■	■	A	N	T	E
R	E	V	■	V	E	S	T	I	G	E	S
■	D	E	L	E	T	I	O	N	■	■	■
■	■	■	E	N	C	L	O	S	E	D	■
M	A	R	A	T	H	O	N	■	L	E	D
A	G	E	S	■	■	■	S	N	A	F	U
C	A	S	H	E	W	S	■	E	P	I	C
A	T	E	■	L	O	U	■	A	S	E	A
W	E	T	■	M	O	P	■	T	E	S	T

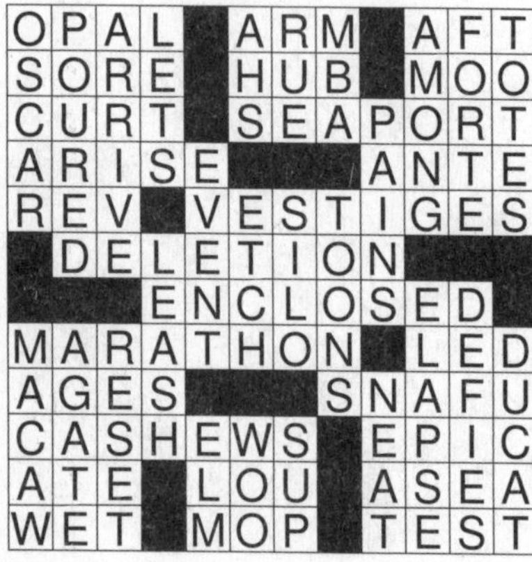

page 66 • **Show of support**

M	Y	N	A	S	■	■	C	R	O	W	D
P	E	A	L	E	D	■	H	A	T	E	D
H	A	G	G	L	E	■	A	N	T	E	S
■	■	■	A	L	B	E	I	T	■	■	■
V	E	N	E	E	R	S	■	S	L	A	M
A	Y	E	■	R	I	C	E	■	I	C	E
M	E	T	■	S	E	A	M	■	N	H	L
P	S	S	T	■	F	L	I	R	T	E	D
■	■	■	I	N	S	A	N	E	■	■	■
L	O	T	T	O	■	T	E	A	C	U	P
I	D	E	A	S	■	E	N	C	A	S	E
P	E	N	N	Y	■	■	T	H	R	E	W

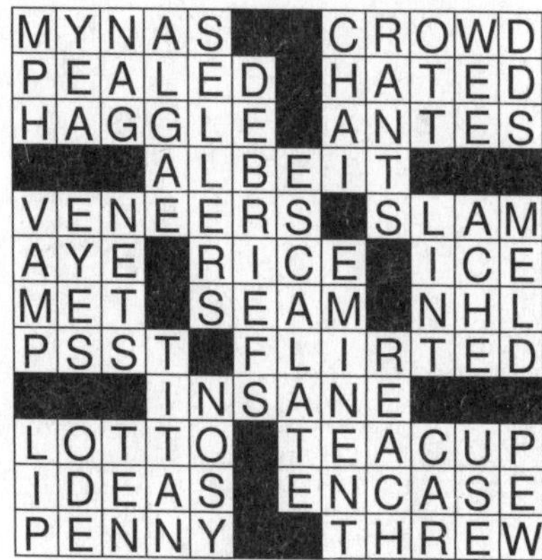

page 67 • **It sets a trap**

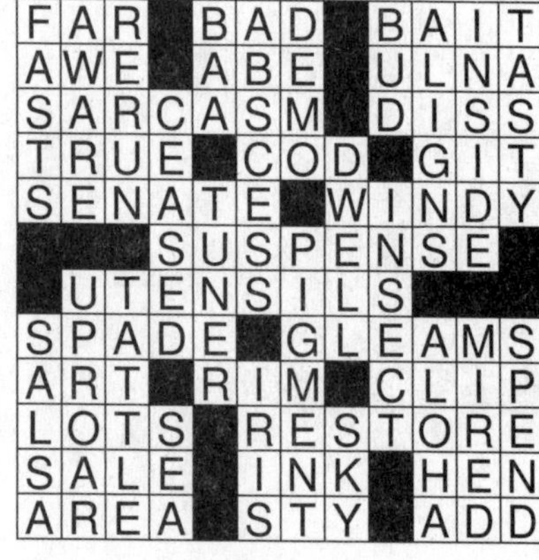

F	A	R	■	B	A	D	■	B	A	I	T
A	W	E	■	A	B	E	■	U	L	N	A
S	A	R	C	A	S	M	■	D	I	S	S
T	R	U	E	■	C	O	D	■	G	I	T
S	E	N	A	T	E	■	W	I	N	D	Y
■	■	■	S	U	S	P	E	N	S	E	■
■	U	T	E	N	S	I	L	S	■	■	■
S	P	A	D	E	■	G	L	E	A	M	S
A	R	T	■	R	I	M	■	C	L	I	P
L	O	T	S	■	R	E	S	T	O	R	E
S	A	L	E	■	I	N	K	■	H	E	N
A	R	E	A	■	S	T	Y	■	A	D	D

page 68 • **Practice**

E	A	T	E	R	■	■	O	T	H	E	R
O	L	I	V	E	S	■	W	E	A	V	E
N	E	P	A	L	I	■	E	M	B	E	D
■	■	■	D	A	N	K	■	P	A	R	S
O	N	S	E	T	■	I	R	O	N	■	■
P	I	E	■	I	S	L	E	■	E	M	S
S	P	A	■	O	A	T	H	■	R	I	P
■	■	S	A	N	G	■	E	P	O	X	Y
L	O	O	T	■	A	F	A	R	■	■	■
A	N	N	O	Y	■	D	R	I	L	L	S
S	C	A	L	E	■	A	S	S	A	I	L
T	E	L	L	S	■	■	E	M	P	T	Y

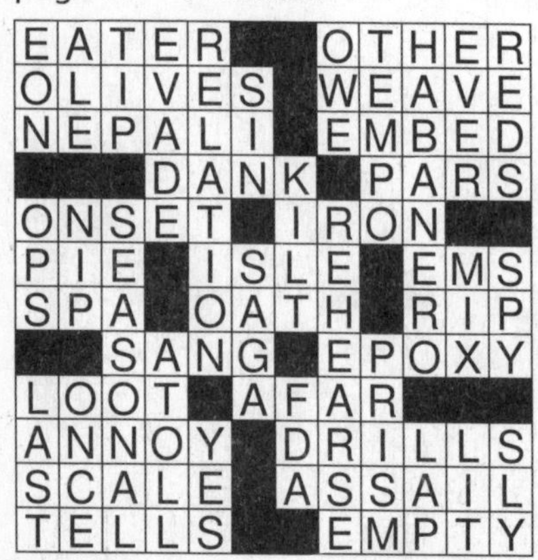

page 69 • **Cry at a clue**

R	O	N	■	V	C	R	■	T	U	F	T
A	P	E	■	A	H	A	■	O	S	L	O
G	E	E	■	T	A	R	■	T	H	O	U
E	N	D	S	■	G	E	L	■	E	R	R
S	E	L	L	E	R	■	A	U	R	A	S
■	R	E	A	L	I	S	T	S	■	■	■
■	■	■	B	O	N	E	H	E	A	D	■
G	R	A	S	P	■	S	E	R	V	E	S
R	E	D	■	E	T	S	■	S	O	A	P
A	V	O	W	■	A	I	R	■	I	R	E
P	U	R	E	■	C	O	O	■	D	I	N
H	E	E	D	■	T	N	T	■	S	E	T

page 70 • **Quite an accomplishment**

I	N	T	R	O	■	■	S	P	O	I	L
M	O	W	E	R	■	S	P	A	R	T	A
P	R	O	U	D	■	H	E	R	E	S	Y
■	■	■	S	E	L	E	C	T	■	■	■
R	E	V	E	R	E	■	■	S	O	F	T
A	X	E	■	L	I	C	K	■	K	E	Y
N	P	R	■	Y	A	R	N	■	R	A	P
G	O	B	S	■	■	A	E	R	A	T	E
■	■	■	P	E	E	W	E	E	■	■	■
L	A	G	O	O	N	■	C	A	V	E	S
A	R	O	U	N	D	■	A	D	I	E	U
D	E	B	T	S	■	■	P	S	A	L	M

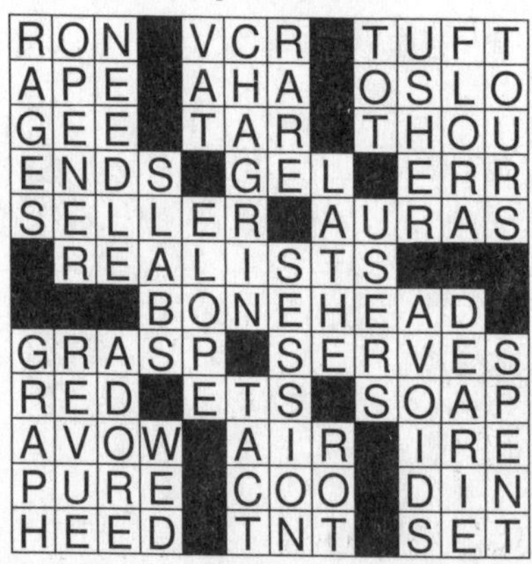

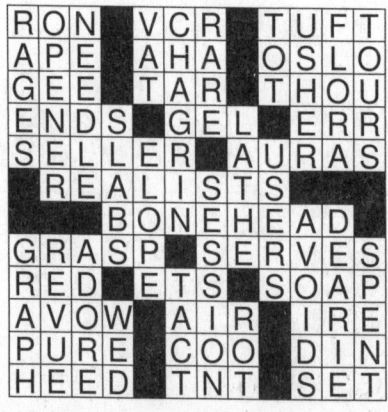

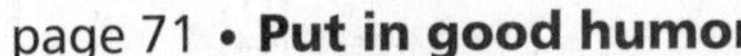

page 71 • **Put in good humor**

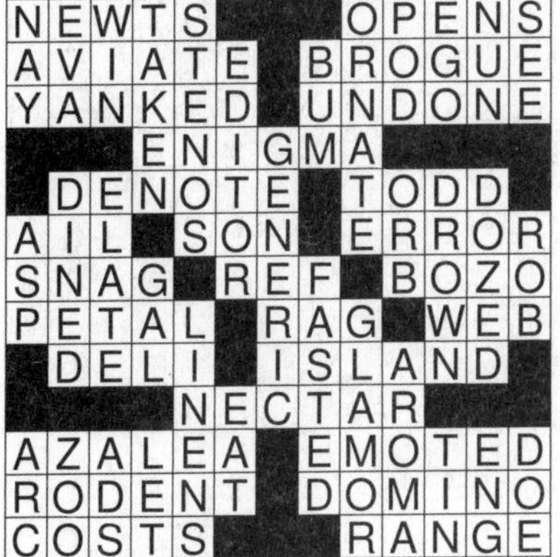

page 72 • **You can dig it**

page 73 • **Verbose**

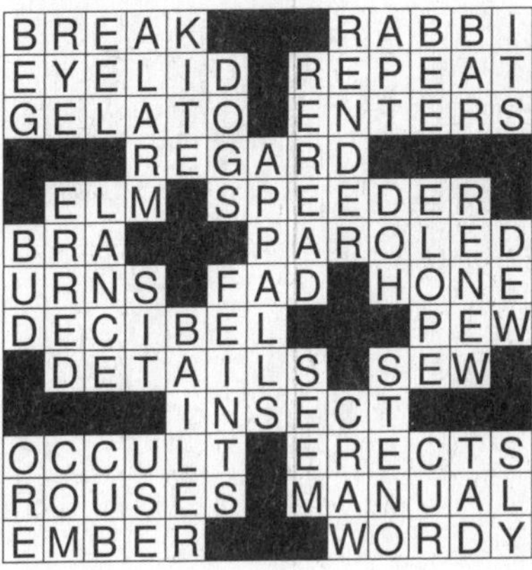

page 74 • **Curious**

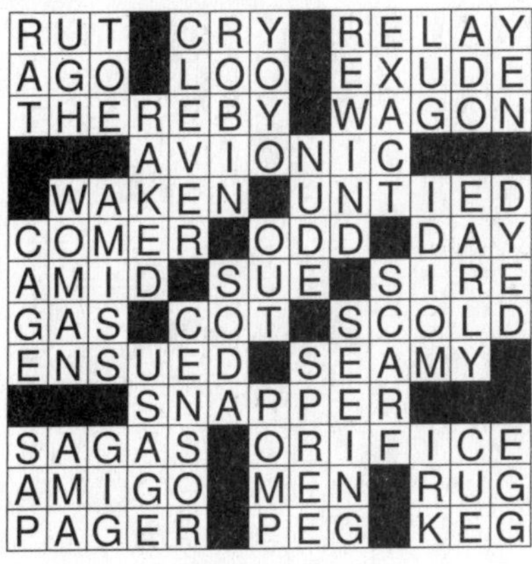

page 75 • **Can I have one?**

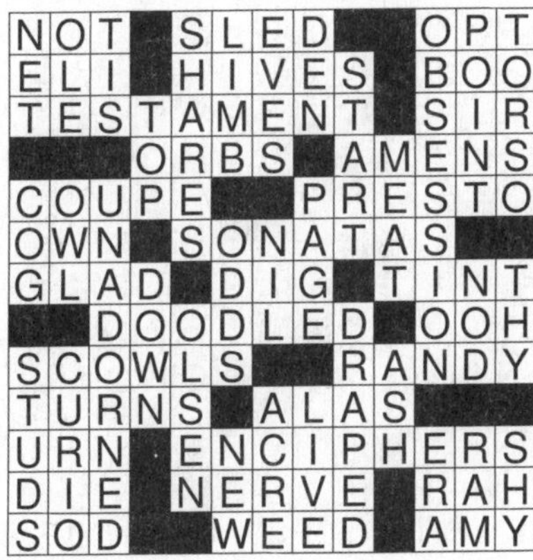

page 76 • **What else?**

page 77 • **Impressive!**

page 78 • **Say it again**

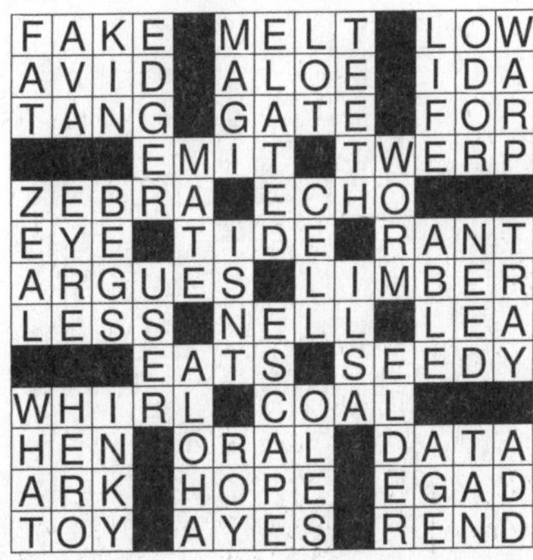

page 79 • **Benevolent**

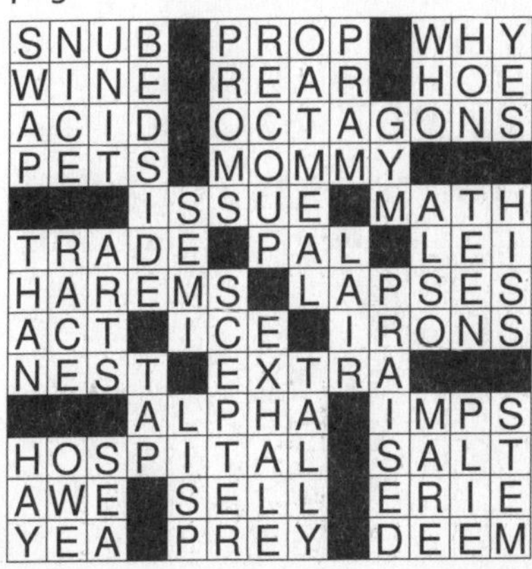

page 82 • **Pacify**

F	R	E	T		S	L	I	P		T	R	O	D
L	A	M	E		M	E	N	U		Y	O	G	I
A	R	M	S		E	A	S	T		C	A	L	M
B	E	A	T		A	N	T		C	O	R	E	S
			E	R	R		A	F	R	O			
S	T	A	R	E		F	L	O	U	N	D	E	R
T	O	N		F	R	I	L	L	S		A	Y	E
I	R	E		E	U	R	E	K	A		Z	E	D
R	E	W	O	R	D	E	D		D	E	E	D	S
			D	E	E	P		S	E	T			
S	L	I	D	E		R	B	I		C	H	I	P
L	O	N	E		D	O	E	S		H	A	R	E
A	R	K	S		W	O	E	S		E	L	M	S
B	E	S	T		I	F	F	Y		S	E	A	T

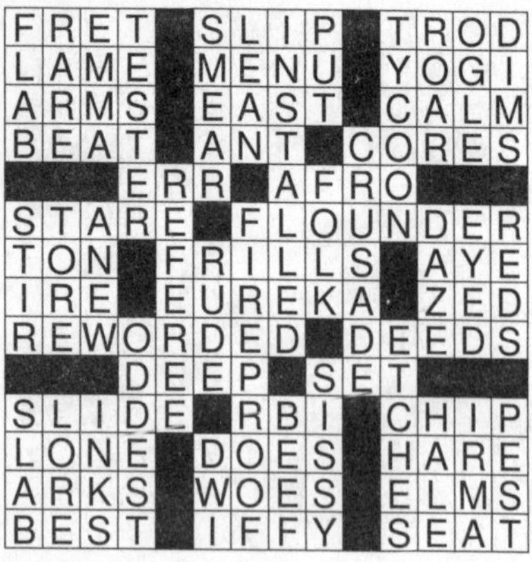

page 83 • **Get over here!**

S	H	O	W		O	P	T	S		O	F	F	S
T	Y	P	E		P	A	R	E		A	L	I	T
A	P	E	S		S	P	I	N		R	O	B	E
R	E	N	T	S		A	C	T	S		R	E	P
				U	G	L	Y		T	S	A	R	S
B	A	H	A	M	A		C	H	O	W			
I	R	I	S		T	E	L	E	P	A	T	H	S
D	E	T	H	R	O	N	E	D		M	O	A	T
			E	A	R	L		G	R	I	T	T	Y
T	E	E	N	S		I	D	E	A				
A	L	E		H	A	V	E		Y	O	K	E	L
P	U	R	R		T	E	N	D		O	N	C	E
E	D	I	E		O	N	T	O		H	O	R	N
S	E	E	D		P	S	S	T		S	T	U	D

page 84 • **For beginners**

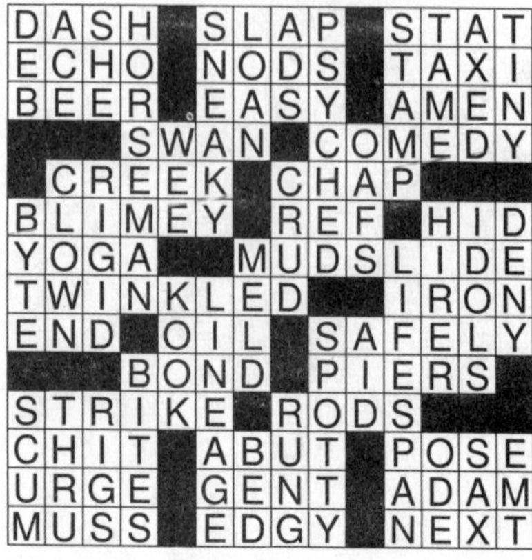

D	A	S	H		S	L	A	P		S	T	A	T
E	C	H	O		N	O	D	S		T	A	X	I
B	E	E	R		E	A	S	Y		A	M	E	N
			S	W	A	N		C	O	M	E	D	Y
	C	R	E	E	K		C	H	A	P			
B	L	I	M	E	Y		R	E	F		H	I	D
Y	O	G	A			M	U	D	S	L	I	D	E
T	W	I	N	K	L	E	D			I	R	O	N
E	N	D		O	I	L		S	A	F	E	L	Y
			B	O	N	D		P	I	E	R	S	
S	T	R	I	K	E		R	O	D	S			
C	H	I	T		A	B	U	T		P	O	S	E
U	R	G	E		G	E	N	T		A	D	A	M
M	U	S	S		E	D	G	Y		N	E	X	T

page 85 • **Start**

R	E	P	O		P	O	S	T		C	O	A	T
O	X	E	N		A	V	O	W		R	U	L	E
T	E	E	S		D	E	L	I		E	R	I	N
S	C	R	E	W		R	O	S	E	S			
			T	E	A	L		T	O	T	E	D	
A	B	S		E	G	O	S		N	E	A	R	S
N	U	T		P	E	O	N	S		D	R	O	P
T	S	A	R		S	K	I	P	S		N	O	R
S	T	R	A	P		S	C	A	N		S	P	Y
	S	K	I	E	R		K	N	O	B			
			M	A	U	D	E		B	R	A	S	H
A	R	T	E		M	E	R	E		I	N	T	O
R	U	I	N		B	E	E	T		S	N	A	P
T	E	N	T		A	D	D	S		K	E	G	S

page 86 • **Passion**

N	A	P	A		L	A	C	K		A	L	P	S
E	X	E	S		U	P	O	N		R	A	I	L
W	I	S	P		G	E	N	E		E	G	G	Y
T	O	T	A	L	S		D	A	D	A			
S	M	O	R	E		B	O	D	E		T	O	W
			T	O	G	A			A	T	O	N	E
N	I	N	A		I	B	U	P	R	O	F	E	N
O	D	O	M	E	T	E	R	S		L	U	S	T
P	O	R	E	D			N	A	P	E			
E	L	M		G	A	B	S		O	R	G	A	N
			V	E	I	L		S	P	A	R	S	E
W	I	F	E		D	U	E	L		B	A	K	E
O	V	E	N		E	R	G	O		L	I	E	D
N	Y	E	T		S	T	O	W		E	N	D	S

page 87 • **Adore**

R	A	M	P	S		A	S	K		P	R	O	F
E	X	A	L	T		W	O	E		L	A	K	E
A	L	G	A	E		E	B	B		O	G	R	E
D	E	N	I	A	L	S		A	P	P	E	A	L
			I	D	L	E		N	B	A			
A	F	T			A	T	E		S	H	A	K	Y
S	O	U	T	H	P	A	W		S	A	U	N	A
A	U	D	I	O		S	E	M	E	S	T	E	R
P	R	E	E	N		T	R	Y			O	E	D
			O	R	E		T	R	A	P			
B	E	F	O	R	E		C	H	E	R	I	S	H
L	U	L	U		A	H	A		F	O	L	I	O
E	R	A	S		P	U	P		E	M	O	T	E
W	O	N	T		S	H	E		R	A	T	E	S

page 88 • **Happiness**

G	A	M		E	T	N	A		A	R	D	O	R
U	S	A		C	R	E	W		C	H	I	V	E
N	P	R		L	I	A	R		T	I	R	E	S
		G	A	I	E	T	Y		I	N	E	R	T
T	R	A	M	P	S			Z	O	O			
H	A	R	E	S		S	K	I	N		P	I	T
I	T	I	N	E	R	A	N	T		M	U	S	H
R	I	N	D		A	V	O	I	D	A	B	L	E
D	O	E		K	N	E	W		R	U	L	E	R
			V	E	G			D	E	V	I	S	E
P	U	R	E	E		P	A	R	S	E	C		
U	S	U	R	P		E	R	O	S		I	T	S
P	E	N	N	E		A	C	N	E		S	E	E
A	S	T	E	R		S	H	E	D		T	A	X

page 89 • **Festive**

H	A	P	P	Y		L	A	V	A		P	R	O
A	W	A	R	E		A	X	I	S		H	O	W
R	A	V	E	N		M	E	S	S		I	L	L
D	Y	E	S		O	B	S	T	A	C	L	E	S
			S	A	T			A	I	L			
A	H	S		I	T	C	H		L	O	T	T	O
S	O	M	B	R	E	R	O	S		S	E	E	N
H	A	U	L		R	A	S	P	B	E	R	R	Y
E	X	T	O	L		G	E	A	R		M	I	X
			W	I	G			C	A	P			
D	O	W	N	G	R	A	D	E		E	B	B	S
O	N	O		H	O	U	R		P	A	U	L	A
E	L	K		T	A	T	E		A	C	R	E	S
R	Y	E		S	N	O	W		R	E	N	D	S

page 90 • **Have fun**

F	A	S	T		C	L	A	M		A	M	P	S
A	M	M	O		A	L	L	Y		R	O	O	T
D	I	O	N		R	A	I	N		C	O	L	A
E	D	G	E	D		M	E	A	T		S	K	I
				O	M	A	N		O	C	E	A	N
L	O	U	N	G	E		A	H	O	Y			
E	L	S	E		R	A	T	E		C	R	A	B
D	E	E	R		I	T	E	M		L	A	M	A
			D	U	T	Y		A	P	E	M	A	N
S	L	A	S	H		P	A	N	E				
M	A	D		F	A	I	R		P	E	T	T	Y
A	I	D	E		A	C	E	S		A	U	R	A
S	T	E	W		R	A	N	K		S	N	I	P
H	Y	D	E		P	L	A	Y		T	A	P	S

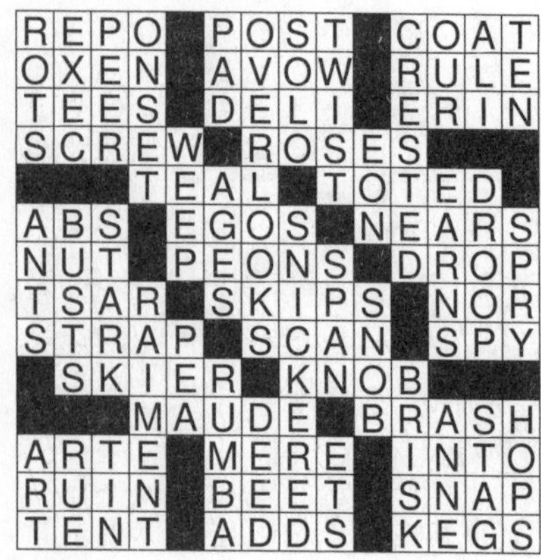

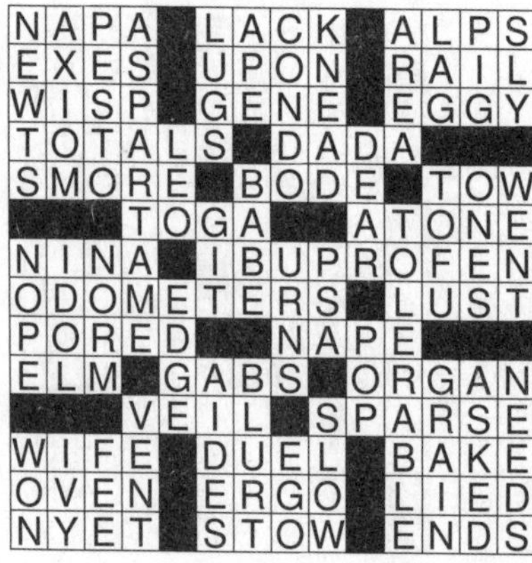

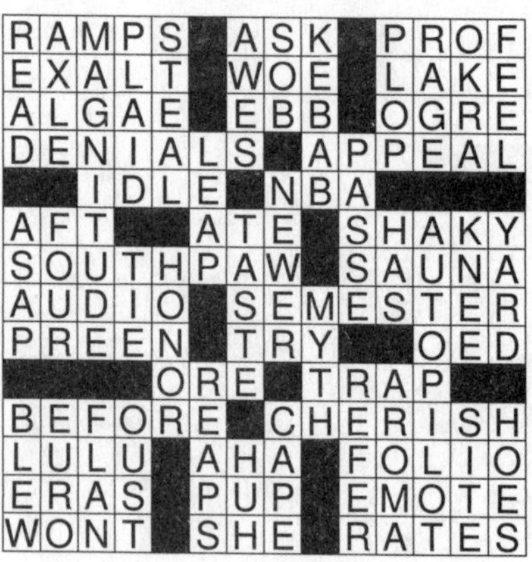

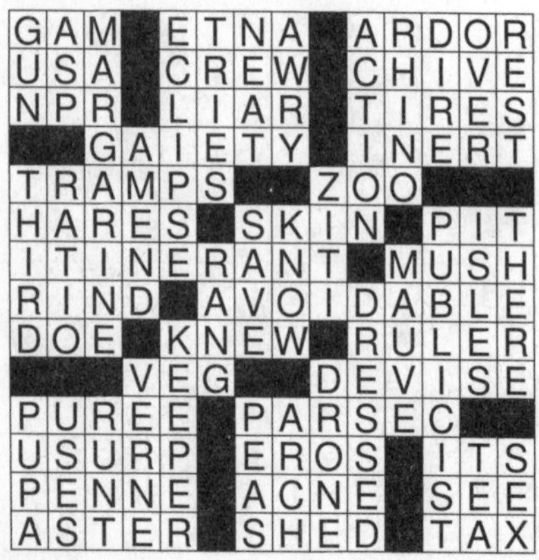

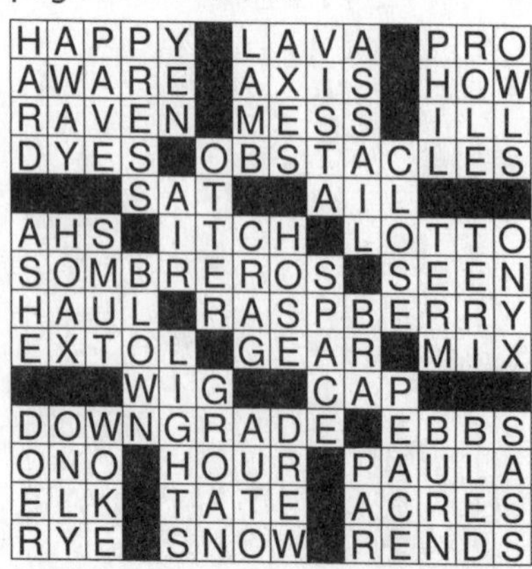

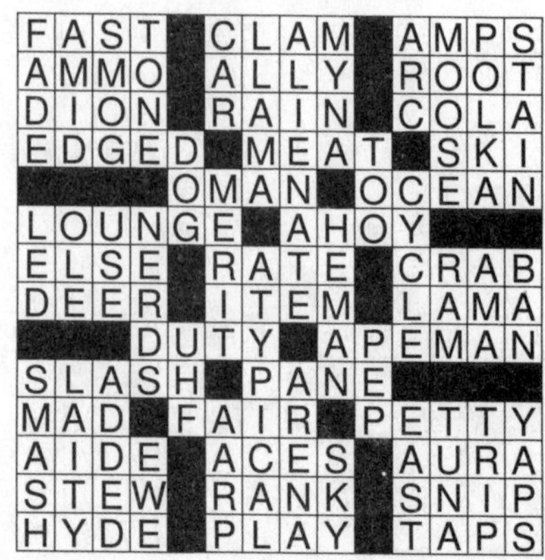

page 91 • Blown away

FEST■SURGE■CASH
LACE■PLANE■ALTO
ACHE■ANNUL■FIAT
THE■BRAG■■GEESE
■■MEEK■EDDY■NHL
SHADE■■■OOPS■■■
OUTING■POT■CHAT
FLIT■AVERT■HUGE
TACO■FEW■YEOMEN
■■■RIFT■■■VOIDS
SAD■MEOW■WILL■■
PLUMP■■HAIL■ICY
LOSE■SPAWN■GALA
ANTE■AILED■ATOM
TEST■WEEDY■LETS

page 92 • Fitting

DART■■GAG■■ASPS
AGER■DRIES■LOOP
MINI■YODEL■TAKE
ELEMENTS■ELOPED
SEW■VAT■DAYS■■■
■■■MEMORIZE■TAB
CASINO■ACE■CORE
ERECT■VIE■CUTIE
LINE■PIN■SHREDS
TAD■RECYCLED■■■
■■■VASE■LIE■CSI
STRIPE■COMPLAIN
TAUT■TEASE■ARCS
ELBA■ARMED■YOKE
PEEL■■APT■■SLOT

page 93 • Enthused

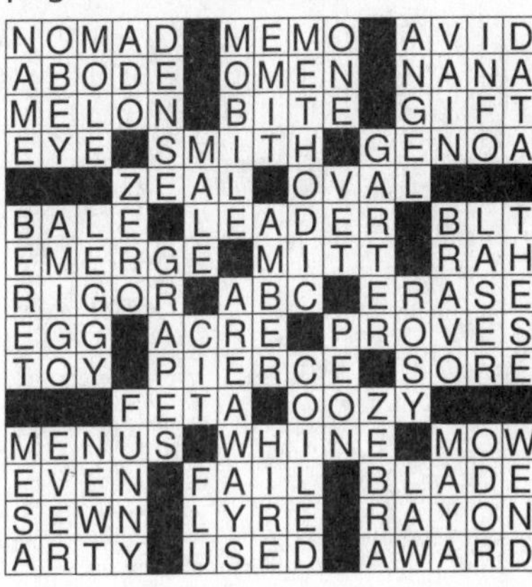

NOMAD■MEMO■AVID
ABODE■OMEN■NANA
MELON■BITE■GIFT
EYE■SMITH■GENOA
■■■ZEAL■OVAL■■■
BALE■LEADER■BLT
EMERGE■MITT■RAH
RIGOR■ABC■ERASE
EGG■ACRE■PROVES
TOY■PIERCE■SORE
■■■FETA■OOZY■■■
MENUS■WHINE■MOW
EVEN■FAIL■BLADE
SEWN■LYRE■RAYON
ARTY■USED■AWARD

page 94 • Oh my!

NAMES■BIAS■STUB
ALAMO■INCH■KITE
POKED■CLAY■EATS
SEER■HEED■■TREE
■■■ADOPTED■CART
FOLLIES■MASH■■■
ABIDED■FIRM■SIN
ROOST■SEA■OBESE
MEN■EGAD■ORACLE
■■■PROP■ALERTED
CZAR■OPPRESS■■■
HOME■■HERS■THUG
OWES■NICE■BOUND
MINT■BRAS■AORTA
PESO■CENT■ALLOY

page 95 • Prized

SHRED■EGGS■STEM
WAIVE■CARP■THOU
ELVES■OPAL■RENT
AVA■KIN■TINIEST
TELL■COVETED■■■
■■■AROMAS■TENSE
PLATONIC■■■■OWE
AIRED■CAN■USUAL
GET■■■■TORRENTS
ESSAY■RETINA■■■
■■■DECODED■RAPT
ACCUSAL■PEN■MAR
LOLL■PLEA■OLIVE
SLAT■REED■VOTES
ODDS■IRKS■ABYSS

page 96 • Moving

CAIN■FREE■PASHA
AFRO■LAWN■ASTIR
ROAD■ODES■CLUNK
TOT■AWASH■TENDS
STEAMER■ROSE■■■
■■■CUR■TON■PSST
ABETS■SAUCE■LOO
RED■EMENDED■ALL
LEI■DINGS■DOMED
OPTS■STY■DID■■■
■■■HATE■NEEDLED
BASIN■NYETS■ARE
ALONG■COVE■ATOP
SIDES■EYES■REDO
START■SORT■FRET

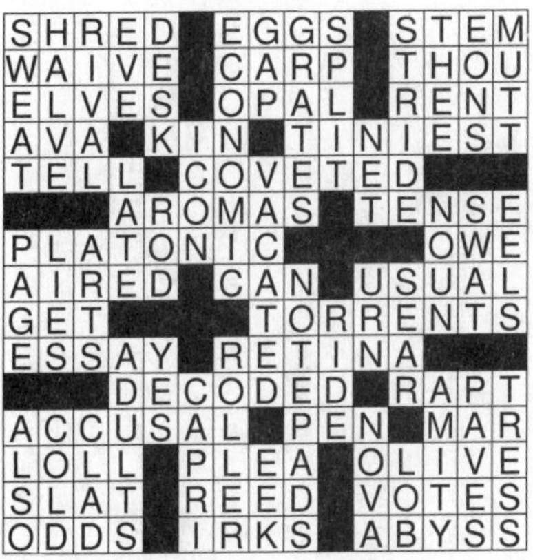

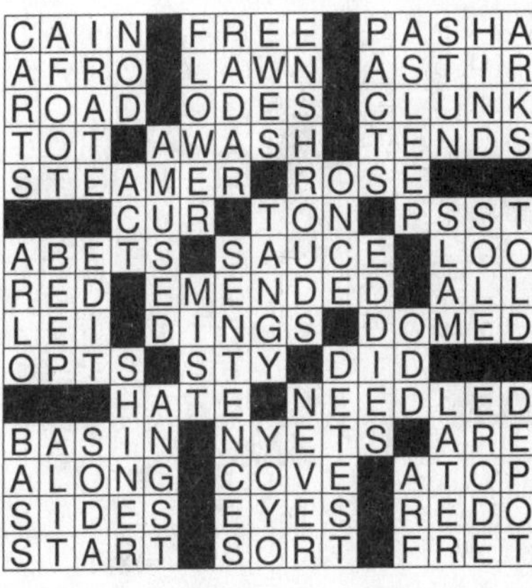

page 97 • Pleased as punch

IGOR■EASY■■OGLE
RODE■GLOAT■ORAL
EVES■OINKS■HERD
■■■IRMA■SAG■AGE
■DISEASE■ROSTER
MITTEN■LASSO■■■
ICE■FIRES■HURLS
SEMI■AIMED■POOH
ORSON■SEARS■BOO
■■■WIDEN■IODINE
BANANA■TIFFANY■
AGO■ERR■STAY■■■
LABS■TABLE■GLAD
SILO■STEER■LILI
ANEW■■SETS■OPEN

page 98 • Some of this and that

JUT■■CRIED■SNAP
ANY■DOODAD■CARE
RIP■EMBERS■RIMS
STEAMBOAT■PIVOT
■■■HOOT■HELPERS
AARON■SUMMIT■■■
BRAY■■■PATE■SUE
LAPSE■TEN■DECRY
ELS■MAIN■■■MAGE
■■■WEIRDO■ACTED
ADDENDA■RARE■■■
BREAD■MINUTEMAN
HALL■LINERS■AMI
OMIT■ASTRAY■MIT
RASH■BUOYS■■ADS

page 99 • I didn't mean it!

NACHO■PEAR■WRAP
ERROR■AXLE■HERE
AGAPE■LIMP■APES
RUM■■FALSE■MOST
SEPARATE■AIM■■■
■■■RUDE■STROLLS
SWEEPS■TASK■OIL
KARAT■ZAP■SPOKE
IDA■USER■WORKED
DESIRED■TIME■■■
■■■REV■MILEPOST
DEMO■EBONY■■WOO
OXEN■NAGS■GONNA
TINE■TRUE■AHEAD
STUD■YELL■SORRY

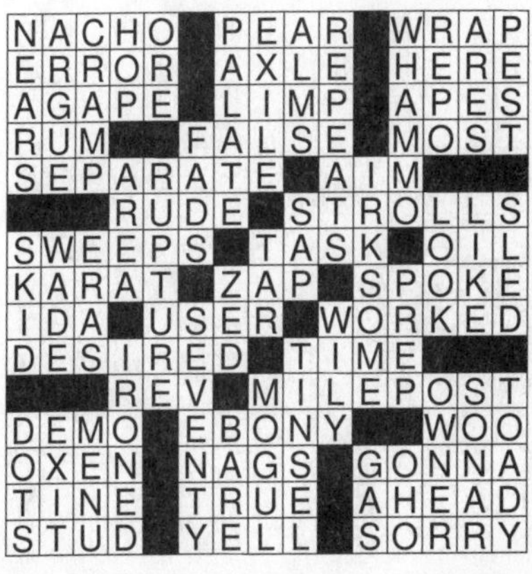

page 102 • **It gets filled out**

FORM HASH LAPS
OKAY FESTER ABET
URNS REHIRE DARE
LATERAL ROB TIE
LEG UPHELD
MUFFIN AISLE
PUP LEARN EASE
ESP MERLIN APPLE
TEENY VISITS RAG
DRAT EVENS ITO
PHASE GARAGE
ODDEST RID
FIR LUG JIMMIES
TOES APEMEN IDLE
EDGE SONATA TOME
NEST NEWS SLOP

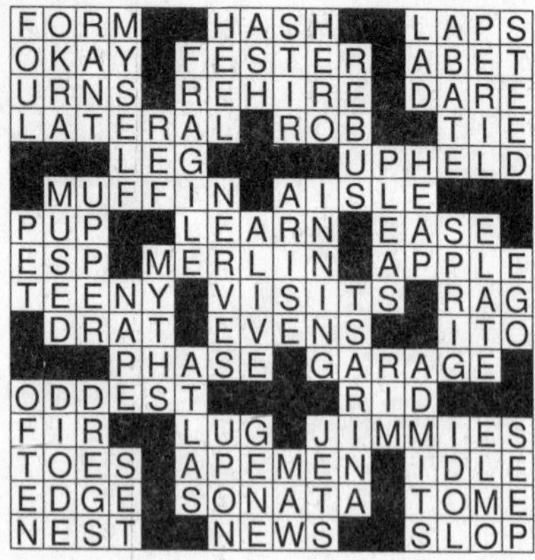

page 103 • **Hear ye, hear ye**

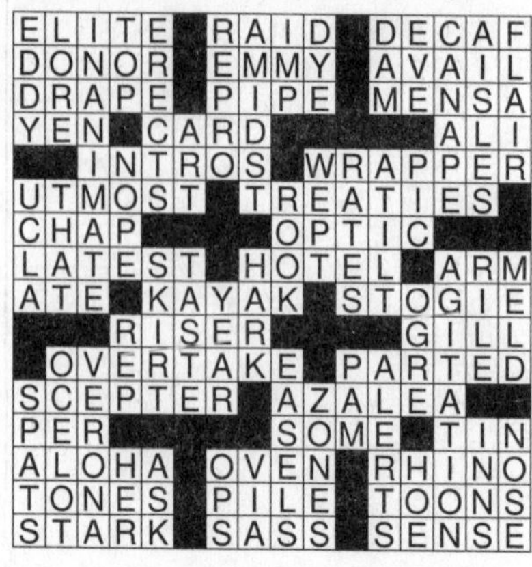

ELITE RAID DECAF
DONOR EMMY AVAIL
DRAPE PIPE MENSA
YEN CARD ALI
INTROS WRAPPER
UTMOST TREATIES
CHAP OPTIC
LATEST HOTEL ARM
ATE KAYAK STOGIE
RISER GILL
OVERTAKE PARTED
SCEPTER AZALEA
PER SOME TIN
ALOHA OVEN RHINO
TONES PILE TOONS
STARK SASS SENSE

page 104 • **Gets cozy**

JOBS TOGA AWOL
EURO SHIELD LIVE
SNOB CELLAR USES
SCISSORS SIMMERS
EEL ELM BUN
ADAM OBLIGED
STORM LITTLE EAR
PAPAYA DOTE YOGI
AHEM LIST DOODLE
WON BITTER TWEED
NESTLES MESH
HON VIE AMA
ACROBAT DEGRADED
COIN TAVERN CODE
HANG EMCEES TRIP
ELKS ERRS SEAT

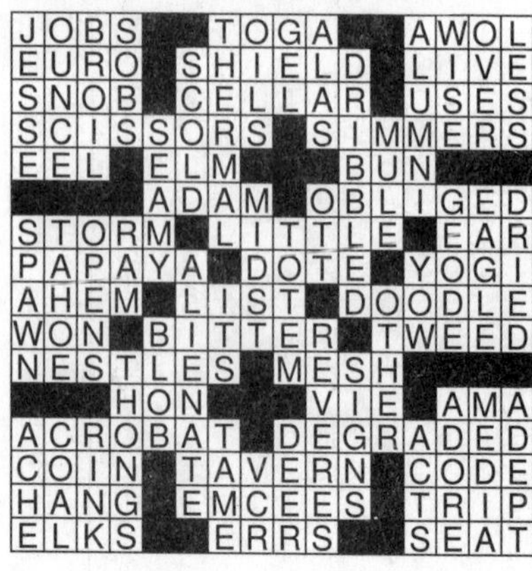

page 105 • **Yes, that's what I said**

IVY STAB ADDED
LIE ANSWER SERVE
LET REALLY PLAIN
SWIMMER LEO UGLY
OAR FIX
BORDER INFLECT
CRUSADE REEK HAT
RATE CHOIR CASH
OVAL BOING ASTI
PEG RAIN HASBEEN
REBUILT SITARS
YET RAN
CLOG SHE SCRATCH
HUMOR EXPIRE AHA
ARENA NEARED BAR
RENEW CREW SIP

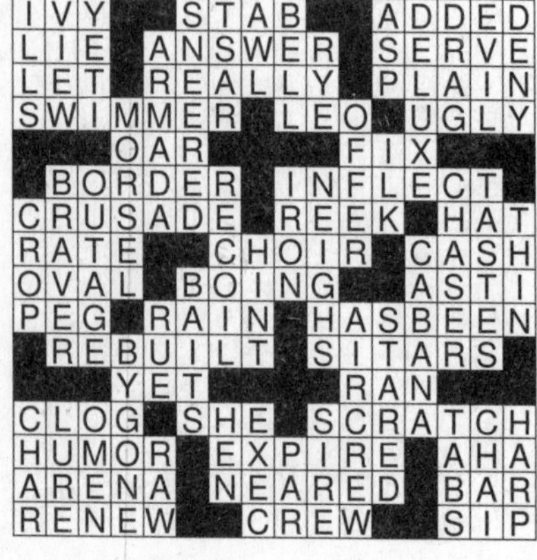

page 106 • **Put away for a rainy day**

JAMB EBBS INFO
OBOE PARIAH GOAL
NONE ORANGE NOTE
AVENGING ERMINES
HEY USE EAT
MESA ASSERTS
CLIMB TIDBIT OAT
RODEOS RUSE POLO
EVEN AWED SORTER
PEA SNORED POSSE
ESSENCE SITE
RAT SIR TIS
ILLOGIC APPARENT
MEAD FORCES UNTO
PAVE YEARLY TERM
SPAS DYES STOP

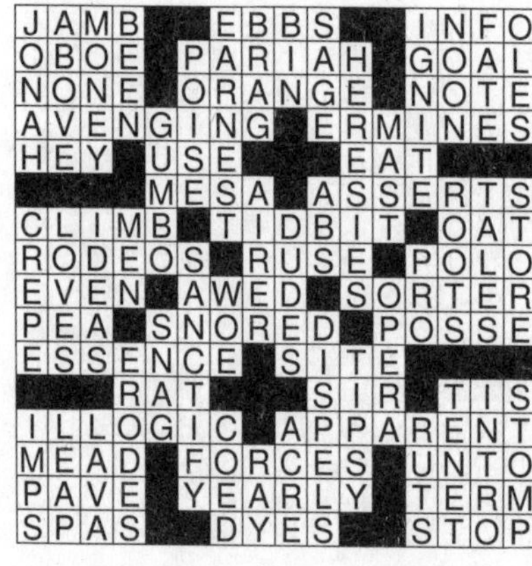

page 107 • **Reverence**

LOAN VATS AMPLE
ELSE PILOT TALLY
VISA ROOMY TRADE
EVER OLE LOUSY
RENE PAD INN TAB
STREET SEE HUE
WRETCH STINT
SAFE DOH ANTS
CLUE RAP EGGS
RITES RETURN
ADO AWE LODGER
GEM YES FLU AXIS
ALIBI LOT ZINC
SATIN SHOVE ELSA
ICING TIRES BEER
NECKS SPAR ODDS

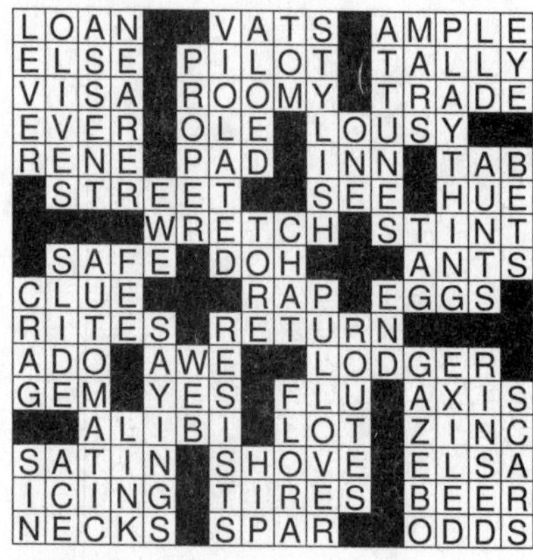

page 108 • **Off yonder**

NICE BLEW BRIAR
ASHY AROMA EERIE
PLIE RACED ASIDE
SENSATION USED
FED DECAL
PUMA ASSORTED
MONORAIL TOE ARF
AMMO BRIDAL SOL
SPA ROTATE DIVE
SOD BAN DERAILED
MELODIES KEYS
EXECS RBI
SLAT CLIENTELE
KILTS HAULS ICON
INSET UPSET PROD
STORY GETS SUPS

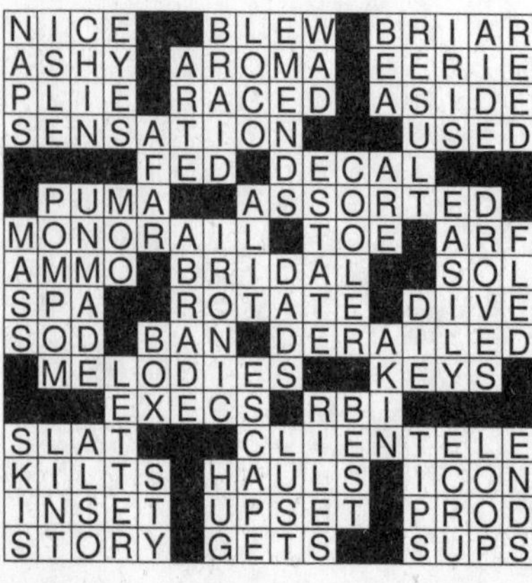

page 109 • **Uncanny ability**

RACES SWAP FAD
AFLOAT PANIC ODE
PRINCE ELDER MAN
TON KNACK INEPT
INSERTS STINTS
TACO TEA PAINTS
ARID SAT ONCE
CIA WOULD SOLO
TANG CARNY PIG
LILY AMP OPAL
SCONES BEE WORE
BEHALF PARTNER
IRATE ESSAY TAM
KEN TRASH LEGUME
ENG SUITE STENOS
DEE TROD SEEKS

page 110 • **Bestow knowledge**

ROLE AMPS ABLE
ORAL GLOATS ROOT
MINK ATONAL MOWS
POD AMOR YOGA
SLEDS PUMAS
EDUCATE BENEFIT
DEGRADE NINE
RAG NEATER STRUM
UNLIT GELATO ESP
STAN INITIAL
HERETIC SEERESS
SEDAN EDICT
IDLE BLED PRY
BLAB EDGIER WHIP
EARL TINDER HOBO
TYKE TUSK ONES

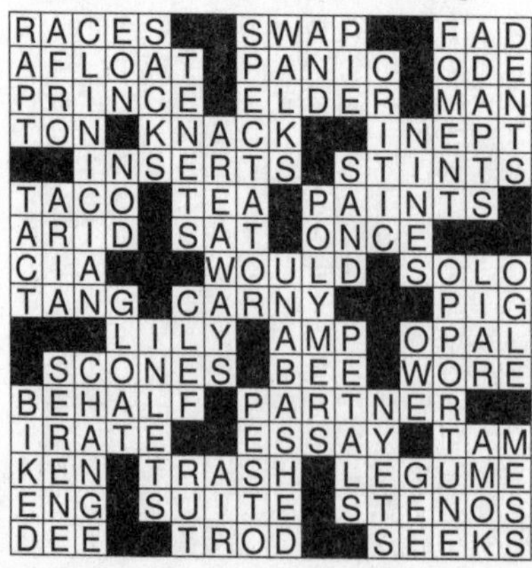

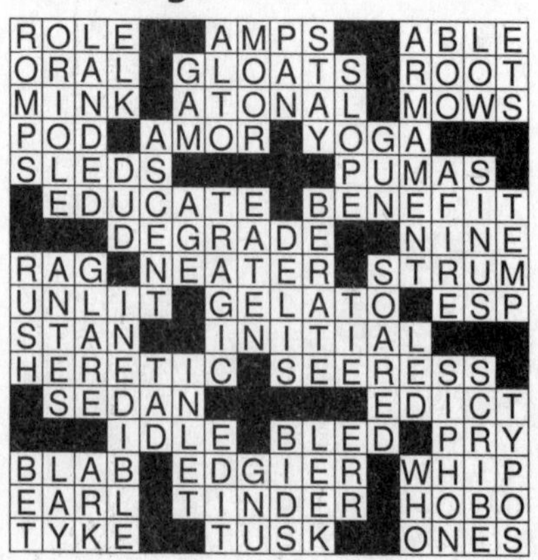

page 111 • **Exceptional**

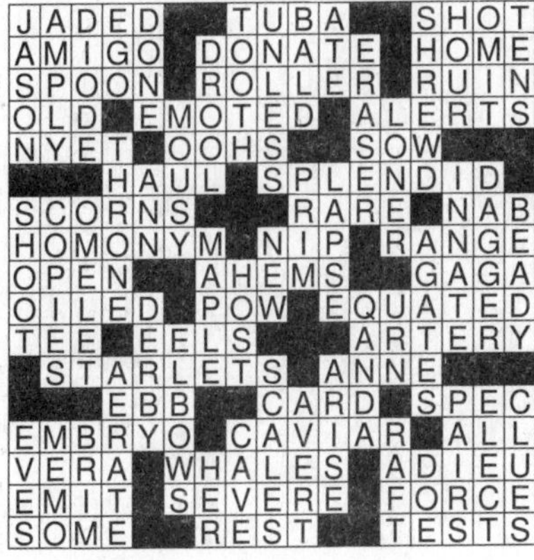

page 112 • **Cunning**

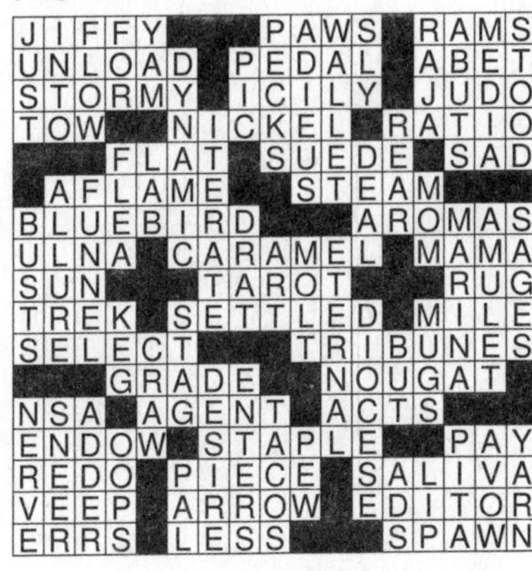

page 113 • **Stuck**

page 114 • **Pickle pusher**

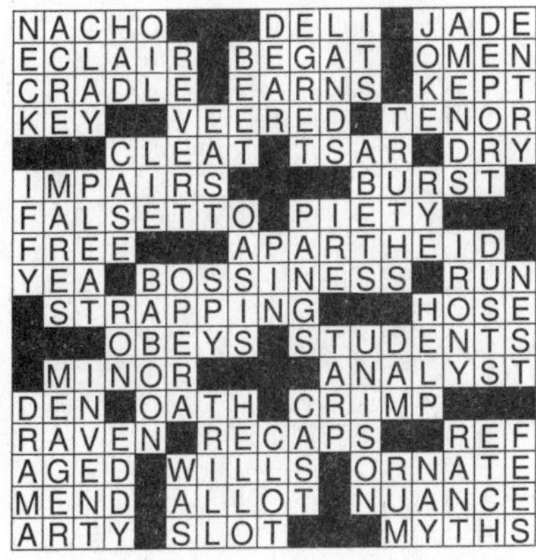

page 115 • **Crossword solver**

page 116 • **Be in charge**

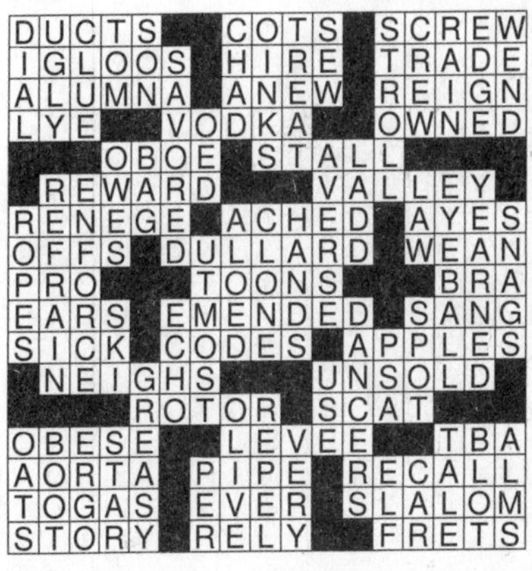

page 117 • **Prized one**

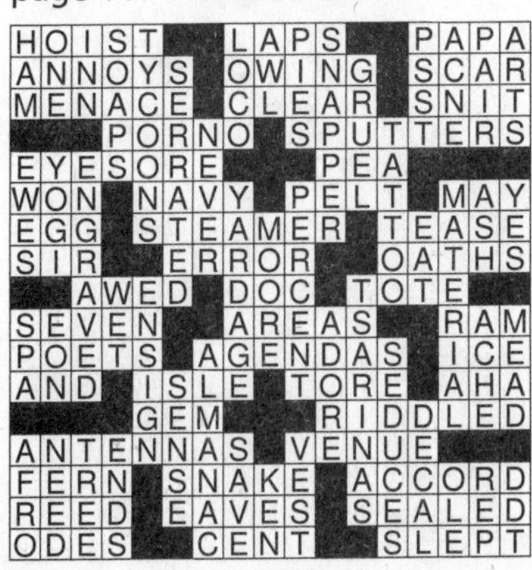

page 118 • **Assortment**

page 119 • **Adorable**

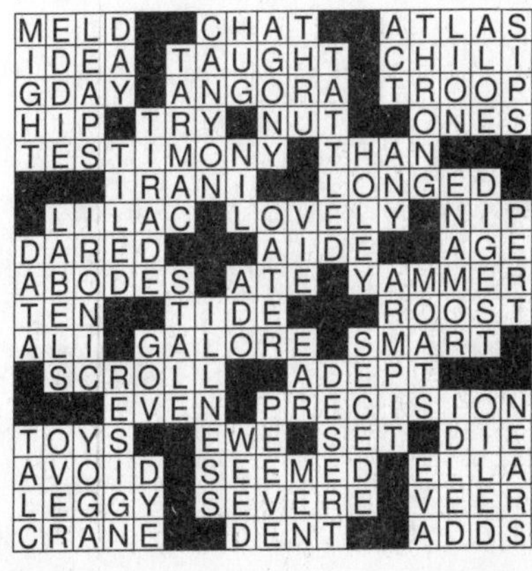

page 122 • **Did you forget something?**

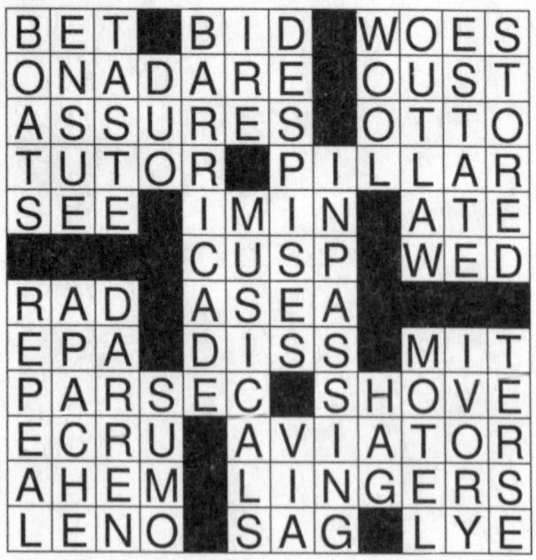

B	E	T		B	I	D		W	O	E	S
O	N	A	D	A	R	E		O	U	S	T
A	S	S	U	R	E	S		O	T	T	O
T	U	T	O	R		P	I	L	L	A	R
S	E	E		I	M	I	N		A	T	E
				C	U	S	P		W	E	D
R	A	D		A	S	E	A				
E	P	A		D	I	S	S		M	I	T
P	A	R	S	E	C		S	H	O	V	E
E	C	R	U		A	V	I	A	T	O	R
A	H	E	M		L	I	N	G	E	R	S
L	E	N	O		S	A	G		L	Y	E

page 123 • **Hassle**

S	O	L	E		E	B	B		A	B	C
P	I	E	R		T	R	I	M	M	E	R
A	L	S	O		E	A	G	E	R	L	Y
M	Y	S	T	E	R	Y		N	A	G	
			I	A	N				D	I	D
F	R	A	C	T	A	L		C	I	A	O
A	U	R	A		L	A	G	O	O	N	S
R	P	M				M	O	M			
	T	O	W		S	P	O	I	L	E	R
C	U	R	A	C	A	O		C	O	D	E
O	R	E	G	A	N	O		A	C	N	E
P	E	R		T	E	N		L	O	A	F

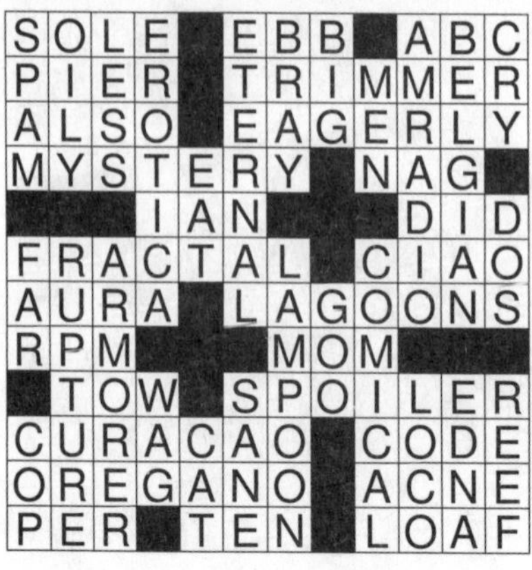

page 124 • **Savvy about**

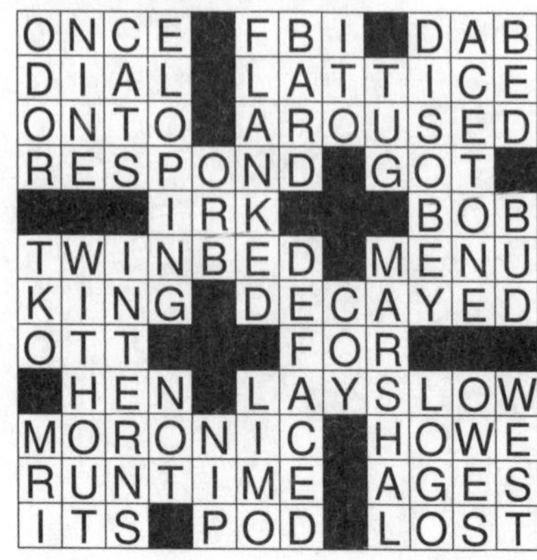

O	N	C	E		F	B	I		D	A	B
D	I	A	L		L	A	T	T	I	C	E
O	N	T	O		A	R	O	U	S	E	D
R	E	S	P	O	N	D		G	O	T	
			I	R	K				B	O	B
T	W	I	N	B	E	D		M	E	N	U
K	I	N	G		D	E	C	A	Y	E	D
O	T	T				F	O	R			
	H	E	N		L	A	Y	S	L	O	W
M	O	R	O	N	I	C		H	O	W	E
R	U	N	T	I	M	E		A	G	E	S
I	T	S		P	O	D		L	O	S	T

page 125 • **Go around**

L	E	A	F	Y		P	A	J	A	M	A
E	A	G	L	E		E	L	U	D	E	D
T	R	E	A	T		R	O	T	A	T	E
S	N	O	W		B	E	E		G	A	P
G	E	L		D	E	N		P	E	L	T
O	R	D	I	N	A	N	C	E			
			V	A	R	I	A	T	I	O	N
P	R	A	Y		D	A	N		R	U	E
L	A	D		I	L	L		S	I	T	E
U	N	D	O	N	E		P	O	S	E	D
S	T	E	E	R	S		I	D	E	A	L
H	O	R	D	E	S		P	A	S	T	E

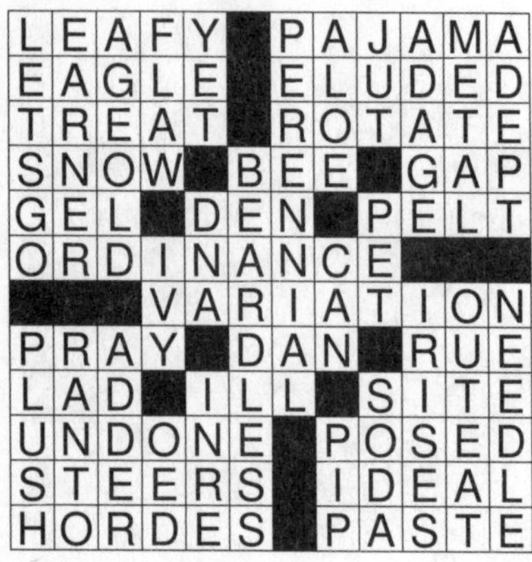

page 126 • **It's off the beaten path**

A	I	L		W	E	B	S		A	P	T
S	N	A	K	E	P	I	T		S	R	O
S	A	N	I	T	I	Z	E		C	O	T
E	R	I	N		C	A	W		O	N	E
S	U	N				R	E	S	T	E	D
S	T	A	G		M	R	D	O			
			E	Y	R	E		B	A	B	Y
S	O	R	T	O	F				B	Y	E
T	W	A		K	I	D		S	A	R	A
A	N	D		E	X	E	C	U	T	O	R
T	E	A		L	I	M	A	B	E	A	N
E	R	R		S	T	O	P		D	D	S

page 127 • **Swallow whole**

R	U	S	H		A	L	A		S	I	R
A	C	H	Y		S	U	P	R	E	M	E
G	L	U	G		S	M	E	A	R	E	D
E	A	T	I	T	U	P		M	I	A	
			E	A	R				A	N	Y
S	T	I	N	G	E	R		P	L	I	E
U	R	G	E		D	E	T	E	S	T	S
M	A	N				C	A	B			
	L	O	B		M	A	R	B	L	E	D
P	A	R	A	G	O	N		L	U	L	U
E	L	E	G	A	N	T		E	T	A	L
P	A	D		G	A	S		S	E	L	L

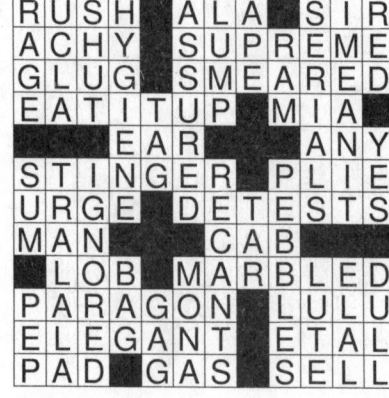

page 128 • **Essential**

T	O	N	E		N	A	P		W	H	U	P
A	V	I	D		O	W	E		A	O	N	E
R	E	N	E		R	A	N		N	U	D	E
T	R	A	N	S	M	I	T		D	R	O	P
				M	A	T	U	R	E			
D	R	E	V	I	L		P	E	R	I	S	H
R	E	G	A	L				V	E	N	U	E
J	O	G	G	E	R		G	I	R	D	E	R
			A	D	O	R	E	S				
G	L	I	B		N	O	T	E	P	A	D	S
M	I	S	O		A	B	S		O	B	I	E
E	V	E	N		L	E	I		P	U	R	E
N	E	E	D		D	D	T		S	T	E	M

page 129 • **Times up**

J	A	V	A		A	C	T		S	C	A	T
O	M	I	T		T	H	E		O	H	N	O
C	E	N	T		B	I	N		A	U	T	O
K	N	E	E		A	L	D	E	R	M	E	N
			N	A	T	I	O	N				
B	A	N	D	B	S		N	A	G	G	E	D
A	L	O	E	S				M	O	O	L	A
H	I	D	D	E	N		C	O	N	V	O	Y
				N	O	M	O	R	E			
P	U	N	C	T	U	A	L		I	C	A	N
U	H	O	H		G	N	U		N	A	M	E
M	U	S	E		A	I	M		T	R	O	T
P	H	E	W		T	A	N		O	A	R	S

page 130 • **Managed**

H	A	S	T	Y		M	R	S		C	O	N
A	R	T	I	E		O	I	L		H	A	Y
R	E	A	P	S		U	P	I		A	T	E
M	A	T		M	A	S	O	C	H	I	S	T
		U	S	A	G	E	F	E	E			
A	T	T	U	N	E		F	R	A	P	P	E
T	H	E	N						D	O	V	E
M	Y	S	T	I	C		C	H	O	I	C	E
			A	D	O	R	N	I	N	G		
I	T	I	N	E	R	A	N	T		N	B	A
S	O	W		A	N	N		S	T	A	L	L
P	R	O		L	E	D		O	W	N	U	P
Y	E	N		S	T	Y		N	O	T	E	S

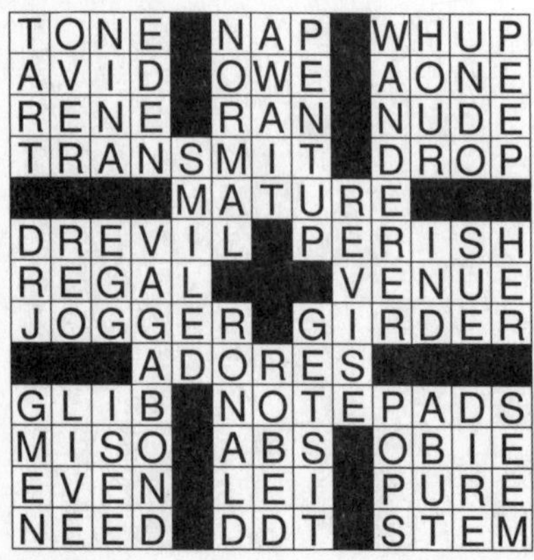

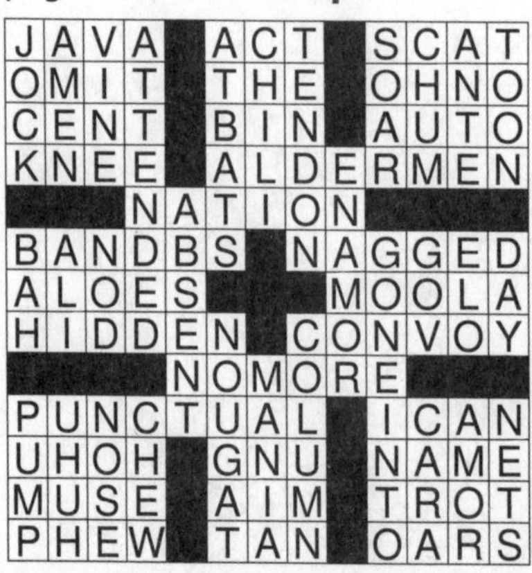

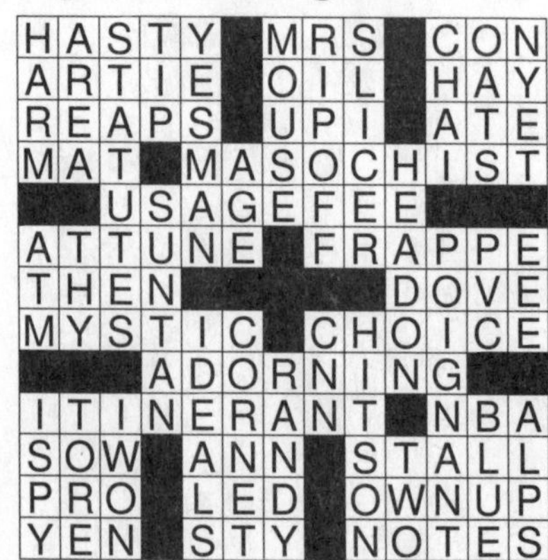

page 131 • **Blameless**

ELF MALL ACHE
DOA ARIA BLOC
INNOCENT LASH
EGGY NEEDEDTO
SPARSE
ABATES TARTAR
HARES READY
SACRED STRODE
TEETHE
ENGRAVER AMOS
GURU IREADYOU
AKIN LIED NHL
DENT SETS ASK

page 132 • **Premiere**

EYED STOW ICY
BEAU TRUE MAO
BASE ROSE PAR
SHELLOUT GUNK
ALTERED
WOEFUL RATEDG
APRON CANOE
STARCH SETTEE
SCHEMER
CLUE LIESBACK
OAR SITS AVON
ACE PUTT SOLO
LES AMSO SWAT

page 133 • **Comfortable**

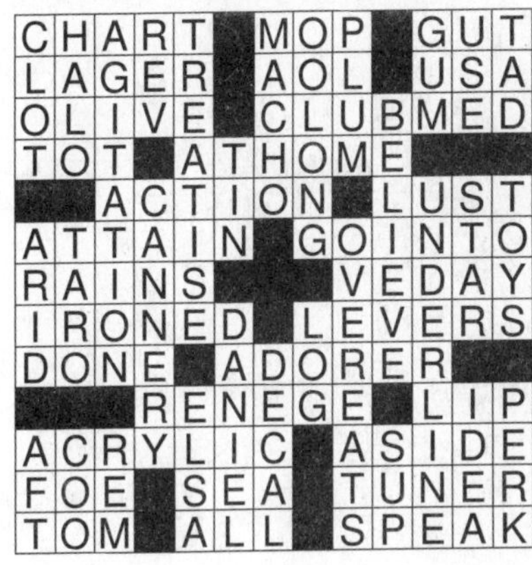

page 134 • **Get ready**

page 135 • **Look at me!**

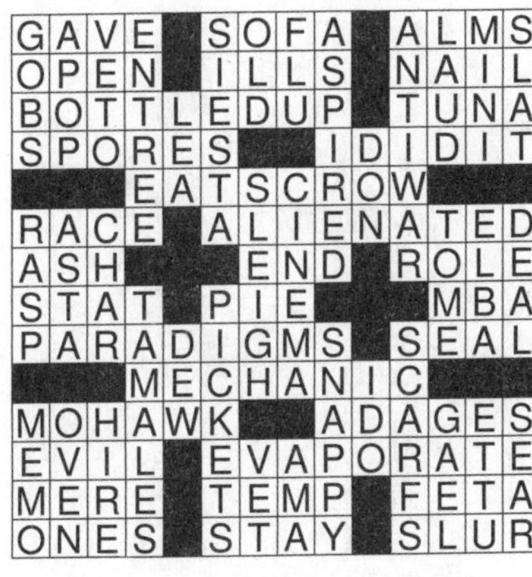

page 136 • **And so on**

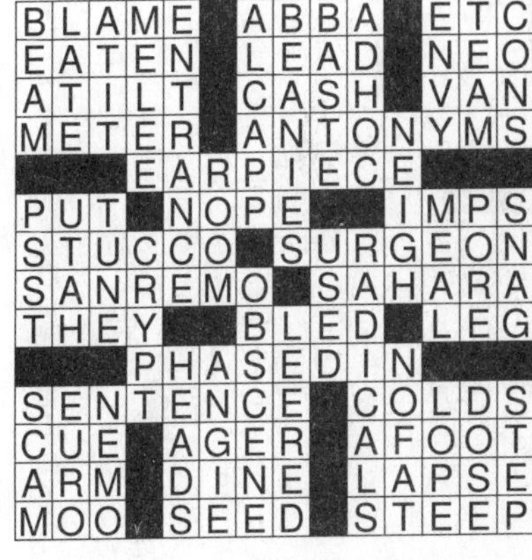

page 137 • **Superior**

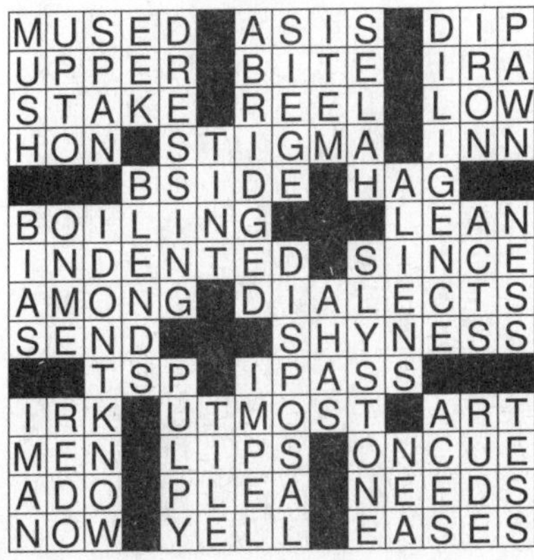

page 138 • **It doesn't hold water**

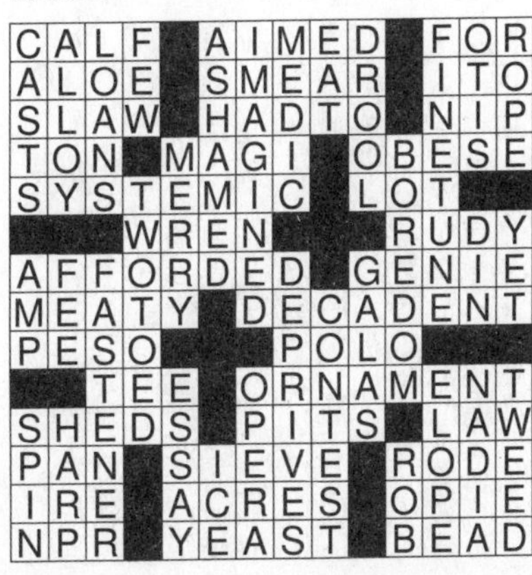

page 139 • **Stretch the truth**

page 142 • **It's hard to see through**

SKIP■HITTER■FDA
NANA■INHALE■OUR
ARTY■FRUGAL■RAM
PARODIED■LIVELY
STOLE■■■■■SIT■■
■■■ALTOS■WHEELS
ROD■VANISH■WEEP
AHA■ENTRIES■TIE
MIST■GOESAT■HAD
POTATO■NITRO■■■
■■APO■■■■■INLET
SCREAM■AIRPLANE
POD■SEDUCE■ODDS
AWL■TOURED■ALOT
SLY■SWEATS■NEWS

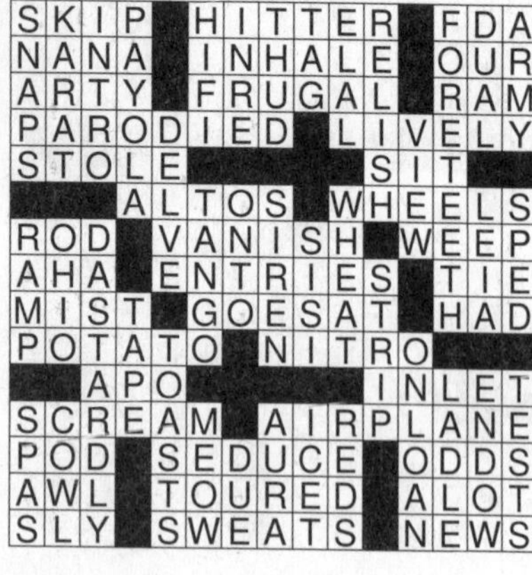

page 143 • **It's a long story**

NONOS■WOK■STEPS
IMOUT■OWE■TOTAL
CERTAINLY■ORATE
ENACTS■■SPOILED
■■■REBEL■EPA■■■
CLAY■NAIVE■MART
HAT■■■SAIL■ODOR
AREA■HEIRS■SAGA
IVAN■OUST■■■GUY
RATS■SPOUT■BEES
■■■WET■NEWER■■■
INCENSE■■INABIT
COURT■GRANDIOSE
OTTER■GAP■UNITE
NEEDY■SHE■PYLON

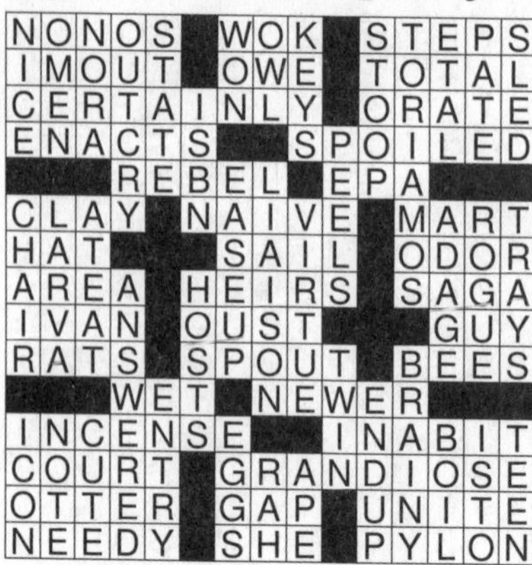

page 144 • **Obviously!**

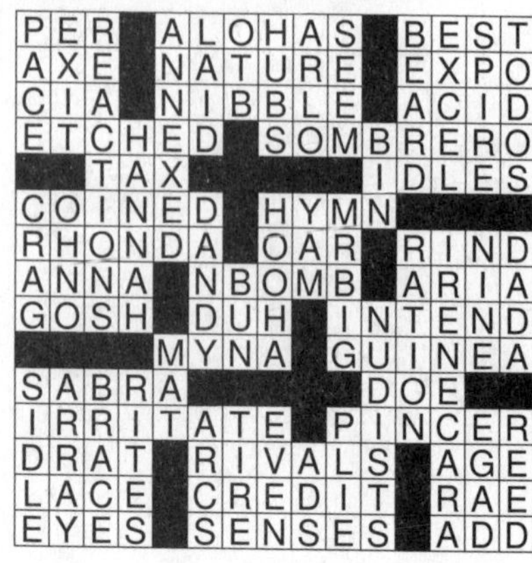

PER■ALOHAS■BEST
AXE■NATURE■EXPO
CIA■NIBBLE■ACID
ETCHED■SOMBRERO
■■TAX■■■■■IDLES
COINED■HYMN■■■■
RHONDA■OAR■RIND
ANNA■NBOMB■ARIA
GOSH■DUH■INTEND
■■■■MYNA■GUINEA
SABRA■■■■■DOE■■
IRRITATE■PINCER
DRAT■RIVALS■AGE
LACE■CREDIT■RAE
EYES■SENSES■ADD

page 145 • **By Jove!**

ISAY■SAWS■LACES
TOGA■TRIP■AWARE
SLAP■ACNE■TOPIC
MAP■STAGE■ELECT
ERECTED■DDS■■■■
■■■RILE■EATCROW
SATINY■TRY■LAVA
WHISK■HIS■VOTED
ISEE■IAN■SEVERE
GODSEND■MANE■■■
■■■■AKA■IVORIES
BURBS■CAROM■RAT
ALERT■LIAR■GAGA
SNAIL■URGE■ONLY
KARMA■EYED■VIES

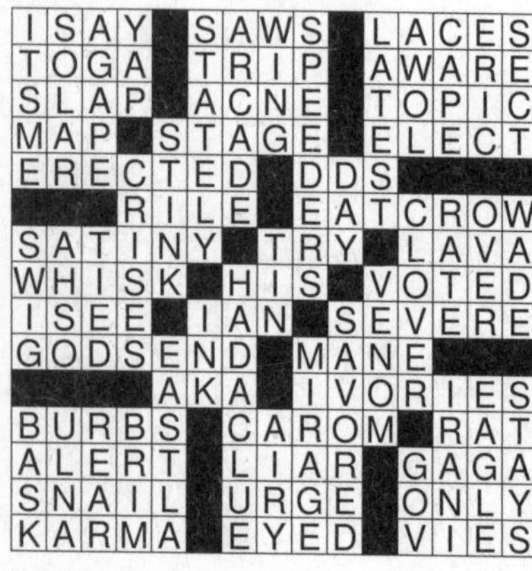

page 146 • **Not even close**

HOP■ACTUP■LASSO
APR■LOUSE■INLAW
STOPLIGHT■KNIFE
■■■RINSE■GEODES
SWOONS■RALLY■■■
TORSO■■■LAYETTE
ARDENT■FAR■DRUM
RTE■ERMINES■ARC
THRU■EAR■DESIRE
SYSTEMS■■■TUTEE
■■■TROTS■WAISTS
OHDEAR■TOAST■■■
WEARS■REALISTIC
LEVEE■ANTED■IDA
SLEDS■POSSE■SOW

page 147 • **Double-crosser**

ELUDE■CENT■MISS
RUNIN■HARE■ALOU
ACTED■IRAN■LOBE
SKI■GILL■OLIVER
EYECANDY■ROGERS
■■■AMOR■■■SNL■■
FASTENED■ASSURE
ORE■■INERT■■CUR
GETSIT■BETRAYER
■■TEN■■■FIAT■■■
DILATE■SERPENTS
OCELOT■PREP■OAT
TADA■HEIR■ECOLI
ERIN■ELLA■RANON
DENT■LOLL■SPENT

page 148 • **Here!**

NABBED■BABA■SHUT
ICEAGE■EXAM■PANS
CHANGE■SIRE■ANTE
KEN■■PRESENT■GIT
■■STREET■■DREADS
ASTOUND■HAMONRYE
STAID■OMELETS■■■
TILLER■IMAN■CAFE
IRKS■EASE■TWOFER
■■■OBSCENE■ENTER
ODOMETER■ABSCESS
CAREER■■GRATER■■
TWA■PISTOLS■■NIL
ONCE■CHAI■IMPOSE
PELT■TORN■CROONS
IDEA■STAG■STINTS

page 149 • **Yikes!**

IMPACT■ASWIM■JAY
TURTLE■PHONY■EGO
ELOPED■TORCH■EEK
MEDEA■■■REHEARSE
■■■ANYONE■ARM■■■
SPEC■ADO■IRONAGE
MATE■KDLANG■OVAL
UGH■■■NERVE■TIME
DENS■PESTO■■■ABC
GRIN■ASSIGN■ATIT
ESCORTS■SUE■NETS
■■■OOH■STEWED■■■
BELPAESE■■■MIDST
RYE■STIES■CORONA
ARF■TILTS■ATONAL
YET■SCOOT■RENEGE

page 150 • **Vision**

LOCK■RIFTS■STUBS
INRE■ADLAI■TYPEA
STAY■TEARS■IRONS
TOMB■EAT■ISLANDS
■■■OLD■■■■MEN■■■
STRAIGHT■BISTROS
THORN■ORBIT■SENT
ERODE■SEALER■HER
EEK■DETAIL■ABIDE
RAID■GETTO■SURGE
STEWARD■SWAPMEET
■■■IRE■■■■GYP■■■
GRANITE■OUR■ICKY
MELDS■LARGE■NANA
APPLE■AISLE■TRIM
NOSES■LLOYD■OPTS

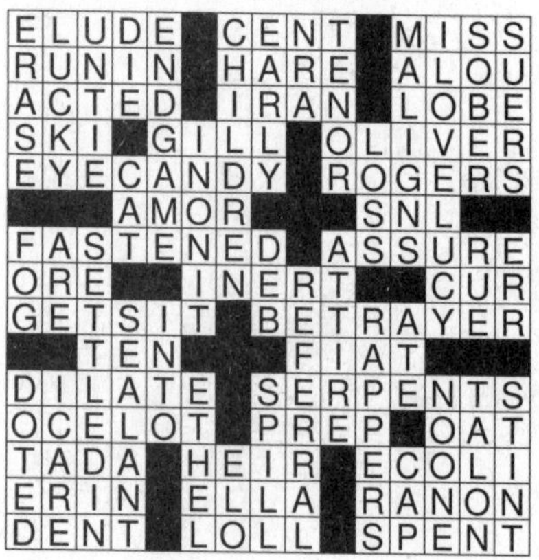

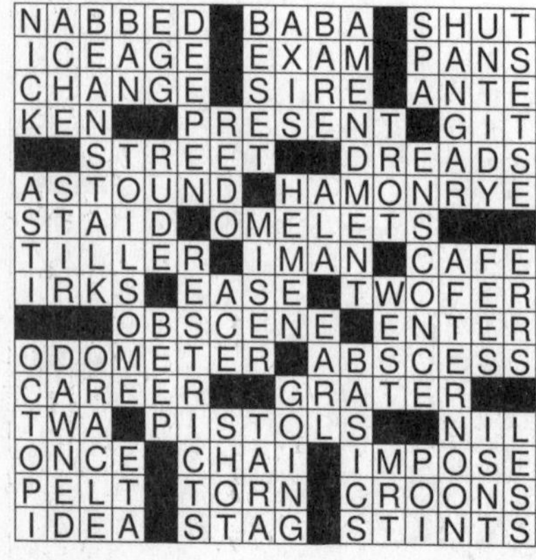

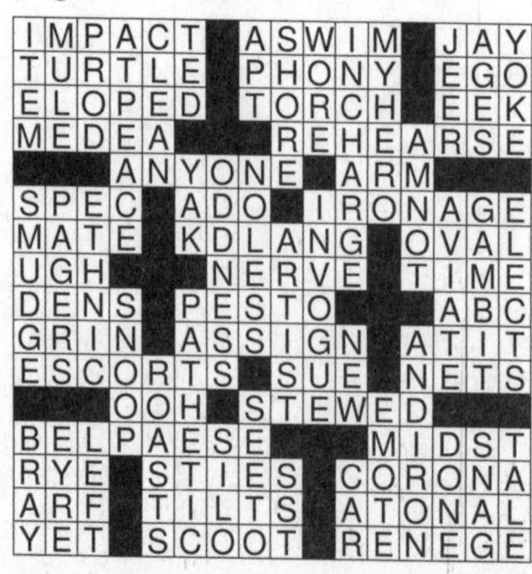

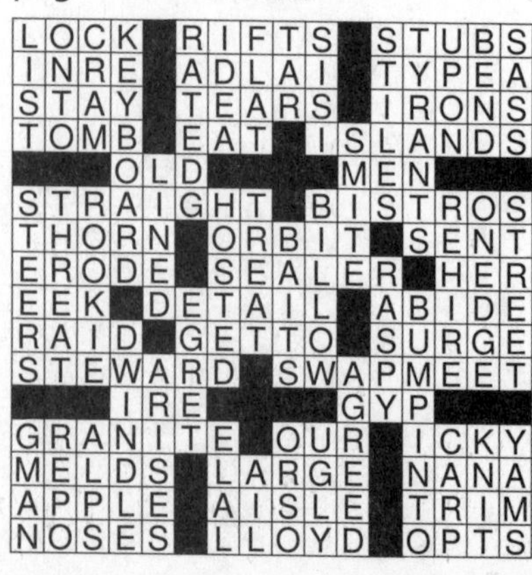

page 151 • **Discovery**

page 152 • **Something to keep**

page 153 • **I'm not kiddin' ya!**

page 154 • **Dish it out**

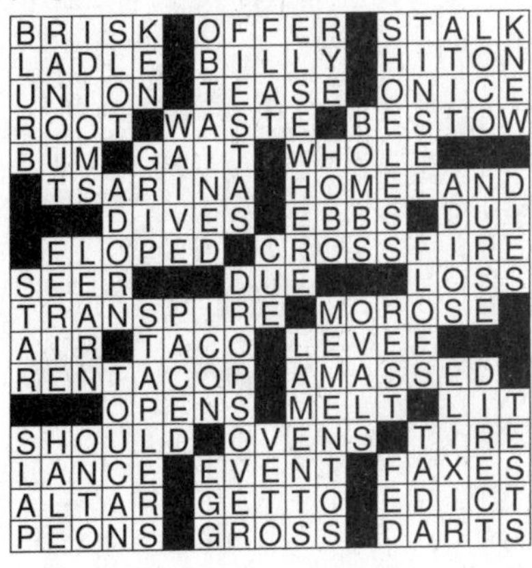

page 155 • **Let 'er rip!**

page 156 • **All clear**

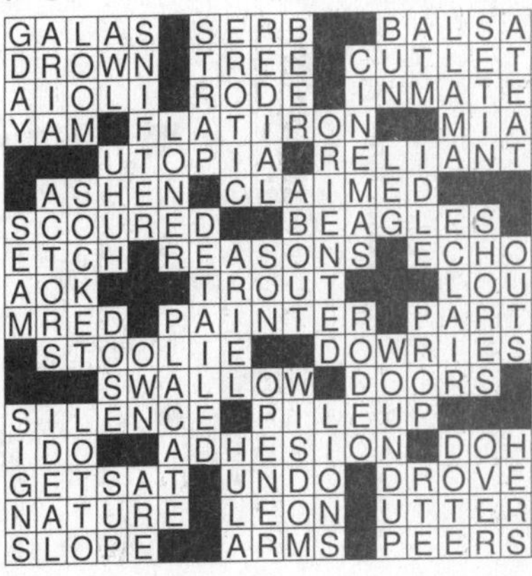

page 157 • **Proceed**

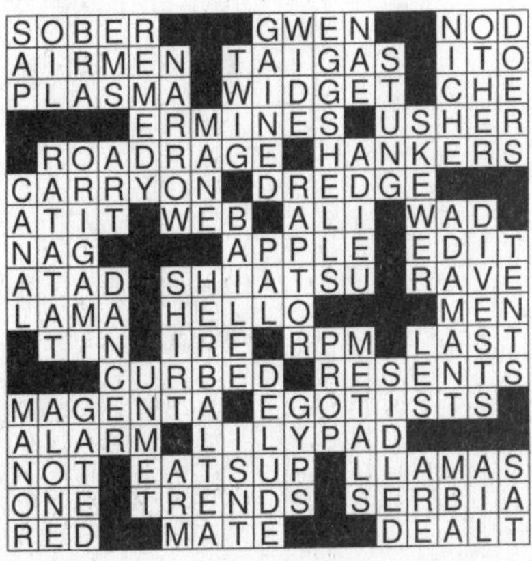

page 158 • **Hint**

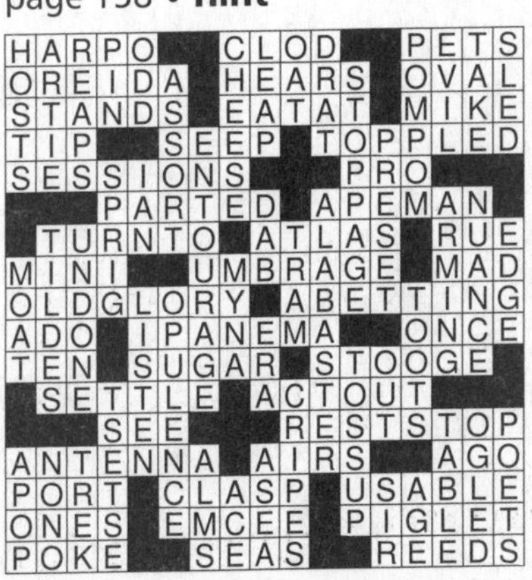

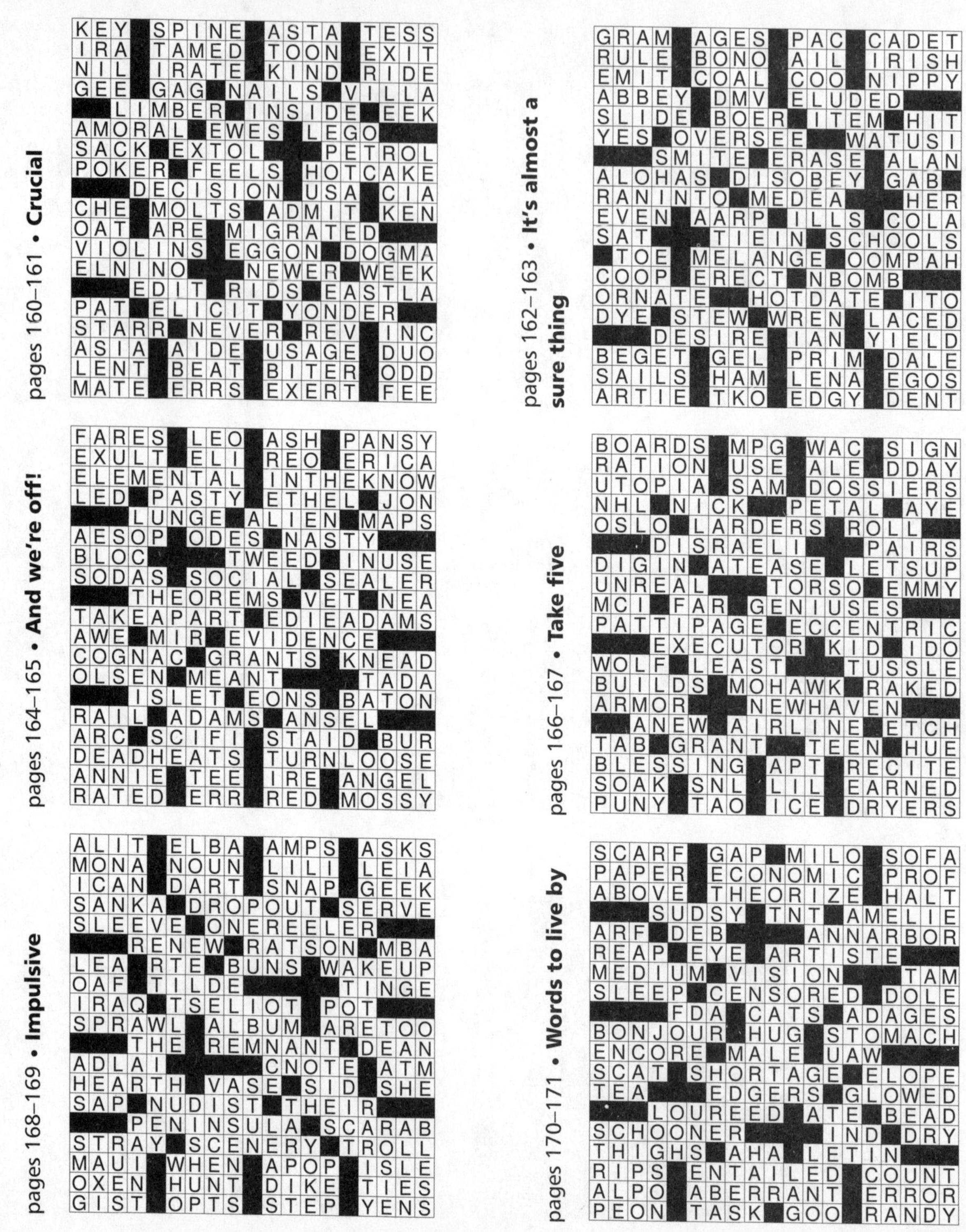

pages 160–161 • Crucial

pages 162–163 • It's almost a sure thing

pages 164–165 • And we're off!

pages 166–167 • Take five

pages 168–169 • Impulsive

pages 170–171 • Words to live by

pages 172–173 • Despicable

PRJOB YEN SPILL NIPS
LAURA ALA CANOE ACLU
UNDER HMS RIDGE VEIN
TUG BOOTH ONES VASES
OPERATOR ELSE SILK
ORB ELAL PATE APR
CONGA DEER POD TOO
LUAU SESAME CPR TEST
ASSERTS VAN ARMRESTS
PTA EATHERE SADAT
RATIO KRATION DDS
COMPLETE EGG SOTHERE
ADAM MUD DINNER IMAN
LOS SET ZEUS CROWD
MRT KNEE NEWT OLE
OMIT RAID HILARITY
DIDUP VAIN PONDS NRA
IDOL AISLE LUG SAFER
GENE FLEET USO IMEAN
SASS TEDDY GET CARTS

pages 176–177 • It's nothing, really

KNIFE BRA PUCKS AWRY
ISLES OAR APRIL THEE
TAKES ACT RHINO TINA
LARRY DOOM PHASER
RIBEYE GULLET MIKES
OVER PLEATED SOON
GOB GOOGLY SLAP EGGS
ERODE PAL IREADYOU
TYPING DEGRADING PAM
SURF OLES NEEDSTO
SPICIER NANA ARLO
TAN NAILSDOWN SEVERS
AGREESTO HOE SELAH
BEEN ETTU NOVELS IDA
TIDE TRALALA SOIL
FLOWN ROTATE BEATIT
LANINA ZERO UPSET
ODIN SMORE DNA RUMOR
ALOE PANEL WIT IRANI
TEND SEEDY ITS ENDED

pages 180–181 • Where you probably are now

STIGMA REF KIM SWEET
PUREES ERR ARE EARTH
ATOLLS VIE RAN ALINE
NUN EUGENE AQUA LEAN
DEMON ZITI ICY
ECRU ELUDED GLACIER
ROARS LEI AHOY MONGO
GOTAWAY ECLAIR EXTRA
OPENED OUTLAY RED
TALC COPE TEAPOTS
IMPERIL SLID ELLA
NOR BICPEN PENPAL
TOOTH MEADOW TSUNAMI
OSSIE BONO ELO TIRES
WEEPERS FEDORA NEXT
SLY HEFT STING
FLAT EDAM CHEERY SIN
EASED IRE HIS ELAPSE
ENTRY NPR ELI ROGUES
LEASE SOY DOT SNORES

pages 174–175 • Lay it on the line

NORAD YAK SCOTT MASS
AMANA ODE TABOO ORAL
PENTHOUSE ENEMY NOTI
ANGELA POESY OMAN
HUSHUP SOW RANK
HAS BUNION PAPA
AMIGO TRUCE UTILIZED
LETINTO SEAMS TOLEDO
ONEDGE PESSIMIST ANN
DONOR EXAM ALAS
GORY WISP IPASS
AVA IDENTICAL MAPOUT
NAGANO TYKES APLENTY
GLUTTONS ENTER ONTAP
TORE SERMON OHO
ABBA SOS MORAYS
CROC CAIRO HANGAR
HIGH BLOND IMBALANCE
EDIE EARNS DOE DIANA
DEED TWEET SON ALTER

pages 178–179 • Crazy one

EATAT FRAN ASHE HELP
ELITE LOSE LOON EVIL
KLEIN OAKS ARTE RENE
STRUM SASE RHONDA
SMASHER BILK EGO SAD
LOCUST LEEMARVIN
ACHE REED SNOOZE TSP
TKO CENT OKEYDOKE
ESOPHAGUS BIKE EDIT
SAT PEDAL DIPLOMA
MALAISE AVAST REV
ETAL LEND ARBORETUM
MARMOSET ISNT UPI
ODD SAVORS NOAH ABET
AMENITIES ASSENT
ABC KEN COST INNARDS
PARIAH BOWL ANDOR
PRAM EMIT AIRS RURAL
LEVI RENT NOTE ELUDE
EDEN ELSA DUST DEEDS

pages 182–183 • Perfect scores

EEE FITS AVAIL BRIAN
MRI OKRA PINTO RONCO
BIGBREAK TONES ITSME
ECHO VIA LOMEIN TEL
RATRACE GDAY ROGER
GNARLED DERIDE
RAF DESI TOT TIRADES
ATOP SEEM CHAIN SEEP
SERENA DISTURBED
PATTERN STANCE ISLAM
STEER ASCEND TARTARE
DONNAREED STAGES
THAT FALSE REPS TENS
BELIEFS TOE BEAM RAY
AMTRAK OSTRICH
RESET SANK ALIASES
ICU TYRANT IAN LIVE
NOISE ALOOF UNCLESAM
OLSEN CARLA RUBE SDI
NAMED KNELT AMSO YES

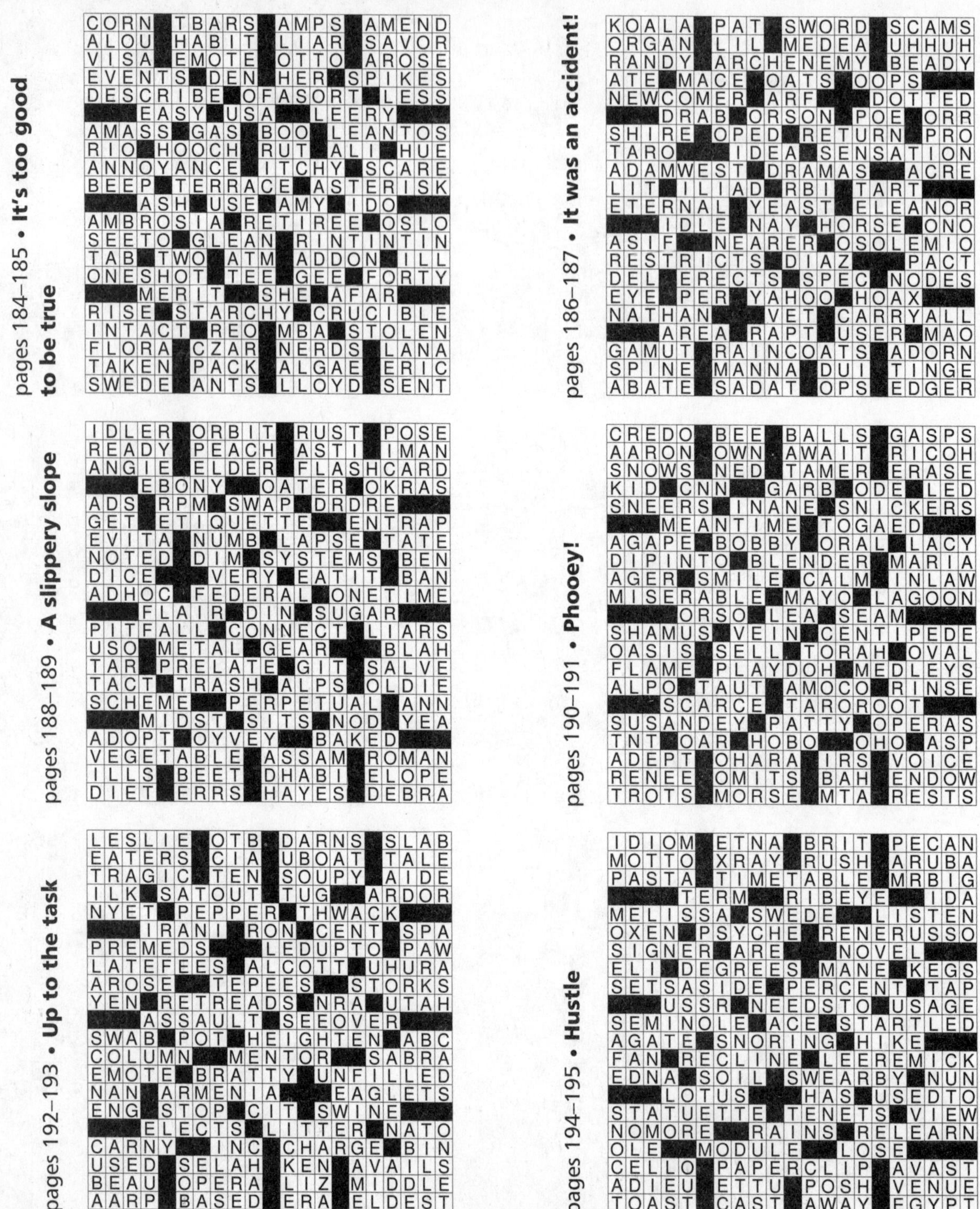
pages 184–185 • It's too good to be true
CORN TBARS AMPS AMEND
ALOU HABIT LIAR SAVOR
VISA EMOTE OTTO AROSE
EVENTS DEN HER SPIKES
DESCRIBE OFASORT LESS
EASY USA LEERY
AMASS GAS BOO LEANTOS
RIO HOOCH RUT ALI HUE
ANNOYANCE ITCHY SCARE
BEEP TERRACE ASTERISK
ASH USE AMY IDO
AMBROSIA RETIREE OSLO
SEETO GLEAN RINTINTIN
TAB TWO ATM ADDON ILL
ONESHOT TEE GEE FORTY
MERIT SHE AFAR
RISE STARCHY CRUCIBLE
INTACT REO MBA STOLEN
FLORA CZAR NERDS LANA
TAKEN PACK ALGAE ERIC
SWEDE ANTS LLOYD SENT
pages 188–189 • A slippery slope
IDLER ORBIT RUST POSE
READY PEACH ASTI IMAN
ANGIE ELDER FLASHCARD
EBONY OATER OKRAS
ADS RPM SWAP DRDRE
GET ETIQUETTE ENTRAP
EVITA NUMB LAPSE TATE
NOTED DIM SYSTEMS BEN
DICE VERY EATIT BAN
ADHOC FEDERAL ONETIME
FLAIR DIN SUGAR
PITFALL CONNECT LIARS
USO METAL GEAR BLAH
TAR PRELATE GIT SALVE
TACT TRASH ALPS OLDIE
SCHEME PERPETUAL ANN
MIDST SITS NOD YEA
ADOPT OYVEY BAKED
VEGETABLE ASSAM ROMAN
ILLS BEET DHABI ELOPE
DIET ERRS HAYES DEBRA
pages 192–193 • Up to the task
LESLIE OTB DARNS SLAB
EATERS CIA UBOAT TALE
TRAGIC TEN SOUPY AIDE
ILK SATOUT TUG ARDOR
NYET PEPPER THWACK
IRANI RON CENT SPA
PREMEDS LEDUPTO PAW
LATEFEES ALCOTT UHURA
AROSE TEPEES STORKS
YEN RETREADS NRA UTAH
ASSAULT SEEOVER
SWAB POT HEIGHTEN ABC
COLUMN MENTOR SABRA
EMOTE BRATTY UNFILLED
NAN ARMENIA EAGLETS
ENG STOP CIT SWINE
ELECTS LITTER NATO
CARNY INC CHARGE BIN
USED SELAH KEN AVAILS
BEAU OPERA LIZ MIDDLE
AARP BASED ERA ELDEST
pages 186–187 • It was an accident!
KOALA PAT SWORD SCAMS
ORGAN LIL MEDEA UHHUH
RANDY ARCHENEMY BEADY
ATE MACE OATS OOPS
NEWCOMER ARF DOTTED
DRAB ORSON POE ORR
SHIRE OPED RETURN PRO
TARO IDEA SENSATION
ADAMWEST DRAMAS ACRE
LIT ILIAD RBI TART
ETERNAL YEAST ELEANOR
IDLE NAY HORSE ONO
ASIF NEARER OSOLEMIO
RESTRICTS DIAZ PACT
DEL ERECTS SPEC NODES
EYE PER YAHOO HOAX
NATHAN VET CARRYALL
AREA RAPT USER MAO
GAMUT RAINCOATS ADORN
SPINE MANNA DUI TINGE
ABATE SADAT OPS EDGER
pages 190–191 • Phooey!
CREDO BEE BALLS GASPS
AARON OWN AWAIT RICOH
SNOWS NED TAMER ERASE
KID CNN GARB ODE LED
SNEERS INANE SNICKERS
MEANTIME TOGAED
AGAPE BOBBY ORAL LACY
DIPINTO BLENDER MARIA
AGER SMILE CALM INLAW
MISERABLE MAYO LAGOON
ORSO LEA SEAM
SHAMUS VEIN CENTIPEDE
OASIS SELL TORAH OVAL
FLAME PLAYDOH MEDLEYS
ALPO TAUT AMOCO RINSE
SCARCE TAROROOT
SUSANDEY PATTY OPERAS
TNT OAR HOBO OHO ASP
ADEPT OHARA IRS VOICE
RENEE OMITS BAH ENDOW
TROTS MORSE MTA RESTS
pages 194–195 • Hustle
IDIOM ETNA BRIT PECAN
MOTTO XRAY RUSH ARUBA
PASTA TIMETABLE MRBIG
TERM RIBEYE IDA
MELISSA SWEDE LISTEN
OXEN PSYCHE RENERUSSO
SIGNER ARE NOVEL
ELI DEGREES MANE KEGS
SETSASIDE PERCENT TAP
USSR NEEDSTO USAGE
SEMINOLE ACE STARTLED
AGATE SNORING HIKE
FAN RECLINE LEEREMICK
EDNA SOIL SWEARBY NUN
LOTUS HAS USEDTO
STATUETTE TENETS VIEW
NOMORE RAINS RELEARN
OLE MODULE LOSE
CELLO PAPERCLIP AVAST
ADIEU ETTU POSH VENUE
TOAST CAST AWAY EGYPT

page 198 • **The riddle**

SHIP SWEAR PANS
AURA MIAMI ISEE
WHATDOESAMYSTIC
BURLY ATILT
MASONED HIHO
ECHOES HONOLULU
SCANS HASTO NIP
SURE SAYTO PROD
USO LURES ARENA
PENNAMES PRESET
ASPS BRITTLE
SORTS MOOSE
THEHOTDOGVENDOR
AIDA ANNIE DOVE
NOON BAKED SNAP

page 199 • **The answer**

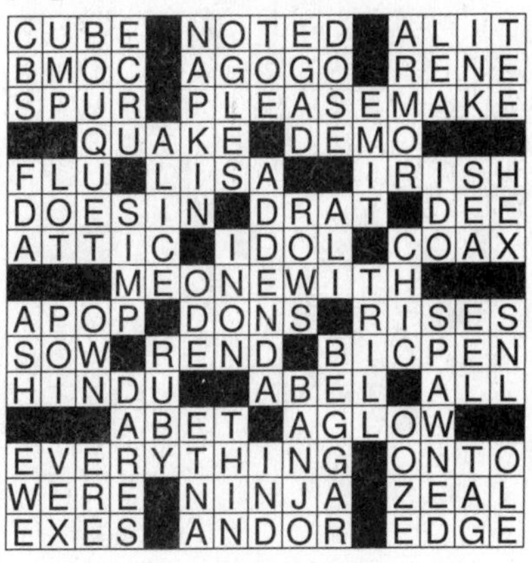

page 200 • **Fab Four by Three**

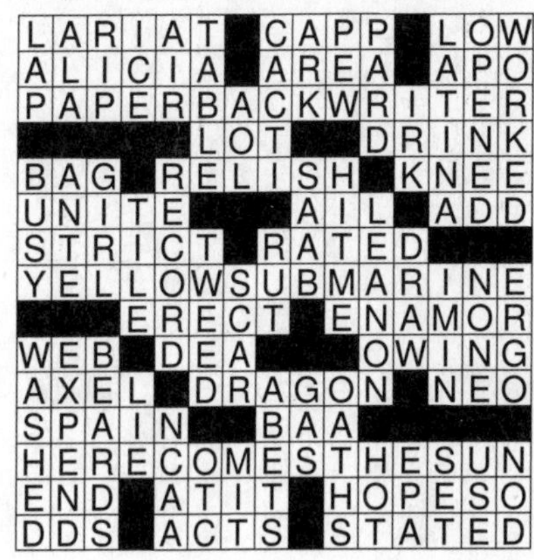

page 201 • **Tic-Tac-Toe**

page 202 • **Clothes encounters**

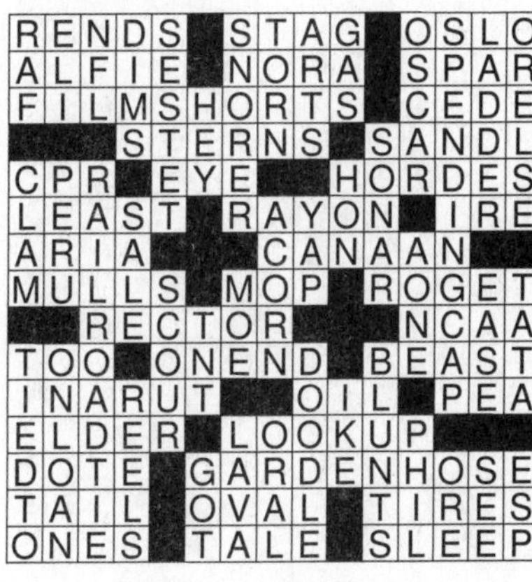

page 203 • **Fruity folk**

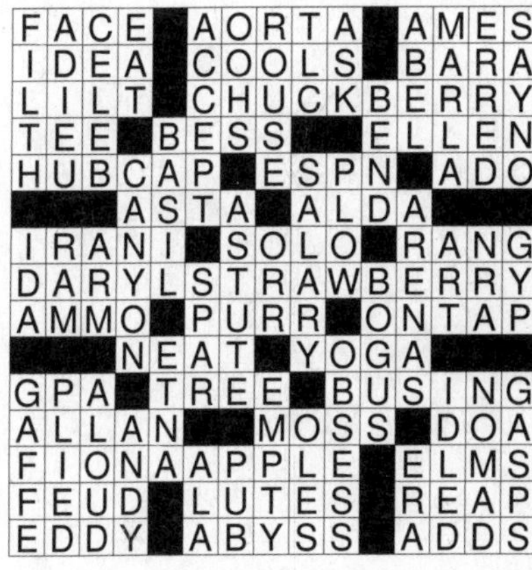

page 204 • **Who goes there?**

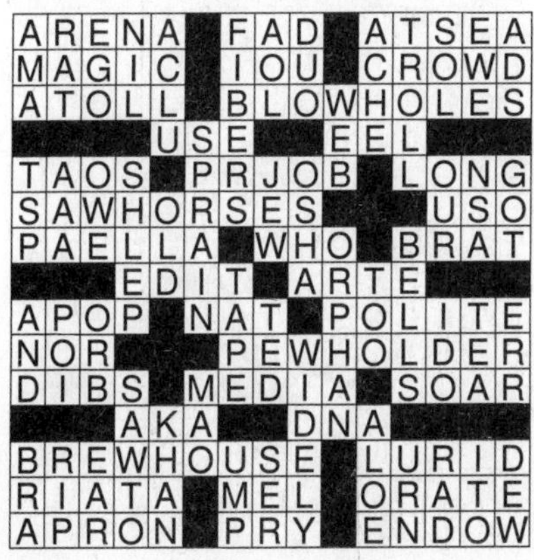

page 205 • **Go figure**

page 206 • **Front and back**

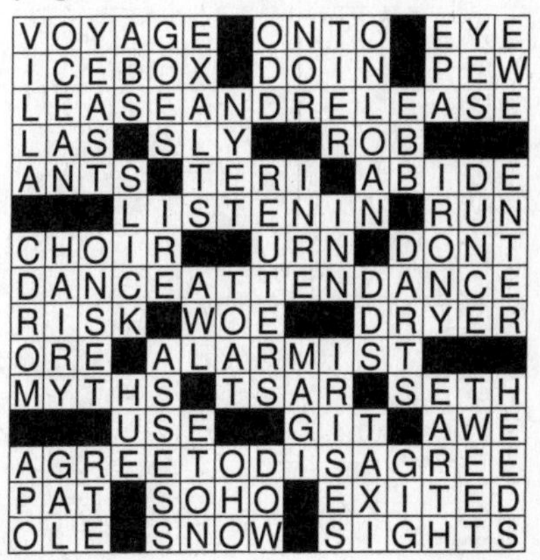

page 207 • **Horsing around**

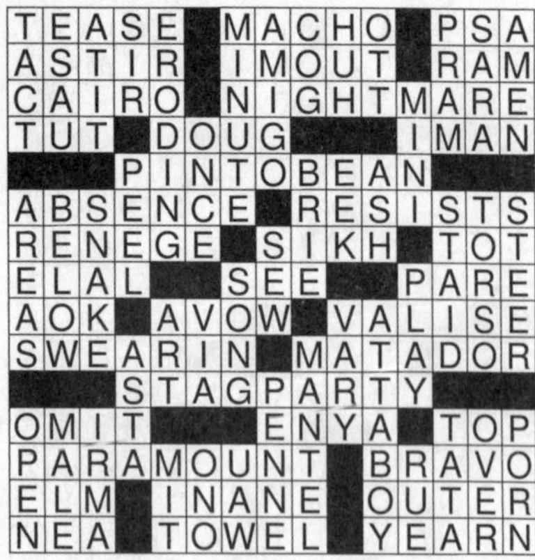

page 208 • **Thrice-heard songs**

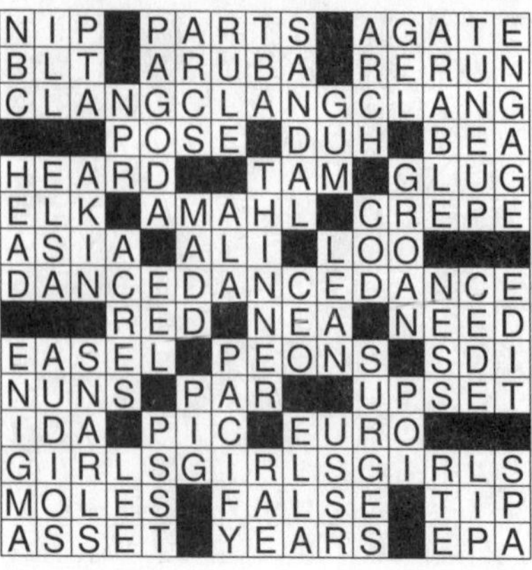

page 209 • **Aye, Aye, Captain**

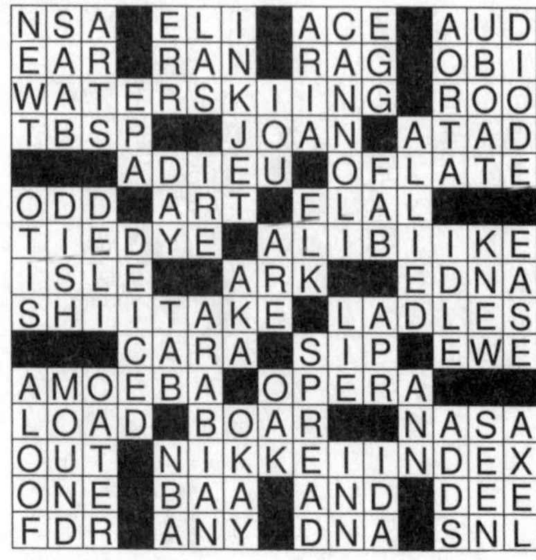

page 210 • **Twofer**

page 211 • **Don't mention the war**

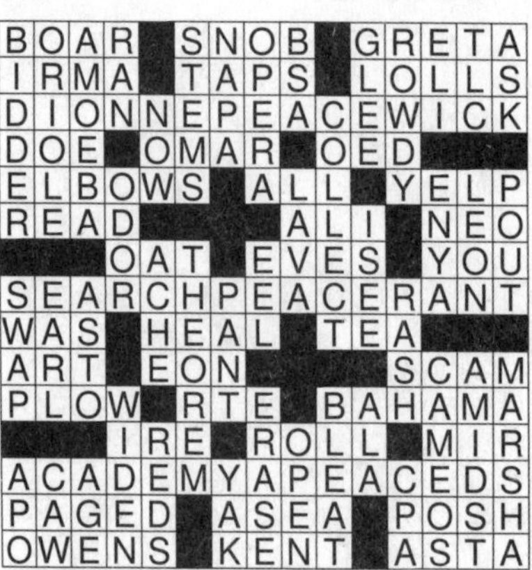

page 212 • **Kids' characters invented for this puzzle #1**

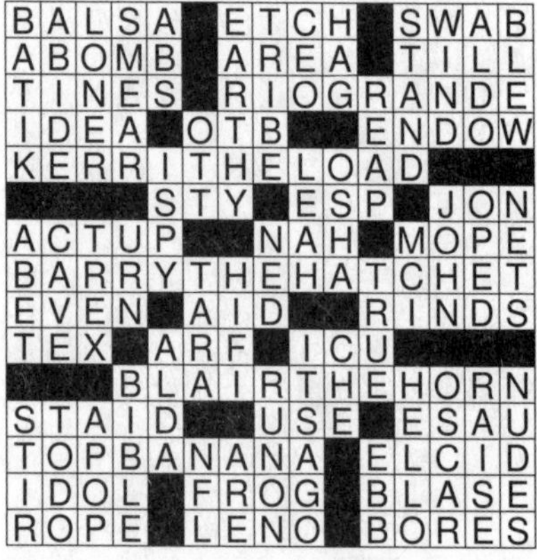

page 213 • **Oh no, not again!**

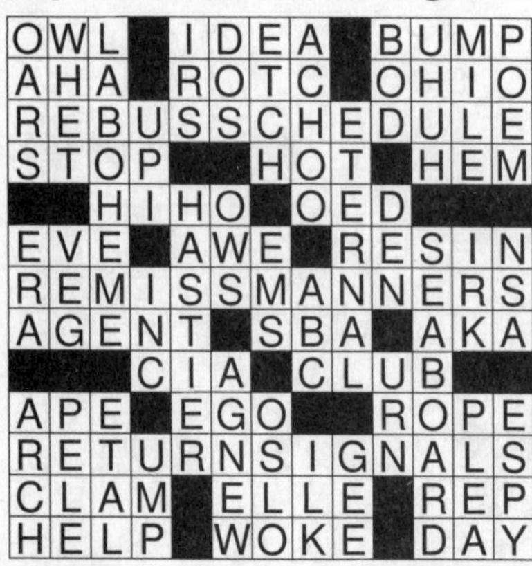

page 214 • **All-American**

VOWS APART ELLE
EPIC MARIA PEAR
REDHEADEDLEAGUE
ADELE GEL ARC
ELM DESI CIT
TBSP AMID AYES
OAK EYES AFT
WHITEBLOODCELLS
IKE BLOC OAR
GMAN BEER DODO
OUT DDAY EEE
BLT ARM SMILE
BLUERIBBONPANEL
LENO NOUNS NCAA
EDEN KOREA DAHL

page 216 • **Kids' characters invented for this puzzle #2**

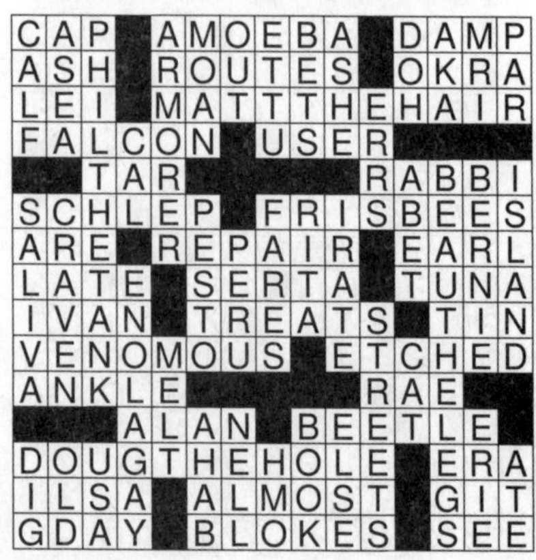

page 217 • **Some kind of mix-up**

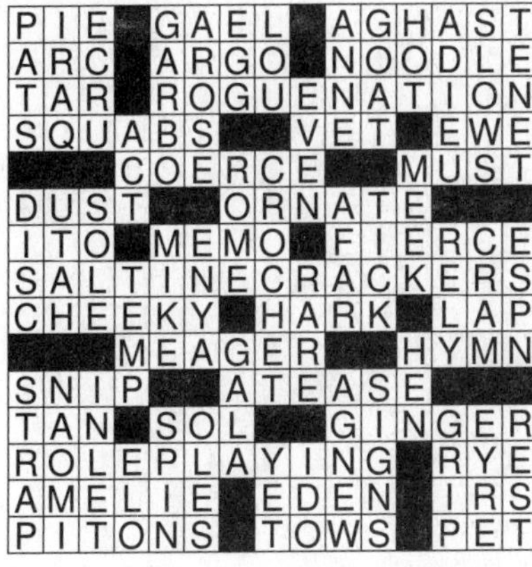

page 218 • **Double-header headlines on 2000 politics**

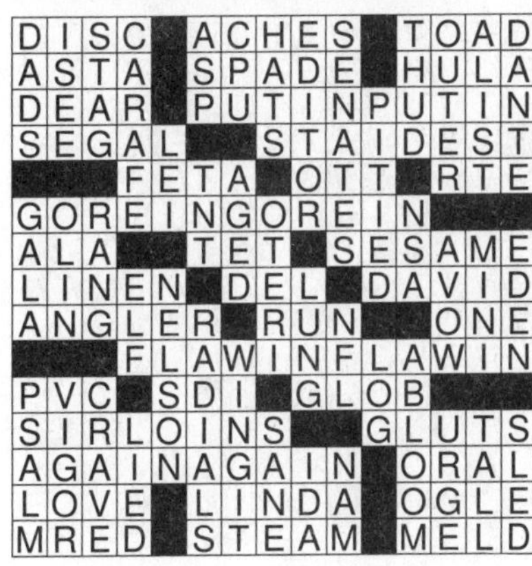

page 219 • **All caught up**

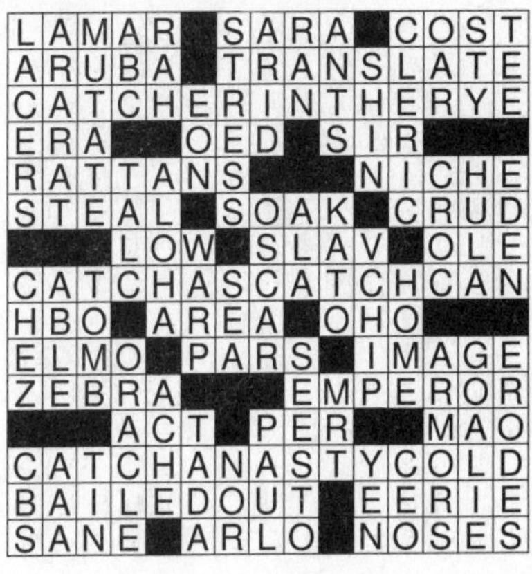

page 220 • **Going to extremes**

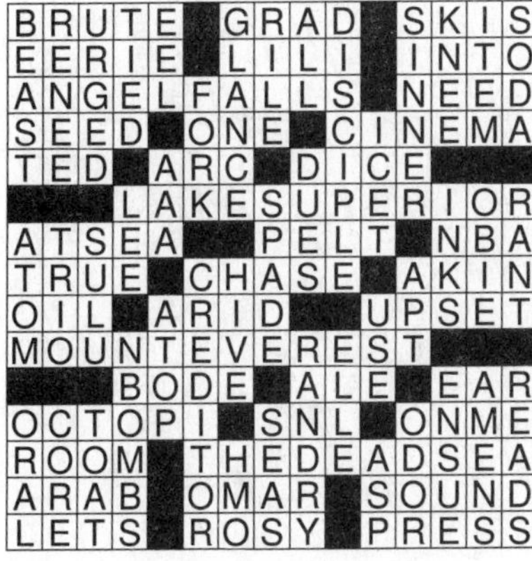

page 221 • **Card game enders**

page 222 • **Sean Connery flicks**

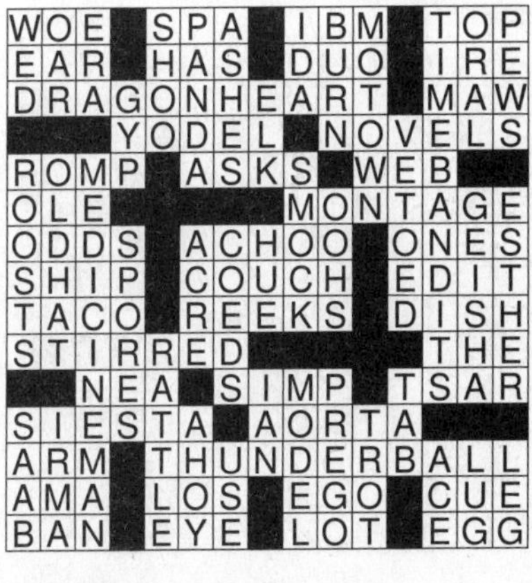

page 223 • **Song clips**

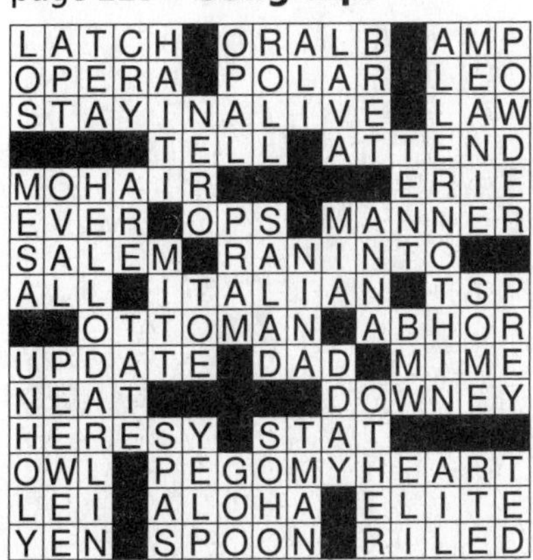

page 224 • **Severe cutbacks**

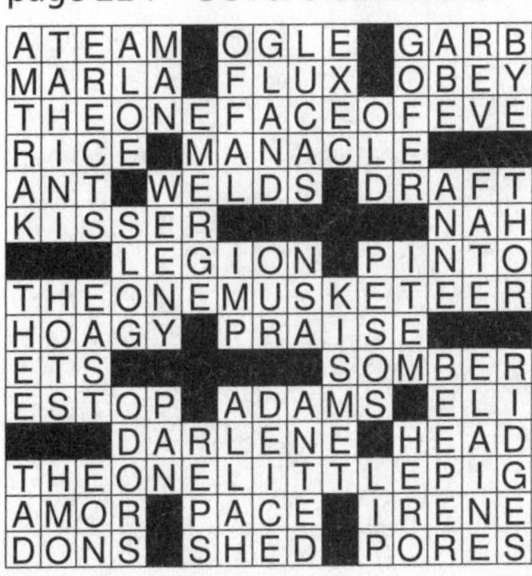

page 225 • **She went that-a-way**

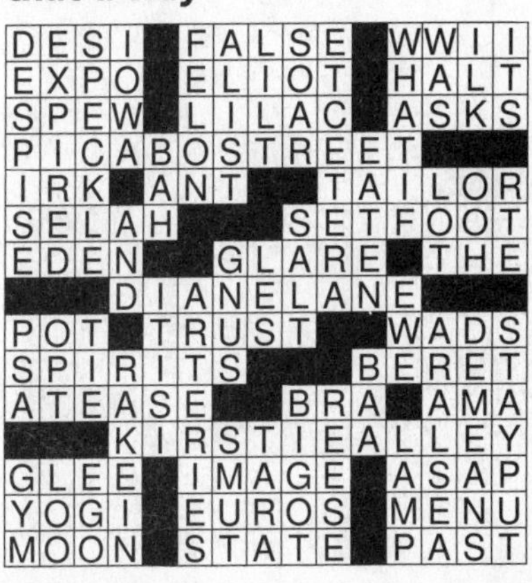

page 226 • **Foreign-born all-Americans**

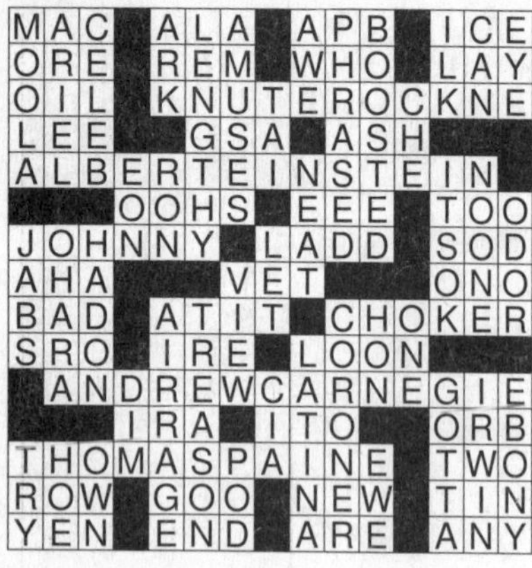

page 227 • **Throw in the towel**

page 228 • **Hits of 1968**

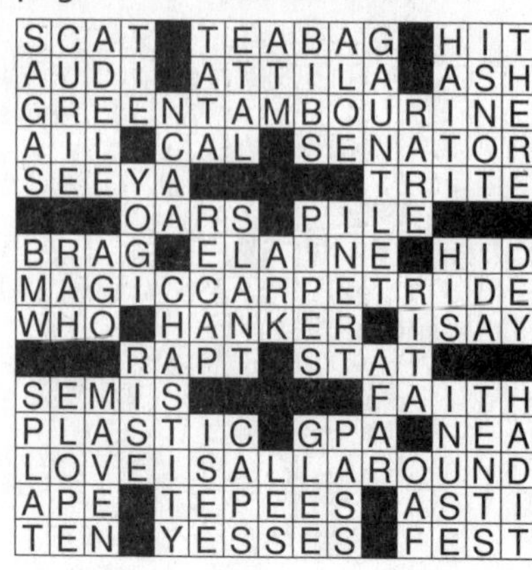

page 229 • **Sides reversed is**

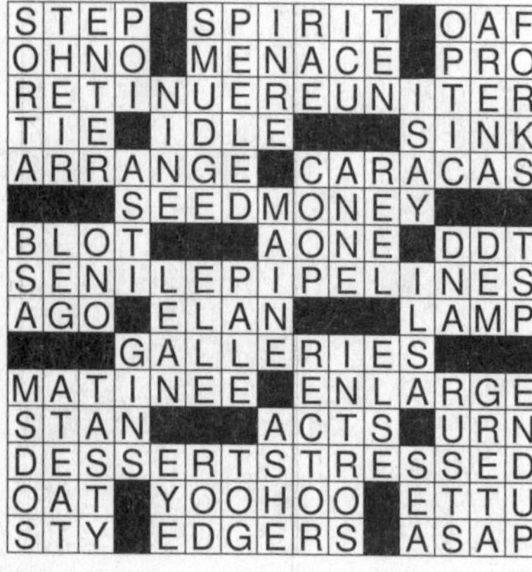

page 230 • **No grade school**

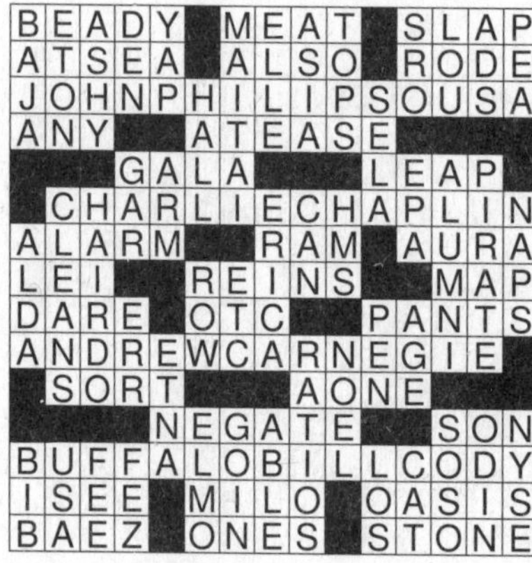

page 231 • **Children's classics**

page 232 • **Dr. Seuss classics**

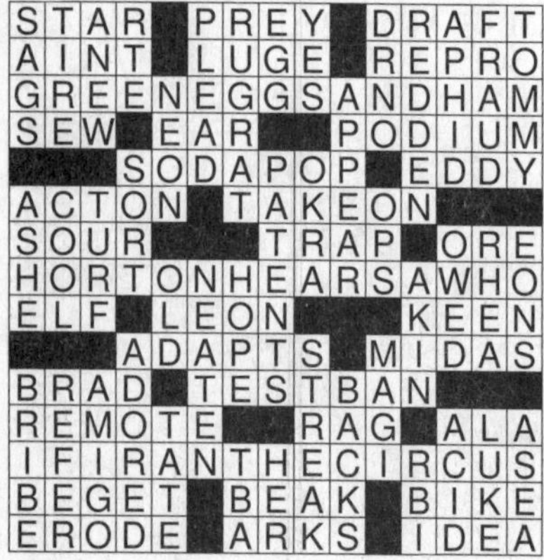

page 234 • **Fill 'Er Up 1**

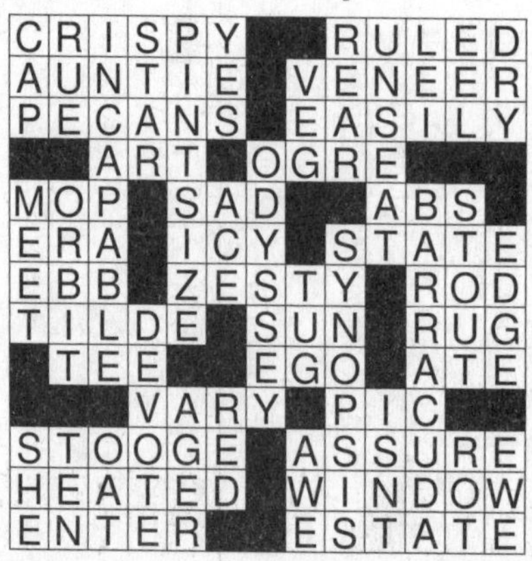

page 235 • **Fill 'Er Up 2**

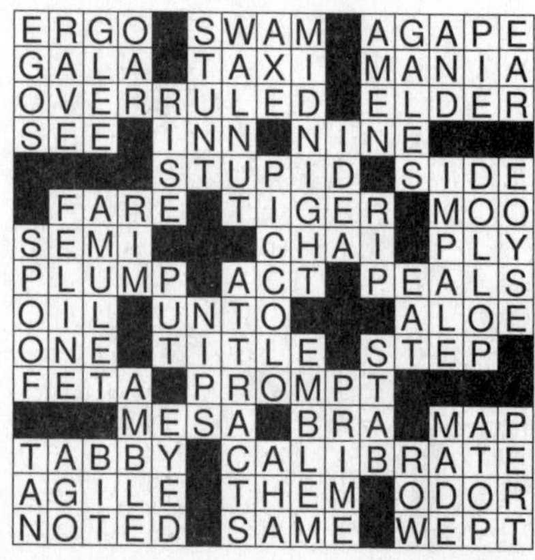

page 236 • **Fill 'Er Up 3**

```
MAR#BAA#HAS#ELF
ARE#ILL#ODE#RUE
JOT#BEG#SOL#GAL
OMITS#AFT#AFOUL
RARE#HER#SHE###
#SENSE#ELK#ZOOM
###EON#QUIT#WHO
VISTA#DUG#ALLOW
ORE#KNEE#OLE###
WEEP#INN#WEARS#
###LOX#CAN#SEAT
VINYL#GYP#JELLY
ERA#ICE#TWO#AMP
TOP#VAN#LEI#TOE
ONE#EWE#YEN#END
```

page 237 • **Fill 'Er Up 4**

```
AFT#OAF#ARCS#PLAN
SAW#OIL#VIOL#RACE
TIE#HOE#IDEA#EVES
ILL##LARDERS#VAST
REV#VISA##CHAI###
#DELI##JADE#PERT#
###ELF#ARE#SEWERS
#BUGLES#EARL#SMUT
FUN#ANOMALIES#ICY
ARIA#CLAW#DELUXE#
BRONZE#ZAP#KEG###
#ONCE#KEYS##PHEW#
###EDGE##SLIT#NAP
ARTS#NEGATED##VIE
QUIT#OPEN#ALL#ITS
UNDO#MEAT#SEA#EEK
AGER#ERRS#TRY#DRY
```

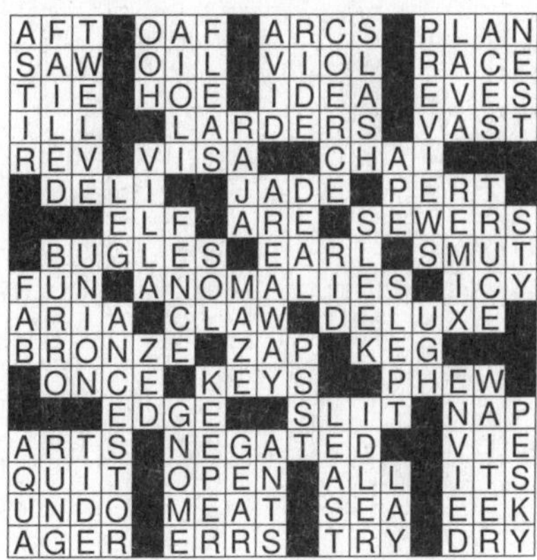

page 238 • **Fill 'Er Up 5**

```
MET#SODA#WOVE
AGO#QUIP#IDEA
COMMUTER#NEXT
###AID#ILK###
#JUMBO#CUSHY#
NANAS#FOG#OOH
ODD##LOT##SUE
WEE#AIR#BATTY
#DRANK#HARSH#
###BYE#ORE###
GAZE#NARRATOR
OMIT#ELSE#EWE
OPTS#DEED#AND
```

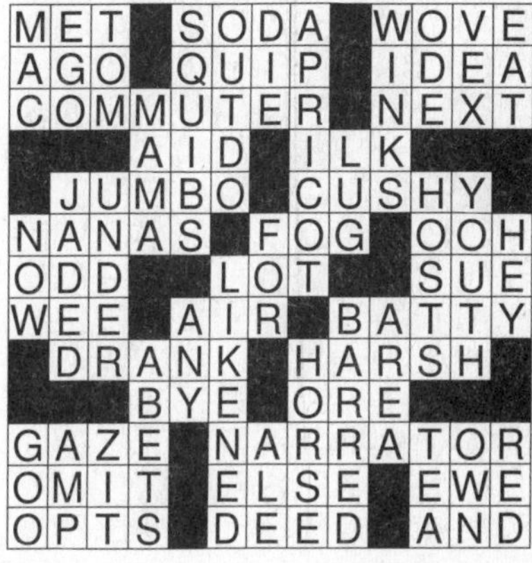

page 239 • **Fill 'Er Up 6**

```
PREY#EDGE#AROMA
SALE#NANA#NEWER
ADDS#CZAR#CLERK
LIE#WOES#BIASES
MORTAR#HOLEY###
###USE##RAN#WHO
QUIT#SLIGHT#HOW
UNCUT#ERA#STOOL
ADO#RAVENS#OAKS
DON#EWE##EGO###
###ISLET#DELETE
TAUNTS#WHAM#JIG
EXPEL#FIAT#GEAR
SLOPE#ANTE#ACRE
TENTS#DEED#STAT
```

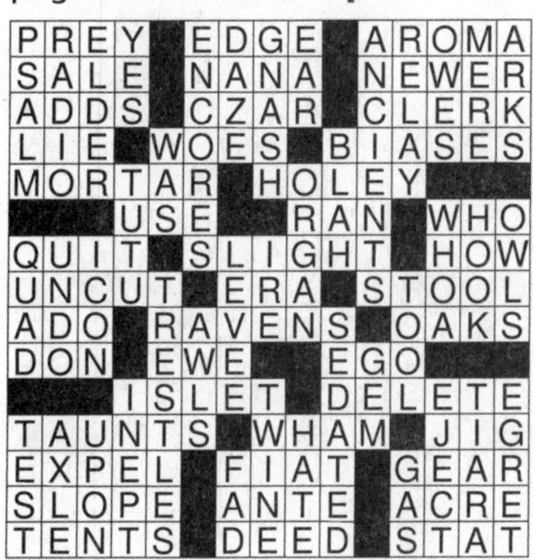

page 240 • **Fill 'Er Up 7**

```
ILK##SING##BUSH
RAN#OTTERS#ONTO
APE#PISTOL#ODOR
TEASER#SCEPTERS
ELDER###EEL#RYE
###TAB#ARTIST##
FACT#YETI#ELATE
IDOL#ENTER#AKIN
TONES#VISA#NEED
##CRITIC#WAD###
SEE#GAS###MEDAL
ARACHNID#VIRILE
TOLL#GORGES#OLD
IDEA#ONIONS#DOG
NERD##SPOT##EYE
```

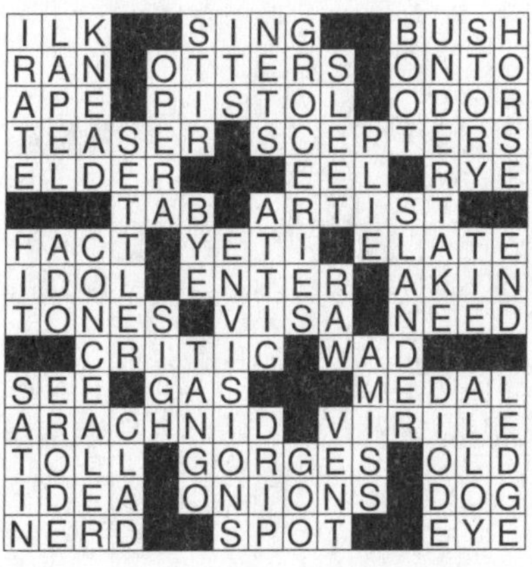

page 242 • **Food, wonderful food 1**

```
EDAM#BARM#SOP
PALE#ADDA#ALE
ALLA#SEAR#CIA
###LBS##ONCOR
SHOYU#SYRAH##
TON#LOCO#MARC
AHI#BIRRA#RIO
ROOT#LAKE#INN
##NOMSG#RANGE
TASTE##TOP###
IKA#DOPE#ROME
EEL#OXEN#OVAL
SET#COAT#NAIL
```

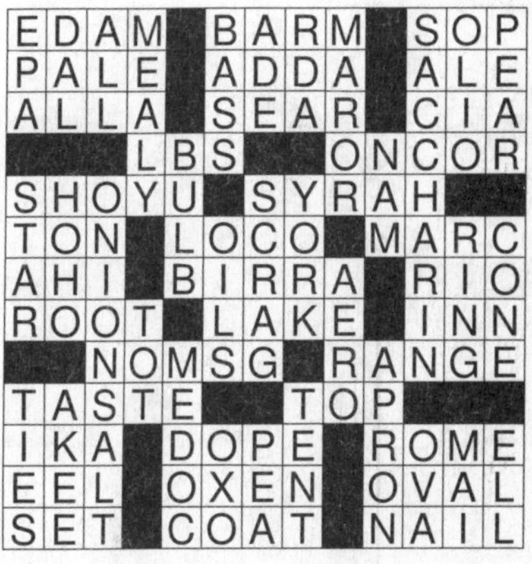

page 243 • **Food, wonderful food 2**

```
DOC#EDAM##POP
AIR#MILAN#EPA
BLUEPLATE#POT
###AIL##SMORE
SCOUR#ASTI###
EEL#EGGO#MASA
ACID#RAY#IRON
LINA#UVAS#NUT
###TUBE#PHILS
DINED##MOO###
OCA#OCEANPOUT
CEP#NOMSG#ADE
GSA##DUKE#TON
```

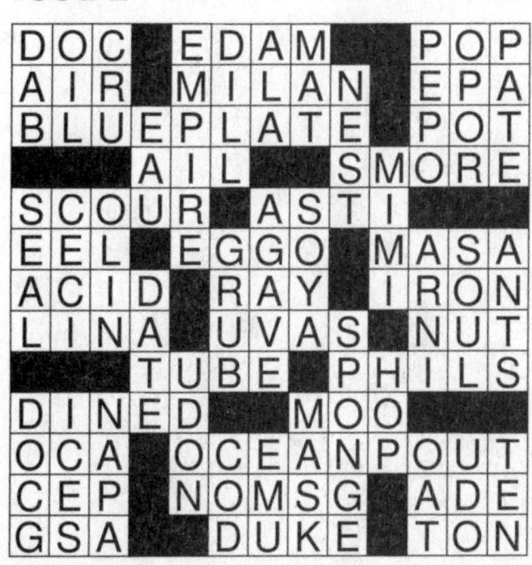

page 244 • **Food, wonderful food 3**

```
CON#OHTA##ALL
UNI#RIOJA#MAI
PEPPERPOT#OIL
###ROE##HASTY
ROPE#SAVOR###
UVA###COLLARD
BATF#AIL#OLIO
SLOEGIN###LBS
###TYRIA#CASE
OSCAR##CEE###
CHA#OPAKAPAKA
HOT#SOBER#NAM
ATE##ICES#TIA
```

page 245 • **Food, wonderful food 4**

```
MOP#EGGO#TAPA
AIL#DRUM#SHAG
MEALTIME#PIPE
###IAN#LBS###
#JAM#DEER#ASH
SUMAC#ATE#PAO
ALA#HOUSE#RUM
FEN#OLD#DHOTE
EPA#KEEP#ONE#
###DOS#EAR###
TOFU#TRANSFAT
BALL#REST#AJO
SKOL#ADES#NIP
```

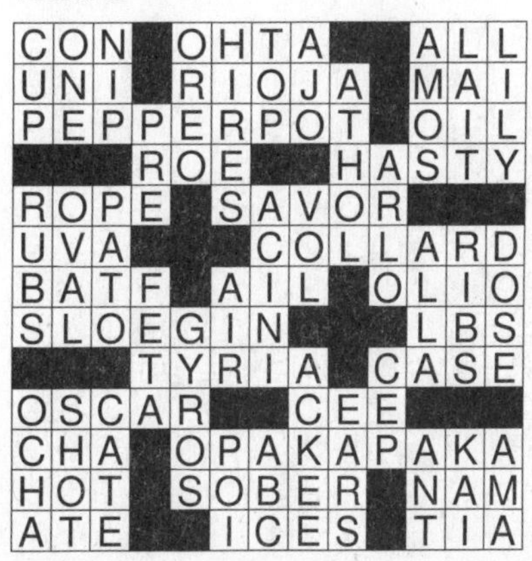

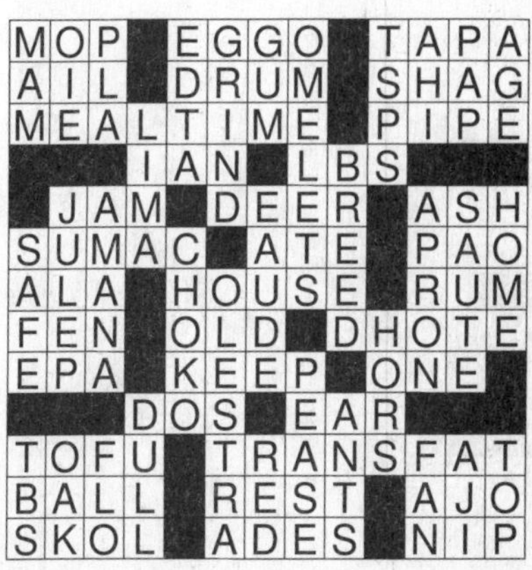

page 246 • **Food, wonderful food 5**

page 247 • **Food, wonderful food 6**

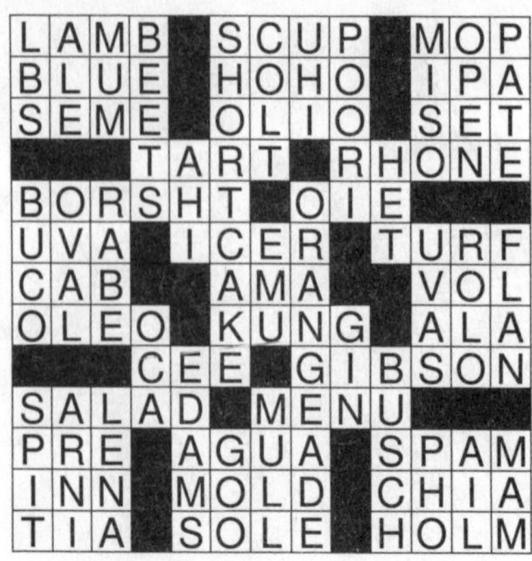

pages 248–249 • **Bible crossword 1**

pages 250–251 • **Bible crossword 2**

pages 252–253 • **Bible crossword 3**

pages 254–255 • **Bible crossword 4**

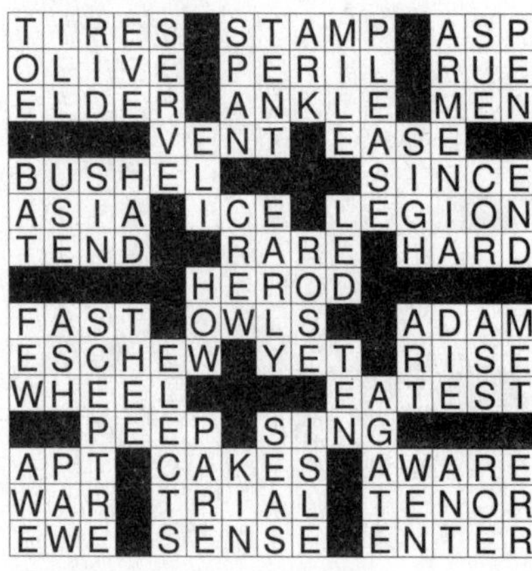

pages 256–257 • **Bible crossword 5**

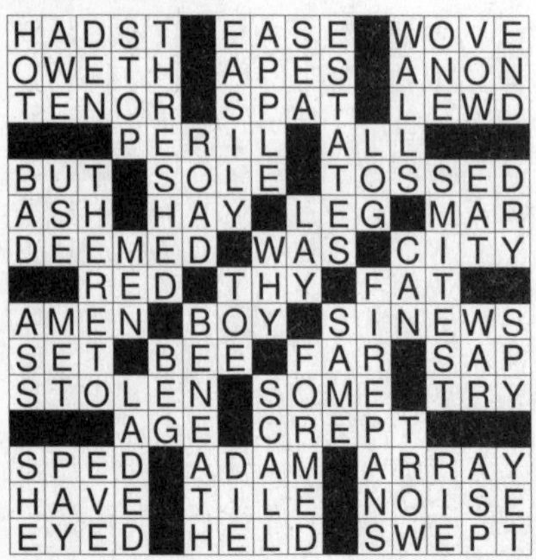

pages 258–259 • **Bible crossword 6**

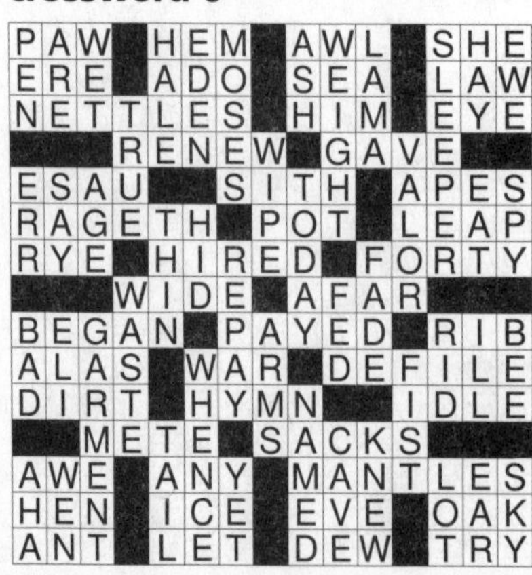

pages 260–261 • **TV/film crossword 1**

pages 262–263 • **TV/film**

crossword 2

pages 264–265 • **TV/film**

crossword 3

pages 266–267 • **TV/film**

crossword 4

pages 268–269 • **TV/film**

crossword 5

pages 270–271 • **TV/film**

crossword 6

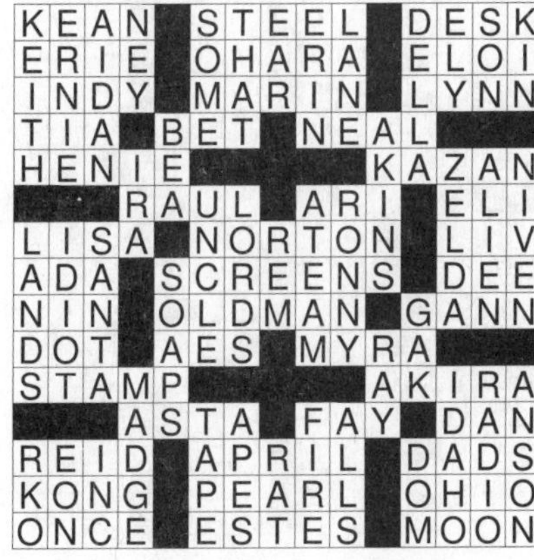

pages 272–273 • **TV/film**

crossword 7

pages 274–275 • **TV/film**

crossword 8

page 278 • **The I's have it 1**

page 279 • **The I's have it 2**

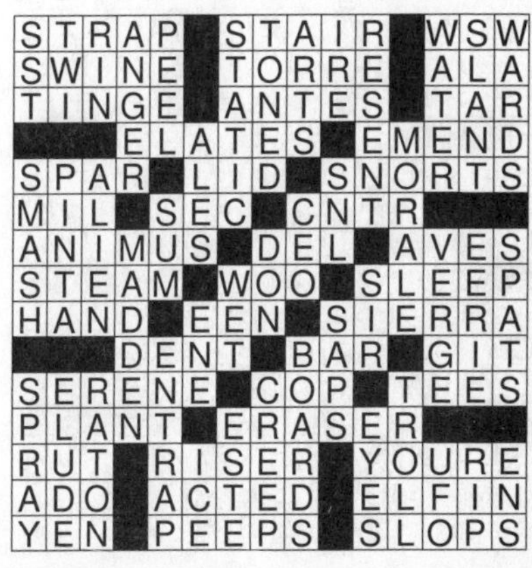

page 280 • **The I's have it 3**

WEEPS CAP GIMP
EERIE ORE AREA
ELATE PREGGERS
HAG EVE SET
DABS RESENT
ELO SALT OPAH
ADO SNL OCTOPI
NESTED RAM SAD
SRTA BATS ERE
ROTATE SSTS
ALC TAN RAN
COLESLAW IOTAS
NOON ENE DROLL
ETDS SAT STRAY

page 281 • **A lot 1**

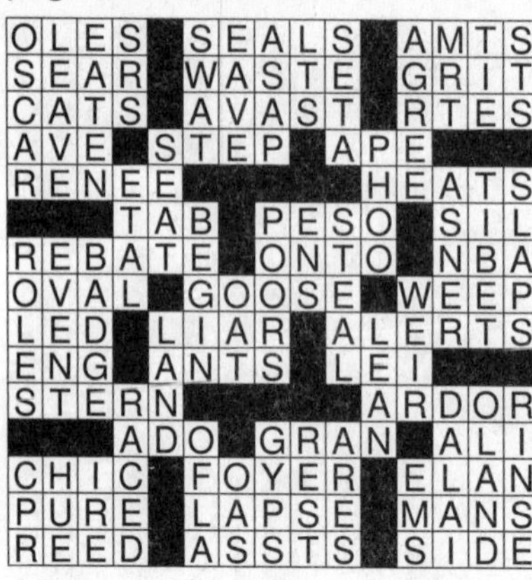
OLES SEALS AMTS
SEAR WASTE GRIT
CATS AVAST RTES
AVE STEP APE
RENEE HEATS
TAB PESO SIL
REBATE ONTO NBA
OVAL GOOSE WEEP
LED LIAR ALERTS
ENG ANTS LEI
STERN ARDOR
ADO GRAN ALI
CHIC FOYER ELAN
PURE LAPSE MANS
REED ASSTS SIDE

page 282 • **A lot 2**

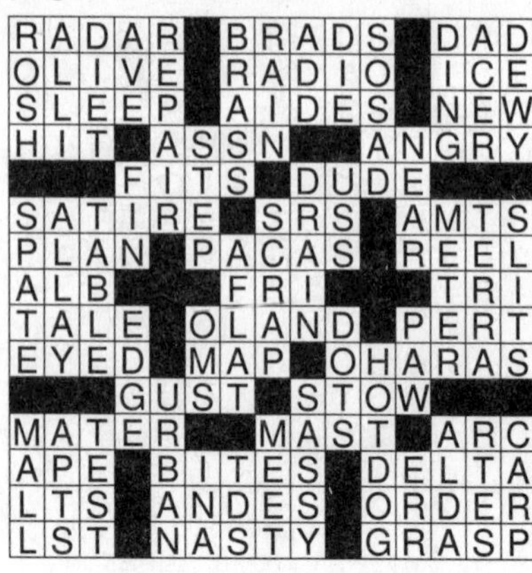
RADAR BRADS DAD
OLIVE RADIO ICE
SLEEP AIDES NEW
HIT ASSN ANGRY
FITS DUDE
SATIRE SRS AMTS
PLAN PACAS REEL
ALB FRI TRI
TALE OLAND PERT
EYED MAP OHARAS
GUST STOW
MATER MAST ARC
APE BITES DELTA
LTS ANDES ORDER
LST NASTY GRASP

page 283 • **A lot 3**

AVE AFC MET HIS
DOT BIO ONE ANT
SWATHES STA SPA
ROSH HIT TUT
ASSERT RECREATE
MALE ALE EOE
IRED SALTS GAGS
GAP LAE SRI
ONTO PAPAS SNAG
RCA SMU TECH
PRETENSE SNARES
LEA ATE SPAR
OMS SHA CENTRAL
TIE EER ANA OLE
STS SRS TDS EGG

page 284 • **4-letter words 1**

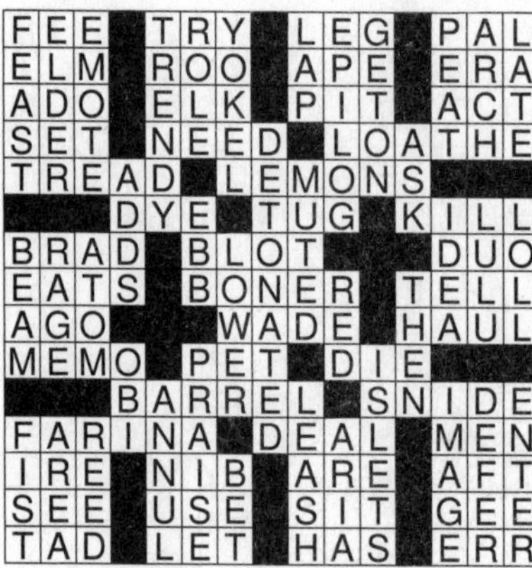
FEE TRY LEG PAL
ELM ROO APE ERA
ADO ELK PIT ACT
SET NEED LOATHE
TREAD LEMONS
DYE TUG KILL
BRAD BLOT DUO
EATS BONER TELL
AGO WADE HAUL
MEMO PET DIE
BARREL SNIDE
FARINA DEAL MEN
IRE NIB ARE AFT
SEE USE SIT GEE
TAD LET HAS ERR

page 285 • **4-letter words 2**

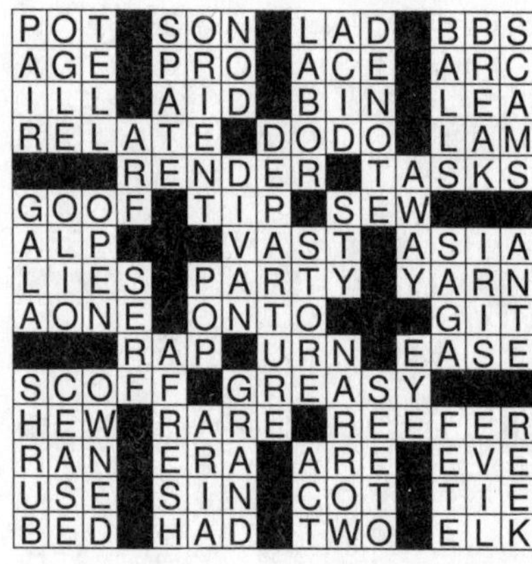
POT SON LAD BBS
AGE PRO ACE ARC
ILL AID BIN LEA
RELATE DODO LAM
RENDER TASKS
GOOF TIP SEW
ALP VAST ASIA
LIES PARTY YARN
AONE ONTO GIT
RAP URN EASE
SCOFF GREASY
HEW RARE REEFER
RAN ERA ARE EVE
USE SIN COT TIE
BED HAD TWO ELK

page 286 • **4-letter words 3**

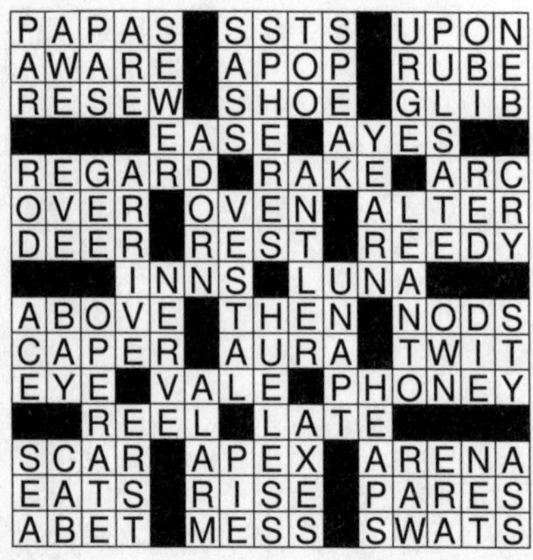
PAPAS SSTS UPON
AWARE APOP RUBE
RESEW SHOE GLIB
EASE AYES
REGARD RAKE ARC
OVER OVEN ALTER
DEER REST REEDY
INNS LUNA
ABOVE THEN NODS
CAPER AURA TWIT
EYE VALE PHONEY
REEL LATE
SCAR APEX ARENA
EATS RISE PARES
ABET MESS SWATS

page 287 • **O sole me O 1**

NOSE ADARE BOSS
IOTA MERES UNIT
PLUG AGENT MARE
SANER RATES NEW
ROBES ELIDES
NET USE BMOC
ERRATA YES HASH
SAUTE TEA RODEO
STET SET BURDEN
IRON TAN SSE
PARCEL PORTE
IDO DADAS OATHS
PEAL COPSE SEEP
ELSE EPEES ELMO
SATE SENSE SLOT

page 288 • **O sole me O 2**

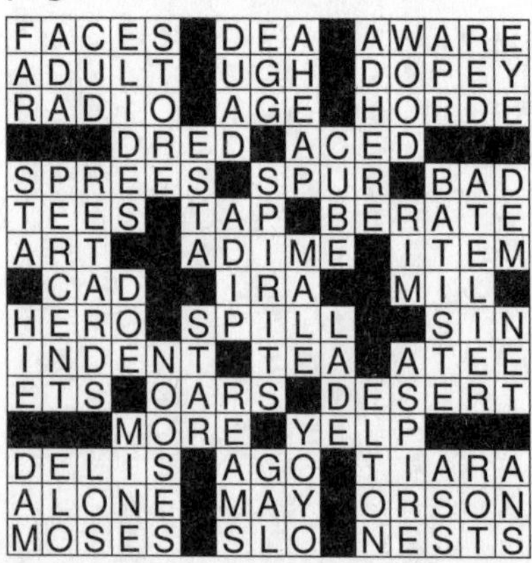
FACES DEA AWARE
ADULT UGH DOPEY
RADIO AGE HORDE
DRED ACED
SPREES SPUR BAD
TEES TAP BERATE
ART ADIME ITEM
CAD IRA MIL
HERO SPILL SIN
INDENT TEA ATEE
ETS OARS DESERT
MORE YELP
DELIS AGO TIARA
ALONE MAY ORSON
MOSES SLO NESTS

page 289 • **O sole me O 3**

page 290 • **Behead before entry 1**

page 291 • **Behead before entry 2**

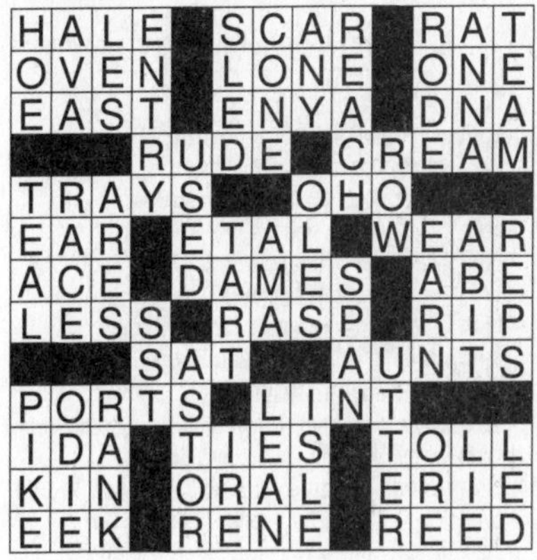

page 292 • **Behead before entry 3**

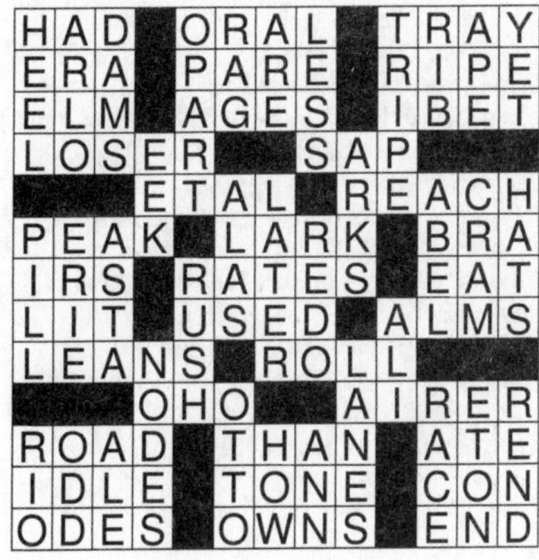

page 293 • **8 sounds good to me 1**

page 294 • **8 sounds good to me 2**

THE EVERYTHING® SERIES!

BUSINESS & PERSONAL FINANCE

Everything® Accounting Book
Everything® Budgeting Book, 2nd Ed.
Everything® Business Planning Book
Everything® Coaching and Mentoring Book, 2nd Ed.
Everything® Fundraising Book
Everything® Get Out of Debt Book
Everything® Grant Writing Book, 2nd Ed.
Everything® Guide to Buying Foreclosures
Everything® Guide to Fundraising, $15.95
Everything® Guide to Mortgages
Everything® Guide to Personal Finance for Single Mothers
Everything® Home-Based Business Book, 2nd Ed.
Everything® Homebuying Book, 3rd Ed., $15.95
Everything® Homeselling Book, 2nd Ed.
Everything® Human Resource Management Book
Everything® Improve Your Credit Book
Everything® Investing Book, 2nd Ed.
Everything® Landlording Book
Everything® Leadership Book, 2nd Ed.
Everything® Managing People Book, 2nd Ed.
Everything® Negotiating Book
Everything® Online Auctions Book
Everything® Online Business Book
Everything® Personal Finance Book
Everything® Personal Finance in Your 20s & 30s Book, 2nd Ed.
Everything® Personal Finance in Your 40s & 50s Book, $15.95
Everything® Project Management Book, 2nd Ed.
Everything® Real Estate Investing Book
Everything® Retirement Planning Book
Everything® Robert's Rules Book, $7.95
Everything® Selling Book
Everything® Start Your Own Business Book, 2nd Ed.
Everything® Wills & Estate Planning Book

COOKING

Everything® Barbecue Cookbook
Everything® Bartender's Book, 2nd Ed., $9.95
Everything® Calorie Counting Cookbook
Everything® Cheese Book
Everything® Chinese Cookbook
Everything® Classic Recipes Book
Everything® Cocktail Parties & Drinks Book
Everything® College Cookbook
Everything® Cooking for Baby and Toddler Book
Everything® Diabetes Cookbook
Everything® Easy Gourmet Cookbook
Everything® Fondue Cookbook
Everything® Food Allergy Cookbook, $15.95
Everything® Fondue Party Book
Everything® Gluten-Free Cookbook
Everything® Glycemic Index Cookbook
Everything® Grilling Cookbook
Everything® Healthy Cooking for Parties Book, $15.95
Everything® Holiday Cookbook
Everything® Indian Cookbook
Everything® Lactose-Free Cookbook
Everything® Low-Cholesterol Cookbook
Everything® Low-Fat High-Flavor Cookbook, 2nd Ed., $15.95
Everything® Low-Salt Cookbook
Everything® Meals for a Month Cookbook
Everything® Meals on a Budget Cookbook
Everything® Mediterranean Cookbook
Everything® Mexican Cookbook
Everything® No Trans Fat Cookbook
Everything® One-Pot Cookbook, 2nd Ed., $15.95
Everything® Organic Cooking for Baby & Toddler Book, $15.95
Everything® Pizza Cookbook
Everything® Quick Meals Cookbook, 2nd Ed., $15.95
Everything® Slow Cooker Cookbook
Everything® Slow Cooking for a Crowd Cookbook
Everything® Soup Cookbook
Everything® Stir-Fry Cookbook
Everything® Sugar-Free Cookbook
Everything® Tapas and Small Plates Cookbook
Everything® Tex-Mex Cookbook
Everything® Thai Cookbook
Everything® Vegetarian Cookbook
Everything® Whole-Grain, High-Fiber Cookbook
Everything® Wild Game Cookbook
Everything® Wine Book, 2nd Ed.

GAMES

Everything® 15-Minute Sudoku Book, $9.95
Everything® 30-Minute Sudoku Book, $9.95
Everything® Bible Crosswords Book, $9.95
Everything® Blackjack Strategy Book
Everything® Brain Strain Book, $9.95
Everything® Bridge Book
Everything® Card Games Book
Everything® Card Tricks Book, $9.95
Everything® Casino Gambling Book, 2nd Ed.
Everything® Chess Basics Book
Everything® Christmas Crosswords Book, $9.95
Everything® Craps Strategy Book
Everything® Crossword and Puzzle Book
Everything® Crosswords and Puzzles for Quote Lovers Book, $9.95
Everything® Crossword Challenge Book
Everything® Crosswords for the Beach Book, $9.95
Everything® Cryptic Crosswords Book, $9.95
Everything® Cryptograms Book, $9.95
Everything® Easy Crosswords Book
Everything® Easy Kakuro Book, $9.95
Everything® Easy Large-Print Crosswords Book
Everything® Games Book, 2nd Ed.
Everything® Giant Book of Crosswords
Everything® Giant Sudoku Book, $9.95
Everything® Giant Word Search Book
Everything® Kakuro Challenge Book, $9.95
Everything® Large-Print Crossword Challenge Book
Everything® Large-Print Crosswords Book
Everything® Large-Print Travel Crosswords Book
Everything® Lateral Thinking Puzzles Book, $9.95
Everything® Literary Crosswords Book, $9.95
Everything® Mazes Book
Everything® Memory Booster Puzzles Book, $9.95
Everything® Movie Crosswords Book, $9.95
Everything® Music Crosswords Book, $9.95
Everything® Online Poker Book
Everything® Pencil Puzzles Book, $9.95
Everything® Poker Strategy Book
Everything® Pool & Billiards Book
Everything® Puzzles for Commuters Book, $9.95
Everything® Puzzles for Dog Lovers Book, $9.95
Everything® Sports Crosswords Book, $9.95
Everything® Test Your IQ Book, $9.95
Everything® Texas Hold 'Em Book, $9.95
Everything® Travel Crosswords Book, $9.95
Everything® Travel Mazes Book, $9.95
Everything® Travel Word Search Book, $9.95
Everything® TV Crosswords Book, $9.95
Everything® Word Games Challenge Book
Everything® Word Scramble Book
Everything® Word Search Book

HEALTH

Everything® Alzheimer's Book
Everything® Diabetes Book
Everything® First Aid Book, $9.95
Everything® Green Living Book
Everything® Health Guide to Addiction and Recovery
Everything® Health Guide to Adult Bipolar Disorder
Everything® Health Guide to Arthritis
Everything® Health Guide to Controlling Anxiety
Everything® Health Guide to Depression
Everything® Health Guide to Diabetes, 2nd Ed.
Everything® Health Guide to Fibromyalgia
Everything® Health Guide to Menopause, 2nd Ed.
Everything® Health Guide to Migraines
Everything® Health Guide to Multiple Sclerosis
Everything® Health Guide to OCD
Everything® Health Guide to PMS
Everything® Health Guide to Postpartum Care
Everything® Health Guide to Thyroid Disease
Everything® Hypnosis Book
Everything® Low Cholesterol Book
Everything® Menopause Book
Everything® Nutrition Book
Everything® Reflexology Book
Everything® Stress Management Book
Everything® Superfoods Book, $15.95

HISTORY

Everything® American Government Book
Everything® American History Book, 2nd Ed.
Everything® American Revolution Book, $15.95
Everything® Civil War Book
Everything® Freemasons Book
Everything® Irish History & Heritage Book
Everything® World War II Book, 2nd Ed.

HOBBIES

Everything® Candlemaking Book
Everything® Cartooning Book
Everything® Coin Collecting Book
Everything® Digital Photography Book, 2nd Ed.

Everything® Drawing Book
Everything® Family Tree Book, 2nd Ed.
Everything® Guide to Online Genealogy, $15.95
Everything® Knitting Book
Everything® Knots Book
Everything® Photography Book
Everything® Quilting Book
Everything® Sewing Book
Everything® Soapmaking Book, 2nd Ed.
Everything® Woodworking Book

HOME IMPROVEMENT

Everything® Feng Shui Book
Everything® Feng Shui Decluttering Book, $9.95
Everything® Fix-It Book
Everything® Green Living Book
Everything® Home Decorating Book
Everything® Home Storage Solutions Book
Everything® Homebuilding Book
Everything® Organize Your Home Book, 2nd Ed.

KIDS' BOOKS

All titles are $7.95

Everything® Fairy Tales Book, $14.95
Everything® Kids' Animal Puzzle & Activity Book
Everything® Kids' Astronomy Book
Everything® Kids' Baseball Book, 5th Ed.
Everything® Kids' Bible Trivia Book
Everything® Kids' Bugs Book
Everything® Kids' Cars and Trucks Puzzle and Activity Book
Everything® Kids' Christmas Puzzle & Activity Book
Everything® Kids' Connect the Dots Puzzle and Activity Book
Everything® Kids' Cookbook, 2nd Ed.
Everything® Kids' Crazy Puzzles Book
Everything® Kids' Dinosaurs Book
Everything® Kids' Dragons Puzzle and Activity Book
Everything® Kids' Environment Book $7.95
Everything® Kids' Fairies Puzzle and Activity Book
Everything® Kids' First Spanish Puzzle and Activity Book
Everything® Kids' Football Book
Everything® Kids' Geography Book
Everything® Kids' Gross Cookbook
Everything® Kids' Gross Hidden Pictures Book
Everything® Kids' Gross Jokes Book
Everything® Kids' Gross Mazes Book
Everything® Kids' Gross Puzzle & Activity Book
Everything® Kids' Halloween Puzzle & Activity Book
Everything® Kids' Hanukkah Puzzle and Activity Book
Everything® Kids' Hidden Pictures Book
Everything® Kids' Horses Book
Everything® Kids' Joke Book
Everything® Kids' Knock Knock Book
Everything® Kids' Learning French Book
Everything® Kids' Learning Spanish Book
Everything® Kids' Magical Science Experiments Book
Everything® Kids' Math Puzzles Book
Everything® Kids' Mazes Book
Everything® Kids' Money Book, 2nd Ed.
Everything® Kids' Mummies, Pharaoh's, and Pyramids Puzzle and Activity Book
Everything® Kids' Nature Book
Everything® Kids' Pirates Puzzle and Activity Book
Everything® Kids' Presidents Book
Everything® Kids' Princess Puzzle and Activity Book
Everything® Kids' Puzzle Book
Everything® Kids' Racecars Puzzle and Activity Book
Everything® Kids' Riddles & Brain Teasers Book
Everything® Kids' Science Experiments Book
Everything® Kids' Sharks Book
Everything® Kids' Soccer Book
Everything® Kids' Spelling Book
Everything® Kids' Spies Puzzle and Activity Book
Everything® Kids' States Book
Everything® Kids' Travel Activity Book
Everything® Kids' Word Search Puzzle and Activity Book

LANGUAGE

Everything® Conversational Japanese Book with CD, $19.95
Everything® French Grammar Book
Everything® French Phrase Book, $9.95
Everything® French Verb Book, $9.95
Everything® German Phrase Book, $9.95
Everything® German Practice Book with CD, $19.95
Everything® Inglés Book
Everything® Intermediate Spanish Book with CD, $19.95
Everything® Italian Phrase Book, $9.95
Everything® Italian Practice Book with CD, $19.95
Everything® Learning Brazilian Portuguese Book with CD, $19.95
Everything® Learning French Book with CD, 2nd Ed., $19.95
Everything® Learning German Book
Everything® Learning Italian Book
Everything® Learning Latin Book
Everything® Learning Russian Book with CD, $19.95
Everything® Learning Spanish Book
Everything® Learning Spanish Book with CD, 2nd Ed., $19.95
Everything® Russian Practice Book with CD, $19.95
Everything® Sign Language Book, $15.95
Everything® Spanish Grammar Book
Everything® Spanish Phrase Book, $9.95
Everything® Spanish Practice Book with CD, $19.95
Everything® Spanish Verb Book, $9.95
Everything® Speaking Mandarin Chinese Book with CD, $19.95

MUSIC

Everything® Bass Guitar Book with CD, $19.95
Everything® Drums Book with CD, $19.95
Everything® Guitar Book with CD, 2nd Ed., $19.95
Everything® Guitar Chords Book with CD, $19.95
Everything® Guitar Scales Book with CD, $19.95
Everything® Harmonica Book with CD, $15.95
Everything® Home Recording Book
Everything® Music Theory Book with CD, $19.95
Everything® Reading Music Book with CD, $19.95
Everything® Rock & Blues Guitar Book with CD, $19.95
Everything® Rock & Blues Piano Book with CD, $19.95
Everything® Rock Drums Book with CD, $19.95
Everything® Singing Book with CD, $19.95
Everything® Songwriting Book

NEW AGE

Everything® Astrology Book, 2nd Ed.
Everything® Birthday Personology Book
Everything® Celtic Wisdom Book, $15.95
Everything® Dreams Book, 2nd Ed.
Everything® Law of Attraction Book, $15.95
Everything® Love Signs Book, $9.95
Everything® Love Spells Book, $9.95
Everything® Palmistry Book
Everything® Psychic Book
Everything® Reiki Book
Everything® Sex Signs Book, $9.95
Everything® Spells & Charms Book, 2nd Ed.
Everything® Tarot Book, 2nd Ed.
Everything® Toltec Wisdom Book
Everything® Wicca & Witchcraft Book, 2nd Ed.

PARENTING

Everything® Baby Names Book, 2nd Ed.
Everything® Baby Shower Book, 2nd Ed.
Everything® Baby Sign Language Book with DVD
Everything® Baby's First Year Book
Everything® Birthing Book
Everything® Breastfeeding Book
Everything® Father-to-Be Book
Everything® Father's First Year Book
Everything® Get Ready for Baby Book, 2nd Ed.
Everything® Get Your Baby to Sleep Book, $9.95
Everything® Getting Pregnant Book
Everything® Guide to Pregnancy Over 35
Everything® Guide to Raising a One-Year-Old
Everything® Guide to Raising a Two-Year-Old
Everything® Guide to Raising Adolescent Boys
Everything® Guide to Raising Adolescent Girls
Everything® Mother's First Year Book
Everything® Parent's Guide to Childhood Illnesses
Everything® Parent's Guide to Children and Divorce
Everything® Parent's Guide to Children with ADD/ADHD
Everything® Parent's Guide to Children with Asperger's Syndrome
Everything® Parent's Guide to Children with Anxiety
Everything® Parent's Guide to Children with Asthma
Everything® Parent's Guide to Children with Autism
Everything® Parent's Guide to Children with Bipolar Disorder
Everything® Parent's Guide to Children with Depression
Everything® Parent's Guide to Children with Dyslexia
Everything® Parent's Guide to Children with Juvenile Diabetes
Everything® Parent's Guide to Children with OCD
Everything® Parent's Guide to Positive Discipline
Everything® Parent's Guide to Raising Boys
Everything® Parent's Guide to Raising Girls
Everything® Parent's Guide to Raising Siblings
Everything® Parent's Guide to Raising Your Adopted Child
Everything® Parent's Guide to Sensory Integration Disorder
Everything® Parent's Guide to Tantrums
Everything® Parent's Guide to the Strong-Willed Child
Everything® Parenting a Teenager Book
Everything® Potty Training Book, $9.95
Everything® Pregnancy Book, 3rd Ed.
Everything® Pregnancy Fitness Book
Everything® Pregnancy Nutrition Book
Everything® Pregnancy Organizer, 2nd Ed., $16.95
Everything® Toddler Activities Book
Everything® Toddler Book
Everything® Tween Book
Everything® Twins, Triplets, and More Book

PETS

Everything® Aquarium Book
Everything® Boxer Book
Everything® Cat Book, 2nd Ed.
Everything® Chihuahua Book
Everything® Cooking for Dogs Book
Everything® Dachshund Book
Everything® Dog Book, 2nd Ed.
Everything® Dog Grooming Book

Everything® Dog Obedience Book
Everything® Dog Owner's Organizer, $16.95
Everything® Dog Training and Tricks Book
Everything® German Shepherd Book
Everything® Golden Retriever Book
Everything® Horse Book, 2nd Ed., $15.95
Everything® Horse Care Book
Everything® Horseback Riding Book
Everything® Labrador Retriever Book
Everything® Poodle Book
Everything® Pug Book
Everything® Puppy Book
Everything® Small Dogs Book
Everything® Tropical Fish Book
Everything® Yorkshire Terrier Book

REFERENCE

Everything® American Presidents Book
Everything® Blogging Book
Everything® Build Your Vocabulary Book, $9.95
Everything® Car Care Book
Everything® Classical Mythology Book
Everything® Da Vinci Book
Everything® Einstein Book
Everything® Enneagram Book
Everything® Etiquette Book, 2nd Ed.
Everything® Family Christmas Book, $15.95
Everything® Guide to C. S. Lewis & Narnia
Everything® Guide to Divorce, 2nd Ed., $15.95
Everything® Guide to Edgar Allan Poe
Everything® Guide to Understanding Philosophy
Everything® Inventions and Patents Book
Everything® Jacqueline Kennedy Onassis Book
Everything® John F. Kennedy Book
Everything® Mafia Book
Everything® Martin Luther King Jr. Book
Everything® Pirates Book
Everything® Private Investigation Book
Everything® Psychology Book
Everything® Public Speaking Book, $9.95
Everything® Shakespeare Book, 2nd Ed.

RELIGION

Everything® Angels Book
Everything® Bible Book
Everything® Bible Study Book with CD, $19.95
Everything® Buddhism Book
Everything® Catholicism Book
Everything® Christianity Book
Everything® Gnostic Gospels Book
Everything® Hinduism Book, $15.95
Everything® History of the Bible Book
Everything® Jesus Book
Everything® Jewish History & Heritage Book
Everything® Judaism Book
Everything® Kabbalah Book
Everything® Koran Book
Everything® Mary Book
Everything® Mary Magdalene Book
Everything® Prayer Book
Everything® Saints Book, 2nd Ed.
Everything® Torah Book
Everything® Understanding Islam Book
Everything® Women of the Bible Book
Everything® World's Religions Book

SCHOOL & CAREERS

Everything® Career Tests Book
Everything® College Major Test Book
Everything® College Survival Book, 2nd Ed.
Everything® Cover Letter Book, 2nd Ed.
Everything® Filmmaking Book
Everything® Get-a-Job Book, 2nd Ed.
Everything® Guide to Being a Paralegal
Everything® Guide to Being a Personal Trainer
Everything® Guide to Being a Real Estate Agent
Everything® Guide to Being a Sales Rep
Everything® Guide to Being an Event Planner
Everything® Guide to Careers in Health Care
Everything® Guide to Careers in Law Enforcement
Everything® Guide to Government Jobs
Everything® Guide to Starting and Running a Catering Business
Everything® Guide to Starting and Running a Restaurant
Everything® Guide to Starting and Running a Retail Store
Everything® Job Interview Book, 2nd Ed.
Everything® New Nurse Book
Everything® New Teacher Book
Everything® Paying for College Book
Everything® Practice Interview Book
Everything® Resume Book, 3rd Ed.
Everything® Study Book

SELF-HELP

Everything® Body Language Book
Everything® Dating Book, 2nd Ed.
Everything® Great Sex Book
Everything® Guide to Caring for Aging Parents, $15.95
Everything® Self-Esteem Book
Everything® Self-Hypnosis Book, $9.95
Everything® Tantric Sex Book

SPORTS & FITNESS

Everything® Easy Fitness Book
Everything® Fishing Book
Everything® Guide to Weight Training, $15.95
Everything® Krav Maga for Fitness Book
Everything® Running Book, 2nd Ed.
Everything® Triathlon Training Book, $15.95

TRAVEL

Everything® Family Guide to Coastal Florida
Everything® Family Guide to Cruise Vacations
Everything® Family Guide to Hawaii
Everything® Family Guide to Las Vegas, 2nd Ed.
Everything® Family Guide to Mexico
Everything® Family Guide to New England, 2nd Ed.
Everything® Family Guide to New York City, 3rd Ed.
Everything® Family Guide to Northern California and Lake Tahoe
Everything® Family Guide to RV Travel & Campgrounds
Everything® Family Guide to the Caribbean
Everything® Family Guide to the Disneyland® Resort, California Adventure®, Universal Studios®, and the Anaheim Area, 2nd Ed.
Everything® Family Guide to the Walt Disney World Resort®, Universal Studios®, and Greater Orlando, 5th Ed.
Everything® Family Guide to Timeshares
Everything® Family Guide to Washington D.C., 2nd Ed.

WEDDINGS

Everything® Bachelorette Party Book, $9.95
Everything® Bridesmaid Book, $9.95
Everything® Destination Wedding Book
Everything® Father of the Bride Book, $9.95
Everything® Green Wedding Book, $15.95
Everything® Groom Book, $9.95
Everything® Jewish Wedding Book, 2nd Ed., $15.95
Everything® Mother of the Bride Book, $9.95
Everything® Outdoor Wedding Book
Everything® Wedding Book, 3rd Ed.
Everything® Wedding Checklist, $9.95
Everything® Wedding Etiquette Book, $9.95
Everything® Wedding Organizer, 2nd Ed., $16.95
Everything® Wedding Shower Book, $9.95
Everything® Wedding Vows Book,3rd Ed., $9.95
Everything® Wedding Workout Book
Everything® Weddings on a Budget Book, 2nd Ed., $9.95

WRITING

Everything® Creative Writing Book
Everything® Get Published Book, 2nd Ed.
Everything® Grammar and Style Book, 2nd Ed.
Everything® Guide to Magazine Writing
Everything® Guide to Writing a Book Proposal
Everything® Guide to Writing a Novel
Everything® Guide to Writing Children's Books
Everything® Guide to Writing Copy
Everything® Guide to Writing Graphic Novels
Everything® Guide to Writing Research Papers
Everything® Guide to Writing a Romance Novel, $15.95
Everything® Improve Your Writing Book, 2nd Ed.
Everything® Writing Poetry Book

Available wherever books are sold! To order, call 800-258-0929, or visit us at ***www.adamsmedia.com.***

Bolded titles are new additions to the series.
All Everything® books are priced at $12.95 or $14.95, unless otherwise stated. Prices subject to change without notice.